C++: The Complete Reference
Second Edition

About the Author...

Herbert Schildt is the world's leading C/C++ author. His programming books have sold more than one-and-a-half million copies worldwide and have been translated into all major foreign languages. He is the author of best-sellers **C: The Complete Reference**, now in its third edition, **Teach Yourself C**, and **Teach Yourself C++**. He has also written **The Annotated ANSI C Standard, C++ from the Ground Up, Schildt's Windows 95 Programming in C and C++,** and numerous other books. Schildt is the president of Universal Computing Laboratories, a software consulting firm in Mahomet, Illinois, and is a member of the ANSI C++ standardization committee. He holds a master's degree in computer science from the University of Illinois.

C++: The Complete Reference
Second Edition

Herbert Schildt

Osborne **McGraw-Hill**

Berkeley New York St. Louis San Francisco
Auckland Bogotá Hamburg London Madrid
Mexico City Milan Montreal New Delhi Panama City
Paris São Paulo Singapore Sydney
Tokyo Toronto

Osborne **McGraw-Hill**
2600 Tenth Street
Berkeley, California 94710
U.S.A.

For information on translations or book distributors outside the U.S.A., or to arrange bulk purchase discounts for sales promotions, premiums, or fundraisers, please contact Osborne **McGraw-Hill** at the above address.

C++: The Complete Reference, Second Edition

567890 DOC 9987

ISBN 0-07-882123-1

Publisher	**Indexer**
Lawrence Levitsky	Sheryl Schildt
Acquisitions Editor	**Computer Designer**
Nancy McLaughlin	Peter F. Hancik
Technical Editor	**Illustrator**
Paul Chui	Rhys Elliott
Copy Editor	**Quality Control Specialist**
Janice Jue	Joe Scuderi
Proofreader	**Cover Design**
Patricia Mannion	Compass Marketing

Contents at a Glance

Part II C++-Specific Features

Part III Some C++ Applications

Contents

PART II

C++-Specific Features

PART III

Some C++ Applications

Preface

This is the second edition of *C++: The Complete Reference*. In the years that have transpired since the first edition, C++ has undergone many changes. Several new features have been added and many small inconsistencies have been cleared up. However, the single most important event is that work on the ANSI C++ standard has begun. Although the standardization process is a slow one, and will probably take several more years, the creation of a C++ standard is the necessary final step in establishing C++ as a world-class professional programming language. Of course, the information contained in this edition reflects the proposed ANSI C++ standard.

Although C++ has been part of the programming universe for several years now, it is good to remember that it still represents a major step forward in programming. Based upon the C language, C++ adds extensions that support object-oriented programming. These extensions also dramatically increase the power of the language, in general. Programming languages (and underlying methodologies) have been constantly evolving since they were first invented in the 1950s. C++ is the next step. While a description of object-oriented programming is found later in this book, the point of it is to let you, the programmer, manage increasingly larger and more complex programs. Toward this end, C++ succeeds admirably.

C++ is built upon C. At the time of this writing, C is still the most popular and important computer programming language in the world. Because C++ is an enhancement of and an extension to C, C++ is expected to continue increasing in acceptance and use. Given the power and versatility of C++, combined with the fact that it is based on the already popular C language, its place in programming history is already assured.

A Book for All Programmers

This book covers both the C-like aspects of C++ and its C++-specific features. However, the greatest emphasis is on those features unique to C++. Since many readers are already familiar with and proficient in C, the C-like features are discussed separately from the C++-specific ones. This approach prevents the knowledgeable C programmer from having to "wade through" reams of information he or she already knows. Instead, the experienced C programmer can simply turn to the sections of this book that cover the C++-specific features.

This C++ reference is designed for all C++ programmers, regardless of their experience level. It does assume, however, a reader able to create at least a simple program. If you are just learning C++, this book will make an excellent companion to any C++ tutorial and serve as a source of answers to your specific questions.

Therefore, whether you are an experienced C programmer moving to C++ or a relative newcomer to programming, you will find this book to be of value.

What's New in the Second Edition

For the most part, I have left the basic structure of this book unchanged from its preceding edition. However, a substantial amount of new material has been added—including two completely new chapters. Since the first edition, two major features have been added to C++: templates and exception handling. The two new chapters discuss these constructs in detail. In addition to the major features, several smaller features have been added, including run-time type information, new casting operators, the **bool** data type, and name spaces.

Many of the new features are the result of the standardization process and are quite new. However, there have also been a few other changes to C++ that are the result of reconciling certain inconsistencies in the language. Thus, there have been several small changes here and there, throughout the book, to reflect these minor modifications. For example, there have been small changes to the **new** and **delete** operators relative to how they function with arrays, and to the procedure used to overload the increment and decrement operators.

What's Inside

This books covers in detail all aspects of the C++ language, including its foundation: C. The book is divided into three parts, covering

- The C language foundation
- The C++ language
- Sample C++ applications

Part One provides a comprehensive discussion of the basis for C++: the C language. This section fully describes ANSI standard C. A thorough understanding of the C language is a prerequisite to learning C++. Part Two discusses in detail the extensions and enhancements to C added by C++. Part Three shows practical examples of applying C++ and object-oriented programming.

Diskette Offer

There are many useful and interesting functions, algorithms, and programs contained in this book. If you're like me, you probably would like to try them, but hate typing them into the computer. When I key in routines from a book it always seems that I type something wrong and spend hours trying to get the program to work. For this reason, I am offering the source code on diskette for all the programs contained in this book for $24.95. Just fill in the order blank on the next page and mail it, along with your payment, to the address shown. Or, if you're in a hurry, just call (217) 586-4021 (the number of my consulting office) and place your order by telephone. You can FAX your order to (217) 586-4997. (VISA and MasterCard accepted.)

Please send me _____ copies, at $24.95 each, of the programs in *C++: The Complete Reference, Second Edition* on an IBM compatible diskette.

(Foreign orders only: Checks must be drawn on a U.S. bank. Please add $5.00 shipping and handling.)

_____
Name

_____
Address

_____   _____   _____
City   State   ZIP

_____
Telephone

Diskette size (check one):   5.25" _____   3.5" _____

Method of payment: Check_____   VISA_____   MC_____

Credit card number: _____

Expiration date: _____

Signature: _____

Send to:

Herbert Schildt
398 County Rd 2500 N
Mahomet, IL 61853

Phone: (217) 586-4021
FAX: (217) 586-4997

For Further Study

C++: The Complete Reference, Second Edition is just one of the many programming books written by Herbert Schildt. Here are some others that you will find of interest.

To learn more about the C++, we recommend:

Teach Yourself C++, Second Edition
C++ From the Ground Up

If you want to learn more about C (which forms the foundation for C++), then the following titles will be of interest:

The Annotated ANSI C Standard
C: The Complete Reference, Third Edition
Teach Yourself C, Second Edition

If you are interested in programming for Windows 95, Schildt has written the definitive guide to this latest version of Windows:

Schildt's Windows 95 Programming in C and C++

To learn more about Windows programming, we recommend the *Osborne Windows Programming Series*, co-authored by Herbert Schildt. You will find it to be invaluable when trying to understand the complexities of Windows. The series titles are:

Volume 1: Programming Fundamentals
Volume 2: General Purpose API Functions
Volume 3: Special Purpose API Functions

Finally, here are some other interesting and useful books about C and C++ written by Herbert Schildt:

The Art of C
The Craft of C
Turbo C/C++: The Complete Reference

When you need solid answers fast, turn to Herbert Schildt, the recognized authority on programming.

PART ONE

The Foundation of C++: The C Language

Part One of this book discusses the C-like features of C++. As you probably know, C++ is built upon the foundation of C. When C++ was invented, the C language was used as the starting point. To C were added several new features and extensions designed to support object-oriented programming (OOP). However, the C-like aspects of C++ were never abandoned.

In its current form, C++ is an enhanced version of ANSI standard C. In fact, the ANSI C standard is a *base document* for the proposed ANSI C++ standard. For this reason, any C++ compiler is by definition also a C compiler. Because C++ is built upon C, you cannot program in C++ unless you know how to program in C. Further, many of the fundamental concepts that form the basis for C also form the foundation for C++.

Since C++ is a superset of C, the material described in this part of the book is fully applicable to C++. The C++-specific features of C++ are detailed in Part Two. The reason that the C-like features of C++ are covered in their own section is to make it easier for the experienced C programmer to quickly and easily find information about C++ without having to "wade through" reams of information that he or she already knows. Throughout Part One, any minor differences between C and C++ are noted.

 NOTE: *Part One of this book is excerpted from my book* C: The Complete Reference, 3rd Edition *(Osborne/McGraw-Hill, 1995). If you are particularly interested in C, you will find this book helpful. It covers the complete ANSI C standard as well as all of the standard C library functions. It also contains several example applications of C.*

Chapter One

An Overview of C

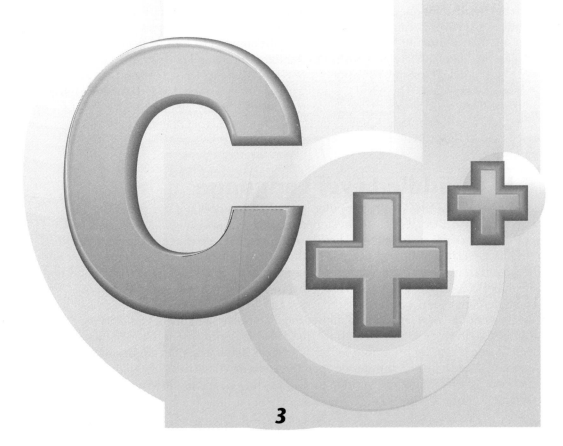

The purpose of this chapter is to present an overview of the C programming language, its origins, its uses, and its underlying philosophy. Since C++ is built upon C, this chapter also provides an important historical perspective on the roots of C++.

The Origins of C

C was invented and first implemented by Dennis Ritchie on a DEC PDP-11 that used the UNIX operating system. C is the result of a development process that started with an older language called BCPL. BCPL was developed by Martin Richards, and it influenced a language called B, which was invented by Ken Thompson. B led to the development of C in the 1970s.

For many years, the de facto standard for C was the version supplied with the UNIX operating system. It was first described in *The C Programming Language* by Brian Kernighan and Dennis Ritchie (Englewood Cliffs, NJ: Prentice-Hall, 1978). With the rise in popularity of personal computers, numerous C implementations were created. In a near miracle, most of these implementations were highly compatible. (That is, a program written for one of them could usually be successfully compiled using another.) However, because no standard existed, there were discrepancies. To remedy this situation, a committee was established in the summer of 1983 to create an ANSI (American National Standards Institute) standard that would define the C language once and for all. The standardization process took six years (much longer than anyone reasonably expected). The ANSI C standard was finally adopted in December of 1989, with the first copies becoming available in early 1990. Today, all mainstream C/C++ compilers comply with the ANSI C standard. Also, the ANSI C standard is a base document of the proposed ANSI C++ standard.

C Is a Middle-Level Language

C is often called a *middle-level* computer language. This does not mean that C is less powerful, harder to use, or less developed than a high-level language such as BASIC or Pascal, nor does it imply that C has the cumbersome nature of assembly language (and its associated troubles). Rather, C is thought of as a middle-level language because it combines the best elements of high-level languages with the control and flexibility of assembly language. Table 1-1 shows how C fits into the spectrum of computer languages.

As a middle-level language, C allows the manipulation of bits, bytes, and addresses—the basic elements with which the computer functions. Despite this fact, C code is also very portable. *Portability* means that it is easy to adapt software written for one type of computer or operating system to another. For example, if you can easily convert a program written for DOS so that it runs under Windows, that program is portable.

Highest level	Ada
	Modula-2
	Pascal
	COBOL
	FORTRAN
	BASIC
Middle level	C++
	C
	FORTH
	Macro-assembler
Lowest level	Assembler

Table 1-1. *C's Place in the World of Computer Languages*

All high-level programming languages support the concept of data types. A *data type* defines a set of values that a variable can store along with a set of operations that can be performed on that variable. Common data types are integer, character, and real. Although C has five basic built-in data types, it is not a strongly typed language, as are Pascal and Ada. C permits almost all type conversions. For example, you may freely intermix character and integer types in an expression.

Unlike a high-level language, C performs almost no run-time error checking. For example, no check is performed to ensure that array boundaries are not overrun. These types of checks are the responsibility of the programmer.

In the same vein, C does not demand strict type compatibility between a parameter and an argument. As you may know from your other programming experience, a high-level computer language will typically require that the type of an argument be (more or less) exactly the same type as the parameter that will receive the argument. However, such is not the case for C. Instead, C allows an argument to be of any type so long as it can be reasonably converted into the type of the parameter. Further, C provides all of the automatic conversions to accomplish this.

C is special in that it allows the direct manipulation of bits, bytes, words, and pointers. This makes it well suited for system-level programming, where these operations are common.

Another important aspect of C is that it has only 32 keywords (27 from the Kernighan and Ritchie de facto standard, and five added by the ANSI standardization committee), which are the commands that make up the C language. High-level languages typically have several times more keywords. As a comparison, consider that most versions of BASIC have well over 100 keywords!

C Is a Structured Language

In your previous programming experience, you may have heard the term *block-structured* applied to a computer language. Although the term "block-structured language" does not strictly apply to C, C is commonly referred to simply as a *structured* language. It has many similarities to other structured languages, such as ALGOL, Pascal, and Modula-2.

NOTE: *The reason that C (and C++) is not, technically, a block-structured language is that block-structured languages permit procedures or functions to be declared inside other procedures or functions. However, since C does not allow the creation of functions within functions, it cannot formally be called block-structured.*

The distinguishing feature of a structured language is *compartmentalization* of code and data. This is the ability of a language to section off and hide from the rest of the program all information and instructions necessary to perform a specific task. One way that you achieve compartmentalization is by using subroutines that employ local (temporary) variables. By using local variables, you can write subroutines so that the events that occur within them cause no side effects in other parts of the program. This capability makes it very easy for C programs to share sections of code. If you develop compartmentalized functions, you only need to know what a function does, not how it does it. Remember, excessive use of global variables (variables known throughout the entire program) may allow bugs to creep into a program by allowing unwanted side effects. (Anyone who has programmed in standard BASIC is well aware of this problem.)

NOTE: *The concept of compartmentalization is greatly expanded by the C++ extensions to C. Specifically, in C++, one part of your program may tightly control which other parts of your program are allowed access.*

A structured language allows you a variety of programming possibilities. It directly supports several loop constructs, such as **while, do-while,** and **for.** In a structured language, the use of **goto** is either prohibited or discouraged and is not the common form of program control (as is the case in standard BASIC and traditional FORTRAN, for example). A structured language allows you to place statements anywhere on a line and does not require a strict field concept (as some older FORTRANs do).

Here are some examples of structured and nonstructured languages:

Nonstructured	Structured
FORTRAN	Pascal
BASIC	Ada
COBOL	C++
	C
	Modula-2

Structured languages tend to be modern. In fact, a mark of an old computer language is that it is nonstructured. Today, most programmers consider structured languages easier to program in and the programs written in those languages easier to maintain.

C's main structural component is the *function*—C's stand-alone subroutine. In C, functions are the building blocks in which all program activity occurs. They allow you to define and code the separate tasks in a program, thus allowing your programs to be modular. After you have created a function, you can rely on it to work properly in various situations without creating side effects in other parts of the program. Being able to create stand-alone functions is extremely critical in larger projects where one programmer's code must not accidentally affect another's.

Another way to structure and compartmentalize code in C is through the use of code blocks. A *code block* is a logically connected group of program statements that is treated as a unit. In C, you create a code block by placing a sequence of statements between opening and closing curly braces. In this example,

```
if (x < 10)   {
    printf("Too low, try again.\n");
    scanf("%d", &x);
}
```

the two statements after the **if** and between the curly braces are both executed if **x** is less than 10. These two statements together with the braces represent a code block. They are a logical unit: one of the statements cannot execute without the other executing also. Note that every statement in C can be either a single statement or a block of statements. Code blocks allow many algorithms to be implemented with clarity, elegance, and efficiency. Moreover, they help the programmer better conceptualize the true nature of the algorithm being implemented.

C Is a Programmer's Language

Surprisingly, not all computer programming languages are for programmers. Consider the classic examples of nonprogrammer languages, COBOL and BASIC.

COBOL was designed not to better the programmer's lot, not to improve the reliability of the code produced, and not even to improve the speed with which code can be written. Rather, COBOL was designed, in part, to enable nonprogrammers to read and presumably (however unlikely) to understand the program. BASIC was created essentially to allow nonprogrammers to program a computer to solve relatively simple problems.

In contrast, C (as well as C++) was created, influenced, and field-tested by working programmers. The end result is that C gives the programmer what the programmer wants: few restrictions, few complaints, block structures, stand-alone functions, and a compact set of keywords. By using C, you can nearly achieve the efficiency of assembly code combined with the structure of ALGOL or Modula-2. It is no wonder that C and C++ are easily the most popular languages among topflight professional programmers.

The fact that you can often use C in place of assembly language is a major factor in its popularity among programmers. Assembly language uses a symbolic representation of the actual binary code that the computer executes directly. Each assembly-language operation maps into a single task for the computer to perform. Although assembly language gives programmers the potential to accomplish tasks with maximum flexibility and efficiency, it is notoriously difficult to work with when developing and debugging a program. Furthermore, since assembly language is unstructured, the final program tends to be spaghetti code—a tangled mess of jumps, calls, and indexes. This lack of structure makes assembly-language programs difficult to read, enhance, and maintain. Perhaps more important, assembly-language routines are not portable between machines with different central processing units (CPUs).

Initially, C was used for systems programming. A *systems program* forms a portion of the operating system of the computer or its support utilities. For example, the following are usually called systems programs:

- Operating systems
- Interpreters
- Editors
- Compilers
- Databases
- Spreadsheets

As C grew in popularity, many programmers began to use it to program all tasks because of its portability and efficiency. Because there are C compilers for virtually all computers, you can take code written for one machine and compile and run it on another with relatively few changes. This portability saves both time and money. C compilers also tend to produce very tight, fast object code—tighter and faster than that of most COBOL compilers, for example.

In addition, programmers use C in all types of programming tasks because they like it! C offers the speed of assembly language and the extensibility of FORTH, but has few of the restrictions of Pascal or Modula-2. Each C programmer can create and maintain a unique library of functions that have been tailored to his or her own programming style and that can be used in many different programs. Because it allows—indeed, encourages—separate compilation, C enables programmers to manage large projects easily, with minimal duplication of effort.

The Form of a C Program

Table 1-2 lists the 32 keywords that, combined with the formal C syntax, form the C programming language. Of these, 27 were defined by the original version of C. These five were added by the ANSI C committee: **enum**, **const**, **signed**, **void**, and **volatile**.

In addition, many C (and C++) compilers have added several keywords that better exploit their operating environment. For example, several compilers include keywords to manage the memory organization of the 8086 family of processors, to support inter-language programming, and to access interrupts. Here is a list of some commonly used extended keywords:

asm	_cs	_ds	_es
_ss	cdecl	far	huge
interrupt	near	pascal	

Your compiler may also support other extensions that help it take better advantage of its specific environment.

All C keywords are lowercase. In C, uppercase and lowercase are different: **else** is a keyword; **ELSE** is not. You may not use a keyword for any other purpose in a C program—that is, you may not use it as a variable or function name.

auto	double	int	struct
break	else	long	switch
case	enum	register	typedef
char	extern	return	union
const	float	short	unsigned
continue	for	signed	void
default	goto	sizeof	volatile
do	if	static	while

Table 1-2.   *The 32 Keywords Defined by the ANSI C Standard*

All C programs consist of one or more functions. The only function that must be present is called **main( )**, which is the first function called when program execution begins. In well-written C code, **main( )** contains what is, in essence, an outline of what the program does. The outline is composed of function calls. Although **main( )** is not a keyword, treat it as if it were. For example, don't try to use **main( )** as the name of a variable because you will probably confuse the compiler.

The general form of a C program is illustrated in Figure 1-1, where **f1( )** through **fN( )** represent user-defined functions.

The Library and Linking

Technically speaking, you can create a useful, functional C program that consists solely of the statements that you actually created. However, this is quite rare because

```
global declarations

return-type main(parameter list)
{
  statement sequence
}

return-type f1(parameter list)
{
  statement sequence
}

return-type f2(parameter list)
{
  statement sequence
}
  .
  .
  .
return-type fN(parameter list)
{
  statement sequence
}
```

Figure 1-1.   *The general form of a C program*

C does not, within the actual definition of the language, provide any method of performing input/output (I/O) operations. As a result, most programs include calls to various functions contained in the *standard library*.

All C compilers come with a standard library of functions that perform most commonly needed tasks. The ANSI C standard specifies a minimal set of functions that will be contained in the library. However, your compiler will probably contain many other functions. For example, the standard library does not define any graphics functions, but your compiler will probably include some.

 NOTE: *It is important to understand that C++ supports the entire ANSI C standard library. Thus, all of the standard C functions are available for use by both C and C++ programs that you write. Of course, C++ also defines several library functions that relate specifically to C++.*

The implementors of your compiler have already written most of the general-purpose functions that you will use. When you call a function that is not part of your program, the compiler "remembers" its name. Later, the linker combines the code you wrote with the object code already found in the standard library. This process is called *linking*. Some compilers have their own linker, while others use the standard linker supplied by your operating system.

The functions in the library are in *relocatable* format. This means that the memory addresses for the various machine-code instructions have not been absolutely defined—only offset information has been kept. When your program links with the functions in the standard library, these memory offsets are used to create the actual addresses used. There are several technical manuals and books that explain this process in more detail. However, you do not need any further explanation of the actual relocation process to program in C or C++.

Many of the functions that you will need as you write programs are in the standard library. They act as building blocks that you combine. If you write a function that you will use again and again, you can place it into a library too. Some compilers allow you to place your function in the standard library; others make you create an additional library. Either way, the code will be there for you to use repeatedly.

Separate Compilation

Most short programs are completely contained within one source file. However, as a program's length grows, so does its compile time (and long compile times make for short tempers). Hence, C allows a program to be contained in many files and lets you compile each file separately. Once you have compiled all files, they are linked, along with any library routines, to form the complete object code. The advantage of separate compilation is that if you change the code of one file, you do not need to recompile the entire program. On all but the most simple projects, this saves a substantial amount of time. The user manual to your C/C++ compiler will contain instructions for compiling multifile programs.

Using a C++ Compiler to Compile C Programs

The programs in Part One of this book are C programs. However, you will probably be using a C++ compiler to compile them. All C++ compilers are also C compilers, so you will have no trouble. However, you must remember one important point when compiling C programs: they must have the .C (not the .CPP) file extension. At the time of this writing, most commercial C++ compilers will automatically compile a file that has the .C extension as a C program. They will compile files that have the .CPP extension as C++ programs. (Some compilers may use a slightly different convention, so check your user manual.) Although C is a subset of C++, there are a few minor differences between the two languages. For this reason, you *must* compile C programs *as C programs* and you *must* compile C++ programs *as C++ programs*.

Chapter Two

Expressions

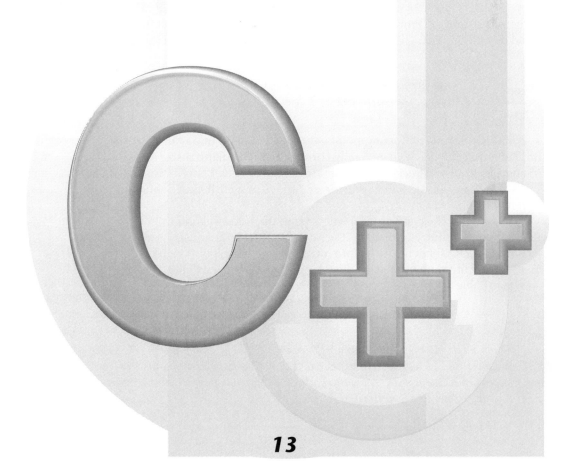

This chapter examines the most fundamental element of the C (as well as the C++) language: the expression. As you will see, expressions in C are substantially more general and more powerful than in most other computer languages. Expressions are formed from the atomic elements of C: *data* and *operators*. Data may be represented either by variables or by constants. C, like most other computer languages, supports a number of types of data. It also provides a wide variety of operators.

The Five Basic Data Types

There are five atomic data types in C: character, integer, floating-point, double floating-point, and valueless (**char**, **int**, **float**, **double**, and **void**, respectively). As you will see, all other data types in C are based upon one of these types. The size and range of these data types may vary with each processor type and between implementations of C. However, in all cases a character is 1 byte. Although an integer is often 2 bytes, you cannot make this assumption if you want your programs to be portable to the widest range of environments. It is important to understand that the ANSI C standard only stipulates the minimal *range* of each data type, not its size in bytes.

NOTE: To the five basic data types defined by C, C++ adds two more: **bool** *and* **wchar_t**. *These are discussed in Part Two of this book.*

The exact format of floating-point values will depend upon how they are implemented. Integers will generally correspond to the natural size of a word on the host computer. Values of type **char** are generally used to hold values defined by the ASCII character set. Values outside that range may be handled differently by different compilers.

The range of **float** and **double** will depend upon the method used to represent the floating-point numbers. Whatever the method, the range is quite large. The ANSI C standard specifies that the minimum range for a floating-point value is 1E–37 to 1E+37. The minimum number of digits of precision for each floating-point type is shown in Table 2-1.

NOTE: The proposed ANSI C++ standard does not specify a minimum size or range for the basic types. Instead, it simply states that they must meet certain requirements. For example, it says that an **int** *will "have the natural size suggested by the machine architecture." However, you can assume that all C++ compilers will meet the minimum ranges specified by the ANSI C standard. Each C++ compiler specifies the size and range of the basic types in the header file* **<climits>**.

Type	Approximate Size in Bits	Minimal Range
char	8	–127 to 127
unsigned char	8	0 to 255
signed char	8	–127 to 127
int	16	–32,767 to 32,767
unsigned int	16	0 to 65,535
signed int	16	Same as **int**
short int	16	Same as **int**
unsigned short int	16	0 to 65,535
signed short int	16	Same as **short int**
long int	32	–2,147,483,647 to 2,147,483,647
signed long int	32	Same as **long int**
unsigned long int	32	0 to 4,294,967,295
float	32	Six digits of precision
double	64	Ten digits of precision
long double	80	Ten digits of precision

Table 2-1.   *All Data Types Defined by the ANSI C Standard*

The type **void** either explicitly declares a function as returning no value or creates generic pointers. Both of these uses are discussed in subsequent chapters.

Modifying the Basic Types

Except type **void**, the basic data types may have various modifiers preceding them. You use a *modifier* to alter the meaning of the base type to fit various situations more precisely. The list of modifiers is shown here:

    signed
    unsigned
    long
    short

You can apply the modifiers **signed**, **short**, **long**, and **unsigned** to integer base types. You can apply **signed** and **unsigned** to characters. You can also apply **long** to **double**.

Table 2-1 shows all data type combinations that adhere to the ANSI C standard, along with their minimal ranges and approximate bit widths. (These values also apply to a typical C++ implementation.)

The use of **signed** on integers is allowed, but redundant because the default integer declaration assumes a signed number. The most important use of **signed** is to modify **char** in implementations in which **char** is unsigned by default.

The difference between signed and unsigned integers is in the way that the high-order bit of the integer is interpreted. If you specify a signed integer, the compiler generates code that assumes that the high-order bit of an integer is to be used as a *sign flag*. If the sign flag is 0, the number is positive; if it is 1, the number is negative.

In general, negative numbers are represented using the *two's complement* approach, which reverses all bits in the number (except the sign flag), adds 1 to this number, and sets the sign flag to 1.

Signed integers are important for a great many algorithms, but they only have half the absolute magnitude of their unsigned brothers. For example, here is 32,767:

0 1 1 1 1 1 1 1   1 1 1 1 1 1 1 1

If the high-order bit were set to 1, the number would be interpreted as –1. However, if you declare this to be an **unsigned int**, the number becomes 65,535 when the high-order bit is set to 1.

Identifier Names

In C/C++, the names of variables, functions, labels, and various other user-defined objects are called *identifiers*. These identifiers can vary from one to several characters. The first character must be a letter or an underscore, and subsequent characters must be either letters, digits, or underscores. Here are some correct and incorrect identifier names:

Correct	**Incorrect**
count	1count
test23	hi!there
high_balance	high...balance

The ANSI C standard states that identifiers may be of any length. However, not all characters will necessarily be significant. If the identifier will be involved in an external link process, then at least the first six characters will be significant. These identifiers, called *external names*, include function names and global variables that are shared between files. If the identifier is not used in an external link process, then at least the first 31 characters will be significant. This type of identifier is called an *internal name* and includes the names of local variables, for example. However, in C++, there is no limit to the length of an identifier and all characters are significant. This difference may be important if you are converting a program from C to C++.

In an identifier, upper- and lowercase are treated as distinct. Hence, **count**, **Count**, and **COUNT** are three separate identifiers.

An identifier cannot be the same as a C or C++ keyword, and should not have the same name as functions that are in the C or C++ library.

Variables

As you probably know, a *variable* is a named location in memory that is used to hold a value that may be modified by the program. All variables must be declared before they can be used. The general form of a declaration is

type variable_list;

Here, *type* must be a valid data type plus any modifiers, and *variable_list* may consist of one or more identifier names separated by commas. Here are some declarations:

```
int i,j,l;
short int si;
unsigned int ui;
double balance, profit, loss;
```

REMEMBER: *in C/C++ the name of a variable has nothing to do with its type.*

Where Variables Are Declared

Variables will be declared in three basic places: inside functions, in the definition of function parameters, and outside of all functions. These are local variables, formal parameters, and global variables.

Local Variables

Variables that are declared inside a function are called *local variables*. In some C/C++ literature, these variables are referred to as *automatic* variables. This book uses the more common term "local variable." Local variables may be referenced only by statements that are inside the block in which the variables are declared. In other words, local variables are not known outside their own code block. Remember, a block of code begins with an opening curly brace and terminates with a closing curly brace.

Local variables exist only while the block of code in which they are declared is executing. That is, a local variable is created upon entry into its block and destroyed upon exit.

The most common code block in which local variables are declared is the function. For example, consider the following two functions.

```
void func1(void)
{
  int x;

  x = 10;
}

void func2(void)
{
  int x;

  x = -199;
}
```

The integer variable **x** is declared twice, once in **func1( )** and once in **func2( )**. The **x** in **func1( )** has no bearing on or relationship to the **x** in **func2( )**. This is because each **x** is only known to the code within the same block as the variable declaration.

The C language contains the keyword **auto**, which you can use to declare local variables. However, since all nonglobal variables are, by default, assumed to be **auto**, this keyword is virtually never used. Hence, the examples in this book will not use it. (It has been said that **auto** was included in C to provide for source-level compatibility with its predecessor B. Further, **auto** is supported in C++ to provide compatibility with C.)

For reasons of convenience and tradition, most programmers declare all the variables used by a function immediately after the function's opening curly brace and before any other statements. However, you may declare local variables within any code block. The block defined by a function is simply a special case. For example,

```
void f(void)
{
  int t;

  scanf("%d",&t);

  if(t==1) {
    char s[80];   /* this is created only upon
                     entry into this block */
    printf("enter name:");
    gets(s);
    /* do something ... */
  }
}
```

Here, the local variable **s** is created upon entry into the **if** code block and destroyed upon exit. Furthermore, **s** is known only within the **if** block and may not be referenced elsewhere—even in other parts of the function that contains it.

One advantage of declaring a local variable within a conditional block is that memory for the variable will only be allocated if needed. This is because local variables do not come into existence until the block in which they are declared is entered. You might need to worry about this when producing code for dedicated controllers (like a garage door opener that responds to a digital security code) in which RAM is in short supply, for example.

Declaring variables within the block of code that uses them also helps prevent unwanted side effects. Since the variable does not exist outside the block in which it is declared, it cannot be accidentally altered.

There is an important difference between C and C++ as to where you can declare local variables. In C, you must declare all local variables at the start of the block in which they are defined, prior to any program statements. For example, the following function is in error if compiled by a C compiler.

```
/* This function is in error if compiled using
   a C compiler, but perfectly acceptable to a
   C++ compiler.
*/
void f(void)
{
  int i;

  i = 10;

  int j;  /* this line will cause an error */

  j = 20;
}
```

However, in C++, this function is perfectly valid because you can define local variables at any point in your program. (C++ variable declaration is discussed in depth in Part Two of this book.)

Because local variables are created and destroyed with each entry and exit from the block in which they are declared, their content is lost once the block is left. This is especially important to remember when calling a function. When a function is called, its local variables are created, and upon its return they are destroyed. This means that local variables cannot retain their values between calls. (However, you can direct the compiler to retain their values by using the **static** modifier.)

Unless otherwise specified, local variables are stored on the stack. The fact that the stack is a dynamic and changing region of memory explains why local variables cannot, in general, hold their values between function calls.

You can initialize a local variable to some known value. This value will be assigned to the variable each time the block of code in which it is declared is entered. For example, the following program prints the number **10** ten times.

```c
#include <stdio.h>

void f(void);

void main(void)
{
  int i;

  for(i=0; i<10; i++)  f();
}

void f(void)
{
  int j = 10;

  printf("%d ", j);

  j++;   /* this line has no lasting effect */
}
```

Formal Parameters

If a function is to use arguments, it must declare variables that will accept the values of the arguments. These variables are called the *formal parameters* of the function. They behave like any other local variables inside the function. As shown in the following program fragment, their declarations occur after the function name and inside parentheses:

```c
/* Return 1 if c is part of string s; 0 otherwise */
is_in(char *s, char c)
{
  while(*s)
    if(*s==c) return 1;
    else s++;

  return 0;
}
```

The function **is_in( )** has two parameters: **s** and **c**. This function returns 1 if the character specified in **c** is contained within the string **s**; 0 if it is not.

You must specify the type of the formal parameters by declaring them as just shown. Then you may use them inside the function as normal local variables. Keep in mind that, as local variables, they are also dynamic and are destroyed upon exit from the function.

As with local variables, you may make assignments to a function's formal parameters or use them in any allowable expression. Even though these variables receive the value of the arguments passed to the function, you can use them like any other local variable.

Global Variables

Unlike local variables, *global variables* are known throughout the program and may be used by any piece of code. Also, they will hold their value throughout the program's execution. You create global variables by declaring them outside of any function. Any expression may access them, regardless of what block of code that expression is in.

In the following program, the variable **count** has been declared outside of all functions. Although its declaration occurs before the **main( )** function, you could have placed it anywhere before its first use as long as it was not in a function. However, it is best to declare global variables at the top of the program.

```c
#include <stdio.h>

int count;   /* count is global */

void func1(void);
void func2(void);

void main(void)
{
  count = 100;
  func1();
}

void func1(void)
{
  int temp;

  temp = count;
  func2();
  printf("count is %d", count); /* will print 100 */
}

void func2(void)
{
  int count;
```

```
    for(count=1; count<10; count++)
      putchar('.');
}
```

Look closely at this program. Notice that although neither **main( )** nor **func1( )** has declared the variable **count**, both may use it. **func2( )**, however, has declared a local variable called **count**. When **func2( )** references **count**, it references only its local variable, not the global one. If a global variable and a local variable have the same name, all references to that variable name inside the code block in which the local variable is declared will refer to that local variable and have no effect on the global variable. This can be convenient, but forgetting this can cause your program to act strangely, even though it looks correct.

Storage for global variables is in a fixed region of memory set aside for this purpose by the compiler. Global variables are helpful when many functions in your program use the same data. You should avoid using unnecessary global variables, however. They take up memory the entire time your program is executing, not just when they are needed. In addition, using a global where a local variable would do makes a function less general because it relies on something that must be defined outside itself. Finally, using a large number of global variables can lead to program errors because of unknown and unwanted side effects. A major problem in developing large programs is the accidental changing of a variable's value because it was used elsewhere in the program. This can happen in C/C++ if you use too many global variables in your programs.

Access Modifiers

There are two modifiers (also referred to as *qualifiers*) that control how variables may be accessed or modified. These qualifiers are **const** and **volatile**. They must precede the type modifiers and the type names that they qualify.

const

Variables of type **const** may not be changed by your program. (A **const** variable can be given an initial value, however.) The compiler is free to place variables of this type into read-only memory (ROM). For example,

```
const int a=10;
```

creates an integer variable called **a** with an initial value of 10 that your program may not modify. However, you can use the variable **a** in other types of expressions. A **const** variable will receive its value either from an explicit initialization or by some hardware-dependent means.

The **const** qualifier can be used to protect the objects pointed to by the arguments of a function from being modified by that function. That is, when a pointer is passed to a function, that function can modify the actual variable pointed to by the pointer. However, if the pointer is specified as **const** in the parameter declaration, the function code won't be able to modify what it points to. For example, the **sp_to_dash( )** function in the following program prints a dash for each space in its string argument. That is, the string "this is a test" will be printed as "this-is-a-test". The use of **const** in the parameter declaration ensures that the code inside the function cannot modify the object pointed to by the parameter.

```
#include <stdio.h>

void sp_to_dash(const char *str);

void main(void)
{
  sp_to_dash("this is a test");
}

void sp_to_dash(const char *str)
{
  while(*str) {
    if(*str== ' ') printf("%c", '-');
    else printf("%c", *str);
    str++;
  }
}
```

If you had written **sp_to_dash( )** in such a way that the string would be modified, it would not compile. For example, if you had coded **sp_to_dash( )** as follows, you would receive a compile-time error.

```
/* This is wrong. */
void sp_to_dash(const char *str)
{
  while(*str) {
    if(*str==' ' ) *str = '-'; /* can't do this */
    printf("%c", *str);
    str++;
  }
}
```

Many functions in the standard library use **const** in their parameter declarations. For example, the **strlen( )** function has this prototype:

size_t strlen(const char *str);

Specifying *str* as **const** ensures that **strlen( )** will not modify the string pointed to by *str*. In general, when a standard library function has no need to modify an object pointed to by a calling argument, the parameter is declared as **const**.

You can also use **const** to verify that your program does not modify a variable. Remember, a variable of type **const** can be modified by something outside your program. For example, a hardware device may set its value. However, by declaring a variable as **const**, you can prove that any changes to that variable occur because of external events.

volatile

The modifier **volatile** tells the compiler that a variable's value may be changed in ways not explicitly specified by the program. For example, a global variable's address may be passed to the operating system's clock routine and used to hold the real time of the system. In this situation, the contents of the variable are altered without any explicit assignment statements in the program. This is important because most C/C++ compilers automatically optimize certain expressions by assuming that a variable's content is unchanging if it does not occur on the left side of an assignment statement; thus, it might not be reexamined each time it is referenced. Also, some compilers change the order of evaluation of an expression during the compilation process. The **volatile** modifier prevents these changes.

You can use **const** and **volatile** together. For example, if 0x30 is assumed to be the value of a port that is changed by external conditions only, the following declaration would prevent any possibility of accidental side effects.

```
const volatile unsigned char *port=0x30;
```

Storage Class Specifiers

There are four storage class specifiers supported by C:

extern
static
register
auto

These specifiers tell the compiler how to store the subsequent variable. The storage specifier precedes the rest of the variable declaration. Its general form is

storage_specifier type var_name

extern

Because C/C++ allows separate modules of a large program to be separately compiled and linked together, there must be some way of telling all the files about the global variables required by the program. Although C technically allows you to declare a global variable more than once, it is not good practice (and may cause problems when linking). More importantly, in C++, you may *only* declare a global variable *once*. How, then, do you inform all the files in your program about the global variables used by the program? The solution is to declare all of your global variables in one file and use **extern** declarations in the other, as in Figure 2-1.

In File 2, the global variable list was copied from File 1 and the **extern** specifier was added to the declarations. The **extern** specifier tells the compiler that the variable types and names that follow it have been declared elsewhere. In other words, **extern** lets the compiler know what the types and names are for these global variables without actually creating storage for them again. When the linker links the two modules, all references to the external variables are resolved.

File 1	File 2
int x,y;	extern int x, y;
char ch;	extern char ch;
main(void)	func22(void)
{	{
.	x = y/10;
.	}
.	
}	func23( )
	{
func1( )	y = 10;
}	{
x=123;	
}	

Figure 2-1. *Using global variables in separately compiled modules*

The **extern** keyword has this general form:

extern *var-list*;

There is another, optional use of **extern** that you may occasionally see. When you use a global variable inside a function, you can declare it as **extern**, as shown here:

```
int first, last;  /* global definition of first
                      and last */

void main(void)
{
  extern int first;  /* optional use of the
                        extern declaration */
   .
   .
   .
}
```

Although **extern** variable declarations as shown in this example are allowed, they are not necessary. If the compiler finds a variable that has not been declared within the current block, the compiler checks if it matches any of the variables declared within enclosing blocks. If it does not, the compiler then checks the global variables. If a match is found, the compiler assumes that the global variable is being referenced.

static Variables

static variables are permanent variables within their own function or file. Unlike global variables, they are not known outside their function or file, but they maintain their values between calls. This feature makes them useful when you write generalized functions and function libraries that other programmers may use. **static** has different effects upon local variables and global variables.

static Local Variables

When you apply the **static** modifier to a local variable, the compiler creates permanent storage for it, much as it creates storage for a global variable. The key difference between a **static** local variable and a global variable is that the **static** local variable remains known only to the block in which it is declared. In simple terms, a **static** local variable is a local variable that retains its value between function calls.

static local variables are very important to the creation of stand-alone functions because several types of routines must preserve a value between calls. If **static** variables were not allowed, globals would have to be used, opening the door to possible side effects. An example of a function that benefits from a **static** local variable is a number-series generator that produces a new value based on the previous one. You could use a global variable to hold this value. However, each time the function is used in a program, you would have to declare that global variable and make sure that it did not conflict with any other global variables already in place. Also, using a global variable would make this function difficult to put into a function library. The better solution is to declare the variable that holds the generated number to be **static**, as in this program fragment:

```
series(void)
{
  static int series_num;

  series_num = series_num+23;
  return series_num;
}
```

In this example, the variable **series_num** stays in existence between function calls, instead of coming and going the way a normal local variable would. This means that each call to **series( )** can produce a new member of the series based on the preceding number without declaring that variable globally.

You can give a **static** local variable an initialization value. This value is assigned only once—not each time the block of code is entered, as with normal local variables. For example, this version of **series( )** initializes **series_num** to 100:

```
series(void)
{
  static int series_num = 100;

  series_num = series_num+23;
  return series_num;
}
```

As the function now stands, the series will always begin with the value 123. While this is acceptable for some applications, most series generators need to let the user specify the starting point. One way to give **series_num** a user-specified value is to make **series_num** a global variable and then set its value as specified. However, not defining **series_num** as global was the point of making it **static**. This leads to the second use of **static**.

static Global Variables

Applying the specifier **static** to a global variable instructs the compiler to create a global variable that is known only to the file in which you declared it. This means that even though the variable is global, routines in other files may have no knowledge of it or alter its contents directly, keeping it free from side effects. For the few situations where a local **static** cannot do the job, you can create a small file that contains only the functions that need the global **static** variable, separately compile that file, and use it without fear of side effects.

To illustrate a global **static**, the series generator example from the previous section is recoded so that a seed value initializes the series through a call to a second function called **series_start( )**. The entire file containing **series( )**, **series_start( )**, and **series_num** is shown here:

```
/* This must all be in one file - preferably by itself. */

static int series_num;
void series_start(int seed);
int series(void);

series(void)
{
  series_num = series_num+23;
  return series_num;
}

/* initialize series_num */
void series_start(int seed)
{
  series_num = seed;
}
```

Calling **series_start( )** with some known integer value initializes the series generator. After that, calls to **series( )** generate the next element in the series.

To review: The names of local **static** variables are known only to the block of code in which they are declared; the names of global **static** variables are known only to the file in which they reside. If you place the **series( )** and **series_start( )** functions in a library, you can use the functions but cannot reference the variable **series_num**, which is hidden from the rest of the code in your program. In fact, you can even declare and use another variable called **series_num** in your program (in another file, of course). In essence, the **static** modifier permits variables that are known only to the functions that need them, without confusing other functions.

static variables enable you to hide portions of your program from other portions. This can be a tremendous advantage when you are trying to manage a very large and complex program.

register Variables

The **register** storage specifier traditionally applied only to variables of type **int** and **char**. However, the ANSI C standard broadened its definition so that you can apply **register** to any type of variable.

Originally, the **register** specifier requested that the compiler keep the value of a variable in a register of the CPU rather than in memory, where normal variables are stored. This meant that operations on a **register** variable could occur much faster than on a normal variable because the value of the **register** variable was actually held in the CPU and did not require a memory access to determine or modify its value.

Today, the definition of **register** has been greatly expanded, and it now may be applied to any type of variable. The ANSI C standard simply states "that access to the object be as fast as possible." (The proposed ANSI C++ standard states that a **register** is a "hint to the compiler that the object so declared will be heavily used.") In practice, characters and integers are still stored in registers in the CPU. Larger objects like arrays obviously cannot be stored in a register, but they may still receive preferential treatment by the compiler. Depending upon the implementation of the C/C++ compiler and its operating environment, **register** variables may be handled in any way deemed fit by the compiler's implementor. In fact, it is technically permissible for a compiler to ignore the **register** specifier altogether and treat variables modified by it as if they weren't, but this is seldom done in practice.

You can only apply the register specifier to local variables and to the formal parameters in a function. Hence, global **register** variables are not allowed. Here is an example that uses **register** variables. This function computes the result of M^e for integers:

```
int_pwr(register int m, register int e)
{
  register int temp;

  temp = 1;

  for(; e; e--) temp = temp * m;
  return temp;
}
```

In this example, **e**, **m**, and **temp** are declared as **register** variables because they are all used within the loop. The fact that **register** variables are optimized for speed makes them ideal for control of or use in loops. Generally, **register** variables are used where they will do the most good, which are often places where many references will be made to the same variable. This is important because you can declare any number of variables as being of type **register**, but not all will receive the same access speed optimization.

The number of **register** variables optimized for speed allowed within any one code block is determined by both the environment and the specific implementation of C/C++. You don't have to worry about declaring too many **register** variables because the compiler automatically transforms **register** variables into nonregister variables when the limit is reached. (This ensures portability of code across a broad line of processors.)

Usually at least two **register** variables of type **char** or **int** can actually be held in the registers of the CPU. Because environments vary widely, consult your compiler's user manual to determine if you can apply any other types of optimization options.

Because a **register** variable may be stored in a register of the CPU, **register** variables do not have addresses. That is, you may not find the address of a **register** variable using the **&** operator (discussed later in this chapter).

Although the ANSI C standard (and the proposed ANSI C++ standard) has broadened the description of **register** beyond its traditional meaning, in practice it still generally has a significant effect only with integer and character types. Thus, you should probably not count on substantial speed improvements for other variable types.

Variable Initializations

You can give a variable a value as you declare it by placing an equal sign and a constant after the variable name. The general form of initialization is

type variable_name = constant;

Some examples are

```
char ch = 'a';
int first = 0;
float balance = 123.23;
```

Global and **static** local variables are initialized only at the start of the program. Local variables (excluding **static** local variables) are initialized each time the block in which they are declared is entered. Local variables that are not initialized have unknown values before the first assignment is made to them. Uninitialized global and **static** local variables are automatically set to zero.

Constants

Constants refer to fixed values that the program may not alter. Constants can be of any of the basic data types. The way each constant is represented depends upon its type. Character constants are enclosed between single quotes. For example 'a' and '%' are both character constants. C also defines multibyte characters (used mostly in non-English language environments).

Integer constants are specified as numbers without fractional components. For example, 10 and –100 are integer constants. Floating-point constants require the decimal point followed by the number's fractional component. For example, 11.123 is a floating-point constant. C also allows you to use scientific notation for floating-point numbers.

There are two floating-point types: **float** and **double**. There are also several variations of the basic types that you can generate using the type modifiers. By default, the C compiler fits a numeric constant into the smallest compatible data type that will hold it. Therefore, 10 is **int** by default, but 60,000 is **unsigned**, and 100,000 is **long**. Even though the value 10 could fit into a character type, the compiler will not cross type boundaries. The only exceptions to the smallest type rule are floating-point constants, which are assumed to be **double**s.

For most programs you will write, the compiler defaults are adequate. However, you can specify precisely the type of numeric constant you want by using a suffix. For floating-point types, if you follow the number with an F, the number is treated as a **float**. If you follow it with an L, the number becomes a **long double**. For integer types, the U suffix stands for **unsigned** and the L for **long**. Here are some examples:

Data Type	Constant Examples
int	1 123 21000 –234
long int	35000L –34L
short int	10 –12 90
unsigned int	10000U 987U 40000
float	123.23F 4.34e–3F
double	123.23 12312333 –0.9876324
long double	1001.2L

Hexadecimal and Octal Constants

It is sometimes easier to use a number system based on 8 or 16 rather than 10 (our standard decimal system). The number system based on 8 is called *octal* and uses the digits 0 through 7. In octal, the number 10 is the same as 8 in decimal. The base 16 number system is called *hexadecimal* and uses the digits 0 through 9 plus the letters A through F, which stand for 10, 11, 12, 13, 14, and 15, respectively. For example, the hexadecimal number 10 is 16 in decimal. Because these two number systems are used frequently, C allows you to specify integer constants in hexadecimal or octal instead of decimal. A hexadecimal constant must consist of a 0x followed by the constant in hexadecimal form. An octal constant begins with a 0. Here are some examples:

```
int hex = 0x80;    /* 128 in decimal */
int oct = 012;     /* 10 in decimal */
```

String Constants

C supports one other type of constant: the string. A *string* is a set of characters enclosed in double quotes. For example, "this is a test" is a string. You have seen examples of strings in some of the **printf( )** statements in the sample programs. Although C allows you to define string constants, it does not formally have a string data type.

You must not confuse strings with characters. A single character constant is enclosed in single quotes, as in 'a'. However, "a" is a string containing only one letter.

Backslash Character Constants

Enclosing character constants in single quotes works for most printing characters. A few, however, such as the carriage return, are impossible to enter into a string from the keyboard. For this reason, C includes the special *backslash character constants*.

C supports several special backslash codes (listed in Table 2-2) so that you may easily enter these special characters as constants. You should use the backslash codes instead of their ASCII equivalents to help ensure portability.

Code	Meaning
\b	Backspace
\f	Form feed
\n	New line
\r	Carriage return
\t	Horizontal tab
\"	Double quote
\'	Single quote
\0	Null
\\	Backslash
\v	Vertical tab
\a	Alert
\N	Octal constant (where N is an octal constant)
\xN	Hexadecimal constant (where N is a hexadecimal constant)

Table 2-2.   *Backslash Codes*

For example, the following program outputs a new line and a tab and then prints the string **This is a test**.

```
#include <stdio.h>

void main(void)
{
   printf("\n\tThis is a test");
}
```

Operators

C is very rich in built-in operators. In fact, it places more significance on operators than do most other computer languages. C defines four classes of operators: *arithmetic*, *relational*, *logical*, and *bitwise*. In addition, C has some special operators for particular tasks.

The Assignment Operator

In C, you can use the assignment operator within any valid expression. This is not the case with most computer languages (including Pascal, BASIC, and FORTRAN), which treat the assignment operator as a special case statement. The general form of the assignment operator is

variable_name = expression;

where an expression may be as simple as a single constant or as complex as you require. Like BASIC and FORTRAN, C uses a single equal sign to indicate assignment (unlike Pascal or Modula-2, which use the := construct). The *target*, or left part, of the assignment must be a variable or a pointer, not a function or a constant.

Frequently in literature on C and in compiler error messages you will see these two terms: lvalue and rvalue. Simply put, an *lvalue* is any object that can occur on the left side of an assignment statement. For all practical purposes, "lvalue" means "variable." The term *rvalue* refers to expressions on the right side of an assignment and simply means the value of an expression.

Type Conversion in Assignments

When variables of one type are mixed with variables of another type, a *type conversion* will occur. In an assignment statement, the type conversion rule is easy: The value of the right side (expression side) of the assignment is converted to the type of the left side (target variable), as illustrated here:

```
int x;
char ch;
float  f;

void func(void)
{
  ch = x;      /* line 1 */
  x = f;       /* line 2 */
  f = ch;      /* line 3 */
  f = x;       /* line 4 */
}
```

In line 1, the left high-order bits of the integer variable **x** are lopped off, leaving **ch** with the lower 8 bits. If **x** were between 256 and 0, **ch** and **x** would have identical values. Otherwise, the value of **ch** would reflect only the lower-order bits of **x**. In line 2, **x** will receive the nonfractional part of **f**. In line 3, **f** will convert the 8-bit integer value stored in **ch** to the same value in the floating-point format. This also happens in line 4, except that **f** will convert an integer value into floating-point format.

When converting from integers to characters and long integers to integers, the appropriate amount of high-order bits will be removed. In many environments, this means that 8 bits will be lost when going from an integer to a character and 16 bits will be lost when going from a long integer to an integer.

Table 2-3 summarizes the assignment type conversions. Remember that the conversion of an **int** to a **float**, or a **float** to a **double**, and so on, does not add any precision or accuracy. These kinds of conversions only change the form in which the value is represented. In addition, some C compilers (and processors) always treat a **char** variable as positive, no matter what value it has, when converting it to an **int** or **float**. Other compilers treat **char** variable values greater than 127 as negative numbers when converting. Generally speaking, you should use **char** variables for characters, and use **int**s, **short int**s, or **signed char**s when needed to avoid possible portability problems.

Target Type	Expression Type	Possible Info Loss
signed char	char	If value > 127, target is negative
char	short int	High-order 8 bits
char	int	High-order 8 bits
char	long int	High-order 24 bits
int	long int	High-order 16 bits
int	float	Fractional part and possibly more
float	double	Precision, result rounded
double	long double	Precision, result rounded

Table 2-3. *Common Type Conversions (Assuming a 16-bit Word)*

To use Table 2-3 to make a conversion not shown, simply convert one type at a time until you finish. For example, to convert from **double** to **int**, first convert from **double** to **float** and then from **float** to **int**.

Multiple Assignments

C allows you to assign many variables the same value by using multiple assignments in a single statement. For example, this program fragment assigns **x**, **y**, and **z** the value 0:

```
x = y = z = 0;
```

In professional programs, variables are frequently assigned common values using this method.

Arithmetic Operators

Table 2-4 lists C's arithmetic operators. In C, the operators **+**, **−**, *****, and **/** work as they do in most other computer languages. You can apply them to almost any built-in data type allowed by C. When you apply **/** to an integer or character, any remainder will be truncated. For example, 5/2 will equal 2 in integer division.

Operator	Action
−	Subtraction, also unary minus
+	Addition
*	Multiplication
/	Division
%	Modulus
− −	Decrement
++	Increment

Table 2-4. *Arithmetic Operators*

The modulus operator, %, also works in C as it does in other languages, yielding the remainder of an integer division. However, you cannot use it on floating-point types. The following code fragment illustrates %.

```
int x, y;

x = 5;
y = 2;

printf("%d", x/y);    /* will display 2 */
printf("%d", x%y);    /* will display 1, the remainder of
                             the integer division */

x = 1;
y = 2;

printf("%d %d", x/y, x%y); /*  will display 0 1 */
```

The last line prints a 0 and a 1 because 1/2 in integer division is 0 with a remainder of 1.

The unary minus multiplies its operand by −1. That is, any number preceded by a minus sign switches its sign.

Increment and Decrement

C includes two useful operators not generally found in other computer languages. These are the increment and decrement operators, **++** and **– –**. The operator **++** adds 1 to its operand, and **– –** subtracts one. In other words:

```
x = x+1;
```

is the same as

```
++x;
```

and

```
x = x-1;
```

is the same as

```
x--;
```

Both the increment and decrement operators can either precede (prefix) or follow (postfix) the operand. For example,

```
x = x+1;
```

can be written

```
++x;
```

or

```
x++;
```

There is, however, a difference between the prefix and postfix forms when you use these operators in an expression. When an increment or decrement operator precedes its operand, C performs the increment or decrement operation before obtaining the value of the operand for use in the expression. If the operator follows its operand, C obtains the value of the operand before incrementing or decrementing it. For instance,

```
x = 10;
y = ++x;
```

sets **y** to 11. However, if you write the code as

```
x = 10;
y = x++;
```

y is set to 10. Either way, **x** is set to 11; the difference is in when it happens.

Most C/C++ compilers produce very fast, efficient object code for increment and decrement operations—code that is better than that generated by using the equivalent assignment statement. For this reason, you should use the increment and decrement operators when you can.

Here is the precedence of the arithmetic operators:

Highest	++ −−
	− (unary minus)
	* / %
Lowest	+ −

Operators on the same level of precedence are evaluated by the compiler from left to right. Of course, you can use parentheses to alter the order of evaluation. C treats parentheses in the same way as virtually all other computer languages. Parentheses force an operation, or set of operations, to have a higher level of precedence.

Relational and Logical Operators

In the term "relational operator," *relational* refers to the relationships that values can have with one another. In the term "logical operator," *logical* refers to the ways these relationships can be connected. Because the relational and logical operators often work together, they are discussed together here.

The idea of true and false underlies the concepts of relational and logical operators. In C, true is any value other than zero. False is zero. Expressions that use relational or logical operators return zero for false and 1 for true.

Table 2-5 shows the relational and logical operators. The truth table for the logical operators is shown here, using 1's and 0's.

p	q	p && q	p ¦¦ q	!p
0	0	0	0	1
0	1	0	1	1
1	1	1	1	0
1	0	0	1	0

Both the relational and logical operators are lower in precedence than the arithmetic operators. That is, an expression like 10 > 1+12 is evaluated as if it were written 10 > (1+12). Of course, the result is false.

You can combine several operations into one expression, as shown here:

10>5 && !(10<9) ¦¦ 3<=4

Relational Operators

Operator	Action
>	Greater than
>=	Greater than or equal
<	Less than
<=	Less than or equal
==	Equal
!=	Not equal

Logical Operators

Operator	Action
&&	AND
¦¦	OR
!	NOT

Table 2-5. *Relational and Logical Operators*

In this case, the result is true.

Although neither C nor C++ contains an exclusive OR (XOR) logical operator, you can easily create a function that performs this task using the other logical operators. The outcome of an XOR operation is true if and only if one operand (but not both) is true. The following program contains the function **xor( )**, which returns the outcome of an exclusive OR operation performed on its two arguments.

```
#include <stdio.h>

int xor(int a, int b);

void main(void)
{
  printf("%d", xor(1, 0));
  printf("%d", xor(1, 1));
  printf("%d", xor(0, 1));
  printf("%d", xor(0, 0));
}

/* Perform a logical XOR operation using the
   two arguments. */
xor(int a, int b)
{
  return (a || b) && !(a && b);
}
```

The following table shows the relative precedence of the relational and logical operators.

Highest	!
	> >= < <=
	== !=
	&&
Lowest	||

As with arithmetic expressions, you can use parentheses to alter the natural order of evaluation in a relational and/or logical expression. For example,

!0 && 0 || 0

is false. However, when you add parentheses to the same expression, as shown here, the result is true:

!(0 && 0) || 0

Remember, all relational and logical expressions produce a result of either 0 or 1. Therefore, the following program fragment is not only correct, but will print the number 1.

```
int x;

x = 100;
printf("%d", x>10);
```

Bitwise Operators

Unlike many other languages, C supports a full complement of bitwise operators. Since C was designed to take the place of assembly language for most programming tasks, it needed to be able to support many operations that can be done in assembler, including operations on bits. *Bitwise operation* refers to testing, setting, or shifting the actual bits in a byte or word, which correspond to C's standard **char** and **int** data types and variants. You cannot use bitwise operations on **float**, **double**, **long double**, **void**, or other more complex types. Table 2-6 lists the operators that apply to bitwise operations. These operations are applied to the individual bits of the operands.

The bitwise AND, OR, and NOT (one's complement) are governed by the same truth table as their logical equivalents, except that they work bit by bit. The exclusive OR has the truth table shown here:

p	**q**	**p ^q**
0	0	0
1	0	1
1	1	0
0	1	1

As the table indicates, the outcome of an XOR is true only if exactly one of the operands is true; otherwise, it is false.

Bitwise operations most often find application in device drivers—such as modem programs, disk file routines, and printer routines—because the bitwise operations can be used to mask off certain bits, such as parity. (The *parity* bit confirms that the rest of the bits in the byte are unchanged. It is usually the high-order bit in each byte.)

Think of the bitwise AND as a way to clear a bit. That is, any bit that is 0 in either operand causes the corresponding bit in the outcome to be set to 0. For example, the

Operator	Action
&	AND
¦	OR
^	Exclusive OR (XOR)
~	One's complement (NOT)
>>	Shift right
<<	Shift left

Table 2-6. *Bitwise Operators*

following function reads a character from the modem port using the function **read_modem( )** and resets the parity bit to 0.

```c
char get_char_from_modem(void)
{
  char ch;

  ch = read_modem(); /* get a character from the
                        modem port */
  return(ch & 127);
}
```

Parity is often indicated by the eighth bit, which is set to 0 by ANDing it with a byte that has bits 1 through 7 set to 1, and bit 8 set to 0. The expression **ch & 127** means to AND together the bits in **ch** with the bits that make up the number 127. The net result is that the eighth bit of **ch** is set to 0. In the following example, assume that **ch** had received the character **A** and had the parity bit set.

Parity bit

```
  1 1 0 0 0 0 0 1     ch containing and "A" with parity set
  0 1 1 1 1 1 1 1     127 in binary
& _____      do bitwise AND
  0 1 0 0 0 0 0 1     "A" without parity
```

The bitwise OR, as the reverse of AND, can be used to set a bit. Any bit that is set to 1 in either operand causes the corresponding bit in the outcome to be set to 1. For example, the following is 128 | 3.

```
  1 0 0 0 0 0 0 0     128 in binary
  0 0 0 0 0 0 1 1     3 in binary
| ─────────────       bitwise OR
  1 0 0 0 0 0 1 1     result
```

An exclusive OR, usually abbreviated XOR, will set a bit on if and only if the bits being compared are different. For example, 127 ^120 is

```
  0 1 1 1 1 1 1 1     127 in binary
  0 1 1 1 1 0 0 0     120 in binary
^ ─────────────       bitwise XOR
  0 0 0 0 0 1 1 1     result
```

REMEMBER: *relational and logical operators always produce a result that is either 0 or 1, whereas the similar bitwise operations may produce any arbitrary value in accordance with the specific operation. In other words, bitwise operations can produce values other than 0 or 1, while logical operators will always evaluate to 0 or 1.*

The bit shift operators, >> and <<, move all bits in a variable to the right or left as specified. The general form of the shift-right statement is

variable >> number of bit positions

The general form of the shift-left statement is

variable << number of bit positions

As bits are shifted off one end, zeros are brought in the other end. (In the case of a signed, negative integer, a right shift will cause a 1 to be brought in so that the sign bit is preserved.) Remember, a shift is not a rotate. That is, the bits shifted off one end do not come back around to the other. The bits shifted off are lost.

Bit-shift operations can be very useful when you are decoding input from an external device, like a D/A converter, and reading status information. The bitwise shift operators can also quickly multiply and divide integers. A shift right effectively divides a number by 2 and a shift left multiplies it by 2, as shown in Table 2-7. The following program illustrates the shift operators.

```c
/* A bit shift example. */
#include <stdio.h>

void main(void)
{
  unsigned int i;
  int j;

  i = 1;

  /* left shifts */
  for(j=0; j<4; j++) {
    i = i << 1;  /* left shift i by 1,
              which is same as a multiply by 2 */
    printf("left shift %d: %d\n", j, i);
  }

  /* right shifts */
  for(j=0; j<4; j++) {
    i = i >> 1;  /* right shift i by 1,
              which is same as a division by 2 */
    printf("right shift %d: %d\n", j, i);
  }
}
```

The one's complement operator, ~, reverses the state of each bit in its operand. That is, all 1's are set to 0, and all 0's are set to 1.

The bitwise operators are often used in cipher routines. If you want to make a disk file appear unreadable, perform some bitwise manipulations on it. One of the simplest methods is to complement each byte by using the one's complement to reverse each bit in the byte, as is shown here:

Original byte	0 0 1 0 1 1 0 0
After 1st complement	1 1 0 1 0 0 1 1
After 2nd complement	0 0 1 0 1 1 0 0

Same

Notice that a sequence of two complements in a row always produces the original number. Hence, the first complement represents the coded version of that byte. The second complement decodes the byte to its original value.

unsigned char x;	x as Each Statement Executes	Value of x
x = 7;	00000111	7
x = x<<1;	00001110	14
x = x<<3;	01110000	112
x = x<<2;	11000000	192
x = x>>1;	01100000	96
x = x>>2;	00011000	24

Each left shift multiplies by 2. Notice that information has been lost after x<<2 because a bit was shifted off the end. Each right shift divides by 2. Notice that subsequent divisions do not bring back any lost bits.

Table 2-7. *Multiplication and Division with Shift Operators*

You could use the **encode( )** function shown here to encode a character:

```
/* A simple cipher function. */
char encode(char ch)
{
  return(~ch); /* complement it */
}
```

The ? Operator

C contains a very powerful and convenient operator that replaces certain statements of the if-then-else form. The ternary operator **?** takes the general form

Exp1 ? *Exp2* : *Exp3*;

where *Exp1*, *Exp2*, and *Exp3* are expressions. Notice the use and placement of the colon.

The **?** operator works like this: *Exp1* is evaluated. If it is true, *Exp2* is evaluated and becomes the value of the expression. If *Exp1* is false, *Exp3* is evaluated and its value becomes the value of the expression. For example, in

```
x = 10;

y = x>9 ? 100 : 200;
```

y is assigned the value 100. If **x** had been less than 9, **y** would have received the value 200. The same code written using the **if-else** statement is

```
x = 10;

if(x>9) y = 100;
else y = 200;
```

The **?** operator will be discussed more fully in Chapter 3 in relationship to C's other conditional statements.

The & and * Pointer Operators

A *pointer* is the memory address of a variable. A *pointer variable* is a variable that is specifically declared to hold a pointer to an object of its specified type. Knowing a variable's address can be of great help in certain types of routines. However, pointers have three main functions in C. They can provide a fast means of referencing array elements. They allow C functions to modify their calling parameters. Lastly, they support linked lists and other dynamic data structures. Chapter 5 is devoted exclusively to pointers. However, this chapter briefly covers the two operators that are used to manipulate pointers.

The first pointer operator is **&**, a unary operator that returns the memory address of its operand. (Remember, a unary operator only requires one operand.) For example,

```
m = &count;
```

places into **m** the memory address of the variable **count**. This address is the computer's internal location of the variable. It has nothing to do with the value of **count**. You can think of **&** as meaning "the address of." Therefore, the preceding assignment statement means "**m** receives the address of **count**."

To better understand this assignment, assume that the variable **count** is at memory location 2000. Also assume that **count** has a value of 100. Then, after the previous assignment, **m** will have the value 2000.

The second pointer operator is *****, which is the complement of **&**. The ***** is a unary operator that returns the value of the variable located at the address that follows it. For example, if **m** contains the memory address of the variable **count**,

```
q = *m;
```

places the value of **count** into **q**. Now **q** has the value 100 because 100 is stored at location 2000, the memory address that was stored in **m**. Think of ***** as meaning "at address." In this case, you could read the statement as "**q** receives the value at address **m**."

Unfortunately, the multiplication symbol and the "at address" symbol are the same, and the symbol for the bitwise AND and the "address of" symbol are the same. These operators have no relationship to each other. Both **&** and ***** have a higher precedence than all other arithmetic operators except the unary minus, with which they share equal precedence.

Variables that will hold pointers must be declared as such. Variables that will hold memory addresses, or pointers as they are called in C, must be declared by putting ***** in front of the variable name. This indicates to the compiler that it will hold a pointer to that type of variable. For example, to declare **ch** as a pointer to a character, write

```
char *ch;
```

Here, **ch** is not a character but a pointer to a character—there is a big difference. The type of data that a pointer points to, in this case **char**, is called the *base type* of the pointer. However, the pointer variable itself is a variable that holds the address to an object of the base type. Hence, a character pointer (or any pointer) is of sufficient size to hold an address as defined by the architecture of the computer that it is running on. However, remember that a pointer should only point to data that is of that pointer's base type.

You can mix both pointer and nonpointer variables in the same declaration statement. For example,

```
int x, *y, count;
```

declares **x** and **count** as integer types and **y** as a pointer to an integer type.

The following program uses ***** and **&** operators to put the value **10** into a variable called **target**. As expected, this program displays the value **10** on the screen.

```
#include <stdio.h>

void main(void)
{
  int target, source;
  int *m;

  source = 10;
  m = &source;
  target = *m;

  printf("%d", target);
}
```

The Compile-Time Operator sizeof

sizeof is a unary compile-time operator that returns the length, in bytes, of the variable or parenthesized type-specifier that it precedes. For example, assuming that integers are 2 bytes and **float**s are 8 bytes,

```
float f;

printf("%d ", sizeof f);
printf("%d", sizeof(int));
```

will display **8 2**.

Remember, to compute the size of a type, you must enclose the type name in parentheses. This is not necessary for variable names, although there is no harm done if you do so.

C defines (using **typedef**) a special type called **size_t**, which corresponds loosely to an unsigned integer. Technically, the value returned by **sizeof** is of type **size_t**. For all practical purposes, however, you can think of it (and use it) as if it were an unsigned integer value.

sizeof primarily helps to generate portable code that depends upon the size of the C built-in data types. For example, imagine a database program that needs to store six integer values per record. If you want to port the database program to a variety of computers, you must not assume the size of an integer, but must determine its actual length using **sizeof**. This being the case, you could use the following routine to write a record to a disk file.

```
/* Write 6 integers to a disk file. */
void put_rec(int rec[6], FILE *fp)
{
  int len;

  len = fwrite(rec, sizeof rec, 1, fp);
  if(len != 1) printf("write error");
}
```

Coded as shown, **put_rec( )** compiles and runs correctly on any computer, no matter how many bytes are in an integer.

One final point: **sizeof** is evaluated at compile time, and the value it produces is treated as a constant within your program.

The Comma Operator

The comma operator strings together several expressions. The left side of the comma operator is always evaluated as **void**. This means that the expression on the right side becomes the value of the total comma-separated expression. For example,

x = (y=3, y+1);

first assigns **y** the value 3 and then assigns **x** the value 4. The parentheses are necessary because the comma operator has a lower precedence than the assignment operator.

Essentially, the comma causes a sequence of operations. When you use it on the right side of an assignment statement, the value assigned is the value of the last expression of the comma-separated list.

The comma operator has somewhat the same meaning as the word "and" in normal English as used in the phrase "do this and this and this."

The Dot (.) and Arrow (–>) Operators

The . (dot) and the –>(arrow) operators reference individual elements of structures and unions. *Structures* and *unions* are aggregate data types that may be referenced under a single name (see Chapter 7).

The dot operator is used when working with the actual structure or union. The arrow operator is used with a pointer to a structure or union. For example, given the fragment

```
struct employee
{
  char name[80];
  int age;
  float wage;
} emp;

struct employee *p = &emp; /* address of emp into p */
```

you would write the following code to assign the value 123.23 to the **wage** member of structure variable **emp.**

```
emp.wage = 123.23;
```

However, the same assignment using a pointer to **emp** would be

```
p->wage = 123.23;
```

The ( ) and [ ] Operators

Parentheses are operators that increase the precedence of the operations inside them. Square brackets perform array indexing (arrays will be discussed fully in Chapter 4). Given an array, the expression within square brackets provides an index into that array. For example,

```
#include <stdio.h>
char s[80];

void main(void)
{
    s[3] = 'X';
    printf("%c", s[3]);
}
```

first assigns the value **'X'** to the fourth element (remember all arrays in C begin at 0) of array **s**, and then prints that element.

Precedence Summary

Table 2-8 lists the precedence of all C operators. Note that all operators, except the unary operators and **?**, associate from left to right. The unary operators (*****, **&**, **–**) and **?** associate from right to left.

NOTE: C++ defines a few additional operators, which are discussed at length in Part Two.

Expressions

Operators, constants, and variables are the constituents of expressions. An *expression* in C is any valid combination of these elements. Because most expressions tend to follow the general rules of algebra, they are often taken for granted. However, a few aspects of expressions relate specifically to C (and C++).

Order of Evaluation

Neither the ANSI C standard nor the proposed ANSI C++ standard specifies the order in which the subexpressions of an expression are evaluated. This leaves the compiler free to rearrange an expression to produce more optimal code. However, it also means that your code should never rely upon the order in which subexpressions are evaluated. For example, the expression

```
x = f1() + f2();
```

does not ensure that **f1( )** will be called before **f2( )**.

Type Conversion in Expressions

When constants and variables of different types are mixed in an expression, they are all converted to the same type. The compiler converts all operands up to the type of the largest operand, which is called *type promotion*. First, all **char** and **short int** values are automatically elevated to **int**. (This process is called *integral promotion*.) Once this

Highest	( ) [] ->.
	! ~ ++ -- - (type) * & sizeof
	* / %
	+ -
	<< >>
	< <= > >=
	== !=
	&
	^
	¦
	&&
	¦¦
	?:
	= += -= *= /= etc.
Lowest	,

Table 2-8. *The Precedence of C Operators*

step has been completed, all other conversions are done operation by operation, as described in the following type conversion algorithm:

IF an operand is a **long double**
THEN the second is converted to **long double**
ELSE IF an operand is a **double**
THEN the second is converted to **double**
ELSE IF an operand is a **float**
THEN the second is converted to **float**
ELSE IF an operand is an **unsigned long**
THEN the second is converted to **unsigned long**
ELSE IF an operand is **long**
THEN the second is converted to **long**
ELSE IF an operand is **unsigned int**
THEN the second is converted to **unsigned int**

There is one additional special case: If one operand is **long** and the other is **unsigned int**, and if the value of the **unsigned int** cannot be represented by a **long**, both operands are converted to **unsigned long**.

Once these conversion rules have been applied, each pair of operands is of the same type and the result of each operation is the same as the type of both operands.

For example, consider the type conversions that occur in Figure 2-2. First, the character **ch** is converted to an integer and **float f** is converted to **double**. Then the outcome of **ch/i** is converted to a **double** because **f*d** is **double**. The final result is **double** because, by this time, both operands are **double**.

Casts

You can force an expression to be of a specific type by using a *cast*. The general form of a cast is

(type) expression

where *type* is a valid data type. For example, to make sure that the expression **x/2** evaluates to type **float**, write

```
(float) x/2
```

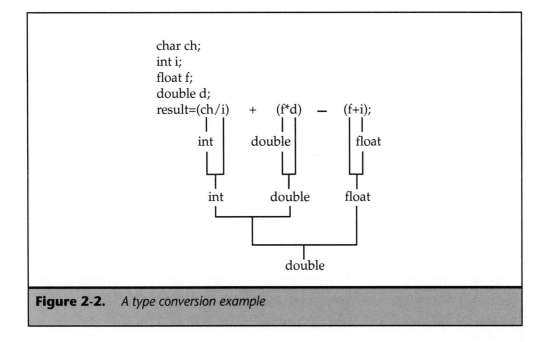

Figure 2-2. *A type conversion example*

Casts are technically operators. As an operator, a cast is unary and has the same precedence as any other unary operator.

Although casts are not common in programming, they can be very useful when needed. For example, suppose you wish to use an integer for loop control, yet to perform computation on it requires a fractional part, as in the following program.

```
#include <stdio.h>

void main(void) /* print i and i/2 with fractions */
{
  int i;

  for(i=1; i<=100; ++i)
    printf("%d / 2 is: %f\n", i, (float) i /2);
}
```

Without the cast **(float)**, only an integer division would have been performed. The cast ensures that the fractional part of the answer is displayed.

NOTE: *The proposed ANSI C++ standard has added several new casting operators, such as **const_cast** and **static_cast**. These operators are discussed in Part Two.*

Spacing and Parentheses

You can add tabs and spaces to C expressions to make them easier to read. For example, the following two expressions are the same.

```
x=10/y~(127/x);

x = 10 / y ~(127/x);
```

Redundant or additional parentheses do not cause errors or slow down the execution of an expression. You should use parentheses to clarify the exact order of evaluation, both for yourself and for others. For example, which of the following two expressions is easier to read?

```
x=y/2-34*temp&127;
x = (y/3) - ((34*temp) & 127);
```

C Shorthand

There is a variation on the assignment statement, sometimes referred to as *C shorthand,* that simplifies the coding of a certain type of assignment operation. For example,

```
x = x+10;
```

can be written as

```
x += 10;
```

The operator **+=** tells the compiler to assign to **x** the value of **x** plus 10.

This shorthand works for all the binary operators (those that require two operands). In general, statements like

var = var operator expression

can be rewritten as

var operator = expression

For another example,

```
x = x-100;
```

is the same as

```
x -= 100;
```

NOTE: *Shorthand notation is widely used in professionally written C/C++ programs; you should become familiar with it.*

Chapter Three

Statements

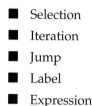

This chapter discusses the statement. In the most general sense, a statement is a part of your program that can be executed. That is, a statement specifies an action. The ANSI C standard (and the proposed ANSI C++ standard) categorizes statements into these groups:

- Selection
- Iteration
- Jump
- Label
- Expression
- Block

Included in the selection statements are **if** and **switch**. (The term *conditional statement* is often used in place of "selection statement.") The iteration statements are **while, for,** and **do-while**. These are also commonly called *loop statements*. The jump statements are **break, continue, goto,** and **return**. The label statements include the **case** and **default** statements (discussed along with the **switch** statement) and the label statement (discussed with **goto**). Expression statements are statements composed of a valid expression. Block statements are simply blocks of code. (Remember, a block begins with a { and ends with a }.) The proposed ANSI C++ standard also refers to block statements as *compound statements*.

NOTE: C++ adds two additional statement types: the **try** block and the declaration statement. These are discussed in Part Two.

Since many statements rely upon the outcome of some conditional test, let's begin by reviewing the concepts of true and false.

True and False in C

Many C statements rely upon a conditional expression that determines what course of action is to be taken. A conditional expression evaluates to either a true or false value. In C, unlike many other computer languages, a true value is any nonzero value, including negative numbers. A false value is 0. This approach to true and false allows a wide range of routines to be coded extremely efficiently, as you will see shortly.

NOTE: While the proposed ANSI C++ standard defines a Boolean data type called **bool** (which can have only the values **true** and **false**), C++ still implements the general concept of true and false in exactly the same way as does C.

Selection Statements

C supports two types of selection statements: **if** and **switch**. In addition, the **?** operator is an alternative to **if** in certain circumstances.

if

The general form of the **if** statement is

> if (*expression*) *statement*;
> else *statement*;

where a *statement* may consist of a single statement, a block of statements, or nothing (in the case of empty statements). The **else** clause is optional.

If *expression* evaluates to true (anything other than 0), the statement or block that forms the target of **if** is executed; otherwise, the statement or block that is the target of **else** will be executed, if it exists. Remember, only the code associated with **if** or the code associated with **else** executes, never both.

The conditional statement controlling **if** must produce a scalar result. A *scalar* is either an integer, character, pointer, or floating-point type. However, it is rare to use a floating-point number to control a conditional statement because this slows execution time considerably. (It takes several instructions to perform a floating-point operation. It takes relatively few instructions to perform an integer or character operation.)

The following program contains an example of **if**. The program plays a very simple version of the "guess the magic number" game. It prints the message ** **Right** ** when the player guesses the magic number. It generates the magic number using C's random number generator **rand( )**, which returns an arbitrary number between 0 and **RAND_MAX** (which defines an integer value that is 32,767 or larger). **rand( )** requires the header file STDLIB.H.

```
/* Magic number program #1. */
#include <stdio.h>
#include <stdlib.h>

void main(void)
{
  int magic; /* magic number */
  int guess; /* user's guess */

  magic = rand(); /* generate the magic number */
```

```
   printf("Guess the magic number: ");
   scanf("%d", &guess);

   if(guess == magic) printf("** Right **");
}
```

Taking the magic-number program further, the next version illustrates the use of the **else** statement to print a message in response to the wrong number.

```
/* Magic number program #2. */
#include <stdio.h>
#include <stdlib.h>

void main(void)
{
  int magic; /* magic number */
  int guess; /* user's guess */

  magic = rand(); /* generate the magic number */

  printf("Guess the magic number: ");
  scanf("%d", &guess);

  if(guess == magic) printf("** Right **");
  else printf("Wrong");
}
```

Nested ifs

A nested **if** is an **if** that is the target of another **if** or **else**. Nested **ifs** are very common in programming. In a nested **if**, an **else** statement always refers to the nearest **if** statement that is within the same block as the **else** and that is not already associated with an **else**. For example,

```
if(i)
{
  if(j) statement 1;
  if(k) statement 2; /* this if */
  else  statement 3; /* is associated with this else */
}
else statement 4; /* associated with if(i) */
```

As noted, the final **else** is not associated with **if(j)** because it is not in the same block. Rather, the final **else** is associated with **if(i)**. Also, the inner **else** is associated with **if(k)**, which is the nearest **if**.

The ANSI C standard specifies that at least 15 levels of nesting must be supported. In practice, most compilers allow substantially more. More importantly, the proposed ANSI C++ standard suggests that at least 256 levels of nested **if**s be allowed in a C++ program. However, nesting beyond a few levels is seldom necessary, and excessive nesting can quickly confuse the meaning of an algorithm.

You can use a nested **if** to further improve the magic number program by providing the player with feedback about a wrong guess.

```c
/* Magic number program #3. */
#include <stdio.h>
#include <stdlib.h>

void main(void)
{
  int magic; /* magic number */
  int guess; /* user's guess */

  magic = rand(); /* get a random number */

  printf("Guess the magic number: ");
  scanf("%d", &guess);

  if (guess == magic) {
    printf("** Right **");
    printf(" %d is the magic number\n", magic);
  }
  else {
    printf("Wrong, ");
    if(guess > magic) printf("too high\n");
    else printf("too low\n");
  }
}
```

The if-else-if Ladder

A common programming construct is the *if-else-if ladder*, sometimes called the *if-else-if staircase* because of its appearance. Its general form is

```
if (expression) statement;
else
  if (expression) statement;
  else
    if (expression) statement;
    .
    .
    .
    else statement;
```

The conditions are evaluated from the top downward. As soon as a true condition is found, the statement associated with it is executed and the rest of the ladder is bypassed. If none of the conditions are true, the final **else** is executed. That is, if all other conditional tests fail, the last **else** statement is performed. If the final **else** is not present, no action takes place if all other conditions are false.

Although the indentation of the preceding if-else-if ladder is technically correct, it can lead to overly deep indentation. For this reason, the if-else-if ladder is generally indented like this:

```
if (expression)
  statement;
else if(expression)
  statement;
else if(expression)
  statement;
  .
  .
  .
else
  statement;
```

Using an if-else-if ladder, the magic number program becomes

```
/* Magic number program #4. */
#include <stdio.h>
#include <stdlib.h>

void main(void)
{
  int magic; /* magic number */
  int guess; /* user's guess */
```

```
   magic = rand(); /* generate the magic number */

   printf("Guess the magic number: ");
   scanf("%d", &guess);

   if(guess == magic) {
     printf("** Right ** ");
     printf("%d is the magic number", magic);
   }
   else if(guess > magic)
     printf("Wrong, too high");
   else printf("Wrong, too low");
}
```

The ? Alternative

You can use the **?** operator to replace **if-else** statements of the general form:

> if(*condition*) *expression*;
> else *expression*;

However, the target of both **if** and **else** must be a single expression—not another statement.

The **?** is called a *ternary operator* because it requires three operands. It takes the general form

> *Exp1* ? *Exp2* : *Exp3*

where *Exp1*, *Exp2*, and *Exp3* are expressions. Notice the use and placement of the colon.

The value of a **?** expression is determined as follows: *Exp1* is evaluated. If it is true, *Exp2* is evaluated and becomes the value of the entire **?** expression. If *Exp1* is false, then *Exp3* is evaluated and its value becomes the value of the expression. For example, consider

```
x = 10;
y = x>9 ? 100 : 200;
```

In this example, **y** is assigned the value 100. If **x** had been less than 9, **y** would have received the value 200. The same code written with the **if-else** statement would be

```
x = 10;
if(x>9) y = 100;
else y = 200;
```

The following program uses the **?** operator to square an integer value entered by the user. However, this program preserves the sign (10 squared is 100 and –10 squared is –100).

```
#include <stdio.h>

void main(void)
{
  int isqrd, i;

  printf("Enter a number: ");
  scanf("%d", &i);

  isqrd = i>0 ? i*i : -(i*i);

  printf("%d squared is %d", i, isqrd);
}
```

The use of the **?** operator to replace **if-else** statements is not restricted to assignments only. Remember, all functions (except those declared as **void**) may return a value. Hence, you can use one or more function calls in an expression. When the function's name is encountered, the function is executed so that its return value may be determined. Therefore, you can execute one or more function calls using the **?** operator by placing the calls in the expressions that form the **?**'s operands, as in

```
#include <stdio.h>

int f1(int n);
int f2(void);

void main(void)
{
  int t;

  printf("Enter a number: ");
```

```
   scanf("%d", &t);

   /* print proper message */
   t ? f1(t) + f2() : printf("zero entered");
}

f1(int n)
{
  printf("%d ", n);
  return 0;
}

f2(void)
{
  printf("entered");
  return 0;
}
```

Entering a 0 in this example calls the **printf( )** function and displays the message **zero entered**. If you enter any other number, both **f1( )** and **f2( )** execute. Note that the value of the **?** expression is discarded in this example. You don't need to assign it to anything.

CAUTION: *Some C/C++ compilers rearrange the order of evaluation of an expression in an attempt to optimize the object code. This could cause functions that form the operands of the* **?** *operator to execute in an unintended sequence.*

Using the **?** operator, you can rewrite the magic number program yet again.

```
/* Magic number program #5. */
#include <stdio.h>
#include <stdlib.h>

void main(void)
{
  int magic;
  int guess;

  magic = rand(); /* generate the magic number */
```

```
printf("Guess the magic number: ");
scanf("%d", &guess);

if(guess == magic) {
  printf("** Right ** ");
  printf("%d is the magic number", magic);
}
else
  guess > magic ? printf("High") : printf("Low");
}
```

Here, the **?** operator displays the proper message based on the outcome of the test **guess > magic**.

The Conditional Expression

Sometimes newcomers to C (and C++) are confused by the fact that you can use any valid expression to control the **if** or the **?** operator. That is, you are not restricted to expressions involving the relational and logical operators (as is the case in languages like BASIC or Pascal). The expression must simply evaluate to either a zero or nonzero value. For example, the following program reads two integers from the keyboard and displays the quotient. It uses an **if** statement, controlled by the second number, to avoid a divide-by-zero error.

```
/* Divide the first number by the second. */

#include <stdio.h>

void main(void)
{
  int a, b;

  printf("Enter two numbers: ");
  scanf("%d%d", &a, &b);

  if(b) printf("%d\n", a/b);
  else printf("Cannot divide by zero.\n");
}
```

This approach works because if **b** is 0, the condition controlling the **if** is false and the **else** executes. Otherwise, the condition is true (nonzero) and the division takes place. However, writing the **if** statement like this:

```
if(b != 0) printf("%d\n", a/b);
```

is redundant and potentially inefficient and is considered bad style.

switch

C has a built-in multiple-branch selection statement, called **switch**, which successively tests the value of an expression against a list of integer or character constants. When a match is found, the statements associated with that constant are executed. The general form of the **switch** statement is

```
switch (expression) {
    case constant1:
        statement sequence
        break;
    case constant2:
        statement sequence
        break;
    case constant3:
        statement sequence
        break;
        .
        .
        .
    default
        statement sequence
}
```

The value of *expression* is tested, in order, against the values of the constants specified in the **case** statements. When a match is found, the statement sequence associated with that **case** is executed until the **break** statement or the end of the **switch** statement is reached. The **default** statement is executed if no matches are found. The **default** is optional and, if it is not present, no action takes place if all matches fail.

The ANSI C standard specifies that a **switch** can have at least 257 **case** statements. The proposed C++ standard recommends that *at least* 16,384 **case** statements be supported. In practice, you will want to limit the number of **case** statements to a smaller amount for efficiency. Although **case** is a label statement, it cannot exist by itself, outside of a **switch**.

The **break** statement is one of C's jump statements. You can use it in loops as well as in the **switch** statement (see the section "Iteration Statements"). When **break** is encountered in a **switch**, program execution "jumps" to the line of code following the **switch** statement. There are three important things to know about the **switch** statement:

■ The **switch** differs from the **if** in that **switch** can only test for equality, whereas **if** can evaluate any type of relational or logical expression.

■ No two **case** constants in the same **switch** can have identical values. Of course, a **switch** statement enclosed by an outer **switch** may have **case** constants that are the same.

■ If character constants are used in the **switch** statement, they are automatically converted to integers.

The **switch** statement is often used to process keyboard commands, such as menu selection. As shown here, the function **menu( )** displays a menu for a spelling-checker program and calls the proper procedures:

```
void menu(void)
{
  char ch;

  printf("1. Check Spelling\n");
  printf("2. Correct Spelling Errors\n");
  printf("3. Display Spelling Errors\n");
  printf("Strike Any Other Key to Skip\n");
  printf("      Enter your choice: ");

  ch = getchar(); /* read the selection from
                     the keyboard */

  switch(ch) {
    case '1':
      check_spelling();
      break;
    case '2':
      correct_errors();
      break;
    case '3':
      display_errors();
      break;
    default :
      printf("No option selected");
  }
}
```

Technically, the **break** statements inside the **switch** statement are optional. They terminate the statement sequence associated with each constant. If the **break** statement is omitted, execution will continue on into the next **case**'s statements until either a **break** or the end of the **switch** is reached. For example, the following function uses the "drop through" nature of the **case**s to simplify the code for a device-driver input handler:

```
/* Process a value */
void inp_handler(int i)
{
  int flag;

  flag = -1;

  switch(i) {
    case 1:  /* these cases have common statement */
    case 2:  /* sequences */
    case 3:
      flag = 0;
      break;
    case 4:
      flag = 1;
    case 5:
      error(flag);
      break;
    default:
      process(i);
  }
}
```

This example illustrates two aspects of **switch**. First, you can have **case** statements that have no statement sequence associated with them. When this occurs, execution simply drops through to the next **case**. In this example, the first three **case**s all execute the same statements, which are

```
flag = 0;
break;
```

Second, execution of one statement sequence continues into the next **case** if no **break** statement is present. If **i** matches 4, **flag** is set to 1 and, because there is no **break** statement at the end of that **case**, execution continues and the call to **error(flag)** is executed. If **i** had matched 5, **error(flag)** would have been called with a flag value of −1 (rather than 1).

The fact that **case**s can run together when no **break** is present prevents the unnecessary duplication of statements, resulting in more efficient code.

Nested switch Statements

You can have a **switch** as part of the statement sequence of an outer **switch**. Even if the **case** constants of the inner and outer **switch** contain common values, no conflicts arise. For example, the following code fragment is perfectly acceptable:

```
switch(x) {
  case 1:
    switch(y) {
      case 0: printf("divide by zero error");
              break;
      case 1: process(x,y);
    }
    break;
  case 2:
    .
    .
    .
```

Iteration Statements

In C, and all other modern programming languages, iteration statements (also called *loops*) allow a set of instructions to be repeatedly executed until a certain condition is reached. This condition may be predefined (as in the **for** loop), or open ended (as in the **while** and **do-while** loops).

The for Loop

The general design of C's **for** loop is reflected in some form or another in all procedural programming languages. However, in C, it provides unexpected flexibility and power.

The general form of the **for** statement is

for(*initialization; condition; increment*) *statement;*

The **for** loop allows many variations. However, the *initialization* is generally an assignment statement that is used to set the loop control variable. The *condition* is a relational expression that determines when the loop exits. The *increment* defines how the loop control variable changes each time the loop is repeated. You must separate these three major sections by semicolons. The **for** loop continues to execute as long as the condition is true. Once the condition becomes false, program execution resumes on the statement following the **for**.

In the following program, a **for** loop is used to display the numbers 1 through 100 on the screen:

```c
#include <stdio.h>

void main(void)
{
  int x;

  for(x=1; x <= 100; x++) printf("%d ", x);
}
```

In the loop, **x** is initially set to 1 and then compared with 100. Since **x** is less than 100, **printf( )** is called and the loop iterates. This causes **x** to be increased by 1 and again tested to see if it is still less than or equal to 100. If it is, **printf( )** is called. This process repeats until **x** is greater than 100, at which point the loop terminates. In this example, **x** is the loop control variable, which is changed and checked each time the loop repeats.

The following example is a **for** loop that iterates multiple statements:

```c
for(x=100; x != 65; x -= 5) {
  z = x*x;
  printf("The square of %d, %f", x, z);
}
```

Both the squaring of **x** and the call to **printf( )** are executed until **x** equals 65. Note that the loop is *negative running:* **x** is initialized to 100, and 5 is subtracted from it each time the loop repeats.

In **for** loops, the conditional test is always performed at the top of the loop. This means that the code inside the loop may not be executed at all if the condition is false to begin with. For example, in

```c
x = 10;
for(y=10; y!=x; ++y) printf("%d", y);
printf("%d", y);   /* this is the only printf()
                    statement that will execute */
```

the loop will never execute because **x** and **y** are equal when the loop is entered. Because this causes the conditional expression to evaluate to false, neither the body of the loop nor the increment portion of the loop executes. Hence, **y** still has the value 10, and the only output produced by the fragment is the number 10 printed once on the screen.

for Loop Variations

The previous discussion described the most common form of the **for** loop. However, several variations of the **for** are allowed that increase its power, flexibility, and applicability to certain programming situations.

One of the most common variations uses the comma operator to allow two or more variables to control the loop. (Remember, you use the comma operator to string together a number of expressions in a "do this and this" fashion. See Chapter 2.) For example, the variables **x** and **y** control the following loop, and both are initialized inside the **for** statement:

```
for(x=0, y=0; x+y<10; ++x) {
  y = getchar();
  y = y-'0'; /* subtract the ASCII code for 0
              from y */
     .
     .
     .
}
```

Commas separate the two initialization statements. Each time the loop repeats, **x** is incremented and **y**'s value is set by keyboard input. Both **x** and **y** must be at the correct value for the loop to terminate. Even though **y**'s value is set by keyboard input, **y** must be initialized to 0 so that its value is defined before the first evaluation of the conditional expression. (If **y** were not defined, it could by chance contain the value 10, making the conditional test false and preventing the loop from executing.)

The **converge( )** function shown next demonstrates multiple loop control variables. The **converge( )** function displays a string by printing characters from both ends, converging in the middle at the specified line. This requires positioning the cursor at various disconnected points on the screen. Because C/C++ runs under a wide variety of environments, it does not define a cursor positioning function. However, virtually all C/C++ compilers supply one, although its name may vary. The following program uses Borland's cursor positioning function, which is called **gotoxy( )**. (It requires the header CONIO.H.)

```
/* Borland version. */
#include <stdio.h>
#include <conio.h>
#include <string.h>

void converge(int line, char *message);

void main(void)
{
  converge(10, "This is a test of converge().");
}

/* This function displays a string starting at the left
   side of the specified line.  It writes characters
   from both the ends, converging at the middle. */
void converge(int line, char *message)
{
  int i, j;

  for(i=1, j=strlen(message); i<j; i++, j--) {
    gotoxy(i, line); printf("%c", message[i-1]);
    gotoxy(j, line); printf("%c", message[j-1]);
  }
}
```

The Microsoft equivalent of **gotoxy( )** is **_settextposition( )**, which uses the header file **graph.h**. The preceding program, recoded for Microsoft C/C++, is shown here:

```
/* Microsoft version. */
#include <stdio.h>
#include <graph.h>
#include <string.h>

void converge(int line, char *message);

void main(void)
{
  converge(10, "This is a test of converge().");
```

```
   }

   /* This function displays a string starting at the left
      side of the specified line.  It writes characters
      from both the ends converging at the middle. */
   void converge(int line, char *message)
   {
     int i, j;

     for(i=1, j=strlen(message); i<j; i++, j--) {
       _settextposition(line, i);
       printf("%c", message[i-1]);
       _settextposition(line, j);
       printf("%c", message[j-1]);
     }
   }
```

If you use a different C/C++ compiler, you will need to check your user manuals for the name of your cursor positioning function.

In both versions of **converge( )**, the **for** loop uses two loop control variables, **i** and **j**, to index the string from opposite ends. As the loop iterates, **i** is increased and **j** is decreased. The loop stops when **i** is equal to or greater than **j**, thus ensuring that all characters are written.

The conditional expression does not have to involve testing the loop control variable against some target value. In fact, the condition may be any relational or logical statement. This means that you can test for several possible terminating conditions.

For example, you could use the following function to log a user onto a remote system. The user has three tries to enter the password. The loop terminates when the three tries are used up or the user enters the correct password.

```
   void sign_on(void)
   {
     char str[20];
     int x;

     for(x=0; x<3 && strcmp(str, "password"); ++x) {
       printf("Enter password please:");
       gets(str);
     }

     if(x==3) return;
     /* else log user in ... */
   }
```

This function uses **strcmp( )**, the standard library function that compares two strings and returns 0 if they match.

Remember that each of the three sections of the **for** loop may consist of any valid expression. The expressions need not actually have anything to do with what the sections are generally used for. With this in mind, consider the following example:

```c
#include <stdio.h>

int sqrnum(int num);
int readnum(void);
int prompt(void);

void main(void)
{
  int t;

  for(prompt(); t=readnum(); prompt())
    sqrnum(t);
}

prompt(void)
{
  printf("Enter a number: ");
  return 0;
}

readnum(void)
{
  int t;

  scanf("%d", &t);
  return t;
}

sqrnum(int num)
{
  printf("%d\n", num*num);
  return num*num;
}
```

Look closely at the **for** loop in **main( )**. Notice that each part of the **for** loop is composed of function calls that prompt the user and read a number entered from the keyboard. If the number entered is 0, the loop terminates because the conditional expression will be false. Otherwise, the number is squared. Thus, this **for** loop uses the initialization and increment portions in a nontraditional but completely valid sense.

Another interesting trait of the **for** loop is that pieces of the loop definition need not be there. In fact, there need not be an expression present for any of the sections—the expressions are optional. For example, this loop will run until the user enters **123**:

```
for(x=0; x!=123; ) scanf("%d", &x);
```

Notice that the increment portion of the **for** definition is blank. This means that each time the loop repeats, **x** is tested to see if it equals 123, but no further action takes place. If you type **123** at the keyboard, however, the loop condition becomes false and the loop terminates.

The initialization often occurs outside the **for** statement. This most frequently happens when the initial condition of the loop control variable must be computed by some complex means, as in this example:

```
gets(s);  /* read a string into s */
if(*s) x = strlen(s); /* get the string's length */
else x = 10;

for( ; x<10; ) {
  printf("%d", x);
  ++x;
}
```

The initialization section has been left blank, and **x** is initialized before the loop is entered.

The Infinite Loop

Although you can use any loop statement to create an infinite loop, **for** is traditionally used for this purpose. Since none of the three expressions that form the **for** loop are required, you can make an endless loop by leaving the conditional expression empty, as shown here:

```
for( ; ; ) printf(" This loop will run forever.\n");
```

When the conditional expression is absent, it is assumed to be true. You may have an initialization and increment expression, but C/C++ programmers more commonly use the **for(;;)** construct to signify an infinite loop.

Actually, the **for(;;)** construct does not guarantee an infinite loop because a **break** statement, encountered anywhere inside the body of a loop, causes immediate termination (**break** is discussed later in this chapter). Program control then resumes at the code following the loop, as shown here:

```
ch = '\0';

for( ; ; ) {
  ch = getchar(); /* get a character */
  if(ch=='A') break; /* exit the loop */
}

printf("you typed an A");
```

This loop will run until the user types an **A** at the keyboard.

for Loops with No Bodies

A statement may be empty. This means that the body of the **for** loop (or any other loop) may also be empty. You can use this fact to improve the efficiency of certain algorithms and to create time delay loops.

Removing spaces from an input stream is a common programming task. For example, a database program may allow a query such as "show all balances less than 400." The database needs to have each word fed to it separately, without spaces. That is, the database input processor recognizes "**show**" but not " **show**". The following loop removes leading spaces from the stream pointed to by **str**.

```
for( ; *str == ' '; str++) ;
```

As you can see, this loop has no body—and no need for one either.

Time delay loops are often used in programs. The following code shows how to create one by using **for**:

```
for(t=0; t<SOME_VALUE; t++) ;
```

The while Loop

The second loop available in C is the **while** loop. Its general form is

while(*condition*) *statement*;

where *statement* is either an empty statement, a single statement, or a block of statements. The *condition* may be any expression, and true is any nonzero value. The loop iterates while the condition is true. When the condition becomes false, program control passes to the line of code immediately following the loop.

The following example shows a keyboard input routine that simply loops until the user types **A**:

```
wait_for_char(void)
{
  char ch;

  ch = '\0';  /* initialize ch */
  while(ch != 'A') ch = getchar();
  return ch;
}
```

First, **ch** is initialized to null. As a local variable, its value is not known when **wait_for_char( )** is executed. The **while** loop then checks to see if **ch** is not equal to **A**. Because **ch** was initialized to null, the test is true and the loop begins. Each time you press a key, the condition is tested again. Once you enter an **A**, the condition becomes false because **ch** equals **A**, and the loop terminates.

Like **for** loops, **while** loops check the test condition at the top of the loop, which means that the body of the loop will not execute if the condition is false to begin with. This feature may eliminate the need to perform a separate conditional test before the loop. The **pad( )** function provides a good illustration of this. It adds spaces to the end of a string to fill the string to a predefined length. If the string is already at the desired length, no spaces are added.

```
#include <stdio.h>
#include <string.h>

void pad(char *s, int length);

void main(void)
{
  char str[80];

  strcpy(str, "this is a test");
  pad(str, 40);
  printf("%d", strlen(str));
}
```

```
/* Add spaces to the end of a string. */
void pad(char *s, int length)
{
  int l;

  l = strlen(s); /* find out how long it is */

  while(l<length) {
    s[l] = ' '; /* insert a space */
    l++;
  }
  s[l]= '\0'; /* strings need to be
                 terminated in a null */
}
```

The two arguments of **pad( )** are **s**, a pointer to the string to lengthen, and **length**, the number of characters that **s** should have. If the length of string **s** is already equal to or greater than **length**, the code inside the **while** loop does not execute. If **s** is shorter than **length**, **pad( )** adds the required number of spaces. The **strlen( )** function, part of the standard library, returns the length of the string.

If several separate conditions need to terminate a **while** loop, a single variable commonly forms the conditional expression. The value of this variable is set at various points throughout the loop. In this example,

```
void func1(void)
{
  int working;

  working = 1; /* i.e., true */

  while(working) {
    working = process1();
    if(working)
      working = process2();
    if(working)
      working = process3();
  }
}
```

any of the three routines may return false and cause the loop to exit.

There need not be any statements in the body of the **while** loop. For example,

```
while((ch=getchar()) != 'A') ;
```

will simply loop until the user types **A**. If you feel uncomfortable putting the assignment inside the **while** conditional expression, remember that the equal sign is just an operator that evaluates to the value of the right-hand operand.

The do-while Loop

Unlike **for** and **while** loops, which test the loop condition at the top of the loop, the **do-while** loop checks its condition at the bottom of the loop. This means that a **do-while** loop always executes at least once. The general form of the **do-while** loop is

```
do{
  statement;
} while(condition);
```

Although the curly braces are not necessary when only one statement is present, they are usually used to avoid confusion (to you, not the compiler) with the **while**. The **do-while** loop iterates until *condition* becomes false.

The following **do-while** loop will read numbers entered from the keyboard until it finds a number less than or equal to 100.

```
do {
  scanf("%d", &num);
} while(num > 100);
```

Perhaps the most common use of the **do-while** loop is in a menu selection function. When the user enters a valid response, it is returned as the value of the function. Invalid responses cause a reprompt. The following code shows an improved version of the spelling-checker menu developed earlier in this chapter:

```
void menu(void)
{
  char ch;

  printf("1. Check Spelling\n");
  printf("2. Correct Spelling Errors\n");
  printf("3. Display Spelling Errors\n");
  printf("      Enter your choice: ");

  do {
```

```
   ch = getchar(); /* read the selection from
                      the keyboard */
   switch(ch) {
     case '1':
       check_spelling();
       break;
     case '2':
       correct_errors();
       break;
     case '3':
       display_errors();
       break;
   }
 } while(ch!='1' && ch!='2' && ch!='3');
}
```

Here, the **do-while** loop is a good choice because you will always want a menu
function to execute at least once. After the options have been displayed, the program
will loop until a valid option is selected.

Jump Statements

C has four statements that perform an unconditional branch: **return**, **goto**, **break**, and
continue. Of these, you may use **return** and **goto** anywhere in your program. You may
use the **break** and **continue** statements in conjunction with any of the loop statements.
As discussed earlier in this chapter, you can also use **break** with **switch**.

The return Statement

The **return** statement is used to return from a function. It is categorized as a jump
statement because it causes execution to return (jump back) to the point at which the
call to the function was made. A **return** may or may not have a value associated with
it. If **return** has a value associated with it, that value becomes the return value of the
function. In C, a non-**void** function does not technically have to return a value. If no
return value is specified, a garbage value is returned. However, in C++, a non-**void**
function *must* return a value. That is, in C++, if a function is specified as returning a
value, any **return** statement within it must have a value associated with it. (Even in C,
if a function is declared as returning a value, it is good practice to actually return one.)

The general form of the **return** statement is

return *expression*;

The *expression* is only present if the function is declared as returning a value. In this case, the value of *expression* will become the return value of the function.

You can use as many **return** statements as you like within a function. However, the function will stop executing as soon as it encounters the first **return**. The } that ends a function also causes the function to return. It is the same as a **return** without any specified value. If this occurs within a non-**void** function, then the return value of the function is undefined.

A function declared as **void** may not contain a **return** statement that specifies a value. (Since a **void** function has no return value, it makes sense that no **return** statement within a **void** function can return a value.)

See Chapter 6 for more information on **return**.

The goto Statement

Since C has a rich set of control structures and allows additional control using **break** and **continue**, there is little need for **goto**. Most programmers' chief concern about the **goto** is its tendency to render programs unreadable. Nevertheless, although the **goto** statement fell out of favor some years ago, it has managed to polish its tarnished image somewhat. There are no programming situations that require **goto**. Rather, it is a convenience, which, if used wisely, can be a benefit in a narrow set of programming situations. As such, **goto** is not used outside of this section.

The **goto** statement requires a label for operation. (A *label* is a valid identifier followed by a colon.) Furthermore, the label must be in the same function as the **goto** that uses it—you cannot jump between functions. The general form of the **goto** statement is

goto *label*;
.
.
.
label:

where *label* is any valid label either before or after **goto**. For example, you could create a loop from 1 to 100 using the **goto** and a label, as shown here:

```
x = 1;
loop1:
  x++;
  if(x<100) goto loop1;
```

The break Statement

The **break** statement has two uses. You can use it to terminate a **case** in the **switch** statement (covered in the section on **switch** earlier in this chapter). You can also use it to force immediate termination of a loop, bypassing the normal loop conditional test.

When the **break** statement is encountered inside a loop, the loop is immediately terminated and program control resumes at the next statement following the loop. For example,

```
#include <stdio.h>

void main(void)
{
  int t;

  for(t=0; t<100; t++) {
    printf("%d ", t);
    if(t==10) break;
  }
}
```

displays the numbers 0 through 10 on the screen. Then the loop terminates because **break** causes immediate exit from the loop, overriding the conditional test **t<100**.

Programmers often use the **break** statement in loops in which a special condition can cause immediate termination. For example, here a keypress can stop the execution of the **look_up( )** function:

```
look_up(char *name)
{
  do {
    /* look up names ... */
    if(kbhit()) break;
  } while(!found);
  /* process match */
}
```

The **kbhit( )** function returns 0 if you do not press a key. Otherwise, it returns a nonzero value. Because of the wide differences between computing environments, neither the ANSI C standard nor the proposed ANSI C++ standard defines **kbhit( )**, but you will almost certainly have it (or one with a slightly different name) supplied with your compiler.

A **break** causes an exit from only the innermost loop. For example,

```
for(t=0; t<100; ++t) {
  count = 1;
  for(;;) {
    printf("%d ", count);
    count++;
    if(count==10) break;
  }
}
```

displays the numbers 1 through 10 on the screen 100 times. Each time the compiler encounters **break**, control is passed back to the outer **for** loop.

A **break** used in a **switch** statement will affect only that **switch**. It does not affect any loop the **switch** happens to be in.

The exit( ) Function

Although **exit( )** is not a program control statement, a short digression that discusses it is in order at this time. Just as you can break out of a loop, you can break out of a program by using the standard library function **exit( )**. This function causes immediate termination of the entire program, forcing a return to the operating system. In effect, the **exit( )** function acts as if it were breaking out of the entire program.

The general form of the **exit( )** function is

void exit(int *return_code*);

The value of *return_code* is returned to the calling process, which is usually the operating system. Zero is generally used as a return code to indicate normal program termination. Other arguments are used to indicate some sort of error.

Programmers frequently use **exit( )** when a mandatory condition for program execution is not satisfied. For example, imagine a virtual-reality computer game that requires a special graphics adapter. The **main( )** function of this game might look like this,

```
void main(void)
{
  if(!virtual_graphics()) exit(1);
  play();
}
```

where **virtual_graphics( )** is a user-defined function that returns true if the virtual-reality graphics adapter is present. If the adapter is not in the system, **virtual_graphics( )** returns false and the program terminates.

As another example, this version of **menu( )** uses **exit( )** to quit the program and return to the operating system:

```
void menu(void)
{
  char ch;

  printf("1. Check Spelling\n");
  printf("2. Correct Spelling Errors\n");
  printf("3. Display Spelling Errors\n");
  printf("4. Quit\n");
  printf("       Enter your choice: ");

  do {
    ch = getchar(); /* read the selection from
                        the keyboard */
      switch(ch) {
        case '1':
          check_spelling();
          break;
        case '2':
          correct_errors();
          break;
        case '3':
          display_errors();
          break;
        case '4':
          exit(0); /* return to OS */
      }
  } while(ch!='1' && ch!='2' && ch!='3');
}
```

The continue Statement

The **continue** statement works somewhat like the **break** statement. Instead of forcing termination, however, **continue** forces the next iteration of the loop to take place, skipping any code in between. For the **for** loop, **continue** causes the increment portions and then the conditional test of the loop to execute. For the **while** and **do-while** loops, program control passes to the conditional tests. For example, the following program counts the number of spaces contained in the string entered by the user:

```
/* Count spaces */
#include <stdio.h>

void main(void)
{
  char s[80], *str;
  int space;

  printf("enter a string: ");
  gets(s);
  str = s;

  for(space=0; *str; str++) {
    if(*str != ' ') continue;
    space++;
  }
  printf("%d spaces\n", space);
}
```

Each character is tested to see if it is a space. If it is not, the **continue** statement forces the **for** to iterate again. If the character *is* a space, **space** is incremented.

The following example shows how you can use **continue** to expedite the exit from a loop by forcing the conditional test to be performed sooner:

```
void code(void)
{
  char done, ch;

  done = 0;
  while(!done) {
    ch = getchar();
    if(ch=='$') {
      done = 1;
      continue;
    }
    putchar(ch+1); /* shift the alphabet one
                      position higher */
  }
}
```

This function codes a message by shifting all characters you type one letter higher. For example, an **A** becomes a **B**. The function will terminate when you type a **$**. After a **$**

has been input, no further output will occur because the conditional test, brought into effect by **continue**, will find **done** to be true and will cause the loop to exit.

Expression Statements

Chapter 2 covers expressions thoroughly. However, a few special points are mentioned here. Remember, an expression statement is simply a valid expression followed by a semicolon, as in

```
func();  /* a function call */
a = b+c; /* an assignment statement */
b+f();   /* a valid, but strange statement */
;        /* an empty statement */
```

The first expression statement executes a function call. The second is an assignment. The third expression, though strange, is still evaluated by the C/C++ compiler because the function **f( )** may perform some necessary task. The final example shows that C allows a statement to be empty (sometimes called a *null statement*).

Block Statements

Block statements are simply groups of related statements that are treated as a unit. The statements that make up a block are logically bound together. A block is begun with a { and terminated by its matching }. Programmers use block statements most commonly to create a multistatement target for some other statement, such as **if**. However, you may place a block statement anywhere you would put any other statement. For example, this is perfectly valid (although unusual) C code:

```
#include <stdio.h>

void main(void)
{
  int i;

  {  /* a block statement */
    i = 120;
    printf("%d", i);
  }
}
```

Chapter Four

Arrays and Strings

A n *array* is a collection of variables of the same type that are referenced by a common name. A specific element in an array is accessed by an index. In C, all arrays consist of contiguous memory locations. The lowest address corresponds to the first element and the highest address to the last element. Arrays may have from one to several dimensions. The most common array in C is the *string*, which is simply an array of characters terminated by a null. This approach to strings gives C greater power and efficiency than other languages.

In C, arrays and pointers are closely related; a discussion of one usually refers to the other. This chapter focuses on arrays, while Chapter 5 looks closely at pointers. You should read both to understand fully these important C constructs.

Single-Dimension Arrays

The general form for declaring a single-dimensioned array is

type var_name[size];

Like other variables, arrays must be explicitly declared so that the compiler may allocate space for them in memory. Here, *type* declares the base type of the array, which is the type of each element in the array. *size* defines how many elements the array will hold. For example, to declare a 100-element array called **balance**, and of type **double**, use this statement:

```
double balance[100];
```

In C, all arrays have 0 as the index of their first element. Therefore, when you write

```
char p[10];
```

you are declaring a character array that has ten elements, **p[0]** through **p[9]**. For example, the following program loads an integer array with the numbers 0 through 99.

```
void main(void)
{
  int x[100]; /* this declares a 100-integer array */
  int t;

  for(t=0; t<100; ++t) x[t] = t;
}
```

The amount of storage required to hold an array is directly related to its type and size. For a single-dimension array, the total size in bytes is computed as shown here:

*total bytes = sizeof(base type) * size of array*

C has no bounds checking on arrays. You could overwrite either end of an array and write into some other variable's data or even into the program's code. As the programmer, it is your job to provide bounds checking where needed. For example, this code will compile without error, but is incorrect because the **for** loop will cause the array **count** to be overrun.

```
int count[10], i;

/* this causes count to be overrun */
for(i=0; i<100; i++) count[i] = i;
```

Single-dimension arrays are essentially lists of information of the same type that are stored in contiguous memory locations in index order. For example, Figure 4-1 shows how array **a** appears in memory if it starts at memory location 1000 and is declared as shown here:

```
char a[7];
```

Generating a Pointer to an Array

You can generate a pointer to the first element of an array by simply specifying the array name, without any index. For example, given

```
int sample[10];
```

Element	a[0]	a[1]	a[2]	a[3]	a[4]	a[5]	a[6]
Address	1000	1001	1002	1003	1004	1005	1006

Figure 4-1.   *A seven-element character array beginning at location 1000*

you can generate a pointer to the first element by using the name **sample**. For example, the following program fragment assigns **p** the address of the first element of **sample**.

```
int *p;
int sample[10];

p = sample;
```

You can also specify the address of the first element of an array using the **&** operator. For example, **sample** and **&sample[0]** both produce the same results. However, in professionally written C/C++ code, you will almost never see **&sample[0]**.

Passing Single-Dimension Arrays to Functions

In C, you cannot pass an entire array as an argument to a function. You can, however, pass to the function a pointer to an array by specifying the array's name without an index. For example, the following program fragment passes the address of **i** to **func1( )**.

```
void main(void)
{
  int i[10];

  func1(i);
  .
  .
  .
}
```

If a function receives a single-dimension array, you can declare its formal parameter in one of three ways: as a pointer, as a sized array, or as an unsized array. For example, to receive **i**, a function called **func1( )** can be declared as

```
void func1(int *x) /* pointer */
{
  .
  .
```

```
      .
}
```

or

```
void func1(int x[10]) /* sized array */
{
      .
      .
      .
}
```

or finally as

```
void func1(int x[]) /* unsized array */
{
      .
      .
      .
}
```

All three declaration methods produce similar results because each tells the compiler that an integer pointer is going to be received. The first declaration actually uses a pointer. The second employs the standard array declaration. In the final version, a modified version of an array declaration simply specifies that an array of type **int** of some length is to be received. As you can see, the length of the array doesn't matter as far as the function is concerned because C performs no bounds checking. In fact, as far as the compiler is concerned,

```
void func1(int x[32])
{
      .
      .
      .
}
```

also works because the C compiler generates code that instructs **func1( )** to receive a pointer—it does not actually create a 32-element array.

Strings

By far the most common use of one-dimensional arrays is as character strings. Remember, in C, a string is defined as a character array that is terminated by a null. A null is specified as `'\0'` and is zero. For this reason, you need to declare character arrays to be one character longer than the largest string that they are to hold. For example, to declare an array **str** that can hold a 10-character string, you would write

```
char str[11];
```

This makes room for the null at the end of the string.

Although C does not have a string data type, it allows string constants. A *string constant* is a list of characters enclosed in double quotes. For example,

```
"hello there"
```

You do not need to add the null to the end of string constants manually—the compiler does this for you automatically.

C supports a wide range of string manipulation functions. The most common are listed here:

Name	Function
strcpy(s1, s2)	Copies s2 into s1
strcat(s1, s2)	Concatenates s2 onto the end of s1
strlen(s1)	Returns the length of s1
strcmp(s1, s2)	Returns 0 if s1 and s2 are the same; less than 0 if s1<s2; greater than 0 if s1>s2
strchr(s1, ch)	Returns a pointer to the first occurrence of ch in s1
strstr(s1, s2)	Returns a pointer to the first occurrence of s2 in s1

These functions use the standard header file STRING.H. The following program illustrates the use of these string functions.

```
#include <stdio.h>
#include <string.h>

void main(void)
{
  char s1[80], s2[80];

  gets(s1);
```

```
    gets(s2);

    printf("lengths: %d %d\n", strlen(s1), strlen(s2));

    if(!strcmp(s1, s2)) printf("The strings are equal\n");

    strcat(s1, s2);
    printf("%s\n", s1);

    strcpy(s1, "This is a test.\n");
    printf(s1);
    if(strchr("hello", 'e')) printf("e is in hello\n");
    if(strstr("hi there", "hi")) printf("found hi");
}
```

If you run this program and enter the strings "**hello**" and "**hello**", the output is

```
lengths: 5 5
The strings are equal
hellohello
This is a test.
e is in hello
found hi
```

> REMEMBER: *strcmp( ) returns false if the strings are equal. Be sure to use the logical operator ! to reverse the condition, as just shown, if you are testing for equality.*

Two-Dimensional Arrays

C supports multidimensional arrays. The simplest form of the multidimensional array is the two-dimensional array. A two-dimensional array is, essentially, an array of one-dimensional arrays. To declare a two-dimensional integer array **d** of size 10,20, you would write

```
int d[10][20];
```

Pay careful attention to the declaration. Most other computer languages use commas to separate the array dimensions; C, in contrast, places each dimension in its own set of brackets.

Similarly, to access point 1,2 of array **d**, you would use

```
d[1][2]
```

The following example loads a two-dimensional array with the numbers 1 through 12 and prints them row by row.

```
#include <stdio.h>

void main(void)
{
  int t, i, num[3][4];

  for(t=0; t<3; ++t)
    for(i=0; i<4; ++i)
      num[t][i] = (t*4)+i+1;

  /* now print them out */
  for(t=0; t<3; ++t) {
    for(i=0; i<4; ++i)
      printf("%3d ", num[t][i]);
    printf("\n");
  }
}
```

In this example, **num[0][0]** has the value 1, **num[0][1]** the value 2, **num[0][2]** the value 3, and so on. The value of **num[2][3]** will be 12. You can visualize the **num** array as shown here:

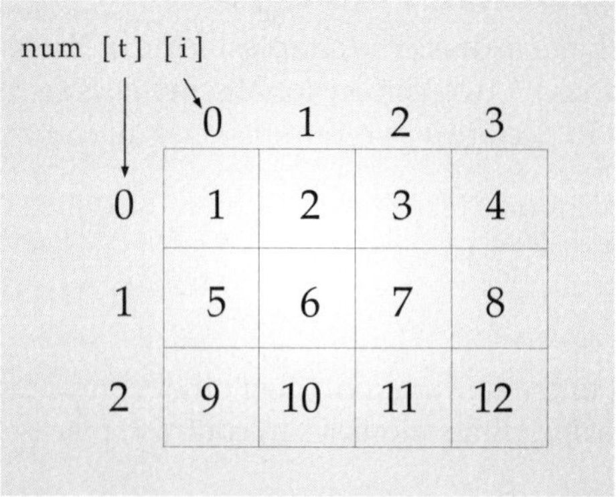

num [t] [i]

	0	1	2	3
0	1	2	3	4
1	5	6	7	8
2	9	10	11	12

Two-dimensional arrays are stored in a row-column matrix, where the first index indicates the row and the second indicates the column. This means that the rightmost index changes faster than the leftmost when accessing the elements in the array in the order in which they are actually stored in memory. See Figure 4-2 for a graphic representation of a two-dimensional array in memory.

In the case of a two-dimensional array, the following formula yields the number of bytes of memory needed to hold it:

bytes = size of 1st index * size of 2nd index * sizeof(base type)

Therefore, assuming 2-byte integers, an integer array with dimensions 10,5 would have

10 * 5 * 2

or 100 bytes allocated.

When a two-dimensional array is used as an argument to a function, only a pointer to the first element is actually passed. However, the parameter receiving a two-dimensional array must define at least the size of the rightmost dimension. This is because the C/C++ compiler needs to know the length of each row if it is to index the

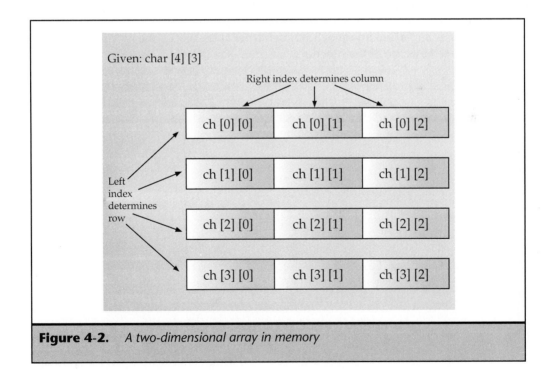

Figure 4-2. *A two-dimensional array in memory*

array correctly. For example, a function that receives a two-dimensional integer array with dimensions 10,10 is declared like this:

```
void func1(int x[][10])
{
    .
    .
    .
}
```

You can specify the left dimension if you like, but it is not necessary. In either case, the compiler needs to know the size of the right dimension in order to correctly execute expressions such as

```
x[2][4]
```

inside the function. If the length of the rows is not known, the compiler cannot determine where the third row begins.

The following short program uses a two-dimensional array to store the numeric grade for each student in a teacher's classes. The program assumes that the teacher has three classes and a maximum of 30 students per class. Notice the way the array **grade** is accessed by each of the functions.

```
#include <stdio.h>
#include <ctype.h>
#include <stdlib.h>

/* A simple student grades database. */

#define CLASSES  3
#define GRADES   30

int grade[CLASSES][GRADES];

void enter_grades(void);
int get_grade(int num);
void disp_grades(int g[][GRADES]);

void main(void)
{
    char ch, str[80];
```

```
  for(;;) {
    do {
      printf("(E)nter grades\n");
      printf("(R)eport grades\n");
      printf("(Q)uit\n");
      gets(str);
      ch = toupper(*str);
    } while(ch!='E' && ch!='R' && ch!='Q');

    switch(ch) {
      case 'E':
        enter_grades();
        break;
      case 'R':
        disp_grades(grade);
        break;
      case 'Q':
        exit(0);
    }
  }
}

/* Enter the student's grades. */
void enter_grades(void)
{
  int t, i;

  for(t=0; t<CLASSES; t++) {
    printf("Class # %d:\n", t+1);
    for(i=0; i<GRADES; ++i)
      grade[t][i] = get_grade(i);
  }
}

/* Read a grade. */
get_grade(int num)
{
  char s[80];

  printf("Enter grade for student # %d:\n", num+1);
  gets(s);
```

```
  return(atoi(s));
}

/* Display grades. */
void disp_grades(int g[][GRADES])
{
  int t, i;

  for(t=0; t<CLASSES; ++t) {
    printf("Class # %d:\n", t+1);
    for(i=0; i<GRADES; ++i)
      printf("Student #%d is %d\n", i+1, g[t][i]);
  }
}
```

Arrays of Strings

It is not uncommon in programming to use an array of strings. For example, the input processor to a database may verify user commands against an array of valid commands. To create an array of strings, use a two-dimensional character array. The size of the left index determines the number of strings, and the size of the right index specifies the maximum length of each string. The following code declares an array of 30 strings, each with a maximum length of 79 characters.

```
char str_array[30][80];
```

It is easy to access an individual string: you simply specify only the left index. For example, the following statement calls **gets( )** with the third string in **str_array**.

```
gets(str_array[2]);
```

The preceding statement is functionally equivalent to

```
gets(&str_array[2][0]);
```

but the first of the two forms is much more common in professionally written C/C++ code.

To understand better how string arrays work, study the following short program, which uses a string array as the basis for a very simple text editor.

```c
#include <stdio.h>

#define MAX 100
#define LEN 80

char text[MAX][LEN];

/* A very simple text editor. */
void main(void)
{
  register int t, i, j;

  printf("Enter an empty line to quit.\n");

  for(t=0; t<MAX; t++) {
    printf("%d: ", t);
    gets(text[t]);
    if(!*text[t]) break; /* quit on blank line */
  }

  for(i=0; i<t; i++) {
    for(j=0; text[i][j]; j++) putchar(text[i][j]);
    putchar('\n');
  }
}
```

This program inputs lines of text until a blank line is entered. Then it redisplays each line one character at a time.

Multidimensional Arrays

C allows arrays of more than two dimensions. The exact limit, if any, is determined by your compiler. The general form of a multidimensional array declaration is

type name[*Size1*][*Size2*][*Size3*]. . .[*SizeN*];

Arrays of three or more dimensions are not often used because of the amount of memory they require. For example, a four-dimensional character array with dimensions 10,6,9,4 requires

10 * 6 * 9 * 4

or 2,160 bytes. If the array held 2-byte integers, 4,320 bytes would be needed. If the array held **doubles** (assuming 8 bytes per **double**), 17,280 bytes would be required. The storage required increases exponentially with the number of dimensions.

In multidimensional arrays, it takes the computer time to compute each index. This means that accessing an element in a multidimensional array can be slower than accessing an element in a single-dimension array.

When passing multidimensional arrays into functions, you must declare all but the leftmost dimension. For example, if you declare array **m** as

```
int m[4][3][6][5];
```

a function, **func1( )**, that receives **m**, would look like this:

```
void func1(int d[][3][6][5])
{
    .
    .
    .
}
```

Of course, you can include the first dimension if you like.

Indexing Pointers

In C, pointers and arrays are closely related. As you know, an array name without an index is a pointer to the first element in the array. For example, consider the following array.

```
char p[10];
```

The following statements are identical:

```
p
&p[0]
```

Put another way,

```
p == &p[0]
```

evaluates to true because the address of the first element of an array is the same as the address of the array.

As stated, an array name without an index generates a pointer. Conversely, a pointer can be indexed as if it were declared to be an array. For example, consider this program fragment:

```
int *p, i[10];
p = i;
p[5] = 100;   /* assign using index */
*(p+5) = 100; /* assign using pointer arithmetic */
```

Both assignment statements place the value 100 in the sixth element of **i**. The first statement indexes **p**; the second uses pointer arithmetic. Either way, the result is the same. (Chapter 5 discusses pointers and pointer arithmetic.)

This same concept also applies to arrays of two or more dimensions. For example, assuming that **a** is a 10-by-10 integer array, these two statements are equivalent:

```
a
&a[0][0]
```

Furthermore, the 0,4 element of **a** may be referenced two ways: either by array indexing, **a[0][4]**, or by the pointer, ***((int*)a+4)**. Similarly, element 1,2 is either **a[1][2]** or ***((int*)a+12)**. In general, for any two-dimensional array

a[j][k]

is equivalent to

$*(a+(j*row\ length)+k)$

Pointers are sometimes used to access arrays because pointer arithmetic is often faster than array indexing.

A two-dimensional array can be reduced to a pointer to an array of one-dimensional arrays. Therefore, using a separate pointer variable is one easy way to use pointers to access elements within a row of a two-dimensional array. The following function illustrates this technique. It will print the contents of the specified row for the global integer array **num**.

```
int num[10][10];
    .
    .
    .
void  pr_row(int j)
{
   int *p, t;

   p = &num[j][0]; /* get address of first
                      element in row j */

   for(t=0; t<10; ++t) printf("%d ", *(p+t));
}
```

You can generalize this routine by making the calling arguments be the row, the row length, and a pointer to the first array element, as shown here:

```
void pr_row(int j, int row_dimension, int *p)
{
   int t;

   p = p + (j * row_dimension);

   for(t=0; t<row_dimension; ++t)
     printf("%d ", *(p+t));
}
```

Arrays of greater than two dimensions may be reduced in a similar way. For example, a three-dimensional array can be reduced to a pointer to a two-dimensional array, which can be reduced to a pointer to a single-dimension array. Generally, an *n*-dimensional array can be reduced to a pointer and an (*n*–1)-dimensional array. This new array can be reduced again with the same method. The process ends when a single-dimension array is produced.

Array Initialization

C allows the initialization of arrays at the time of their declaration. The general form of array initialization is similar to that of other variables, as shown here:

type_specifier array_name[size1]. . .[sizeN] = { value_list };

The *value_list* is a comma-separated list of constants whose type is compatible with *type_specifier*. The first constant is placed in the first position of the array, the second constant in the second position, and so on. Note that a semicolon follows the }.

In the following example, a 10-element integer array is initialized with the numbers 1 through 10:

```
int i[10] = {1, 2, 3, 4, 5, 6, 7, 8, 9, 10};
```

This means that **i[0]** will have the value 1 and **i[9]** will have the value 10.

Character arrays that hold strings allow a shorthand initialization that takes the form:

char *array_name[size]* = "*string*";

For example, the following code fragment initializes **str** to the phrase "I like C++".

```
char str[11] = "I like C++";
```

This is the same as writing

```
char str[11] = {'I', ' ', 'l', 'i', 'k', 'e',' ', 'C',
                '+', '+', '\0'};
```

Because all strings in C end with a null, you must make sure that the array you declare is long enough to include the null. This is why **str** is 11 characters long even though "I like C++" is only 10. When you use the string constant, the compiler automatically supplies the null terminator.

Multidimensional arrays are initialized the same as single-dimension ones. For example, the following initializes **sqrs** with the numbers 1 through 10 and their squares.

```
int sqrs[10][2] = {
  1,1,
  2,4,
  3,9,
  4,16,
  5,25,
  6,36,
  7,49,
  8,64,
  9,81,
  10,100
};
```

Unsized Array Initializations

Imagine that you are using array initialization to build a table of error messages, as shown here:

```
char e1[12] = "Read error\n";
char e2[13] = "Write error\n";
char e3[18] = "Cannot open file\n";
```

As you might guess, it is tedious to count the characters in each message manually to determine the correct array dimension. You can let the compiler automatically calculate the dimensions of the arrays by using unsized arrays. If, in an array initialization statement, the size of the array is not specified, the C/C++ compiler automatically creates an array big enough to hold all the initializers present. This is called an *unsized array*. If you use this approach, the message table becomes

```
char e1[] = "Read error\n";
char e2[] = "Write error\n";
char e3[] = "Cannot open file\n";
```

Given these initializations, this statement

```
printf("%s has length %d\n", e2, sizeof e2);
```

will print

Write error has length 13

Besides being less tedious, unsized array initialization allows you to change any of the messages without fear of using incorrect array dimensions.

Unsized array initializations are not restricted to one-dimensional arrays. For multidimensional arrays, you must specify all but the leftmost dimension. (The other dimensions are needed to allow the C/C++ compiler to index the array properly.) In this way, you can build tables of varying lengths, and the compiler automatically allocates enough storage for them. For example, the declaration of **sqrs** as an unsized array is shown here:

```
int sqrs[][2] = {
   1,1,
   2,4,
   3,9,
   4,16,
   5,25,
   6,36,
   7,49,
   8,64,
   9,81,
   10,100
};
```

The advantage of this declaration over the sized version is that you can lengthen or shorten the table without changing the array dimensions.

A Tic-Tac-Toe Example

The longer example that follows illustrates many of the ways that you can manipulate arrays with C. Two-dimensional arrays are commonly used to simulate board game matrices. This section develops a simple tic-tac-toe program.

The computer plays a very simple game. When it is the computer's turn, it uses **get_computer_move( )** to scan the matrix, looking for an unoccupied cell. When it finds one, it puts an **O** there. If it cannot find an empty location, it reports a draw game and exits. The **get_player_move( )** function asks you where you want to place an **X**. The upper-left corner is location 1,1; the lower-right corner is 3,3.

The matrix array is initialized to contain spaces. Each move made by the player or the computer changes a space into either an X or an O. This makes it easy to display the matrix on the screen.

Each time a move has been made, the program calls the **check( )** function. This function returns a space if there is no winner yet, an X if you have won, or an O if the computer has won. It scans the rows, the columns, and then the diagonals, looking for one that contains either all Xs or all Os.

The **disp_matrix( )** function displays the current state of the game. Notice how initializing the matrix with spaces simplified this function.

The routines in this example all access the **matrix** array differently. Study them to make sure that you understand each array operation.

```c
/* A simple Tic Tac Toe game. */
#include <stdio.h>
#include <stdlib.h>

char matrix[3][3];  /* the tic tac toe matrix */

char check(void);
void init_matrix(void);
void get_player_move(void);
void get_computer_move(void);
void disp_matrix(void);

void main(void)
{
  char done;

  printf("This is the game of Tic Tac Toe.\n");
  printf("You will be playing against the computer.\n");

  done = ' ';
  init_matrix();
  do{
    disp_matrix();
    get_player_move();
    done = check(); /* see if winner */
    if(done!= ' ') break; /* winner!*/
    get_computer_move();
    done = check(); /* see if winner */
  } while(done== ' ');
  if(done=='X') printf("You won!\n");
  else printf("I won!!!!\n");
  disp_matrix(); /* show final positions */
}

/* Initialize the matrix. */
void init_matrix(void)
{
  int i, j;
```

```
  for(i=0; i<3; i++)
    for(j=0; j<3; j++) matrix[i][j] = ' ';
}

/* Get a player's move. */
void get_player_move(void)
{
  int x, y;

  printf("Enter coordinates for your X: ");
  scanf("%d%d", &x, &y);

  x--; y--;

  if(matrix[x][y]!= ' '){
    printf("Invalid move, try again.\n");
    get_player_move();
  }
  else matrix[x][y] = 'X';
}

/* Get a move from the computer. */
void get_computer_move(void)
{
  int i, j;
  for(i=0; i<3; i++){
    for(j=0; j<3; j++)
      if(matrix[i][j]==' ') break;
    if(matrix[i][j]==' ') break;
  }

  if(i*j==9)  {
    printf("draw\n");
    exit(0);
  }
  else
    matrix[i][j] = 'O';
}

/* Display the matrix on the screen. */
void disp_matrix(void)
```

```
{
  int t;

  for(t=0; t<3; t++) {
    printf(" %c | %c | %c ",matrix[t][0],
           matrix[t][1], matrix [t][2]);
    if(t!=2) printf("\n---|---|---\n");
  }
  printf("\n");
}

/* See if there is a winner. */
char check(void)
{
  int i;

  for(i=0; i<3; i++)  /* check rows */
    if(matrix[i][0]==matrix[i][1] &&
       matrix[i][0]==matrix[i][2]) return matrix[i][0];

  for(i=0; i<3; i++)  /* check columns */
    if(matrix[0][i]==matrix[1][i] &&
       matrix[0][i]==matrix[2][i]) return matrix[0][i];

  /* test diagonals */
  if(matrix[0][0]==matrix[1][1] &&
     matrix[1][1]==matrix[2][2])
       return matrix[0][0];

  if(matrix[0][2]==matrix[1][1] &&
     matrix[1][1]==matrix[2][0])
       return matrix[0][2];

  return ' ';
}
```

Chapter Five

Pointers

111

The correct understanding and use of pointers is critical to successful C (and C++) programming. There are three reasons for this: First, pointers provide the means by which functions can modify their calling arguments. Second, pointers support dynamic allocation. Third, pointers can improve the efficiency of certain routines. Also, as you will see in Part Two, pointers take on additional, important roles in C++.

Pointers are one of C's strongest but also one of its most dangerous features. For example, uninitialized pointers (or pointers containing invalid values) can cause your system to crash. Perhaps worse, it is easy to use pointers incorrectly, causing bugs that are very difficult to find.

Because of both their importance and their potential for abuse, this chapter examines the subject of pointers in detail.

What Are Pointers?

A *pointer* is a variable that holds a memory address. This address is the location of another object (typically another variable) in memory. For example, if one variable contains the address of another variable, the first variable is said to *point to* the second. Figure 5-1 illustrates this situation.

Pointer Variables

If a variable is going to hold a pointer, it must be declared as such. A pointer declaration consists of a base type, an *, and the variable name. The general form for declaring a pointer variable is

   *type *name;*

where *type* is the base type of the pointer and can be any valid type. The name of the pointer variable is specified by *name*.

The base type of the pointer defines what type of variables the pointer can point to. Technically, any type of pointer can point anywhere in memory. However, all pointer arithmetic is done relative to its base type, so it is important to declare the pointer correctly. (Pointer arithmetic is discussed later in this chapter.)

The Pointer Operators

There are two special pointer operators: * and &. The & is a unary operator that returns the memory address of its operand. (Remember, a unary operator only requires one operand.) For example,

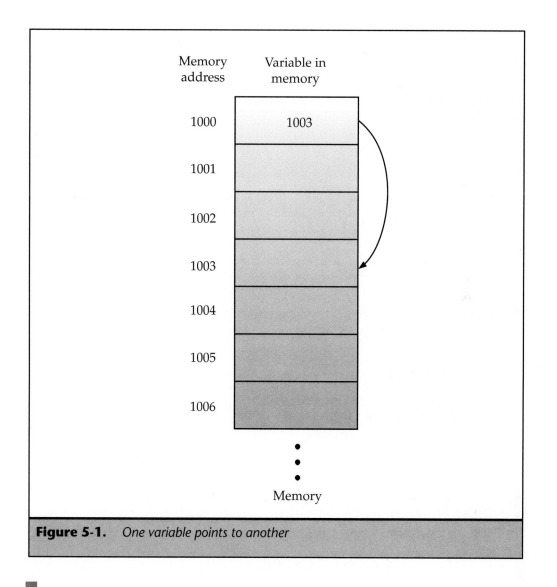

Figure 5-1.   *One variable points to another*

```
m = &count;
```

places into **m** the memory address of the variable **count**. This address is the computer's internal location of the variable. It has nothing to do with the value of **count**. You can think of **&** as returning "the address of." Therefore, the preceding assignment statement means "**m** receives the address of **count**."

To understand the above assignment better, assume that the variable **count** uses memory location 2000 to store its value. Also assume that **count** has a value of 100. Then, after the preceding assignment, **m** will have the value 2000.

The second pointer operator, *, is the complement of &. It is a unary operator that returns the value located at the address that follows. For example, if **m** contains the memory address of the variable **count**,

```
q = *m;
```

places the value of **count** into **q**. Thus, **q** will have the value 100 because 100 is stored at location 2000, which is the memory address that was stored in **m**. You can think of * as "at address." In this case, the preceding statement means "**q** receives the value at address **m**."

It is sometimes confusing to beginners that the multiplication sign and the "at address" sign are the same, and the bitwise AND and the "address of" sign are the same. These operators have no relationship to each other. Both & and * have a higher precedence than all other arithmetic operators except the unary minus, with which they have equal precedence.

You must make sure that your pointer variables always point to the correct type of data. For example, when you declare a pointer to be of type **int**, the compiler assumes that any address that it holds points to an integer variable—whether it actually does or not. Because C allows you to assign any address to a pointer variable, the following code fragment compiles with no error messages (or only warnings, depending upon your compiler) but does not produce the desired result.

```
void main(void)
{
  float x, y;
  int  *p;

  /* The next statement causes p (which is an
     integer pointer) to point to a float. */
  p = &x;

  /* The next statement does not operate as
     expected. */
  y = *p;
}
```

This will not assign the value of **x** to **y**. Because **p** is declared as an integer pointer, only 2 bytes of information will be transferred to **y**, not the 8 bytes that normally make up a floating-point number.

NOTE: In C++, it is illegal to convert one type of pointer into another without the use of an explicit type cast. For this reason, the preceding program will not even compile if you try to compile it as a C++ (rather than as a C) program. However, the type of error described can still occur in C++ in a more roundabout manner.

Pointer Expressions

In general, expressions involving pointers conform to the same rules as other expressions. This section examines a few special aspects of pointer expressions.

Pointer Assignments

As with any variable, you can use a pointer on the right-hand side of an assignment statement to assign its value to another pointer. Here is an example:

```
#include <stdio.h>

void main(void)
{
  int x;
  int *p1, *p2;

  p1 = &x;
  p2 = p1;

  printf(" %p", p2); /* print the address of x,
                        not x's value! */
}
```

Both **p1** and **p2** now point to **x**. The address of **x** is displayed by using the %p **printf( )** format specifier, which causes **printf( )** to display an address in the format used by the host computer.

Pointer Arithmetic

There are only two arithmetic operations that you can use on pointers: addition and subtraction. To understand what occurs in pointer arithmetic, let **p1** be an integer pointer with a current value of 2000. Also, assume integers are 2 bytes long. After the expression

```
p1++;
```

p1 contains 2002, not 2001. The reason for this is that each time **p1** is incremented, it will point to the next integer. The same is true of decrements. For example, assuming that **p1** has the value 2000, the expression

```
p1--;
```

causes **p1** to have the value 1998.

Generalizing from the preceding example, the following rules govern pointer arithmetic. Each time a pointer is incremented, it points to the memory location of the next element of its base type. Each time it is decremented, it points to the location of the previous element. When applied to character pointers, this will appear as "normal" arithmetic because characters are always 1 byte long. However, all other pointers will increase or decrease by the length of the data type they point to. This approach ensures that a pointer is always pointing to an appropriate element of its base type. Figure 5-2 illustrates this concept.

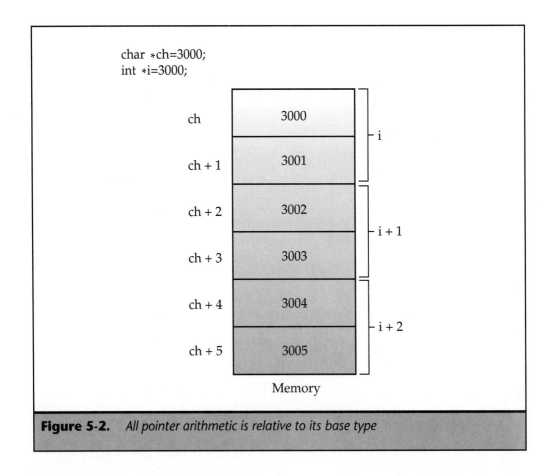

Figure 5-2.   *All pointer arithmetic is relative to its base type*

You are not limited to the increment and decrement operators. For example, you can add or subtract integers to or from pointers. The expression

```
p1 = p1 + 12;
```

makes **p1** point to the 12th element of **p1**'s type beyond the one it currently points to.

Besides addition and subtraction of a pointer and an integer, only one other arithmetic operation is allowed: you can subtract one pointer from another in order to find the number of objects of their base type that separate the two pointers. All other arithmetic operations are prohibited. Specifically, you can not multiply or divide pointers; you can not add two pointers; you can not apply the bitwise operators to them; and you can not add or subtract type **float** or **double** to or from pointers.

Pointer Comparisons

You can compare two pointers in a relational expression. For instance, given two pointers **p** and **q**, the following statement is perfectly valid:

```
if(p<q) printf("p points to lower memory than q\n");
```

Generally, pointer comparisons are used when two or more pointers point to a common object, such as an array. As an example, a pair of stack routines are developed that store and retrieve integer values. A stack is a list that uses first-in, last-out accessing. It is often compared to a stack of plates on a table—the first one set down is the last one to be used. Stacks are used frequently in compilers, interpreters, spreadsheets, and other system-related software. To create a stack, you need two functions: **push( )** and **pop( )**. The **push( )** function places values on the stack and **pop( )** takes them off. These routines are shown here with a simple **main( )** function to drive them. The program puts the values you enter into the stack. If you enter **0**, a value is popped from the stack. To stop the program, enter **–1**.

```
#include <stdio.h>
#include <stdlib.h>

#define SIZE 50

void push(int i);
int pop(void);
```

```
int  *tos, *p1, stack[SIZE];

void main(void)
{
  int value;

  tos = stack; /* tos points to the top of stack */
  p1 = stack; /* initialize p1 */

  do {
    printf("Enter value: ");
    scanf("%d", &value);
    if(value!=0) push(value);
    else printf("value on top is %d\n", pop());
  } while(value!=-1);
}

void push(int i)
{
  p1++;
  if(p1==(tos+SIZE)) {
    printf("Stack Overflow");
    exit(1);
  }
  *p1 = i;
}

pop(void)
{
  if(p1==tos) {
    printf("Stack Underflow");
    exit(1);
  }
  p1--;
  return *(p1+1);
}
```

You can see that memory for the stack is provided by the array **stack**. The pointer **p1** is set to point to the first byte in **stack**. The **p1** variable actually accesses the stack. The variable **tos** holds the memory address of the top of the stack. The value of **tos** prevents stack overflows and underflows. Once the stack has been initialized, **push( )** and **pop( )** can be used. Both the **push( )** and **pop( )** functions perform a relational test on the pointer **p1** to detect limit errors. In **push( )**, **p1** is tested against the end of **stack** by adding **SIZE** (the size of the stack) to **tos**. This prevents an overflow. In **pop( )**, **p1** is checked against **tos** to be sure that a stack underflow has not occurred.

In **pop( )**, the parentheses are necessary in the return statement. Without them, the statement would look like this:

```
return *p1 +1;
```

In this form, the statement would return the value at location **p1** plus one, not the value of the location **p1+1**.

Pointers and Arrays

There is a close relationship between pointers and arrays. Consider this program fragment:

```
char str[80], *p1;
p1 = str;
```

Here, **p1** has been set to the address of the first array element in **str**. To access the fifth element in **str**, you could write

```
str[4]
```

or

```
*(p1+4)
```

Both statements will return the fifth element. Remember, arrays start at 0. To access the fifth element, you must use 4 to index **str**. You also add 4 to the pointer **p1** to access the fifth element because **p1** currently points to the first element of **str**. (Recall that an array name without an index returns the starting address of the array, which is the address of the first element.)

C provides two methods of accessing array elements: pointer arithmetic and array indexing. Pointer arithmetic can be faster than array indexing. Since speed is often a consideration in programming, C/C++ programmers commonly use pointers to access array elements.

These two versions of **putstr( )**—one with array indexing and one with pointers—illustrate how you can use pointers in place of array indexing. The **putstr( )** function writes a string to the standard output device one character at a time.

```
/* Index s as an array. */
void putstr(char *s)
{
  register int t;

  for(t=0; s[t]; ++t) putchar(s[t]);
}

/* Access s as a pointer. */
void putstr(char *s)
{
  while(*s) putchar(*s++);
}
```

Most professional C/C++ programmers would find the second version easier to read and understand. In fact, the pointer version is the way routines of this sort are commonly written in C/C++.

Arrays of Pointers

Pointers may be arrayed like any other data type. The declaration for an **int** pointer array of size 10 is

```
int *x[10];
```

To assign the address of an integer variable called **var** to the third element of the pointer array, write

```
x[2] = &var;
```

To find the value of **var**, write

```
*x[2]
```

If you want to pass an array of pointers into a function, you can use the same method that you use to pass other arrays—simply call the function with the array name without any indexes. For example, a function that receives array **x** looks like this:

```
void display_array(int *q[])
{
  int t;

  for(t=0; t<10; t++)
    printf("%d ", *q[t]);
}
```

Keep in mind that **q** is not a pointer to integers, but rather a pointer to an array of pointers to integers. Therefore you need to declare the parameter **q** as an array of integer pointers, as just shown. You cannot declare **q** simply as an integer pointer because that is not what it is.

Pointer arrays are often used to hold pointers to strings. You can create a function that outputs an error message given its code number, as shown here:

```
void syntax_error(int num)
{
  static char *err[] = {
    "Cannot Open File\n",
    "Read Error\n",
    "Write Error\n",
    "Media Failure\n"
  };

  printf("%s", err[num]);
}
```

The array **err** holds pointers to each string. As you can see, **printf( )** inside **syntax_error( )** is called with a character pointer that points to one of the various error messages indexed by the error number passed to the function. For example, if **num** is passed a 2, the message **Write Error** is displayed.

As a point of interest, note that the command line argument **argv** is an array of character pointers (see Chapter 6).

Multiple Indirection

You can have a pointer point to another pointer that points to the target value. This situation is called *multiple indirection,* or *pointers to pointers.* Pointers to pointers can be confusing. Figure 5-3 helps clarify the concept of multiple indirection. As you can see, the value of a normal pointer is the address of the object that contains the value desired. In the case of a pointer to a pointer, the first pointer contains the address of the second pointer, which points to the object that contains the value desired.

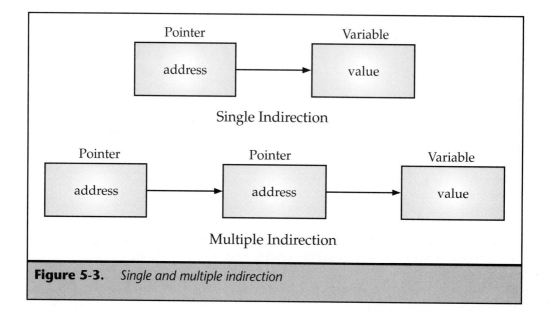

Figure 5-3.   *Single and multiple indirection*

Multiple indirection can be carried on to whatever extent desired, but more than a pointer to a pointer is rarely needed. In fact, excessive indirection is difficult to follow and prone to conceptual errors.

NOTE: *Do not confuse multiple indirection with high-level data structures, such as linked lists, that use pointers. These are two fundamentally different concepts.*

A variable that is a pointer to a pointer must be declared as such. You do this by placing an additional asterisk in front of the variable name. For example, the following declaration tells the compiler that **newbalance** is a pointer to a pointer of type **float**.

```
float **newbalance;
```

You should understand that **newbalance** is not a pointer to a floating-point number but rather a pointer to a **float** pointer.

To access the target value indirectly pointed to by a pointer to a pointer, you must apply the asterisk operator twice, as in the following example:

```
#include <stdio.h>

void main(void)
{
  int x, *p, **q;

  x = 10;
  p = &x;
  q = &p;

  printf("%d", **q); /* print the value of x */
}
```

Here, **p** is declared as a pointer to an integer and **q** as a pointer to a pointer to an integer. The call to **printf( )** prints the number **10** on the screen.

Initializing Pointers

After a pointer is declared but before it has been assigned a value, it may contain an unknown value.

CAUTION: *Should you try to use the pointer before giving it a valid value, you will probably crash your program—and possibly your computer's operation system as well—a very nasty type of error!*

There is an important convention that most C/C++ programmers follow when working with pointers: A pointer that does not currently point to a valid memory location is given the value null (which is zero). By convention, any pointer that is null implies that it points to nothing and should not be used. However, just because a pointer has a null value does not make it "safe." The use of null is simply a convention that programmers follow. It is not part of the C or C++ language. For example, if you use a null pointer on the left side of an assignment statement, you still run the risk of crashing your program or operating system.

Because a null pointer is assumed to be unused, you can use the null pointer to make many of your pointer routines easier to code and more efficient. For example, you could use a null pointer to mark the end of a pointer array. A routine that accesses that array knows that it has reached the end when it encounters the null value. The **search( )** function shown here illustrates this type of approach.

```
/* look up a name */
search(char *p[], char *name)
{
  register int t;

  for(t=0; p[t]; ++t)
    if(!strcmp(p[t], name)) return t;

    return -1; /* not found */
}
```

The **for** loop inside **search( )** runs until either a match is found or a null pointer is encountered. Assuming the end of the array is marked with a null, the condition controlling the loop fails when it is reached.

C/C++ programmers commonly initialize strings. You saw an example of this in the **syntax_error( )** function in the section "Arrays of Pointers." Another variation on the initialization theme is the following type of string declaration:

```
char *p = "hello world";
```

As you can see, the pointer **p** is not an array. The reason this sort of initialization works is because of the way the compiler operates. All C/C++ compilers create what is called a *string table*, which is used internally by the compiler to store the string constants used by the program. Therefore, the preceding declaration statement places the address of **hello world**, as stored in the string table, into the pointer **p**. Throughout a program, **p** can be used like any other string. For example, the following program is perfectly valid:

```
#include <stdio.h>
#include <string.h>

char *p = "hello world";

void main(void)
{
  register int t;

  /* print the string forward and backwards */
  printf(p);
  for(t=strlen(p)-1; t>-1; t--) printf("%c", p[t]);
}
```

Pointers to Functions

A confusing yet powerful feature of C is the *function pointer*. Even though a function is not a variable, it has a physical location in memory that can be assigned to a pointer. A function's address is the entry point of the function. Because of this, a function pointer can be used to call a function.

To understand how function pointers work, you must know a little about how a function is compiled and called. First, as each function is compiled, source code is transformed into object code and an entry point is established. When a call is made to a function while your program is running, a machine-language call is made to this entry point. Therefore, if a pointer contains the address of a function's entry point, it can be used to call that function.

You obtain the address of a function by using the function's name without any parentheses or arguments. (This is similar to the way an array's address is obtained when only the array name, without indexes, is used.) To see how this is done, study the following program, paying close attention to the declarations.

```c
#include <stdio.h>
#include <string.h>

void check(char *a, char *b,
           int (*cmp)(const char *, const char *));

void main(void)
{
  char s1[80], s2[80];
  int (*p)(const char *, const char *);

  p = strcmp;

  gets(s1);
  gets(s2);

  check(s1, s2, p);
}

void check(char *a, char *b,
           int (*cmp)(const char *, const char *))
{
  printf("testing for equality\n");
  if(!(*cmp)(a, b)) printf("equal");
  else printf("not equal");
}
```

When the **check( )** function is called, two character pointers and one function pointer are passed as parameters. Inside the function **check( )**, the arguments are declared as character pointers and a function pointer. Notice how the function pointer is declared. You must use a similar form when declaring other function pointers, although the return type and parameters of the function may differ. The parentheses around the ***cmp** are necessary for the compiler to interpret this statement correctly.

Inside **check( )**, the expression

```
(*cmp)(a, b)
```

calls **strcmp( )**, which is pointed to by **cmp**, with the arguments **a** and **b**. Again, the parentheses around ***cmp** are necessary. This example also illustrates the general method for using a function pointer to call the function it points to.

Note that you can call **check( )** by using **strcmp( )** directly, as shown here:

```
check(s1, s2, strcmp);
```

This eliminates the need for an additional pointer variable.

You may wonder why anyone would write a program in this way. Obviously, nothing is gained and significant confusion is introduced in the previous example. However, at times it is advantageous to pass functions as parameters or to create an array of functions. For example, when a compiler or interpreter is written, the parser (the part that evaluates expressions) often calls various support functions, such as those that compute mathematical operations (sine, cosine, tangent, and so on), perform I/O, or access system resources. Instead of having a large **switch** statement with all of these functions listed in it, an array of function pointers can be created. In this approach, the proper function is selected by its index. You can get the flavor of this type of usage by studying the expanded version of the previous example. In this program, **check( )** can be made to check for either alphabetical equality or numeric equality by simply calling it with a different comparison function.

```
#include <stdio.h>
#include <ctype.h>
#include <stdlib.h>
#include <string.h>

void check(char *a, char *b,
           int (*cmp)(const char *, const char *));
int numcmp(const char *a, const char *b);
```

```
void main(void)
{
  char s1[80], s2[80];

  gets(s1);
  gets(s2);

  if(isalpha(*s1))
        check(s1, s2, strcmp);
  else
        check(s1, s2, numcmp);
}

void check(char *a, char *b,
          int (*cmp)(const char *, const char *))
{
  printf("testing for equality\n");
  if(!(*cmp)(a, b)) printf("equal");
  else printf("not equal");
}

numcmp(const char *a, const char *b)
{
  if(atoi(a)==atoi(b)) return 0;
  else return 1;
}
```

C's Dynamic Allocation Functions

Pointers provide necessary support for C's powerful dynamic allocation system. *Dynamic allocation* is the means by which a program can obtain memory while it is running. As you know, global variables are allocated storage at compile time. Local variables use the stack. However, neither global nor local variables can be added during program execution. Yet there will be times when the storage needs of a program cannot be known ahead of time. For example, a word processor or a database should take advantage of all the RAM in a system. However, because the amount of available RAM varies between computers, such programs will not be able to do so using normal variables. Instead, these and other programs must allocate memory as they need it using C's dynamic allocation system.

> *NOTE:* *Although C++ fully supports C's dynamic allocation system, it also defines its own approach, which contains several improvements over that used by C. C++'s dynamic allocation system is discussed in Part Two.*

Memory allocated by C's dynamic allocation functions is obtained from the *heap*—the region of free memory that lies between your program and its permanent storage area and the stack. Although the size of the heap is unknown, it generally contains a fairly large amount of free memory.

The core of C's allocation system consists of the functions **malloc( )** and **free( )**. (Most compilers supply several other dynamic allocation functions, but these two are the most important.) These functions work together using the free memory region to establish and maintain a list of available storage. The **malloc( )** function allocates memory and the **free( )** function releases it. That is, each time a **malloc( )** memory request is made, a portion of the remaining free memory is allocated. Each time a **free( )** memory release call is made, memory is returned to the system. Any program that uses these functions should include the header file STDLIB.H.

The **malloc( )** function has this prototype:

void *malloc(size_t *number_of_bytes*);

Here, *number_of_bytes* is the number of bytes of memory you wish to allocate. (The type **size_t** is defined in STDLIB.H as (more or less) an **unsigned** integer.) The **malloc( )** function returns a pointer of type **void**, which means that you can assign it to any type of pointer. After a successful call, **malloc( )** returns a pointer to the first byte of the region of memory allocated from the heap. If there is not enough available memory to satisfy the **malloc( )** request, an allocation failure occurs and **malloc( )** returns a null.

The code fragment shown here allocates 1000 bytes of contiguous memory:

```
char *p;
p = malloc(1000); /* get 1000 bytes */
```

After the assignment, **p** points to the first of 1000 bytes of free memory.

Notice that no type cast is needed to assign the return value of **malloc( )** to **p**. In C, a **void *** pointer is automatically converted to the type of the pointer on the left side of an assignment. However, it is important to understand that this automatic conversion *does not* occur in C++. Further, in C++, an explicit type cast is needed when a **void *** pointer is assigned to another type of pointer. Thus, in C++, the preceding assignment must be written as follows:

```
p = (char *) malloc(1000);
```

As a general rule, in C++ you must use a type cast when assigning (or otherwise converting) one type of pointer to another. This is one of the few fundamental differences between C and C++.

The next example allocates space for 50 integers. Notice the use of **sizeof** to ensure portability.

```
int *p;
p = malloc(50*sizeof(int));
```

Since the heap is not infinite, whenever you allocate memory, you must check the value returned by **malloc( )** to make sure that it is not null before using the pointer. Using a null pointer will almost certainly crash your program. The proper way to allocate memory and test for a valid pointer is illustrated in this code fragment:

```
if(!(p=malloc(100)) {
  printf("Out of memory.\n");
  exit(1);
}
```

Of course, you can substitute some other sort of error handler in place of the call to **exit( )**. Just make sure that you do not use the pointer **p** if it is null.

The **free( )** function is the opposite of **malloc( )** in that it returns previously allocated memory to the system. Once the memory has been freed, it may be reused by a subsequent call to **malloc( )**. The function **free( )** has this prototype:

void free(void *p);

Here, p is a pointer to memory that was previously allocated using **malloc( )**. It is critical that you *never* call **free( )** with an invalid argument; this will destroy the free list.

Problems with Pointers

Nothing will get you into more trouble than a wild pointer! Pointers are a mixed blessing. They give you tremendous power and are necessary for many programs. At the same time, when a pointer accidentally contains a wrong value, it can be the most difficult bug to find.

An erroneous pointer is difficult to find because the pointer, itself, is not the problem. The problem is that each time you perform an operation using the bad pointer, you are reading or writing to some unknown piece of memory. If you read from it, the worst that can happen is that you get garbage. However, if you write to it, you might be writing over other pieces of your code or data. This may not show up until later in the execution of your program and may lead you to look for the bug in the wrong place. There may be little or no evidence to suggest that the pointer is the original cause of the problem. This type of bug causes programmers to lose sleep time and time again. Because pointer errors are such nightmares, you should do your best never to generate one. To help you avoid them, a few of the more common errors are discussed here.

The classic example of a pointer error is the *uninitialized pointer.* Consider this program:

```
/* This program is wrong. */
void main(void)
{
  int x, *p;

  x = 10;
  *p = x;
}
```

This program assigns the value 10 to some unknown memory location. Here is why. Since the pointer **p** has never been given a value, it contains an unknown value when the assignment ***p = x** takes place. This causes the value of **x** to be written to some unknown memory location. This type of problem often goes unnoticed when your program is small because the odds are in favor of **p** containing a "safe" address—one that is not in your code, data area, or operating system. However, as your program grows, the probability increases of **p** pointing to something vital. Eventually, your program stops working. The solution is to always make sure that a pointer is pointing at something valid before it is used.

A second common error is caused by a simple misunderstanding of how to use a pointer. Consider the following:

```
/* This program is wrong. */
#include <stdio.h>

void main(void)
{
  int x, *p;
```

```
    x = 10;
    p = x;

    printf("%d", *p);
}
```

The call to **printf( )** does not print the value of **x**, which is 10, on the screen. It prints some unknown value because the assignment

```
p = x;
```

is wrong. That statement assigns the value 10 to the pointer **p**. However, **p** is supposed to contain an address, not a value. To correct the program, write

```
p = &x;
```

Another error that sometimes occurs is caused by incorrect assumptions about the placement of variables in memory. You can never know where your data will be placed in memory, or if it will be placed there the same way again, or whether each compiler will treat it in the same way. For these reasons, making any comparisons between pointers that do not point to a common object may yield unexpected results. For example,

```
char s[80], y[80];
char *p1, *p2;

p1 = s;
p2 = y;
if(p1 < p2) . . .
```

is generally an invalid concept. (In very unusual situations, you might use something like this to determine the relative position of the variables. But this would be rare.)

A related error results when you assume that two adjacent arrays may be indexed as one by simply incrementing a pointer across the array boundaries, as shown here:

```
int first[10], second[10];
int *p, t;

p = first;
for(t=0; t<20; ++t)   *p++ = t;
```

This is not a good way to initialize the arrays **first** and **second** with the numbers 0 through 19. Even though it may work on some compilers under certain circumstances, it assumes that both arrays will be placed back to back in memory with **first** first. This may not always be the case.

The next program illustrates a very dangerous type of bug. See if you can find it.

```c
/* This program has a bug. */
#include <string.h>
#include <stdio.h>

void main(void)
{
  char *p1;
  char s[80];

  p1 = s;
  do {
    gets(s);  /* read a string */

    /* print the decimal equivalent of each
       character */
    while(*p1) printf(" %d", *p1++);

  } while(strcmp(s, "done"));
}
```

This program uses **p1** to print the ASCII values associated with the characters contained in **s**. The problem is that **p1** is assigned the address of **s** only once. The first time through the loop, **p1** points to the first character in **s**. However, the second time through, it continues where it left off because it is not reset to the start of **s**. This next character may be part of the second string, another variable, or a piece of the program! The proper way to write this program is shown here:

```c
/* This program is now correct. */
#include <string.h>
#include <stdio.h>

void main(void)
{
  char *p1;
  char s[80];
```

```
do {
  p1 = s;
  gets(s);   /* read a string */
  /* print the decimal equivalent of each
     character */
  while(*p1) printf(" %d", *p1++);

} while(strcmp(s, "done"));
}
```

Here, each time the loop iterates, **p1** is set to the start of the string. In general, you should remember to reinitialize a pointer if it is to be reused.

The fact that handling pointers incorrectly can cause tricky bugs is no reason to avoid using them. Just be careful, and make sure that you know where each pointer is pointing before you use it.

Chapter Six

Functions

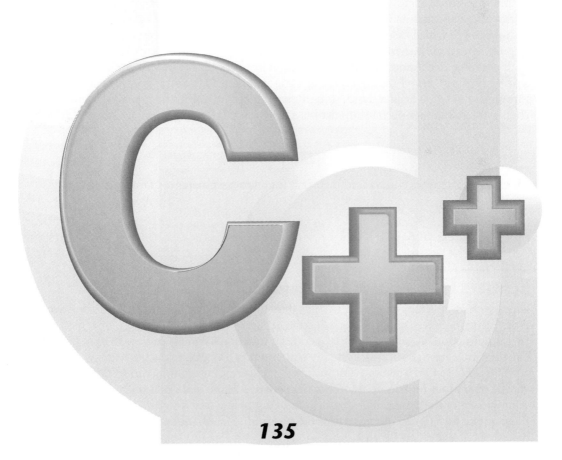

135

Functions are the building blocks of C and the place where all program activity occurs. They are one of C's most important features.

The General Form of a Function

The general form of a function is

```
type_specifier function_name(parameter list)
{
    body of the function
}
```

The *type_specifier* specifies the type of data that the function returns. A function can return any type of data except an array. If no type is specified, the compiler assumes that the function returns an integer result. The *parameter list* is a comma-separated list of variable names and their associated types that receive the values of the arguments when the function is called. A function may be without parameters, in which case the parameter list is empty. However, even if there are no parameters, the parentheses are still required.

In variable declarations, you can declare many variables to be of a common type by using a comma-separated list of variable names. In contrast, all function parameters must be declared individually, each including both the type and name. That is, the parameter declaration list for a function takes this general form:

f(type varname1, type varname2, . . . , type varnameN)

For example, here are correct and incorrect function parameter declarations:

```
f(int i, int k, int j) /* correct */
f(int i, k, float j)   /* incorrect */
```

Scope Rules of Functions

The *scope rules* of a language are the rules that govern whether a piece of code knows about or has access to another piece of code or data.

Each function is a discrete block of code. A function's code is private to that function and cannot be accessed by any statement in any other function except through a call to that function. (For instance, you cannot use **goto** to jump into the middle of another function.) The code that constitutes the body of a function is hidden from the rest of the program and, unless it uses global variables or data, it can neither affect nor be affected by other parts of the program. Stated another way, the code and data that are defined within one function cannot interact with the code or data defined in another function because the two functions have a different scope.

Variables that are defined within a function are called *local variables*. A local variable comes into existence when the function is entered and is destroyed upon exit. That is, local variables cannot hold their value between function calls. The only exception to this rule is when the variable is declared with the **static** storage class specifier. This causes the compiler to treat the variable as if it were a global variable for storage purposes, but still to limit its scope to within the function. (Chapter 2 covers global and local variables in depth.)

In C (and C++), all functions are at the same scope level. That is, you cannot define a function within a function. This is why neither C nor C++ is technically a block-structured language.

Function Arguments

If a function is to use arguments, it must declare variables that accept the values of the arguments. These variables are called the *formal parameters* of the function. They behave like other local variables inside the function and are created upon entry into the function and destroyed upon exit. As shown in the following function, the parameter declarations occur after the function name.

```
/* Return 1 if c is part of string s; 0 otherwise. */
is_in(char *s,  char c)
{
  while(*s)
    if(*s==c) return 1;
    else s++;
  return 0;
}
```

The function **is_in( )** has two parameters: **s** and **c**. This function returns 1 if the character **c** is part of the string **s**; otherwise, it returns 0.

As with local variables, you can make assignments to a function's formal parameters or use them in any allowable expression. Even though these variables perform the special task of receiving the value of the arguments passed to the function, you can use them as you do any other local variable.

Call by Value, Call by Reference

In general, subroutines can be passed arguments in one of two ways. The first is called *call by value*. This method copies the *value* of an argument into the formal parameter of the subroutine. In this case, changes made to the parameter have no effect on the argument.

Call by reference is the second way of passing arguments to a subroutine. In this method, the *address* of an argument is copied into the parameter. Inside the subroutine, the address is used to access the actual argument used in the call. This means that changes made to the parameter affect the argument.

With a few exceptions, C uses call by value to pass arguments. In general, this means that code within a function cannot alter the arguments used to call the function. Consider the following program:

```c
#include <stdio.h>

int sqr(int x);

void main(void)
{
    int t=10;

    printf("%d %d", sqr(t), t);
}

sqr(int x)
{
    x = x*x;
    return(x);
}
```

In this example, the value of the argument to **sqr( )**, 10, is copied into the parameter **x**. When the assignment x = x*x takes place, only the local variable **x** is modified. The variable **t**, used to call **sqr( )**, still has the value 10. Hence, the output is **100 10**.

REMEMBER: It is a copy of the value of the argument that is passed into a function. What occurs inside the function has no effect on the variable used in the call.

Creating a Call by Reference

Even though C's parameter-passing convention is call by value, you can create a call by reference by passing a pointer to an argument, instead of the argument itself. Since the address of the argument is passed to the function, code within the function can change the value of the argument outside the function.

Pointers are passed to functions just like any other value. Of course, you need to declare the parameters as pointer types. For example, the function **swap( )**, which exchanges the value of the two integer variables pointed to by its arguments, shows how.

```
void swap(int *x, int *y)
{
  int temp;

  temp = *x;   /* save the value at address x */
  *x = *y;     /* put y into x */
  *y = temp;   /* put x into y */
}
```

swap( ) is able to exchange the values of the two variables pointed to by **x** and **y** because their addresses (not their values) are passed. Thus, within the function, the contents of the variables can be accessed using standard pointer operations. Hence, the contents of the variables used to call the function are swapped.

Keep in mind that **swap( )**, or any other function that uses pointer parameters, must be called with the *addresses of the arguments*. The following program shows the correct way to call **swap( )**.

```
void swap(int *x, int *y);

void main(void)
{
  int i, j;

  i = 10;
  j = 20;

  swap(&i, &j); /* pass the addresses of i and j */
}
```

In this example, the variable **i** is assigned the value 10, and **j** is assigned the value 20. Then **swap( )** is called with the addresses of **i** and **j**. (The unary operator **&** is used to produce the address of the variables.) Therefore, the addresses of **i** and **j**, not their values, are passed into the function **swap( )**.

Calling Functions with Arrays

Arrays are covered in detail in Chapter 4. However, this section discusses passing arrays as arguments to functions because it is an exception to the standard call-by-value parameter passing.

When an array is used as a function argument, its address is passed to a function. This is an exception to C's call-by-value parameter passing convention. In this case, the code inside the function is operating on, and potentially altering, the actual contents of the array used to call the function. For example, consider the function **print_upper( )**, which prints its string argument in uppercase.

```c
#include <stdio.h>
#include <ctype.h>

void print_upper(char *string);

void main(void)
{
  char s[80];

  gets(s);
  print_upper(s);
}

/* Print a string in uppercase. */
void print_upper(char *string)
{
  register int t;

  for(t=0; string[t]; ++t)  {
    string[t] = toupper(string[t]);
    putchar(string[t]);
  }
}
```

After the call to **print_upper( )**, the contents of array **s** in **main( )** will have been changed to uppercase. If this is not what you want, you could write the program like this:

```c
#include <stdio.h>
#include <ctype.h>

void print_upper(char *string);

void main(void)
{
  char s[80];

  gets(s);
  print_upper(s);
}
```

```
void print_upper(char *string)
{
  register int t;

  for(t=0; string[t]; ++t)
    putchar(toupper(string[t]));
}
```

In this version, the contents of array **s** remain unchanged because its values are not altered.

The standard library function **gets( )** is a classic example of passing arrays into functions. Although the **gets( )** in your standard library is more sophisticated and complex, the following simpler version, called **xgets( )**, will give you an idea of how it works.

```
/* A very simple version of the standard
   gets() library function. */
char *xgets(char *s)
{
  char ch, *p;
  int t;

  p = s;  /* gets() returns a pointer to s */

  for(t=0; t<80; ++t){
    ch = getchar();

    switch(ch) {
      case '\n':
        s[t] = '\0'; /* terminate the string */
        return p;
      case '\b':
        if(t>0) t--;
        break;
      default:
        s[t] = ch;
    }
  }
  s[80] = '\0';
  return p;
}
```

The **xgets( )** function must be called with a character pointer, which can be either a variable declared as a character pointer, or the name of a character array, which by definition is a character pointer. Upon entry, **xgets( )** establishes a **for** loop from 0 to 80. This prevents larger strings from being entered at the keyboard. If more than 80 characters are entered, the function returns. (The real **gets( )** function does not have this restriction.) Because C has no built-in bounds checking, you should make sure that any array used to call **xgets( )** can accept at least 80 characters. As you type characters on the keyboard, they are placed in the string. If you type a backspace, the counter **t** is reduced by 1, effectively removing the previous character from the array. When you press ENTER, a null is placed at the end of the string, signaling its termination. Because the actual array used to call **xgets( )** is modified, upon return it contains the characters that you type.

argc and argv—Arguments to main( )

Sometimes it is useful to pass information into a program when you run it. Generally, you pass information into the **main( )** function via command line arguments. A *command line argument* is the information that follows the program's name on the command line of the operating system. For example, when you compile programs, you might type something like the following after the screen prompt:

cc *program_name*

where *program_name* is a command line argument that specifies the name of the program you wish to compile.

There are two special built-in arguments, **argc** and **argv**, that are used to receive command line arguments. The **argc** parameter holds the number of arguments on the command line and is an integer. It is always at least 1 because the name of the program qualifies as the first argument. The **argv** parameter is a pointer to an array of character pointers. Each element in this array points to a command line argument. All command line arguments are strings—any numbers will have to be converted by the program into the proper internal format. For example, this simple program prints **Hello** and your name on the screen if you type it directly after the program name.

```
#include <stdio.h>
#include <stdlib.h>

void main(int argc, char *argv[])
{
  if(argc!=2) {
    printf("You forgot to type your name.\n");
    exit(1);
```

```
    }
    printf("Hello %s", argv[1]);
}
```

If you called this program **name** and your name were Tom, you would type **name Tom** to run the program. The output from the program would be **Hello Tom**.

In many environments, each command line argument must be separated by a space or a tab. Commas, semicolons, and the like are not considered separators. For example,

```
run Spot, run
```

is made up of three strings, while

```
Herb,Rick,Fred
```

is a single string, since commas are not generally legal separators.

Some environments allow you to enclose within double quotes a string containing spaces. This causes the entire string to be treated as a single argument. Check your operating system manual for details on the definition of command line parameters for your system.

You must declare **argv** properly. The most common method is

```
char *argv[];
```

The empty brackets indicate that the array is of undetermined length. You can now access the individual arguments by indexing **argv**. For example, **argv[0]** points to the first string, which is always the program's name; **argv[1]** points to the first argument, and so on.

Another short example using command line arguments is the program called **countdown**, shown here. It counts down from a starting value (which is specified on the command line) and beeps when it reaches 0. Notice that the first argument containing the number is converted into an integer by the standard function **atoi( )**. If the string "display" is the second command line argument, the countdown will also be displayed on the screen.

```
/* Countdown program. */
#include <stdio.h>
#include <stdlib.h>
include <ctype.h>
```

```
include <string.h>

void main(int argc, char *argv[])
{
  int disp, count;

  if(argc<2) {
    printf("You must enter the length of the count\n");
    printf("on the command line.  Try again.\n");
    exit(1);
  }

  if(argc==3 && !strcmp(argv[2], "display")) disp = 1;
  else disp = 0;

  for(count=atoi(argv[1]); count; --count)
    if(disp) printf("%d\n", count);

  putchar('\a');  /* this will ring the bell on most
                     computers */
  printf("Done");
}
```

Notice that if no command line arguments have been specified, an error message is printed. A program with command line arguments often issues instructions if the user attempts to run the program without entering the proper information.

To access an individual character in one of the command strings, add a second index to **argv**. For example, the next program displays all of the arguments with which it was called, one character at a time.

```
#include <stdio.h>

void main(int argc, char *argv[])
{
  int t, i;

  for(t=0; t<argc; ++t) {
    i = 0;

    while(argv[t][i]) {

      putchar(argv[t][i]);
      ++i;
```

```
      }
    }
  }
```

Keep in mind that the first index accesses the string, and the second index accesses the individual characters of the string.

Usually, you use **argc** and **argv** to get initial commands into your program. In theory, you can have up to 32,767 arguments, but most operating systems do not allow more than a few. You normally use these arguments to indicate a filename or an option. Using command line arguments gives your program a professional appearance and facilitates its use in batch files.

When a C program does not require command line parameters, it is common practice to explicitly declare **main** as having no parameters by using the **void** keyword in its parameter list. This is the approach used by several of the programs in Part One of this book. However, if you like, you can simply specify an empty parameter list. (Also, in C++, the use of **void** to indicate an empty parameter list is redundant.)

The names **argc** and **argv** are traditional but arbitrary. You can name these two parameters to **main( )** anything you like. Also, some compilers may support additional arguments to **main( )**, so be sure to check your user's manual.

The return Statement

The **return** statement has two important uses. First, it causes an immediate exit from the function that it is in. That is, it causes program execution to return to the calling code. Second, it can be used to return a value. Both of these are examined in this section.

Returning from a Function

There are two ways that a function terminates execution and returns to the caller. The first occurs when the last statement in the function has executed and, conceptually, the function's ending curly brace (}) is encountered. (Of course, the curly brace isn't actually present in the object code, but you can think of it in this way.) For example, the **pr_reverse( )** function in this program simply prints the string "I like C++" backwards on the screen and then returns.

```
#include <string.h>
#include <stdio.h>

void pr_reverse(char *s);

void main(void)
{
  pr_reverse("I like C++");
```

```
}

void pr_reverse(char *s)
{
  register int t;

  for(t=strlen(s)-1; t>=0; t--) putchar(s[t]);
}
```

Once the string has been displayed, there is nothing left for **pr_reverse( )** to do, so it returns to the place it was called from.

Actually, not many functions use this default method of terminating their execution. Most functions rely on the **return** statement to stop execution either because a value must be returned, or to make a function's code simpler and more efficient.

Keep in mind that a function can contain several **return** statements. For example, the **find_substr( )** function in the following program returns the starting position of a substring within a string, or returns –1 if no match is found.

```
#include <stdio.h>

int find_substr(char *s1, char *s2);

void main(void)
{
  if(find_substr("C is fun", "is") != -1)
    printf("substring is found");
}

/* Return index of first match of s2 in s1. */
find_substr(char *s1, char *s2)
{
  register int t;
  char *p, *p2;

  for(t=0; s1[t]; t++) {
    p = &s1[t];
    p2 = s2;

    while(*p2 && *p2==*p) {
      p++;
      p2++;
```

```
    }
    if(!*p2) return t; /* 1st return */
  }
  return -1; /* 2nd return */
}
```

Returning Values

All functions, except those of type **void**, return a value. This value is explicitly specified by the **return** statement. If no **return** statement is present, then the return value of the function is technically undefined. (Generally, C/C++ compiler implementors return 0 when no explicit return value is specified, but you should not count on this if portability is a concern.) In other words, as long as a function is not declared as **void**, you can use it as an operand in any valid expression. Therefore, each of the following expressions is valid:

```
x = power(y);
if(max(x,y) > 100) printf("greater");
for(ch=getchar(); isdigit(ch); ) ... ;
```

However, as a general rule, a function cannot be the target of an assignment. A statement such as

```
swap(x,y) = 100; /* incorrect statement */
```

is wrong. The C/C++ compiler will flag it as an error and will not compile a program that contains it. (As is discussed in Part Two, C++ allows some interesting exceptions to this general rule, enabling some types of functions to occur on the left side of an assignment.)

When you write programs, your functions generally will be of three types. The first type is simply computational. These functions are specifically designed to perform operations on their arguments and return a value based on that operation. A computational function is a "pure" function. Examples are the standard library functions **sqrt( )** and **sin( )**, which compute the square root and sine of their arguments.

The second type of function manipulates information and returns a value that simply indicates the success or failure of that manipulation. An example is the library function **fclose( )**, which is used to close a file. If the close operation is successful, the function returns 0; if the operation is unsuccessful, it returns an error code.

The last type of function has no explicit return value. In essence, the function is strictly procedural and produces no value. An example is **exit( )**, which terminates a program. All functions that do not return values should be declared as returning type

void. By declaring a function as **void**, you keep it from being used in an expression, thus preventing accidental misuse.

Sometimes, functions that really don't produce an interesting result return something anyway. For example, **printf( )** returns the number of characters written. Yet, it would be unusual to find a program that actually checked this. In other words, although all functions, except those of type **void**, return values, you don't have to use the return value for anything. A common question concerning function return values is, "Don't I have to assign this value to some variable since a value is being returned?" The answer is no. If there is no assignment specified, the return value is simply discarded. Consider the following program, which uses the function **mul( )**.

```c
#include <stdio.h>

int mul(int a, int b);

void main(void)
{
   int x, y, z;

   x = 10;    y = 20;
   z = mul(x, y);            /* 1 */
   printf("%d", mul(x,y));   /* 2 */
   mul(x, y);                /* 3 */
}

mul(int a, int b)
{
   return a*b;
}
```

In line 1, the return value of **mul( )** is assigned to **z**. In line 2, the return value is not actually assigned, but it is used by the **printf( )** function. Finally, in line 3, the return value is lost because it is neither assigned to another variable nor used as part of an expression.

Functions That Return Noninteger Values

When the return type of a function is not explicitly declared, it automatically defaults to **int**. For many functions, this default will work. However, when a different data type is required, the process involves two steps. First, the function must be given an explicit type specifier. Second, the return type of the function must be identified before the first call is made to it. Only in this way can the compiler generate correct code for functions returning noninteger values.

Functions may be declared to return any valid data type (except arrays). Declaring functions is similar to declaring variables: the type specifier precedes the function name. The type specifier tells the compiler what type of data the function is to return. This information is critical if the program is going to run correctly because different data types have different sizes and internal representations.

Before you can use a function that returns a noninteger type, its type must be made known to the rest of the program. This is because, unless directed to the contrary, the compiler assumes that a function will return an integer value. If your program calls a function that returns a different type prior to that function's declaration, the compiler mistakenly generates the wrong code for the function call. To prevent this, you must use a special form of declaration statement near the top of your program to tell the compiler what value that function is really returning.

There are two ways to declare a function before it is used: the traditional way and the modern prototype method. The traditional approach was the only method available when C was first invented, but is now obsolete. Prototypes were added by the ANSI C standard. The traditional approach is still allowed by the ANSI C standard in order to provide compatibility with older code, but new uses of it are strongly discouraged.

NOTE: C++ does not support the traditional function declaration method. Instead, C++ requires prototypes. The material presented in this section applies only to the C language.

Although outdated, this section briefly describes the traditional function declaration method. Even though it is obsolete, many existing programs still use it, so you should be familiar with it. Moreover, the prototype method is basically an extension of the traditional concept. (Function prototypes are discussed in the following section.)

Using the obsolete function declaration method, you specify the function's return type and name near the start of your program to inform the compiler that a function will return some type of value other than an integer, as illustrated here:

```
#include <stdio.h>

float sum();   /* declare the function */
float first, second;

void main(void)
{
  first = 123.23;
  second = 99.09;
```

```
   printf("%f", sum());
}

float sum()
{
   return first + second;
}
```

The first function type declaration tells the compiler that **sum( )** returns a floating-point data type. This allows the compiler to correctly generate code for calls to **sum( )**. Without the declaration, the compiler will flag a type mismatch error.

The traditional function type declaration statement has the general form

type_specifier function_name( );

Notice that the parameter list is empty. Even if the function were to take arguments, none would be listed in its type declaration.

Without the type declaration statement, a mismatch occurs between the type of data the function returns and the type of data the calling routine expects. The results will be bizarre and unpredictable. If both functions are in the same file, the compiler catches the type mismatch and does not compile the program. However, if the functions are in different files, the compiler does not detect the error. In C, type checking is not done at link time or run time, only at compile time. For this reason, you must make sure that both types are compatible.

NOTE: *When a character is returned from a function declared to be of type **int**, the character value is converted into an integer. Because C cleanly handles the conversion from character to integer and back again, a function that returns a character value is often not declared as returning a character value. The programmer instead relies upon the default type conversion of characters into integers and back again. This sort of thing is found frequently in older C code and is not technically considered an error.*

Function Prototypes

The traditional function declaration (described in the preceding section) only allowed the return type of a function to be declared. The ANSI C standard expanded the traditional function declaration by allowing the number and types of the function's arguments to be declared in addition to its return type. This expanded definition is called a *function prototype*. As mentioned, function prototypes were not part of the original C language. They are, however, one of the most important additions made to C when it was standardized. They are also *required* by C++. In this book, all examples include full function prototypes. Prototypes enable C to provide stronger type checking, somewhat like that provided by languages such as Pascal. When you use prototypes, the compiler can find and report any illegal type conversions between the type of arguments used to call a function and the type definition of its parameters. The compiler will also catch differences between the number of arguments used to call a function and the number of parameters in the function.

The general form of a function prototype definition is

type func_name(type parm_name1, type parm_name2,. . .,
             type parm_nameN);

The use of parameter names is optional. However, they enable the compiler to identify any type mismatches by name when an error occurs, so it is a good idea to include them.

The following program illustrates the value of function prototypes. It produces an error message because it contains an attempt to call **sqr_it( )** with an integer argument instead of the integer pointer required. (It is illegal to convert an integer into a pointer.)

```
/* This program uses a function prototype to
   enforce strong type checking. */

void sqr_it(int *i); /* prototype */

void main(void)
{
   int x;

   x = 10;
   sqr_it(x);   /* type mismatch */
}

void sqr_it(int *i)
{
   *i = *i * *i;
}
```

Because of the need for compatibility with the original version of C, some special rules apply to function prototypes. First, when a function's return type is declared, but the parameter list is empty, the compiler simply assumes that *no parameter information is given*. As far as the compiler is concerned, the function could have several parameters or no parameters. Therefore, how does one prototype a function that does not have any parameters? The answer is this: When a function has no parameters, its prototype uses **void** inside the parameter list. For example, if a function called **f( )** returns a **float** and has no parameters, its prototype looks like this:

```
float f(void);
```

This tells the compiler that the function has no parameters, and any call to that function that has parameters is an error.

NOTE: *In C++, f( ) and f(void) are equivalent.*

Prototyping affects C's automatic type promotions. When a nonprototyped function is called, all characters are converted to integers and all **float**s into **double**s. These somewhat odd type promotions have to do with the characteristics of the original environment in which C was developed. However, if you prototype a function, the types specified in the prototype are maintained and no type promotions will occur.

Function prototypes help you trap bugs before they occur. In addition, they help verify that your program is working correctly by not allowing functions to be called with mismatched arguments.

Keep one fact firmly in mind: Although the use of function prototypes in a C program is strongly recommended, it is not technically an error if there is no prototype for a function. This is necessary to support pre-prototype C code. Nevertheless, your code should, in general, include full prototyping information. The earlier discussion of the traditional function declaration method is included in this book only for the sake of completeness.

REMEMBER: *Although prototypes are optional in C, they are required by C++. This means that every function in a C++ program must be fully prototyped.*

Returning Pointers

Although functions that return pointers are handled just like any other type of function, a few important concepts need to be discussed.

Pointers to variables are neither integers nor unsigned integers. They are the memory addresses of a certain type of data. The reason for this distinction is because pointer arithmetic is relative to the base type. For example, if an integer pointer is incremented, it will contain a value that is 2 greater than its previous value (assuming 2-byte integers). In general, each time a pointer is incremented (or decremented), it points to the next (or previous) data item of its type. Since each data type may be of different length, the compiler must know what type of data the pointer is pointing to. For this reason, a function that returns a pointer must declare explicitly what type of pointer it is returning.

To return a pointer, a function must be declared as having a pointer return type. For example, this function returns a pointer to the first occurrence of the character **c** in string **s**:

```
/* Return pointer of first occurrence of c in s. */
char *match(char c, char *s)
{
   while(c!=*s && *s) s++;
   return(s);
}
```

If no match is found, a pointer to the null terminator is returned. Here is a short program that uses **match( )**:

```
#include <stdio.h>

char *match(char c, char *s);  /* prototype */

void main(void)
{
   char s[80], *p, ch;

   gets(s);
   ch = getchar();
   p = match(ch, s);

   if(*p)  /* there is a match */
     printf("%s ", p);
   else
     printf("No match found.");
}
```

This program reads a string and then a character. If the character is in the string, the program prints the string from the point of match. Otherwise, it prints **No match found**.

Functions of Type void

One of **void**'s uses is to explicitly declare functions that do not return values. This prevents their use in an expression and helps avert accidental misuse. For example, the function **print_vertical( )** prints its string argument vertically down the side of the screen. Since it returns no value, it is declared as **void**.

```
void print_vertical(char *str)
{
  while(*str)
    printf("%c\n", *str++);
}
```

Before you can use any **void** function, you must declare its prototype. If you don't, the compiler assumes that it is returning an integer, and when the compiler actually reaches the function, it declares a type mismatch. The following program shows a proper example that prints a single command line argument vertically on the screen.

```
#include <stdio.h>

void print_vertical(char *str);  /* prototype */

void main(int argc, char *argv[])
{
  if(argc) print_vertical(argv[1]);
}

void print_vertical(char *str)
{
  while(*str)
    printf("%c\n", *str++);
}
```

Before the ANSI C standard defined **void**, functions that did not return values were simply allowed to default to a return type of **int**. Therefore, don't be surprised to see many examples of this in older code.

What Does main( ) Return?

The **main( )** function returns an integer to the calling process, which is generally the operating system. Returning a value from **main( )** is the equivalent of calling **exit( )** with the same value. If **main( )** does not explicitly return a value, the value passed to the calling process is technically undefined. In practice, most C/C++ compilers automatically return 0, but do not rely on this if portability is a concern.

You can also declare **main( )** as **void** if it does not return a value. (Many of the programs in this book take this approach.) Some compilers issue a warning message if a function is not declared as **void** and also does not return a value. So, if you choose not to return a value from **main( )**, you will want to declare its return type as **void**.

Recursion

In C, a function can call itself. A function is said to be *recursive* if a statement in the body of the function calls itself. Recursion is the process of defining something in terms of itself, and is sometimes called *circular definition*.

A simple example of a recursive function is **factr( )**, which computes the factorial of an integer. The factorial of a number **n** is the product of all the whole numbers between 1 and **n**. For example, 3 factorial is 1 x2 x3, or 6. Both **factr( )** and its iterative equivalent are shown here:

```
factr(int n)  /* recursive */
{
  int answer;

  if(n==1) return(1);
  answer = factr(n-1)*n; /* recursive call */
  return(answer);
}

fact(int n)     /* non-recursive */
{
  int t, answer;

  answer = 1;

  for(t=1; t<=n; t++)
    answer=answer*(t);

  return(answer);
}
```

The nonrecursive version of **fact( )** should be clear. It uses a loop that runs from 1 to **n** and progressively multiplies each number by the moving product.

The operation of the recursive **factr( )** is a little more complex. When **factr( )** is called with an argument of 1, the function returns 1. Otherwise, it returns the product of **factr(n–1)*n**. To evaluate this expression, **factr( )** is called with **n–1**. This happens until **n** equals 1 and the calls to the function begin returning.

For example, when computing the factorial of 2, the first call to **factr( )** causes a second, recursive call with the argument of 1. This call returns 1, which is then multiplied by 2 (the original **n** value). The answer is then 2. Try working through the computation of 3 factorial on your own. (You might want to insert **printf( )** statements into **factr( )** to see the level of each call and what the intermediate answers are.)

When a function calls itself, a new set of local variables and parameters are allocated storage on the stack, and the function code is executed from the top with these new variables. A recursive call does not make a new copy of the function. Only the arguments are new. As each recursive call returns, the old local variables and parameters are removed from the stack, and execution resumes at the point of the function call inside the function. Recursive functions could be said to "telescope" out and back.

Most recursive routines do not significantly reduce code size or improve memory utilization. Also, the recursive versions of most routines may execute a bit slower than their iterative equivalents because of the overhead of the repeated function calls. In fact, many recursive calls to a function could cause a stack overrun. Because storage for function parameters and local variables is on the stack and each new call creates a new copy of these variables, the stack could possibly overwrite some other data or program memory. However, you probably will not have to worry about this unless a recursive function runs wild.

The main advantage to recursive functions is that you can use them to create clearer and simpler versions of several algorithms. For example, the quicksort algorithm is quite difficult to implement in an iterative way. Also, some problems, especially ones related to artificial intelligence, lend themselves to recursive solutions. Finally, some people seem to think recursively more easily than iteratively.

When writing recursive functions, you must have an **if** statement somewhere to force the function to return without the recursive call being executed. If you don't, the function will never return once you call it. Omitting the **if** is a common error when writing recursive functions. Use **printf( )** and **getchar( )** liberally during program development so that you can watch what is going on and abort execution if you see a mistake.

Declaring Variable-Length Parameter Lists

You can specify a function that has a variable number of parameters. The most common example is **printf( )**. To tell the compiler that an unknown number of arguments may be passed to a function, you must end the declaration of its parameters using three periods. For example, this prototype specifies that **func( )** will have at least two integer parameters and an unknown number (including 0) of parameters after that.

```
func(int a, int b, ...);
```

This form of declaration is also used by a function's definition.

Any function that uses a variable number of parameters must have at least one actual parameter. For example, this is incorrect:

```
func(...); /* illegal */
```

Classic Versus Modern Function Parameter Declarations

The original version of C used a different parameter declaration method, sometimes called the *classic* form. This book uses a declaration approach called the *modern* form. The ANSI standard for C supports both forms, but strongly recommends the modern form. The proposed ANSI C++ standard only supports the modern parameter declaration method. However, you should know the classic form because many older C programs still use it. (But, you should not use it for any new code that you write.)

The classic function parameter declaration consists of two parts: a parameter list, which goes inside the parentheses that follow the function name, and the actual parameter declarations, which go between the closing parenthesis and the function's opening curly brace. The general form of the classic parameter definition is shown here:

type func_name(parm1, parm2, . . .parmN)
type parm1;
type parm2;
    .
    .
    .
type parmN;
{
  function code
}

For example, this modern declaration

```
float f(int a, int b, char ch)
{
   /* ... */
}
```

will look like this in its classic form:

```
float f(a, b, ch)
int a, b;
char ch;
{
    /* ... */
}
```

Notice that the classic form allows the declaration of more than one parameter in a list after the type name.

REMEMBER: *The classic form of parameter declaration is designated as obsolete by the C language and is not supported by C++.*

Implementation Issues

There are a few important things to remember when you create functions that affect their efficiency and usability. These issues are the subject of this section.

Parameters and General-Purpose Functions

A general-purpose function is one that will be used in a variety of situations, perhaps by many different programmers. Typically, you should not base general-purpose functions on global data. If possible, all of the information a function needs should be passed to it by its parameters.

Besides making your functions general-purpose, parameters keep your code readable and less susceptible to bugs resulting from side effects.

Efficiency

Functions are the building blocks of C and are crucial to all but the simplest programs. However, in certain specialized applications, you may need to eliminate a function and replace it with *inline* code. Inline code performs the same actions as a function, but without the overhead associated with a function call. For this reason, inline code is often used instead of function calls when execution time is critical.

Inline code is faster than a function call for two reasons. First, a CALL instruction takes time to execute. Second, if there are arguments to pass, these have to be placed on the stack, which also takes time. For most applications, this very slight increase in execution time is of no significance. But if it is, remember that each function call uses time that would be saved if the function's code were placed in line. For example, the following are two versions of a program that prints the square of the numbers from 1 to 10. The inline version runs faster than the other because the function call takes time.

Inline

```
#include <stdio.h>


void main(void)
{
   int x;

   for(x=1; x<11; ++x)
     printf("%d", x*x);
}
```

Function Call

```
#include <stdio.h>
int sqr(int a);


void main(void)
{
   int x;

   for(x=1; x<11; ++x)
     printf("%d", sqr(x));
}


sqr(int a)
{
    return a*a;
}
```

NOTE: *In C++, the concept of inline functions is expanded and formalized. In fact, inline functions are an important component of the C++ language.*

Chapter Seven

Structures, Unions, Enumerations, and User-Defined Types

The C language allows you to create custom data types five different ways. The first is the *structure,* which is a grouping of variables under one name and is called a *compound* data type. (The term *aggregate* or *conglomerate* is also commonly used.) The second user-defined type is the *bit-field,* which is a variation on the structure and allows easy access to individual bits. The third is the *union,* which enables the same piece of memory to be defined as two or more different types of variables. A fourth custom data type is the *enumeration,* which is a list of named integer constants. The final user-defined type is created through the use of **typedef** and defines a new name for an existing type.

Structures

A structure is a collection of variables referenced under one name, providing a convenient means of keeping related information together. A *structure declaration* forms a template that can be used to create structures. The variables that make up the structure are called *members* of the structure. (Structure members are also commonly referred to as *elements* or *fields.*)

Generally, all of the members of a structure are logically related. For example, the name and address information in a mailing list would normally be represented in a structure. The following code fragment shows how to declare a structure that defines the name and address fields. The keyword **struct** tells the compiler that a structure is being declared.

```
struct addr
{
  char name[30];
  char street[40];
  char city[20];
  char state[3];
  unsigned long int zip;
};
```

Notice that the declaration is terminated by a semicolon. This is because a structure declaration is a statement. Also, the structure tag **addr** identifies this particular data structure and is its type specifier.

At this point, *no variable has actually been created.* Only the form of the data has been defined. To declare a variable of type **addr**, write

```
struct addr addr_info;
```

This declares a variable of type **struct addr** called **addr_info**. When you define a structure, you are defining a compound variable type, not a variable. Not until you declare a variable of that type does one actually exist.

> **NOTE:** *In C++, once a structure has been declared, you can declare variables of its type using only its tag name, without preceding it with the keyword* **struct**. *For example, in C++, to declare a structure variable of type* **addr** *you could write:*
>
> ```
> addr addr_info;
> ```
>
> *The reason for this difference between C and C++ is that in C, a structure tag name is not a complete type name. However, in C++, it is. Keep in mind, however, that it is still perfectly legal to use the C-style declaration in a C++ program.*

When a structure variable (such as **addr_info**) is declared, the C/C++ compiler automatically allocates sufficient memory to accommodate all of its members. Figure 7-1 shows how **addr_info** appears in memory assuming 1-byte characters and 4-byte long integers.

You can also declare one or more structure variables when you declare a structure. For example,

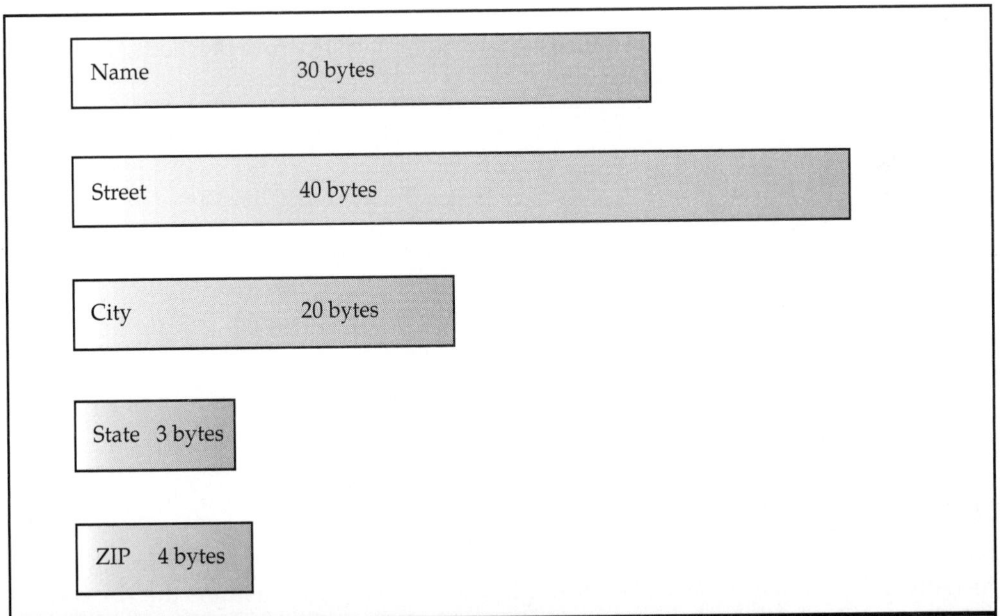

Figure 7-1. *The **addr_info** structure in memory*

```
struct addr {
  char name[30];
  char street[40];
  char city[20];
  char state[3];
  unsigned long int zip;
} addr_info, binfo, cinfo;
```

defines a structure type called **addr** and declares variables **addr_info**, **binfo**, and **cinfo** of that type.

If you only need one structure variable, the structure tag is not needed. That means that

```
struct {
  char name[30];
  char street[40];
  char city[20];
  char state[3];
  unsigned long int zip;
} addr_info;
```

declares one variable named **addr_info** as defined by the structure preceding it.

The general form of a structure declaration is

```
struct tag {
  type member_name;
  type member_name;
  type member_name;
  .
  .
  .
} structure_variables;
```

where either *tag* or *structure_variables* can be omitted, but not both.

Accessing Structure Members

Individual members of a structure are accessed through the use of the **.** operator (usually called the *dot operator*). For example, the following code assigns the ZIP code 12345 to the **zip** field of the structure variable **addr_info** declared earlier.

```
addr_info.zip = 12345;
```

The structure variable name followed by a period and the member name references that individual member. The general form for accessing a member of a structure is

structure_name.member_name

Therefore, to print the ZIP code on the screen, write

```
printf("%d", addr_info.zip);
```

This prints the ZIP code contained in the **zip** member of the structure variable **addr_info**.

In the same fashion, the character array **addr_info.name** can be used in a call to **gets( )**, as shown here:

```
gets(addr_info.name);
```

This passes a character pointer to the start of **name**.

Since **name** is a character array, you can access the individual characters of **addr_info.name** by indexing **name**. For example, you can print the contents of **addr_info.name** one character at a time by using the following code:

```
register int t;

for(t=0; addr_info.name[t]; ++t)
  putchar(addr_info.name[t]);
```

Structure Assignments

The information contained in one structure can be assigned to another structure of the same type using a single assignment statement. That is, you do not need to assign the value of each member separately. The following program illustrates structure assignments.

```
#include <stdio.h>

void main(void)
{
  struct {
    int a;
    int b;
  } x, y;
```

```
   x.a = 10;

   y = x;   /* assign one structure to another */

   printf("%d", y.a);
}
```

After the assignment, **y.a** will contain the value 10.

Arrays of Structures

Perhaps the most common use of structures is in arrays of structures. To declare an array of structures, you must first define a structure and then declare an array variable of that type. For example, to declare a 100-element array of structures of type **addr,** defined earlier, write

```
struct addr addr_info[100];
```

This creates 100 sets of variables that are organized as defined in the structure **addr.**

To access a specific structure, index the array name. For example, to print the ZIP code of structure 3, write

```
printf("%d", addr_info[2].zip);
```

Like all array variables, arrays of structures begin indexing at 0.

Passing Structures to Functions

This section discusses passing structures and their members to functions.

Passing Structure Members to Functions

When you pass a member of a structure to a function, you are actually passing the value of that member to the function. Therefore, you are passing a simple variable (unless, of course, that element is compound, such as an array of characters). For example, consider this structure:

```
struct fred
{
```

```
     char x;
     int y;
     float z;
     char s[10];
   } mike;
```

Here are examples of each member being passed to a function:

```
func(mike.x);   /* passes character value of x */
func2(mike.y); /* passes integer value of y */
func3(mike.z); /* passes float value of z */
func4(mike.s); /* passes address of string s */
func(mike.s[2]); /* passes character value of s[2] */
```

If you wish to pass the *address* of an individual structure member, put the **&** operator before the structure name. For example, to pass the address of the members of the structure **mike**, write

```
func(&mike.x);   /* passes address of character x */
func2(&mike.y); /* passes address of integer y */
func3(&mike.z); /* passes address of float z */
func4(mike.s); /* passes address of string s */
func(&mike.s[2]); /* passes address of character s[2] */
```

Keep in mind that the **&** operator precedes the structure name, not the individual member name. Note also that **s** already signifies an address, so no **&** is required.

Passing Entire Structures to Functions

When a structure is used as an argument to a function, the entire structure is passed using the standard call-by-value method. Of course, this means that any changes made to the contents of the structure inside the function to which it is passed do not affect the structure used as an argument.

When using a structure as a parameter, remember that the type of the argument must match the type of the parameter. For example, in the following program both the argument **arg** and the parameter **parm** are declared as the same type of structure.

```
#include <stdio.h>

/* Define a structure type. */
```

```
struct struct_type {
  int a, b;
  char ch;
} ;

void f1(struct struct_type parm);

void main(void)
{
  struct struct_type arg;

  arg.a = 1000;

  f1(arg);
}

void f1(struct struct_type parm)
{
  printf("%d", parm.a);
}
```

As this program illustrates, if you will be declaring parameters that are structures, you must make the declaration of the structure type global so that all parts of your program can use it. For example, had **struct_type** been declared inside **main( )**, then it would not have been visible to **f1( )**.

As just stated, when passing structures, the type of the argument must match the type of the parameter. It is not sufficient for them to simply be physically similar; their type names must match. For example, the following version of the preceding program is incorrect and will not compile because the type name of the argument used to call **f1( )** differs from the type name of its parameter.

```
/* This program is incorrect and will not compile. */
#include <stdio.h>

/* Define a structure type. */
struct struct_type {
  int a, b;
  char ch;
} ;
```

```
/* Define a structure similar to struct_type,
   but with a different name. */
struct struct_type2 {
  int a, b;
  char ch;
} ;

void f1(struct struct_type2 parm);

void main(void)
{
  struct struct_type arg;

  arg.a = 1000;

  f1(arg); /* type mismatch */
}

void f1(struct struct_type2 parm)
{
  printf("%d", parm.a);
}
```

Structure Pointers

C allows pointers to structures just as it allows pointers to any other type of variable. However, there are some special aspects to structure pointers that you should know.

Declaring a Structure Pointer

Like other pointers, structure pointers are declared by placing * in front of a structure variable's name. For example, assuming the previously defined structure **addr**, the following declares **addr_pointer** as a pointer to data of that type.

```
struct addr *addr_pointer;
```

Remember, in C++ it is not necessary to precede this declaration with the keyword **struct**.

Using Structure Pointers

There are two primary uses for structure pointers: to generate a call by reference parameter to a function, and to create linked lists and other dynamic data structures using C's dynamic allocation system. This chapter covers the first use.

There is one major drawback to passing all but the simplest structures to functions: the overhead needed to push the structure onto the stack when the function call is executed. (Recall that arguments are passed to functions on the stack.) For simple structures with few members, this overhead is not too great. If the structure contains many members, however, or if some of its members are arrays, run-time performance may degrade to unacceptable levels. The solution to this problem is to pass only a pointer to the function.

When a pointer to a structure is passed to a function, only the address of the structure is pushed on the stack. This makes for very fast function calls. A second advantage, in some cases, is when a function needs to reference the actual structure used as the argument, instead of a copy. By passing a pointer, the function can modify the contents of the structure used in the call.

To find the address of a structure variable, place the **&** operator before the structure's name. For example, given the following fragment,

```
struct bal {
  float balance;
  char name[80];
} person;

struct bal *p;  /* declare a structure pointer */
```

then

```
p = &person;
```

places the address of the structure **person** into the pointer **p**.

To access the members of a structure using a pointer to that structure, you must use the **->** operator. For example, this references the **balance** field:

```
p->balance
```

The **->** is usually called the *arrow operator* and consists of the minus sign followed by a greater-than sign. The arrow is used in place of the dot operator when you are accessing a structure member through a pointer to the structure.

To see how a structure pointer can be used, examine this simple program, which prints the hours, minutes, and seconds on your screen using a software timer.

```c
/* Display a software timer. */
#include <stdio.h>

#define DELAY 128000

struct my_time {
  int hours;
  int minutes;
  int seconds;
} ;

void display(struct my_time *t);
void update(struct my_time *t);
void delay(void);

void main(void)
{
  struct my_time systime;

  systime.hours = 0;
  systime.minutes = 0;
  systime.seconds = 0;

  for(;;) {
    update(&systime);
    display(&systime);
  }
}

void update(struct my_time *t)
{
  t->seconds++;
  if(t->seconds==60) {
    t->seconds = 0;
    t->minutes++;
  }


  if(t->minutes==60) {
    t->minutes = 0;
```

```
  t->hours++;
  }

  if(t->hours==24) t->hours = 0;
  delay();
}

void display(struct my_time *t)
{
  printf("%02d:", t->hours);
  printf("%02d:", t->minutes);
  printf("%02d\n", t->seconds);
}

void delay(void)
{
  long int t;

  /* change this as needed */
  for(t=1; t<DELAY; ++t) ;
}
```

The timing of this program is adjusted by changing the definition of **DELAY**.

As you can see, a global structure called **my_time** is defined. Inside **main( )**, the structure variable **systime** is declared and initialized to 00:00:00. This means that **systime** is known directly only to the **main( )** function.

The functions **update( )**, which changes the time, and **display( )**, which prints the time, are passed the address of **systime**. In both functions, their arguments are declared as a pointer to a **my_time** structure.

Inside **update( )** and **display( )**, each member of **systime** is accessed via a pointer. Because **update( )** receives a pointer to the **systime** structure, it can update its value. For example, to set the hours back to 0 when 24:00:00 is reached, **update( )** contains this line of code:

```
if(t->hours==24) t->hours = 0;
```

This tells the compiler to use the address contained in **t**, which points to **systime** in **main( )**, to reset **hours** to zero.

REMEMBER: *Use the dot operator to access structure elements when operating on the structure itself. When you have a pointer to a structure, use the arrow operator.*

Arrays and Structures Within Structures

A member of a structure can be either a simple or compound type. A simple member is one that is of any of the built-in data types, such as integer or character. You have already seen one type of compound element: the character arrays used in **addr**. Other compound data types include one-dimensional and multidimensional arrays of the other data types and structures.

A member of a structure that is an array is treated as you might expect from the earlier examples. For example, consider this structure:

```
struct x {
  int a[10][10]; /* 10 x 10 array of ints */
  float b;
} y;
```

To reference integer 3,7 in **a** of structure **y**, write

```
y.a[3][7]
```

When a structure is a member of another structure, it is called a *nested structure*. For example, the structure **address** is nested inside **emp** in this example:

```
struct emp {
  struct addr address; /* nested structure */
  float wage;
} worker;
```

Here, structure **emp** has been defined as having two members. The first is a structure of type **addr**, which contains an employee's address. The other is **wage**, which holds the employee's wage. The following code fragment assigns 93456 to the **zip** element of **address**.

```
worker.address.zip = 93456;
```

As you can see, the members of each structure are referenced from outermost to innermost. The ANSI C standard specifies that structures can be nested to at least 15 levels. The proposed ANSI C++ standard suggests that at least 256 levels of nesting be allowed.

Bit-Fields

Unlike most other computer languages, C has a built-in feature, called a *bit-field,* that allows you to access a single bit. Bit-fields can be useful for a number of reasons:

- If storage is limited, you can store several *Boolean* (true/false) variables in one byte.
- Certain devices transmit information encoded into bits.
- Certain encryption routines need to access the bits within a byte.

Although these tasks can be performed using the bitwise operators, a bit-field can add more structure (and possibly efficiency) to your code.

To access bits, C uses a method based on the structure. In fact, a bit-field is really just a special type of structure member that defines how long, in bits, the field is to be. The general form of a bit-field definition is

```
struct tag {
  type name1 : length;
  type name2 : length;
  .
  .
  .
  type nameN : length;
} variable_list;
```

Here, *type* specifies the type of the bit-field, which must be either **int**, **unsigned**, or **signed**. Bit-fields of length 1 should be declared as **unsigned** because a single bit cannot have a sign. (Some compilers may only allow **unsigned** bit-fields.) The number of bits in the bit-field is specified by *length.*

Bit-fields are frequently used when analyzing input from a hardware device. For example, the status port of a serial communications adapter might return a status byte organized like this:

Bit	Meaning When Set
0	Change in clear-to-send line
1	Change in data-set-ready
2	Trailing edge detected
3	Change in receive line
4	Clear-to-send
5	Data-set-ready
6	Telephone ringing
7	Received signal

This declaration does not create any variables. You can declare a variable either by placing its name at the end of the declaration, or by using a separate declaration statement. To declare a **union** variable **cnvt** of type **u_type** using the definition just given, write

```
union u_type cnvt;
```

In **cnvt**, both integer **i** and character **ch** share the same memory location. (Of course, **i** occupies 2 bytes and **ch** uses only 1.) Figure 7-2 shows how **i** and **ch** share the same address. At any point in your program, you can refer to the data stored in a **cnvt** as either an integer or a character.

When a **union** variable is declared, the compiler automatically allocates enough storage to hold the largest member of the **union**. For example, (assuming 2-byte integers) **cnvt** is 2 bytes long, so that it can hold **i**, even though **ch** requires only 1 byte.

To access a member of a **union**, use the same syntax that you would use for structures: the dot and arrow operators. If you are operating on the **union** directly, use the dot operator. If the **union** is accessed through a pointer, use the arrow operator. For example, to assign the integer 10 to element **i** of **cnvt**, write

```
cnvt.i = 10;
```

In the next example, a pointer to **cnvt** is passed to a function:

```
void func1(union u_type *un)
{
  un->i = 10; /* assign 10 to cnvt using
                function */
}
```

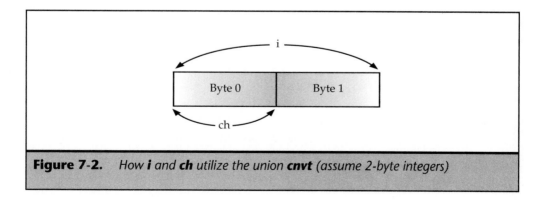

Figure 7-2.   *How **i** and **ch** utilize the union **cnvt** (assume 2-byte integers)*

Using a **union** can aid in the production of machine-independent (portable) code. Because the compiler keeps track of the actual sizes of the **union** members, no machine dependencies are produced. That is, you need not worry about the size of an **int**, **long**, **float**, or whatever.

Unions are used frequently when specialized type conversions are needed because you can refer to the data held in the **union** in fundamentally different ways. For example, you may use a **union** to manipulate the bytes that comprise a **double** in order to alter its precision or to perform some unusual type of rounding.

To get an idea of the usefulness of a **union** when nonstandard type conversions are needed, consider the problem of writing an integer to a disk file. The C/C++ standard library defines no function specifically designed to write an integer to a file. While you can write any type of data (including an integer) to a file using **fwrite( )**, using **fwrite( )** is overkill for such a simple operation. However, using a **union** you can easily create a function called **putw( )**, which writes the binary representation of an integer to a file one byte at a time. To see how, first create a **union** consisting of one integer and a 2-byte character array:

```
union pw {
   int i;
   char ch[2];
};
```

Now, you can use **pw** to create the version of **putw( )** shown in the following program:

```
#include <stdio.h>
union pw {
   int i;
   char ch[2];
};

putw(int num, FILE *fp);

void main(void)
{
   FILE *fp;

   fp = fopen("test.tmp", "w+");

   putw(1000, fp);  /* write the value 1000 as an integer */
   fclose(fp);
}
```

```
putw(int num, FILE *fp)
{
  union pw word;

  word.i = num;

  putc(word.ch[0], fp); /* write first half */
  return putc(word.ch[1], fp); /* write second half */
}
```

Although **putw( )** is called with an integer, it can still use the standard function **putc( )** to write each byte in the integer to a disk file one byte at a time.

NOTE: C++ supports a special type of union called an anonymous union, which is discussed in Part Two of this book.

Enumerations

An *enumeration* is a set of named integer constants that specify all the legal values a variable of that type may have. Enumerations are common in everyday life. For example, an enumeration of the coins used in the United States is

penny, nickel, dime, quarter, half-dollar, dollar

Enumerations are defined much like structures; the keyword **enum** signals the start of an enumeration type. The general form for enumerations is

enum *tag { enumeration list } variable_list;*

Here, both the enumeration tag and the variable list are optional. As with structures, the enumeration tag name is used to declare variables of its type. The following code fragment defines an enumeration called **coin** and declares **money** to be of that type.

```
enum coin { penny, nickel, dime, quarter,
            half_dollar, dollar};
enum coin money;
```

Given these declarations, the following types of statements are perfectly valid:

```
money = dime;
if(money==quarter) printf("Money is a quarter.\n");
```

The key point to understand about an enumeration is that each of the symbols stands for an integer value. As such, they can be used anywhere that an integer can be used. Each symbol is given a value one greater than the symbol that precedes it. The value of the first enumeration symbol is 0. Therefore,

```
printf("%d %d", penny, dime);
```

displays **0 2** on the screen.

You can specify the value of one or more of the symbols by using an initializer. Do this by following the symbol with an equal sign and an integer value. Symbols that appear after initializers are assigned values greater than the previous initialization value. For example, the following code assigns the value of 100 to **quarter**.

```
enum coin { penny, nickel, dime, quarter=100,
            half_dollar, dollar};
```

Now, the values of these symbols are

penny	0
nickel	1
dime	2
quarter	100
half_dollar	101
dollar	102

One common but erroneous assumption about enumerations is that the symbols can be input and output directly. This is not the case. For example, the following code fragment will not perform as desired.

```
/* this will not work */
money = dollar;
printf("%s", money);
```

Remember, **dollar** is simply a name for an integer; it is not a string. For the same reason, you cannot use this code to achieve the desired results:

```
/* this code is wrong */
strcpy(money, "dime");
```

That is, a string that contains the name of a symbol is not automatically converted to that symbol.

Actually, creating code to input and output enumeration symbols is quite tedious (unless you are willing to settle for their integer values). For example, you need the following code to display, in words, the kind of coin that **money** contains.

```
switch(money) {
  case penny: printf("penny");
    break;
  case nickel: printf("nickel");
    break;
  case dime: printf("dime");
    break;
  case quarter: printf("quarter");
    break;
  case half_dollar: printf("half_dollar");
    break;
  case dollar: printf("dollar");
}
```

Sometimes, you can declare an array of strings and use the enumeration value as an index to translate that value into its corresponding string. For example, this code also outputs the proper string:

```
char name[][12]={
  "penny",
  "nickel",
  "dime",
  "quarter",
  "half_dollar",
  "dollar"
};
printf("%s", name[money]);
```

Of course, this only works if no symbol is initialized because the string array must be indexed starting at 0.

Since enumeration values must be converted manually to their human-readable string values for I/O operations, they are most useful in routines that do not make such conversions. An enumeration is often used to define a compiler's symbol table, for example. Enumerations are also used to help prove the validity of a program by providing a compile-time redundancy check confirming that a variable is assigned only valid values.

Using sizeof to Ensure Portability

You have seen that structures and unions can be used to create variables of different sizes, and that the actual size of these variables may change from machine to machine. The **sizeof** operator computes the size of any variable or type and can help eliminate machine-dependent code from your programs. This operator is especially useful where structures or unions are concerned.

For the following discussion, assume an implementation, common to many C/C++ compilers, which has the sizes for data types shown here:

Type	Size in Bytes
char	1
int	2
float	4

Therefore, the following code will print the numbers 1, 2, and 4 on the screen.

```
char ch;
int i;
float f;

printf("%d", sizeof(ch));
printf("%d", sizeof(i));
printf("%d", sizeof(f));
```

The size of a structure is equal to *or greater than* the sum of the sizes of its members, as in this example:

```
struct s {
  char ch;
  int i;
  float f;
} s_var;
```

Here, **sizeof(s_var)** is at least 7 (4 + 2 + 1). However, the size of **s_var** might be greater because the compiler is allowed to pad a structure in order to achieve word or paragraph alignment. (A paragraph is 16 bytes.) Since the size of a structure may be greater than the sum of the sizes of its members, you should always use **sizeof** when you need to know the size of a structure.

Since **sizeof** is a compile-time operator, all the information necessary to compute the size of any variable is known at compile time. This is especially meaningful for **union**s, because the size of a **union** is always equal to the size of its largest member. For example, consider

```
union u {
   char ch;
   int i;
   float f;
} u_var;
```

Here, **sizeof(u_var)** is 4. At run time, it does not matter what **u_var** is actually holding. All that matters is the size of its largest member, because any **union** must be as large as its largest element.

typedef

C allows you to explicitly define new data type names by using the keyword **typedef**. You are not actually *creating* a new data type, but rather defining a new name for an existing type. This process can help make machine-dependent programs more portable. If you define your own type name for each machine-dependent data type used by your program, then only the **typedef** statements have to be changed when compiling for a new environment. **typedef** also can aid in self-documenting your code by allowing descriptive names for the standard data types. The general form of the **typedef** statement is

typedef *type newname*;

where *type* is any valid data type and *newname* is the new name for this type. The new name you define is in addition to, not a replacement for, the existing type name.

For example, you could create a new name for **float** by using

```
typedef float balance;
```

This statement tells the compiler to recognize **balance** as another name for **float**. Next, you could create a **float** variable using **balance**:

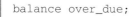

```
balance over_due;
```

Here, **over_due** is a floating-point variable of type **balance**, which is another word for **float**.

Now that **balance** has been defined, it can be used in another **typedef**. For example,

```
typedef balance overdraft;
```

tells the compiler to recognize **overdraft** as another name for **balance**, which is another name for **float**.

Using **typedef** can make your code easier to read and easier to port to a new machine. But remember, you are not creating any new data types.

Chapter Eight

Console I/O

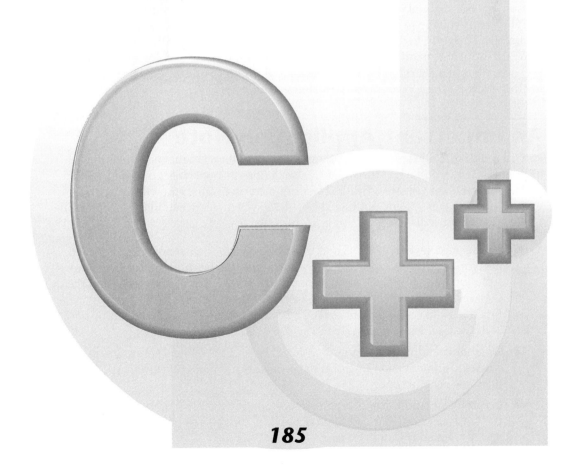

T his and the next chapter discuss the C I/O system. In C, input and output are accomplished through library functions. C's I/O system is an elegant piece of engineering that offers a flexible yet cohesive mechanism for transferring data between devices. However, C's I/O system is quite large and involves several different functions.

C supports both console and file I/O. Technically, C makes little distinction between console I/O and file I/O. However, they are conceptually very different worlds. This chapter examines in detail the console I/O functions. The next chapter presents the file I/O system and describes how the two systems relate.

With one exception, this chapter covers only console I/O functions defined by the ANSI C standard. The ANSI C standard does not define any functions that perform various screen control operations (such as cursor positioning) or that display graphics, because these operations vary widely between machines. Instead, the standard C console I/O functions perform only TTY-based output. However, most compilers include in their libraries screen control and graphics functions that apply to the specific environment in which the compiler is designed to run. (You will need to consult the user manual for your compiler about nonstandard I/O functions.)

This chapter refers to the console I/O functions as performing input from the keyboard and output to the screen. However, these functions actually have the standard input and standard output of the system as the target and/or source of their I/O operations. Furthermore, standard input and standard output may be redirected to other devices. These concepts are covered in Chapter 9.

An Important Application Note

Part One of this book uses the I/O system defined by the C language. Although C++ fully supports the C-like I/O functions, it also defines its own object-oriented I/O system. Therefore, if you are writing object-oriented programs, you will want to use the C+++-specific I/O system, not the ANSI C I/O system described in this chapter. The C-like I/O system is discussed in this book for three reasons:

- For the next several years, C and C++ will coexist. Also, many programs will be hybrids of both C and C++ code. Further, it will be common for C programs to be "upgraded" into C++ programs. Thus, knowledge of both the C and the C++ I/O system will be necessary. For example, to change the C-like I/O functions into C++ object-oriented I/O functions, you will need to know how both the C and C++ I/O systems operate.

- An understanding of the basic principles behind the C-like I/O system is crucial to an understanding of the C++ object-oriented I/O system. (Both share the same general concepts.)

- In certain situations (for example, in very short programs), it may be easier to use C's non-object-oriented approach to I/O than it is to use the object-oriented I/O defined by C++.

In addition, there is an unwritten rule that any C++ programmer must also be a C programmer. If you don't know how to use the C I/O system, you will be limiting your professional horizons.

Reading and Writing Characters

The simplest of the console I/O functions are **getchar( )**, which reads a character from the keyboard, and **putchar( )**, which prints a character on the screen. The **getchar( )** function waits until a key is pressed and then returns its value. The key pressed is also automatically echoed to the screen. The **putchar( )** function writes a character to the screen at the current cursor position. The prototypes for **getchar( )** and **putchar( )** are shown here:

```
int getchar(void);
int putchar(int c);
```

The header file for these functions is STDIO.H. As its prototype shows, the **getchar( )** function is declared as returning an integer. However, you can assign this value to a **char** variable, as is usually done, because the character is contained in the low-order byte. (The high-order byte is usually zero.) **getchar( )** returns **EOF** if an error occurs.

In the case of **putchar( )**, even though it is declared as taking an integer parameter, you will generally call it using a character argument. Only the low-order byte of its parameter is actually output to the screen. The **putchar( )** function returns the character written, or **EOF** if an error occurs. (The **EOF** macro is defined in STDIO.H and is generally equal to −1.)

The following program illustrates **getchar( )** and **putchar( )**. It inputs characters from the keyboard and displays them in reverse case. That is, it prints uppercase as lowercase and lowercase as uppercase. To stop the program, enter a period.

```c
#include <stdio.h>
#include <ctype.h>

void main(void)
{
  char ch;

  printf("Enter some text (type a period to quit).\n");
  do {
    ch = getchar();

    if(islower(ch)) ch = toupper(ch);
    else ch = tolower(ch);
```

```
    putchar(ch);
  } while (ch != '.');
}
```

A Problem with getchar( )

There are some potential problems with **getchar( )**. The ANSI C standard defines **getchar( )** to be compatible with the original, UNIX-based version of C. Unfortunately, in its original form, **getchar( )** buffers input until ENTER is pressed. This is called *line-buffered* input and it was the method used by the original UNIX systems—that is, you had to press ENTER before anything you typed was actually sent to your program. Also, since **getchar( )** inputs only one character each time it is called, line-buffering may leave one or more characters waiting in the input queue, which is annoying in interactive environments. Even though the ANSI C standard specifies that **getchar( )** can be implemented as an interactive function, it seldom is. Therefore, if the preceding program did not behave as you expected, you now know why.

Alternatives to getchar( )

getchar( ) might not be implemented by your compiler in such a way that it is useful in an interactive environment. If this is the case, you will probably want to use a different function to read characters from the keyboard. The ANSI C standard does not define any function that is guaranteed to provide interactive input, but virtually all C compilers do. Although these functions are not defined by ANSI, they are commonly used since **getchar( )** does not fill the needs of most programmers.

Two of the most common alternative functions, **getch( )** and **getche( )**, have these prototypes:

```
int getch(void);
int getche(void);
```

For most compilers, the prototypes for these functions are found in CONIO.H. The **getch( )** function waits for a keypress after which it returns immediately. It does not echo the character to the screen. The **getche( )** function is the same as **getch( )**, but the key is echoed. This book often uses **getche( )** or **getch( )** instead of **getchar( )** when a character needs to be read from the keyboard in an interactive program. However, if your compiler does not support these alternative functions, or if **getchar( )** is implemented as an interactive function by your compiler, you should substitute **getchar( )** when necessary.

For example, the previous program is shown here using **getch( )** instead of **getchar( )**:

```
#include <stdio.h>
#include <conio.h>
#include <ctype.h>

void main(void)
{
  char ch;

  printf("Enter some text (type a period to quit).\n");
  do {
    ch = getch();

    if(islower(ch)) ch = toupper(ch);
    else ch = tolower(ch);

    putchar(ch);
  } while (ch != '.');
}
```

Reading and Writing Strings

The next step up in console I/O, in terms of complexity and power, are the functions **gets( )** and **puts( )**. They enable you to read and write strings of characters at the console.

The **gets( )** function reads a string of characters entered at the keyboard and places them at the address pointed to by its argument. You may type characters at the keyboard until you strike a carriage return. The carriage return does not become part of the string; instead, a null terminator is placed at the end and **gets( )** returns. In fact, you cannot use **gets( )** to return a carriage return (although **getchar( )** can do so). You can correct typing mistakes by using the backspace key before pressing ENTER. The prototype for **gets( )** is

    char *gets(char *str);

where *str* is a character array that receives the characters input by the user. **gets( )** also returns *str*. The prototype for **gets( )** is in STDIO.H. The following program reads a string into the array **str** and prints its length.

```
#include <stdio.h>
#include <string.h>

void main(void)
```

```
{
  char str[80];

  gets(str);
  printf("Length is %d", strlen(str));
}
```

The **puts( )** function writes its string argument to the screen followed by a newline. Its prototype is

int puts(const char *str);

puts( ) recognizes the same backslash codes as **printf( )**, such as '\t' for tab. A call to **puts( )** requires far less overhead than the same call to **printf( )** because **puts( )** can only output a string of characters—it cannot output numbers or do format conversions. Therefore, **puts( )** takes up less space and runs faster than **printf( )**. For this reason, the **puts( )** function is often used when it is important to have highly optimized code. The **puts( )** function returns **EOF** if an error occurs. Otherwise, it returns a nonnegative value. However, when writing to the console, you can usually assume that no error will occur, so the return value of **puts( )** is seldom monitored. The following statement displays **hello**.

```
puts("hello");
```

Table 8-1 summarizes the basic console I/O functions.

Function	Operation
getchar( )	Reads a character from the keyboard; waits for carriage return.
getche( )	Reads a character with echo; does not wait for carriage return; not defined by ANSI standard C, but a common extension.
getch( )	Reads a character without echo; does not wait for carriage return; not defined by ANSI standard C, but a common extension.
putchar( )	Writes a character to the screen.
gets( )	Reads a string from the keyboard.
puts( )	Writes a string to the screen.

Table 8-1. *The Basic I/O Functions*

The following program, a simple computerized dictionary, demonstrates several of the basic console I/O functions. It prompts the user to enter a word and then checks to see if the word matches one in its built-in database. If a match is found, the program prints the word's meaning. Pay special attention to the indirection used in this program. If you have any trouble understanding it, remember that the **dic** array is an array of pointers to strings. Notice that the list must be terminated by two nulls.

```c
/* A simple dictionary. */
#include <stdio.h>
#include <conio.h>
#include <string.h>
#include <ctype.h>

/* list of words and meanings */
char  *dic[][40] = {
  "atlas", "a volume of maps",
  "car", "a motorized vehicle",
  "telephone", "a communication device",
  "airplane", "a flying machine",
  "", ""   /* null terminate the list */
};

void main(void)
{
  char word[80], ch;
  char **p;

  do {
    puts("\nEnter word: ");
    gets(word);

    p = (char **)dic;

    /* find matching word and print its meaning */
    do {
      if(!strcmp(*p, word)) {
        puts("meaning:");
        puts(*(p+1));
        break;
      }
      if(!strcmp(*p, word)) break;
      p = p + 2;   /* advance through the list */
    } while(*p);
```

```
    if(!*p) puts("word not in dictionary");
    printf("another? (y/n): ");
    ch = getche();
  } while(toupper(ch) != 'N');
}
```

Formatted Console I/O

The functions **printf( )** and **scanf( )** perform formatted output and input—that is, they can read and write data in various formats that are under your control. The **printf( )** function writes data to the console. The **scanf( )** function, its complement, reads data from the keyboard. Both functions can operate on any of the built-in data types, including characters, strings, and numbers.

printf( )

The prototype for **printf( )** is

  int printf(const char *control_string, ...);

The prototype for **printf( )** is in STDIO.H. The **printf( )** function returns the number of characters written or a negative value if an error occurs.

The *control_string* consists of two types of items. The first type is composed of characters that will be printed on the screen. The second type contains format specifiers that define the way the subsequent arguments are displayed. A format specifier begins with a percent sign and is followed by the format code. There must be exactly the same number of arguments as there are format specifiers, and the format specifiers and the arguments are matched in order from left to right. For example, this **printf( )** call

```
printf("I like %c %s", 'C', "++ very much!");
```

displays

```
I like C++ very much!
```

The **printf( )** function accepts a wide variety of format specifiers, as shown in Table 8-2.

Code	Format
%c	Character
%d	Signed decimal integers
%i	Signed decimal integers
%e	Scientific notation (lowercase e)
%E	Scientific notation (uppercase E)
%f	Decimal floating point
%g	Uses %e or %f, whichever is shorter
%G	Uses %E or %f, whichever is shorter
%o	Unsigned octal
%s	String of characters
%u	Unsigned decimal integers
%x	Unsigned hexadecimal (lowercase letters)
%X	Unsigned hexadecimal (uppercase letters)
%p	Displays a pointer
%n	Associated argument is an integer pointer into which the number of characters written so far is placed
%%	Prints a % sign

Table 8-2.   *printf( ) Format Specifiers*

Printing Characters

To print an individual character, use **%c**. This causes its matching argument to be output, unmodified, to the screen.

To print a string, use **%s**.

Printing Numbers

You can use either **%d** or **%i** to indicate a signed decimal number. These format specifiers are equivalent; both are supported for historical reasons.

To output an unsigned value, use **%u**.

The **%f** format specifier displays numbers in floating point.

The **%e** and **%E** specifiers tell **printf( )** to display a **double** argument in scientific notation. Numbers represented in scientific notation take this general form:

x.ddddE+/−yy

If you want to display the letter "E" in uppercase, use the **%E** format; otherwise use **%e**.

You can tell **printf( )** to use either **%f** or **%e** by using the **%g** or **%G** format specifiers. This causes **printf( )** to select the format specifier that produces the shortest output. Where applicable, use **%G** if you want "E" shown in uppercase; otherwise, use **%g**. The following program demonstrates the effect of the **%g** format specifier.

```c
#include <stdio.h>

void main(void)
{
  double f;

  for(f=1.0; f<1.0e+10; f=f*10)
    printf("%g ", f);
}
```

It produces the following output:

```
1 10 100 1000 10000 100000 1e+06 1e+07 1e+08 1e+09
```

You can display unsigned integers in octal or hexadecimal format using **%o** and **%x**, respectively. Since the hexadecimal number system uses the letters A through F to represent the numbers 10 through 15, you can display these letters in either upper- or lowercase. For uppercase, use the **%X** format specifier; for lowercase, use **%x**, as shown here:

```c
#include <stdio.h>

void main(void)
{
  unsigned num;

  for(num=0; num<255; num++) {
    printf("%o ", num);
    printf("%x ", num);
    printf("%X\n", num);
  }
}
```

Displaying an Address

If you wish to display an address, use **%p**. This format specifier causes **printf( )** to display a machine address in a format compatible with the type of addressing used by the computer. The next program displays the address of **sample**.

```
#include <stdio.h>

int sample;

void main(void)
{
  printf("%p", &sample);
}
```

The %n Specifier

The **%n** format specifier is different from the others. Instead of telling **printf( )** to display something, it causes **printf( )** to load the variable pointed to by its corresponding argument with a value equal to the number of characters that have been output. In other words, the value that corresponds to the **%n** format specifier must be a pointer to a variable. After the call to **printf( )** has returned, this variable will hold the number of characters output, up to the point at which the **%n** was encountered. Examine this program to understand this somewhat unusual format code.

```
#include <stdio.h>

void main(void)
{
  int count;

  printf("this%n is a test\n", &count);
  printf("%d", count);
}
```

This program displays **this is a test** followed by the number 4. The **%n** format specifier is used primarily to enable your program to perform dynamic formatting.

Format Modifiers

Many format specifiers may take modifiers that alter their meaning slightly. For example, you can specify a minimum field width, the number of decimal places, and left justification. The format modifier goes between the percent sign and the format code. These modifiers are discussed next.

The Minimum Field Width Specifier

An integer placed between the % sign and the format code acts as a *minimum field width specifier*. This pads the output with spaces to ensure that it reaches a certain minimum length. If the string or number is longer than that minimum, it will still be printed in full. The default padding is done with spaces. If you wish to pad with 0's, place a 0 before the field width specifier. For example, **%05d** will pad a number of less than five digits with 0's so that its total length is five. The following program demonstrates the minimum field width specifier.

```
#include <stdio.h>

void main(void)
{
  double item;

  item = 10.12304;

  printf("%f\n", item);
  printf("%10f\n", item);
  printf("%012f\n", item);
}
```

This program produces the following output:

```
10.123040
 10.123040
00010.123040
```

The minimum field width modifier is most commonly used to produce tables in which the columns line up. For example, the next program produces a table of squares and cubes for the numbers between 1 and 19.

```
#include <stdio.h>
```

```
void main(void)
{
  int i;

  /* display a table of squares and cubes */
  for(i=1; i<20; i++)
    printf("%8d %8d %8d\n", i, i*i, i*i*i);
}
```

A sample of its output is shown here:

```
 1       1       1
 2       4       8
 3       9      27
 4      16      64
 5      25     125
 6      36     216
 7      49     343
 8      64     512
 9      81     729
10     100    1000
11     121    1331
12     144    1728
13     169    2197
14     196    2744
15     225    3375
16     256    4096
17     289    4913
18     324    5832
19     361    6859
```

The Precision Specifier

The *precision specifier* follows the minimum field width specifier (if there is one). It consists of a period followed by an integer. Its exact meaning depends upon the type of data it is applied to.

When you apply the precision specifier to floating-point data using the **%f**, **%e**, or **%E** specifier, it determines the number of decimal places displayed. For example, **%10.4f** displays a number at least ten characters wide with four decimal places. If you don't specify the precision, a default of six is used.

When the precision specifier is applied to **%g** or **%G**, it specifies the number of significant digits.

Applied to strings, the precision specifier specifies the maximum field length. For example, **%5.7s** displays a string at least five and not exceeding seven characters long. If the string is longer than the maximum field width, the end characters will be truncated.

When applied to integer types, the precision specifier determines the minimum number of digits that will appear for each number. Leading zeros are added to achieve the required number of digits.

The following program illustrates the precision specifier.

```
#include <stdio.h>

void main(void)
{
  printf("%.4f\n", 123.1234567);
  printf("%3.8d\n", 1000);
  printf("%10.15s\n", "This is a simple test.");
}
```

It produces the following output:

```
123.1235
00001000
This is a simpl
```

Justifying Output

By default, all output is right-justified. That is, if the field width is larger than the data printed, the data will be placed on the right edge of the field. You can force output to be left-justified by placing a minus sign directly after the %. For example, **%–10.2f** left-justifies a floating-point number with two decimal places in a 10-character field.

The following program illustrates left justification.

```
#include <stdio.h>

void main(void)
{
  printf("right-justified:%8d\n", 100);
  printf("left-justified:%-8d\n", 100);
}
```

Handling Other Data Types

There are two format modifiers that allow **printf( )** to display **short** and **long** integers. These modifiers can be applied to the **d**, **i**, **o**, **u**, and **x** type specifiers. The **l** (*ell*) modifier tells **printf( )** that a **long** data type follows. For example, **%ld** means that a **long int** is to be displayed. The **h** modifier instructs **printf( )** to display a **short** integer. For instance, **%hu** indicates that the data is of type **short unsigned int**.

The **L** modifier can prefix the floating-point specifiers **e**, **f**, and **g** and indicates that a **long double** follows.

The * and # Modifiers

The **printf( )** function supports two additional modifiers to some of its format specifiers: * and #.

Preceding **g**, **G**, **f**, **E**, or **e** specifier with a # ensures that there will be a decimal point even if there are no decimal digits. If you precede the **x** or **X** format specifier with a #, the hexadecimal number will be printed with a **0x** prefix. Preceding the **o** specifier with # causes the number to be printed with a leading zero. You cannot apply # to any other format specifiers.

Instead of constants, the minimum field width and precision specifiers may be provided by arguments to **printf( )**. To accomplish this, use an * as a placeholder. When the format string is scanned, **printf( )** will match the * to an argument in the order in which they occur. For example, in Figure 8-1, the minimum field width is 10, the precision is 4, and the value to be displayed is **123.3**.

The following program illustrates both # and *.

```
#include <stdio.h>

void main(void)
{
  printf("%x %#x\n", 10, 10);
  printf("%*.*f", 10, 4, 1234.34);
}
```

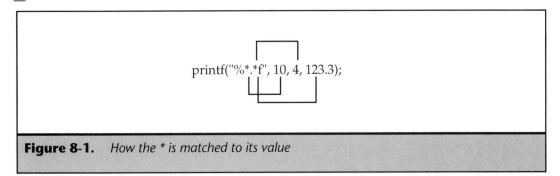

Figure 8-1.   *How the * is matched to its value*

scanf( )

scanf( ) is the general-purpose console input routine. It can read all the built-in data types and automatically convert numbers into the proper internal format. It is much like the reverse of **printf( )**. The prototype for **scanf( )** is

    int scanf(const char *control_string, ...);

The prototype for **scanf( )** is in STDIO.H. The **scanf( )** function returns the number of data items successfully assigned a value. If an error occurs, **scanf( )** returns **EOF**. The *control_string* determines how values are read into the variables pointed to in the argument list.

The control string consists of three classifications of characters:

- Format specifiers
- White-space characters
- Non-white-space characters

Let's take a look at each of these now.

Format Specifiers

The input format specifiers are preceded by a % sign and tell **scanf( )** what type of data is to be read next. These codes are listed in Table 8-3. The format specifiers are

Code	Meaning
%c	Read a single character.
%d	Read a decimal integer.
%i	Read a decimal integer.
%e	Read a floating-point number.
%f	Read a floating-point number.
%g	Read a floating-point number.
%o	Read an octal number.
%s	Read a string.
%x	Read a hexadecimal number.
%p	Read a pointer.
%n	Receive an integer value equal to the number of characters read so far.
%u	Read an unsigned integer.
%[]	Scan for a set of characters.

Table 8-3. *scanf( ) Format Specifiers*

matched, in order from left to right, with the arguments in the argument list. Let's look at some examples.

Inputting Numbers

To read a decimal number, use the **%d** or **%i** specifier. (These specifiers, which do the same thing, are both included for compatibility with older versions of C.)

To read a floating-point number represented in either standard or scientific notation, use **%e**, **%f**, or **%g**. (Again, these specifiers, which do precisely the same thing, are included for compatibility with older versions of C.)

You can use **scanf( )** to read integers in either octal or hexadecimal form by using the **%o** and **%x** format commands, respectively. The **%x** may be in either upper- or lowercase. Either way, you may enter the letters A through F in either case when entering hexadecimal numbers. The following program reads an octal and hexadecimal number.

```c
#include <stdio.h>

void main(void)
{
  int i, j;

  scanf("%o%x", &i, &j);
  printf("%o %x", i, j);
}
```

The **scanf( )** function stops reading a number when the first nonnumeric character is encountered.

Inputting Unsigned Integers

To input an unsigned integer, use the **%u** format specifier. For example,

```c
unsigned num;
scanf("%u", &num);
```

reads an unsigned number and puts its value into **num**.

Reading Individual Characters Using scanf( )

As you learned earlier in this chapter, you can read individual characters using **getchar( )** or a derivative function. You can also use **scanf( )** for this purpose if you use the **%c** format specifier. However, like most implementations of **getchar( )**, **scanf( )** will generally line-buffer input when the **%c** specifier is used. This makes it somewhat troublesome in an interactive environment.

Although spaces, tabs, and newlines are used as field separators when reading other types of data, when reading a single character, white-space characters are read like any other character. For example, with an input stream of "**x y**," this code fragment

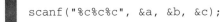

```
scanf("%c%c%c", &a, &b, &c);
```

returns with the character **x** in **a**, a space in **b**, and the character **y** in **c**.

Reading Strings

The **scanf( )** function can be used to read a string from the input stream using the **%s** format specifier. Using **%s** causes **scanf( )** to read characters until it encounters a white-space character. The characters that are read are put into the character array pointed to by the corresponding argument and the result is null terminated. As it applies to **scanf( )**, a white-space character is either a space, a newline, a tab, a vertical tab, or a form feed. Unlike **gets( )**, which reads a string until a carriage return is typed, **scanf( )** reads a string until the first white space is entered. This means that you cannot use **scanf( )** to read a string like "this is a test" because the first space terminates the reading process. To see the effect of the **%s** specifier, try this program using the string "hello there".

```
#include <stdio.h>

void main(void)
{
  char str[80];

  printf("Enter a string: ");
  scanf("%s", str);
  printf("Here's your string: %s", str);
}
```

The program responds with only the "hello" portion of the string.

Inputting an Address

To input a memory address, use the **%p** format specifier. This specifier causes **scanf( )** to read an address in the format defined by the architecture of the CPU. For example, the following program inputs an address and then displays what is at that memory address.

```
#include <stdio.h>

void main(void)
{
  char *p;

  printf("Enter an address: ");
  scanf("%p", &p);
  printf("Value at location %p is %c\n", p, *p);
}
```

The %n Specifier

The %n specifier instructs **scanf( )** to assign the number of characters read from the input stream at the point at which the **%n** was encountered to the variable pointed to by the corresponding argument.

Using a Scanset

The **scanf( )** function supports a general-purpose format specifier called a scanset. A *scanset* defines a set of characters. When **scanf( )** processes the scanset, it will input characters as long as those characters are part of the set defined by the scanset. The characters read will be assigned to the character array that is pointed to by the scanset's corresponding argument. You define a scanset by putting the characters to scan for inside square brackets. The beginning square bracket must be prefixed by a percent sign. For example, the following scanset tells **scanf( )** to read only the characters X, Y, and Z.

```
%[XYZ]
```

When you use a scanset, **scanf( )** continues to read characters and put them into the corresponding character array until it encounters a character that is not in the scanset. Upon return from **scanf( )**, this array will contain a null-terminated string that consists of the characters that have been read. To see how this works, try this program:

```
#include <stdio.h>

void main(void)
{
  int i;
  char str[80], str2[80];
```

```
    scanf("%d%[abcdefg]%s", &i, str, str2);
    printf("%d %s %s", i, str, str2);
}
```

Enter **123abcdtye** followed by ENTER. The program will then display **123 abcd tye**. Because the "t" is not part of the scanset, **scanf( )** stops reading characters into **str** when it encounters the "t." The remaining characters are put into **str2**.

You can specify an inverted set if the first character in the set is a ^. The ^ instructs **scanf( )** to accept any character that is *not* defined by the scanset.

You can specify a range using a hyphen. For example, this tells **scanf( )** to accept the characters A through Z:

```
%[A-Z]
```

One important point to remember is that the scanset is case sensitive. If you want to scan for both upper- and lowercase letters, you must specify them individually.

Discarding Unwanted White Space

A white-space character in the control string causes **scanf( )** to skip over one or more white-space characters in the input stream. A white-space character is either a space, a tab, vertical tab, form feed, or a newline. In essence, one white-space character in the control string causes **scanf( )** to read, but not store, any number (including zero) of white-space characters up to the first non-white-space character.

Non-White-Space Characters in the Control String

A non-white-space character in the control string causes **scanf( )** to read and discard matching characters in the input stream. For example, **"%d,%d"** causes **scanf( )** to read an integer, read and discard a comma, and then read another integer. If the specified character is not found, **scanf( )** terminates. If you wish to read and discard a percent sign, use %% in the control string.

You Must Pass scanf( ) Addresses

All the variables used to receive values through **scanf( )** must be passed by their addresses. This means that all arguments must be pointers to the variables that actually receive input. Recall that this is C's way of creating a call by reference, and it allows a function to alter the contents of an argument. For example, to read an integer into the variable **count**, you would use the following **scanf( )** call:

```
scanf("%d", &count);
```

Strings will be read into character arrays, and the array name, without any index, is the address of the first element of the array. So, to read a string into the character array **str**, you would use

```
scanf("%s", str);
```

In this case, **str** is already a pointer and need not be preceded by the **&** operator.

Format Modifiers

As with **printf( )**, **scanf( )** allows a number of its format specifiers to be modified.

The format specifiers can include a maximum field length modifier. This is an integer, placed between the % and the format specifier, that limits the number of characters read for that field. For example, to read no more than 20 characters into **str**, write

```
scanf("%20s", str);
```

If the input stream is greater than 20 characters, a subsequent call to input begins where this call leaves off. For example, if you enter

ABCDEFGHIJKLMNOPQRSTUVWXYZ

as the response to the **scanf( )** call in this example, only the first 20 characters, or up to the "T," are placed into **str** because of the maximum field width specifier. This means that the remaining characters, UVWXYZ, have not yet been used. If another **scanf( )** call is made, such as

```
scanf("%s", str);
```

the letters UVWXYZ are placed into **str**. Input for a field may terminate before the maximum field length is reached if a white space is encountered. In this case, **scanf( )** moves on to the next field.

To read a long integer, put an **l** (*ell*) in front of the format specifier. To read a short integer, put an **h** in front of the format specifier. These modifiers can be used with the **d, i, o, u**, and **x** format codes.

By default, the **f**, **e**, and **g** specifiers instruct **scanf( )** to assign data to a **float**. If you put an **l** (*ell*) in front of one of these specifiers, **scanf( )** assigns the data to a **double**. Using an **L** tells **scanf( )** that the variable receiving the data is a **long double**.

Suppressing Input

You can tell **scanf( )** to read a field but not assign it to any variable by preceding that field's format code with an *. For example, given

```
scanf("%d%*c%d", &x, &y);
```

you could enter the coordinate pair **10,10**. The comma would be correctly read, but not assigned to anything. Assignment suppression is especially useful when you need to process only a part of what is being entered.

Chapter Nine

File I/O

A s mentioned in Chapter 8, the C language does not contain any I/O statements. Instead, all I/O operations take place through calls to functions in the C standard library. This approach makes C's file system extremely powerful and flexible. C's I/O system also allows data to be transferred in either its internal binary representation or in a human-readable text format. This makes it easy to create files to fit any need.

ANSI C I/O Versus Unix I/O

The ANSI C standard defines a complete set of I/O functions that can be used to read and write any type of data. In contrast, the old Unix C standard contains two distinct file systems that handle I/O operations. The first method loosely parallels the one defined by the ANSI C standard and is sometimes called the *buffered* file system (sometimes the term *formatted* or *high-level* is used instead). The second is the *Unix-like* file system (sometimes called either *unformatted* or *unbuffered*) and is defined under only the old Unix standard. The ANSI C standard does not define the Unix-like file system because, among other things, the two file systems are largely redundant and the Unix-like file system may not be applicable to certain environments that could otherwise support C.

For similar reasons, the Unix-like file system is also not defined or supported by the proposed ANSI C++ standard. However, *all C++ compilers support the ANSI C file system*. Since the Unix-like file system is not particularly relevant to C++ programming and is not defined by either ANSI C or the proposed ANSI C++ standard, it is not discussed in this book.

C Versus C++ I/O

Because C forms the foundation for C++, there is sometimes a question of how C's file system relates to C++. The following short discussion answers this question.

C++ supports the entire ANSI C file system. Thus, if you will be porting older C code to C++ sometime in the future, you will not have to change all of your I/O routines. However, C++ also defines its own, object-oriented I/O system, which includes both I/O functions and I/O operators. The C++ I/O system completely duplicates the functionality of the ANSI C I/O system. In general, if you will be using C++ to write object-oriented programs, you will want to use the object-oriented I/O system. Otherwise, you are free to use either the object-oriented file system or the ANSI C file system. (However, most C++ programmers elect to use the C++ I/O system for reasons that are made clear in Part Two of this book.)

Streams and Files

Before beginning our discussion of the ANSI C file system, it is important to understand the difference between the terms *streams* and *files*. The C I/O system supplies a consistent interface to the C programmer independent of the actual device being accessed. That is, the C I/O system provides a level of abstraction between the programmer and the device. This abstraction is called a *stream,* and the actual device is called a *file.* It is important to understand how streams and files interact.

> **NOTE:** *The concept of streams and files is also important to the C++ I/O system discussed in Part Two of this book.*

Streams

The C file system is designed to work with a wide variety of devices, including terminals, disk drives, and tape drives. Even though each device is very different, the C file system transforms each into a logical device called a stream. All streams behave similarly. Because streams are largely device independent, the same function that can write to a disk file can also be used to write to another type of device, such as the console. There are two types of streams: text and binary.

Text Streams

A *text stream* is a sequence of characters. The ANSI C standard allows (but does not require) a text stream to be organized into lines terminated by a newline character. However, the newline character is optional on the last line, and its use is determined by the implementation (Actually, most C/C++ compilers do not terminate text streams with newline characters.) In a text stream, certain character translations may occur as required by the host environment. For example, a newline may be converted to a carriage return/linefeed pair. Therefore, there may not be a one-to-one relationship between the characters that are written (or read) and those on the external device. Also, because of possible translations, the number of characters written (or read) may not be the same as those on the external device.

Binary Streams

A *binary stream* is a sequence of bytes with a one-to-one correspondence to those in the external device—that is, no character translations occur. Also, the number of bytes written (or read) is the same as the number on the external device. However, an implementation-defined number of null bytes may be appended to a binary stream. These null bytes might be used to pad the information so that it fills a sector on a disk, for example.

Files

In C, a *file* can be anything from a disk file to a terminal or printer. You associate a stream with a specific file by performing an open operation. Once a file is open, information can be exchanged between it and your program.

Not all files have the same capabilities. For example, a disk file can support random access while a modem port cannot. This brings up an important point about the C I/O system: All streams are the same but all files are not.

If the file can support *position requests*, opening that file also initializes the *file position indicator* to the start of the file. As each character is read from or written to the file, the position indicator is incremented, ensuring progression through the file.

You disassociate a file from a specific stream with a close operation. If you close a file opened for output, the contents, if any, of its associated stream are written to the external device. This process is generally referred to as *flushing* the stream and guarantees that no information is accidentally left in the disk buffer. All files are closed automatically when your program terminates normally, either by **main( )** returning to the operating system or by a call to **exit( )**. Files are not closed when a program terminates abnormally, such as when it crashes or when it calls **abort( )**.

Each stream that is associated with a file has a file control structure of type **FILE**. This structure is defined in the header STDIO.H. Never modify this file control block.

If you are new to programming, C's separation of streams and files may seem unnecessary or contrived. Just remember that its main purpose is to provide a consistent interface. In C, you need only think in terms of streams and use only one file system to accomplish all I/O operations. The C I/O system automatically converts the raw input or output from each device into an easily managed stream.

File System Basics

The ANSI C file system is composed of several interrelated functions. The most common of these are shown in Table 9-1. These functions require that the header file STDIO.H be included in any program in which they are used. Notice that most of the functions begin with the letter "f." This is a holdover from the Unix C standard, which defined two file systems. The Unix I/O functions did not begin with a prefix, and most of the formatted I/O system functions were prefixed with the "f." The C standardization committee elected to maintain this naming convention in the interest of continuity.

The header file STDIO.H provides the prototypes for the I/O functions and defines these three types: **size_t**, **fpos_t**, and **FILE**. The **size_t** type is some variety of unsigned integer, as is **fpos_t**. The **FILE** type is discussed in the next section.

STDIO.H also defines several macros. The ones relevant to this chapter are **NULL**, **EOF**, **FOPEN_MAX**, **SEEK_SET**, **SEEK_CUR**, and **SEEK_END**. The **NULL** macro defines a null pointer. The **EOF** macro is generally defined as –1 and is the value returned when an input function tries to read past the end of the file. **FOPEN_MAX**

Name	Function
fopen( )	Opens a file
fclose( )	Closes a file
putc( )	Writes a character to a file
fputc( )	Same as putc( )
getc( )	Reads a character from a file
fgetc( )	Same as getc( )
fseek( )	Seeks to a specified byte in a file
fprintf( )	Is to a file what printf( ) is to the console
fscanf( )	Is to a file what scanf( ) is to the console
feof( )	Returns true if end-of-file is reached
ferror( )	Returns true if an error has occurred
rewind( )	Resets the file position indicator to the beginning of the file
remove( )	Erases a file
fflush( )	Flushes a file

Table 9-1. *The Most Common ANSI C File-System Functions*

defines an integer value that determines the number of files that can be open at any one time. The other macros are used with **fseek( )**, which is the function that performs random access on a file.

The File Pointer

The file pointer is the common thread that unites the ANSI C I/O system. A *file pointer* is a pointer to information that defines various things about the file, including its name, status, and the current position of the file. In essence, the file pointer identifies a specific disk file and is used by the associated stream to direct the operation of the I/O functions. A file pointer is a pointer variable of type **FILE**. To read or write files, your program needs to use file pointers. To obtain a file pointer variable, use a statement like this:

```
FILE *fp;
```

Opening a File

The **fopen( )** function opens a stream for use and links a file with that stream. Then it returns the file pointer associated with that file. Most often (and for the rest of this discussion) the file is a disk file. The **fopen( )** function has this prototype:

FILE *fopen(const char *_filename_, const char *_mode_);

Here, _filename_ is a pointer to a string of characters that make up a valid filename and may include a path specification. The string pointed to by _mode_ determines how the file will be opened. Table 9-2 shows the legal values for _mode_. Strings like "r+b" can also be represented as "rb+."

As stated, the **fopen( )** function returns a file pointer. Your program should never alter the value of this pointer. If an error occurs when it is trying to open the file, **fopen( )** returns a null pointer.

As Table 9-2 shows, a file can be opened in either text or binary mode. In most implementations, in text mode, carriage return/linefeed sequences are translated to newline characters on input. On output, the reverse occurs: Newlines are translated to carriage return/linefeeds. No such translations occur on binary files.

The following fragment uses **fopen( )** to open a file named TEST for output.

```
FILE *fp;
fp = fopen("test", "w");
```

While technically correct, you will usually see the preceding code written like this:

```
FILE *fp;

if ((fp = fopen("test","w"))==NULL) {
  printf("Cannot open file.\n");
  exit(1);
}
```

This method will detect any error in opening a file, such as a write-protected or a full disk, before your program attempts to write to it. In general, you will always want to confirm that **fopen( )** succeeded before attempting any other operations on the file.

If you use **fopen( )** to open a file for writing, any preexisting file by that name will be erased and a new file started. If no file by that name exists, one will be created. If you want to add to the end of the file, you must use mode "a." You can only open existing files for read operations. If the file does not exist, an error is returned. Finally, if a file is opened for read/write operations, it will not be erased if it exists. However, if it does not exist it will be created.

The number of files that can be open at any one time is specified by **FOPEN_MAX**. This value will usually be at least 8, but you must check your compiler manual for its exact value.

Mode	Meaning
r	Open a text file for reading.
w	Create a text file for writing.
a	Append to a text file.
rb	Open a binary file for reading.
wb	Create a binary file for writing.
ab	Append to a binary file.
r+	Open a text file for read/write.
w+	Create a text file for read/write.
a+	Append or create a text file for read/write.
r+b	Open a binary file for read/write.
w+b	Create a binary file for read/write.
a+b	Append or create a binary file for read/write.

Table 9-2. *The Legal Mode Values*

Closing a File

The **fclose( )** function closes a stream that was opened by a call to **fopen( )**. It writes any data still remaining in the disk buffer to the file and does a formal operating-system-level close on the file. Failure to close a stream invites all kinds of trouble, including lost data, destroyed files, and possible intermittent errors in your program. **fclose( )** also frees the file control block associated with the stream, making it available for reuse. In most cases, there is an operating system limit to the number of open files you can have at any one time, so you can have to close one file before opening another.

The **fclose( )** function has this prototype:

int fclose(FILE *fp);

Here, *fp* is the file pointer returned by the call to **fopen( )**. A return value of zero signifies a successful close operation. The function returns **EOF** if an error occurs. You can use the standard function **ferror( )** (discussed shortly) to determine and report any problems. Generally, **fclose( )** will only fail when a disk has been prematurely removed from the drive or there is no more space on the disk.

Writing a Character

The ANSI C I/O system defines two equivalent functions that output a character: **putc( )** and **fputc( )**. (Actually, **putc( )** is implemented as a macro.) There are two identical functions simply to preserve compatibility with older versions of C. This book uses **putc( )**, but you can use **fputc( )** if you like.

The **putc( )** function writes characters to a file that was previously opened for writing using the **fopen( )** function. The prototype of this function is

    int putc(int *ch*, FILE *fp*);

where *fp* is the file pointer returned by **fopen( )** and *ch* is the character to be output. The file pointer tells **putc( )** which disk file to write to. For historical reasons, *ch* is defined as an **int**, but only the low-order byte is used.

If a **putc( )** operation is successful, it returns the character written. Otherwise, it returns **EOF**.

Reading a Character

There are also two equivalent functions that input a character: **getc( )** and **fgetc( )**. Both are defined to preserve compatibility with older versions of C. This book uses **getc( )** (which is actually implemented as a macro), but you can use **fgetc( )** if you like.

The **getc( )** function reads characters from a file opened in read mode by **fopen( )**. The prototype of **getc( )** is

    int getc(FILE *fp*);

where *fp* is a file pointer of type **FILE** returned by **fopen( )**. For historical reasons, **getc( )** returns an integer, but the high-order byte is zero.

The **getc( )** function returns an **EOF** when the end of the file has been reached. Therefore, to read to the end of a text file, you could use the following code:

```
do {
  ch = getc(fp);
} while(ch!=EOF);
```

However, **getc( )** also returns **EOF** if an error occurs. You can use **ferror( )** to determine precisely what has occurred.

Using fopen( ), getc( ), putc( ), and fclose( )

The functions **fopen( )**, **getc( )**, **putc( )**, and **fclose( )** constitute the minimal set of file routines. The following program, KTOD, is a simple example of using **putc( )**, **fopen( )**, and **fclose( )**. It simply reads characters from the keyboard and writes them to a disk file until the user types a dollar sign. The filename is specified from the command line. For example, if you call the following program KTOD, typing **KTOD TEST** allows you to enter lines of text into the file called TEST.

```
/* KTOD: A key to disk program. */
#include <stdio.h>
#include <stdlib.h>

void main(int argc, char *argv[])
{
  FILE *fp;
  char ch;

  if(argc!=2) {
    printf("You forgot to enter the filename.\n");
    exit(1);
  }

  if((fp=fopen(argv[1], "w"))==NULL) {
    printf("Cannot open file.\n");
    exit(1);
  }

  do {
    ch = getchar();
    putc(ch, fp);
  } while (ch!='$');

  fclose(fp);
}
```

The complementary program DTOS, shown next, reads any ASCII file and displays the contents on the screen.

```
/* DTOS: A program that reads files and displays them
        on the screen. */
#include <stdio.h>
#include <stdlib.h>

void main(int argc, char *argv[])
{
  FILE *fp;
  char ch;

  if(argc!=2) {
    printf("You forgot to enter the filename.\n");
```

```
    exit(1);
  }

  if((fp=fopen(argv[1], "r"))==NULL) {
    printf("Cannot open file.\n");
    exit(1);
  }

  ch = getc(fp);    /* read one character */

  while (ch!=EOF) {
    putchar(ch);  /* print on screen */
    ch = getc(fp);
  }

  fclose(fp);
}
```

Try these two programs. First use KTOD to create a text file. Then read its contents using DTOS.

Using feof( )

As stated earlier, the ANSI C file system can also operate on binary data. When a file is opened for binary input, an integer value equal to the **EOF** mark may be read. This would cause the input routine to indicate an end-of-file condition even though the physical end of the file had not been reached. To solve this problem, C includes the function **feof( )**, which determines when the end of the file has been encountered. The **feof( )** function has this prototype.

int feof(FILE *fp);

Like the other file functions, its prototype is in STDIO.H. **feof( )** returns true if the end of the file has been reached; otherwise, it returns 0. Therefore, the following routine reads a binary file until the end of the file is encountered.

```
while(!feof(fp)) ch = getc(fp);
```

Of course, you can apply this method to text files as well as binary files.

The following program, which copies text or binary files, contains an example of **feof( )**. The files are opened in binary mode and **feof( )** checks for the end of the file.

```
/* Copy a file. */
#include <stdio.h>
#include <stdlib.h>

void main(int argc, char *argv[])
{
  FILE *in, *out;
  char ch;

  if(argc!=3) {
    printf("You forgot to enter a filename.\n");
    exit(1);
  }

  if((in=fopen(argv[1], "rb"))==NULL) {
    printf("Cannot open source file.\n");
    exit(1);
  }
  if((out=fopen(argv[2], "wb")) == NULL) {
    printf("Cannot open destination file.\n");
    exit(1);
  }

  /* This code actually copies the file. */
  while(!feof(in)) {
    ch = getc(in);
    if(!feof(in)) putc(ch, out);
  }

  fclose(in);
  fclose(out);
}
```

Working with Strings: fputs( ) and fgets( )

In addition to **getc( )** and **putc( )**, C supports the related functions **fputs( )** and **fgets( )**, which read and write character strings from and to a disk file. These functions work just like **putc( )** and **getc( )**, but instead of reading or writing a single character, they read or write strings. They have the following prototypes:

int fputs(const char *str, FILE *fp);

char *fgets(char *str, int *length*, FILE *fp);

The prototypes for **fputs( )** and **fgets( )** are in STDIO.H.

The **fputs( )** function writes the string pointed to by *str* to the specified stream. It returns **EOF** if an error occurs.

The **fgets( )** function reads a string from the specified stream until either a newline character is read or *length*–1 characters have been read. If a newline is read, it will be part of the string (unlike the **gets( )** function). The resultant string will be null terminated. The function returns *str* if successful and a null pointer if an error occurs.

The following program demonstrates **fputs( )**. It reads strings from the keyboard and writes them to the file called TEST. To terminate the program, enter a blank line. Since **gets( )** does not store the newline character, one is added before each string is written to the file, so that the file can be read more easily.

```c
#include <stdio.h>
#include <stdlib.h>
#include <string.h>

void main(void)
{
  char str[80];
  FILE *fp;

  if((fp = fopen("TEST", "w"))==NULL) {
    printf("Cannot open file.\n");
    exit(1);
  }

  do {
    printf("Enter a string (CR to quit):\n");
    gets(str);
    strcat(str, "\n");  /* add a newline */
    fputs(str, fp);
  } while(*str!='\n');
}
```

rewind( )

The **rewind( )** function resets the file position indicator to the beginning of the file specified as its argument. That is, it "rewinds" the file. Its prototype is

void rewind(FILE *fp);

where *fp* is a valid file pointer. The prototype for **rewind( )** is in STDIO.H.

To see an example of **rewind( )**, you can modify the program from the previous section so that it displays the contents of the file just created. To accomplish this, the program rewinds the file after input is complete and then uses **fgets( )** to read back the file. Notice that the file must now be opened in read/write mode, using "w+" for the mode parameter.

```
#include <stdio.h>
#include <stdlib.h>
#include <string.h>

void main(void)
{
  char str[80];
  FILE *fp;

  if((fp = fopen("TEST", "w+"))==NULL) {
    printf("Cannot open file.\n");
    exit(1);
  }

  do {
    printf("Enter a string (CR to quit):\n");
    gets(str);
    strcat(str, "\n");  /* add a newline */
    fputs(str, fp);
  } while(*str!='\n');

  /* now, read and display the file */
  rewind(fp);  /* reset file position indicator to
                  start of the file. */
  while(!feof(fp)) {
    fgets(str, 79, fp);
    printf(str);
  }
}
```

ferror( )

The **ferror( )** function determines whether a file operation has produced an error. The **ferror( )** function has this prototype:

  int ferror(FILE *fp);

Here, fp is a valid file pointer. It returns true if an error has occurred during the last file operation; otherwise, it returns false. Because each file operation sets the error condition, **ferror( )** should be called immediately after each file operation; otherwise, an error may be lost. The prototype for **ferror( )** is in STDIO.H.

The following program illustrates **ferror( )** by removing tabs from a text file and substituting the appropriate number of spaces. The tab size is defined by **TAB_SIZE**. Notice how **ferror( )** is called after each disk operation. To use the program, specify the names of the input and output files on the command line.

```
/* The program substitutes spaces for tabs
   in a text file and supplies error checking. */

#include <stdio.h>
#include <stdlib.h>

#define TAB_SIZE 8
#define IN 0
#define OUT 1

void err(int e);

void main(int argc, char *argv[])
{
  FILE *in, *out;
  int tab, i;
  char ch;

  if(argc!=3) {
    printf("usage: detab <in> <out>\n");
    exit(1);
  }

  if((in = fopen(argv[1], "rb"))==NULL) {
    printf("Cannot open %s.\n", argv[1]);
    exit(1);
  }

  if((out = fopen(argv[2], "wb"))==NULL) {
    printf("Cannot open %s.\n", argv[1]);
    exit(1);
  }

  tab = 0;
  do {
```

```
      ch = getc(in);
      if(ferror(in)) err(IN);

      /* if tab found, output appropriate number of spaces */
      if(ch=='\t') {
        for(i=tab; i<8; i++) {
          putc(' ', out);
          if(ferror(out)) err(OUT);
        }
        tab = 0;
      }
      else {
        putc(ch, out);
        if(ferror(out)) err(OUT);
        tab++;
        if(tab==TAB_SIZE) tab = 0;
        if(ch=='\n' || ch=='\r') tab = 0;
      }
    } while(!feof(in));
    fclose(in);
    fclose(out);
}

void err(int e)
{
  if(e==IN) printf("Error on input.\n");
  else printf("Error on output.\n");
  exit(1);
}
```

Erasing Files

The **remove( )** function erases the specified file. Its prototype is

    int remove(const char *filename);

It returns zero if successful. Otherwise, it returns a nonzero value.

The following program erases the file specified on the command line. However, it first gives you a chance to change your mind. A utility like this might be useful to new computer users.

```
/* Double check before erasing. */
#include <stdio.h>
#include <stdlib.h>
#include <ctype.h>

main(int argc, char *argv[])
{
  char str[80];

  if(argc!=2) {
    printf("usage: xerase <filename>\n");
    exit(1);
  }

  printf("Erase %s? (Y/N): ", argv[1]);
  gets(str);

  if(toupper(*str)=='Y')
    if(remove(argv[1])) {
      printf("Cannot erase file.\n");
      exit(1);
    }
  return 0;  /* return success to OS */
}
```

Flushing a Stream

If you wish to flush the contents of an output stream, use the **fflush( )** function, whose prototype is shown here:

int fflush(FILE *fp);

This function writes the contents of any buffered data to the file associated with fp. If you call **fflush( )** with fp being null, all files opened for output are flushed.

The **fflush( )** function returns 0 if successful; otherwise, it returns **EOF**.

fread( ) and fwrite( )

To read and write data types that are longer than one byte, the ANSI C file system provides two functions: **fread( )** and **fwrite( )**. These functions allow the reading and writing of blocks of any type of data. Their prototypes are

size_t fread(void *buffer, size_t num_bytes, size_t count, FILE *fp);

size_t fwrite(const void *buffer, size_t num_bytes, size_t count, FILE *fp);

For **fread( )**, *buffer* is a pointer to a region of memory that will receive the data from the file. For **fwrite( )**, *buffer* is a pointer to the information that will be written to the file. The value of *count* determines how many items are read or written, with each item being *num_bytes* bytes in length. (Remember, the type **size_t** is defined in STDIO.H and is more or less an unsigned integer.) Finally, *fp* is a file pointer to a previously opened stream. The prototypes for both of the functions are defined in STDIO.H.

The **fread( )** function returns the number of items read. This value may be less than *count* if the end of the file is reached or an error occurs. The **fwrite( )** function returns the number of items written. This value will equal *count* unless an error occurs.

Using fread( ) and fwrite( )

As long as the file has been opened for binary data, **fread( )** and **fwrite( )** can read and write any type of information. For example, the following program writes and then reads back a **double**, an **int**, and a **long** to and from a disk file. Notice how it uses **sizeof** to determine the length of each data type.

```c
/* Write some non-character data to a disk file
   and read it back.  */
#include <stdio.h>
#include <stdlib.h>

void main(void)
{
  FILE *fp;
  double d = 12.23;
  int i = 101;
  long l = 123023L;

  if((fp=fopen("test", "wb+"))==NULL) {
    printf("Cannot open file.\n");
    exit(1);
  }

  fwrite(&d, sizeof(double), 1, fp);
  fwrite(&i, sizeof(int), 1, fp);
  fwrite(&l, sizeof(long), 1, fp);

  rewind(fp);

  fread(&d, sizeof(double), 1, fp);
  fread(&i, sizeof(int), 1, fp);
```

```
    fread(&l, sizeof(long), 1, fp);

    printf("%f %d %ld", d, i, l);

    fclose(fp);
}
```

As this program illustrates, the buffer can be (and often is) simply the memory used to hold a variable. In this simple program, the return values of **fread( )** and **fwrite( )** are ignored. In the real world, however, you should check their return values for errors.

One of the most useful applications of **fread( )** and **fwrite( )** involves reading and writing user-defined data types, especially structures. For example, given this structure,

```
struct struct_type {
    float balance;
    char name[80];
} cust;
```

the following statement writes the contents of **cust** to the file pointed to by **fp**.

```
fwrite(&cust, sizeof(struct struct_type), 1, fp);
```

fseek( ) and Random-Access I/O

You can perform random read and write operations using the ANSI C I/O system with the help of **fseek( )**, which sets the file position indicator. Its prototype is shown here:

int fseek(FILE *fp, long numbytes, int origin);

Here, fp is a file pointer returned by a call to **fopen( )**. numbytes is the number of bytes from origin that will become the new current position, and origin is one of the following macros defined in STDIO.H.

Origin	Macro Name
Beginning of file	SEEK_SET
Current position	SEEK_CUR
End of file	SEEK_END

Therefore, to seek *numbytes* from the start of the file, *origin* should be **SEEK_SET**. To seek from the current position, use **SEEK_CUR**, and to seek from the end of the file, use **SEEK_END**. The **fseek( )** function returns 0 when successful and a nonzero value if an error occurs.

The following fragment illustrates **fseek( )**. It seeks to and displays the specified byte in the specified file. Specify the filename and then the byte to seek to on the command line.

```
#include <stdio.h>
#include <stdlib.h>

void main(int argc, char *argv[])
{
  FILE *fp;

  if(argc!=3) {
    printf("Usage: SEEK filename byte\n");
    exit(1);
  }

  if((fp = fopen(argv[1], "r"))==NULL) {
    printf("Cannot open file.\n");
    exit(1);
  }

  if(fseek(fp, atol(argv[2]), SEEK_SET)) {
    printf("Seek error.\n");
    exit(1);
  }

  printf("Byte at %ld is %c.\n", atol(argv[2]), getc(fp));
  fclose(fp);
}
```

You can use **fseek( )** to seek in multiples of any type of data by simply multiplying the size of the data by the number of the item you want to reach. For example, assume that you have a mailing-list that consists of structures of type **list_type**. To seek to the tenth address in the file that holds the addresses, use this statement:

```
fseek(fp, 9*sizeof(struct list_type), SEEK_SET);
```

fprintf( ) and fscanf( )

In addition to the basic I/O functions already discussed, the ANSI C I/O system includes **fprintf( )** and **fscanf( )**. These functions behave exactly like **printf( )** and **scanf( )** except that they operate with files. The prototypes of **fprintf( )** and **fscanf( )** are

int fprintf(FILE *fp, const char *control_string,. . .);

int fscanf(FILE *fp, const char *control_string,. . .);

where *fp* is a file pointer returned by a call to **fopen( )**. **fprintf( )** and **fscanf( )** direct their I/O operations to the file pointed to by *fp*.

As an example, the following program reads a string and an integer from the keyboard and writes them to a disk file called TEST. The program then reads the file and displays the information on the screen. After running this program, examine the TEST file. As you will see, it contains human-readable text.

```c
/* fscanf() - fprintf() example */
#include <stdio.h>
#include <io.h>
#include <stdlib.h>

void main(void)
{
  FILE *fp;
  char s[80];
  int t;

  if((fp=fopen("test", "w")) == NULL) {
    printf("Cannot open file.\n");
    exit(1);
  }

  printf("Enter a string and a number: ");
  fscanf(stdin, "%s%d", s, &t); /* read from
                                    keyboard */

  fprintf(fp, "%s %d", s, t); /* write to file */
  fclose(fp);

  if((fp=fopen("test","r")) == NULL) {
    printf("Cannot open file.\n");
    exit(1);
```

```
    }

    fscanf(fp, "%s%d", s, &t); /* read from file */
    fprintf(stdout, "%s %d", s, t); /* print on
                                          screen */
}
```

CAUTION: *Although* **fprintf( )** *and* **fscanf( )** *often are the easiest way to write and read assorted data to and from disk files, they are not always the most efficient. Because formatted ASCII data is being written as it would appear on the screen (instead of in binary), extra overhead is incurred with each call. So, if speed or file size is a concern, you should probably use* **fread( )** *and* **fwrite( ).**

The Standard Streams

Whenever a C program starts execution, three streams are opened automatically. They are **stdin** (standard input), **stdout** (standard output), and **stderr** (standard error). Normally, these streams refer to the console, but they may be redirected by the operating system to some other device in environments that support redirectable I/O. (Redirectable I/O is supported by Windows, DOS, Unix, and OS/2, for example.)

Because the standard streams are file pointers, they can be used by the ANSI C file system to perform I/O operations on the console. For example, **putchar( )** could be defined like this:

```
putchar(char c)
{
  return putc(c, stdout);
}
```

In general, **stdin** is used to read from the console, and **stdout** and **stderr** are used to write to the console. You can use **stdin**, **stdout**, and **stderr** as file pointers in any function that uses a variable of type **FILE ***. For example, you can use **fputs( )** to output a string to the console using a call like this:

```
fputs("hello there", stdout);
```

Keep in mind that **stdin**, **stdout**, and **stderr** are not variables in the normal sense and, cannot be assigned values using **fopen( )**. Also, just as these file pointers are created automatically at the start of your program, they are closed automatically at the end; you should not try to close them.

The Console I/O Connection

Recall from Chapter 8 that C makes little distinction between console I/O and file I/O. The console I/O functions described in Chapter 8 actually direct their I/O operations to either **stdin** or **stdout**. In essence, the console I/O functions are simply special versions of their parallel file functions. The reason they exist is as a convenience to you, the programmer.

As described in the previous section, you can perform console I/O using any of C's file system functions. However, what might surprise you is that you can perform disk file I/O using console I/O functions, such as **printf( )**! This is because all of the console I/O functions described in Chapter 8 operate on **stdin** and **stdout**. In environments that allow redirection of I/O, this means that **stdin** and **stdout** could refer to a device other than the keyboard and screen. For example, consider this program:

```
#include <stdio.h>

void main(void)
{
  char str[80];

  printf("Enter a string: ");
  gets(str);
  printf(str);
}
```

Assume that this program is called TEST. If you execute TEST normally, it displays its prompt on the screen, reads a string from the keyboard, and displays that string on the display. However, in an environment that supports I/O redirection, either **stdin**, **stdout**, or both could be redirected to a file. For example, in a DOS or Windows environment, executing TEST like this

```
TEST > OUTPUT
```

causes the output of TEST to be written to a file called OUTPUT. Executing TEST as follows

```
TEST < INPUT > OUTPUT
```

directs **stdin** to the file called INPUT and sends output to the file called OUTPUT.

> **REMEMBER:**   *When a C program terminates, any redirected streams are automatically reset to their default status.*

Using freopen( ) to Redirect the Standard Streams

You can redirect the standard streams by using the **freopen( )** function. This function associates an existing stream with a new file. Hence, you can use it to associate a standard stream with a new file. Its prototype is

FILE *freopen(const char *filename*, const char *mode*, FILE *stream*);

where *filename* is a pointer to the filename you wish associated with the stream pointed to by *stream*. The file is opened using the value of *mode*, which may have the same values as those used with **fopen( )**. **freopen( )** returns *stream* if successful or NULL on failure.

The following program uses **freopen( )** to redirect **stdout** to a file called OUTPUT.

```
#include <stdio.h>

void main(void)
{
  char str[80];

  freopen("OUTPUT", "w", stdout);

  printf("Enter a string: ");
  gets(str);
  printf(str);
}
```

In general, redirecting the standard streams by using **freopen( )** is useful in special situations, such as debugging. However, performing disk I/O using redirected **stdin** and **stdout** is not as efficient as using functions like **fread( )** or **fwrite( )**.

Chapter Ten

The Preprocessor and Comments

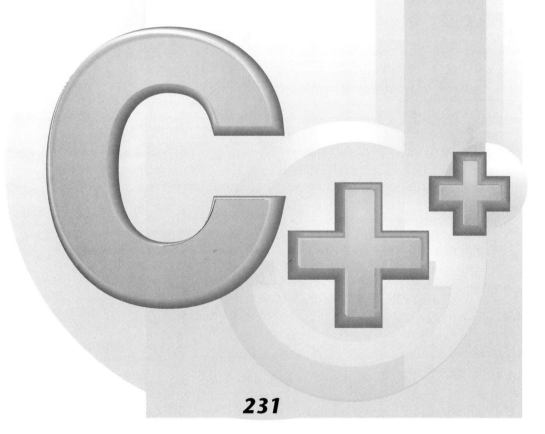

231

Y ou can include various instructions to the compiler in the source code of a C or C++ program. These are called *preprocessor directives,* and although not actually part of the C or C++ language, they expand the scope of the C/C++ programming environment. This chapter also examines comments.

The Preprocessor

The preprocessor contains the following directives:

#if	#include
#ifdef	#define
#ifndef	#undef
#else	#line
#elif	#error
#endif	#pragma

As you can see, all preprocessor directives begin with a # sign. In addition, each preprocessing directive must be on its own line. For example,

```
#include <stdio.h>  #include <stdlib.h>
```

will not work.

#define

The **#define** directive defines an identifier and a character sequence (that is, a set of characters) that will be substituted for the identifier each time the identifier is encountered in the source file. The identifier is referred to as a *macro name* and the replacement process as *macro replacement*. The general form of the directive is

#define *macro_name char-sequence*

Notice that there is no semicolon in this statement. There can be any number of spaces between the identifier and the character sequence, but once the character sequence begins, it is terminated only by a newline.

For example, if you wish to use the word **TRUE** for the value 1 and the word **FALSE** for the value 0, you could declare these two macro **#define**s

```
#define TRUE 1
#define FALSE 0
```

This causes the compiler to substitute a 1 or a 0 each time **TRUE** or **FALSE** is encountered in your source file. For example, the following prints **0 1 2** on the screen.

```
printf("%d %d %d", FALSE, TRUE, TRUE+1);
```

Once a macro name has been defined, it may be used as part of the definition of other macro names. For example, this code defines the values of **ONE**, **TWO**, and **THREE**:

```
#define ONE     1
#define TWO     ONE+ONE
#define THREE   ONE+TWO
```

Macro substitution is simply the replacement of an identifier by the character sequence associated with it. Therefore, if you wish to define a standard error message, you might write something like this:

```
#define E_MS "standard error on input\n"
/* ... */
printf(E_MS);
```

The compiler will actually substitute the string "standard error on input\n" when the identifier **E_MS** is encountered. To the compiler, the **printf( )** statement will actually appear to be

```
printf("standard error on input\n");
```

No text substitutions occur if the identifier is within a quoted string. For example,

```
#define XYZ this is a test

printf("XYZ");
```

does not print **this is a test**, but rather **XYZ**.

If the character is longer than one line, you can continue it on the next by placing a backslash at the end of the line, as shown here:

```
#define LONG_STRING "this is a very long \
string that is used as an example"
```

C/C++ programmers commonly use uppercase letters for defined identifiers. This convention helps anyone reading the program know at a glance that a macro replacement will take place. Also, it is best to put all **#define**s at the start of the file or in a separate header file rather than sprinkling them throughout the program.

Macros are most frequently used to define names for "magic numbers" that occur in a program. For example, you may have a program that defines an array and has several routines that access that array. Instead of "hard-coding" the array's size with a constant, you should define the size using a **#define** statement and then use that macro name whenever the array size is needed. In this way, if you need to change the size of the array, you will only need to change the **#define** statement and then recompile your program. For example,

```
#define MAX_SIZE 100

/* ... */

float balance[MAX_SIZE];

/* ... */

for(i=0; i<MAX_SIZE; i++) printf("%f", balance[i]);
```

Since **MAX_SIZE** defines the size of the array **balance**, if the size of **balance** needs to be changed in the future, you need only change the definition of **MAX_SIZE**. All subsequent references to it will be automatically updated when you recompile your program.

Defining Function-like Macros

The **#define** directive has another powerful feature: The macro name can have arguments. Each time the macro name is encountered, the arguments used in its definition are replaced by the actual arguments found in the program. This form of a macro is called a *function-like macro*. For example,

```
#include <stdio.h>

#define ABS(a)   (a)<0 ? -(a) : (a)

void main(void)
{
  printf("abs of -1 and 1: %d %d", ABS(-1), ABS(1));
}
```

When this program is compiled, **a** in the macro definition will be substituted with the values –1 and 1. The parentheses that enclose **a** ensure proper substitution in all cases. For example, if the parentheses around **a** were removed, this expression

```
ABS(10-20)
```

would be converted to

```
10-20<0 ? -10-20 : 10-20
```

and would yield the wrong result.

The use of a function-like macro in place of real functions has one major benefit: It increases the execution speed of the code because there is no function call overhead. However, if the size of the function-like macro is very large, this increased speed may be paid for with an increase in the size of the program because of duplicated code.

> **NOTE:** *Although parameterized macros are a valuable feature, you will see in Part Two of this book that C++ has a better way of creating inline code that does not rely upon macros.*

#error

The **#error** directive forces the compiler to stop compilation. It is used primarily for debugging. The general form of the **#error** directive is

#error *error_message*

The *error_message* is not between double quotes. When the **#error** directive is encountered, the error message is displayed, possibly along with other information defined by the creator of the compiler.

#include

The **#include** directive instructs the compiler to read another source file in addition to the one that contains the **#include** directive. The name of the additional source file must be enclosed between double quotes or angle brackets. For example,

```
#include "stdio.h"
#include <stdio.h>
```

both instruct the C/C++ compiler to read and compile the header for the file system library functions.

Include files can have **#include** directives in them. Such directives are referred to as *nested include*s. The number of levels of nesting allowed varies between compilers. However, the ANSI C standard stipulates that at least eight nested inclusions will be available. The proposed ANSI C++ standard recommends that at least 256 levels of nesting be supported.

Whether the filename is enclosed by quotes or by angle brackets determines how the search for the specified file is conducted. If the filename is enclosed in angle brackets, the file is searched for in a manner defined by the creator of the compiler. Often, this means searching some special directory set aside for include files. If the filename is enclosed in quotes, the file is looked for in another implementation-defined manner. For many compilers, this means searching the current working directory. If the file is not found, the search is repeated as if the filename had been enclosed in angle brackets.

Typically, most programmers use angle brackets to include the standard header files. The use of quotes is generally reserved for including files specifically related to the program at hand. However, there is no hard and fast rule that demands this usage.

Conditional Compilation Directives

There are several directives that allow you to selectively compile portions of your program's source code. This process is called *conditional compilation* and is used widely by commercial software houses that provide and maintain many customized versions of one program.

#if, #else, #elif, and #endif

Perhaps the most commonly used conditional compilation directives are the **#if**, **#else**, **#elif**, and **#endif**. These directives allow you to conditionally include portions of code based upon the outcome of a constant expression.

The general form of **#if** is

```
#if constant_expression
   statement sequence
#endif
```

If the constant expression following **#if** is true, the code that is between it and **#endif** is compiled. Otherwise, the intervening code is skipped. The **#endif** directive marks the end of an **#if** block. For example,

```
/* Simple #if example. */
#include <stdio.h>

#define MAX 100

void main(void)
{
#if MAX>99
  printf("compiled for array greater than 99\n");
#endif
}
```

This program displays the message on the screen because **MAX** is greater than 99. This example illustrates an important point. The expression that follows the **#if** is evaluated at compile time. Therefore, it must contain only previously defined identifiers and constants—no variables can be used.

The **#else** directive works much like the **else** that is part of the C language: It establishes an alternative if **#if** fails. The previous example can be expanded as shown here:

```
/* Simple #if/#else example. */
#include <stdio.h>

#define MAX 10

void main(void)
{
#if MAX>99
  printf("compiled for array greater than 99\n");
#else
  printf("compiled for small array\n");
#endif
}
```

In this case, **MAX** is defined to be less than 99, so the **#if** portion of the code is not compiled. The **#else** alternative is compiled, however, and the message **compiled for small array** is displayed.

Notice that **#else** is used to mark both the end of the **#if** block and the beginning of the **#else** block. This is necessary because there can only be one **#endif** associated with any **#if**.

The **#elif** directive means "else if" and establishes an if-else-if chain for multiple compilation options. **#elif** is followed by a constant expression. If the expression is true, that block of code is compiled and no other **#elif** expressions are tested. Otherwise, the next block in the series is checked. The general form for **#elif** is

```
#if expression
    statement sequence
#elif expression 1
    statement sequence
#elif expression 2
    statement sequence
#elif expression 3
    statement sequence
#elif expression 4
    .
    .
    .
#elif expression N
    statement sequence
#endif
```

For example, the following fragment uses the value of **ACTIVE_COUNTRY** to define the currency sign.

```
#define US 0
#define ENGLAND 1
#define FRANCE 2

#define ACTIVE_COUNTRY US

#if ACTIVE_COUNTRY == US
  char currency[] = "dollar";
#elif ACTIVE_COUNTRY == ENGLAND
  char currency[] = "pound";
#else
  char currency[] = "franc";
#endif
```

The ANSI C standard states that **#if**s and **#elif**s can be nested to at least eight levels. The proposed ANSI C++ standard suggests that at least 256 levels of nesting be allowed. When nested, each **#endif**, **#else**, or **#elif** associates with the nearest **#if** or **#elif**. For example, the following is perfectly valid:

```
#if MAX>100
  #if SERIAL_VERSION
    int port=198;
  #elif
    int port=200;
  #endif
#else
  char out_buffer[100];
#endif
```

#ifdef and #ifndef

Another method of conditional compilation uses the directives **#ifdef** and **#ifndef**, which mean "if defined" and "if not defined," respectively. The general form of **#ifdef** is

#ifdef *macro_name*
   statement sequence
#endif

If *macro_name* has been previously defined in a **#define** statement, the block of code will be compiled.

The general form of **#ifndef** is

#ifndef *macro_name*
   statement sequence
#endif

If *macro_name* is currently undefined by a **#define** statement, the block of code is compiled.

Both **#ifdef** and **#ifndef** can use an **#else** statement, but not **#elif**. For example,

```
#include <stdio.h>

#define TED 10

void main(void)
```

```
{
#ifdef TED
  printf("Hi Ted\n");
#else
  printf("Hi anyone\n");
#endif
#ifndef RALPH
  printf("RALPH not defined\n");
#endif
}
```

will print **Hi Ted** and **RALPH not defined**. However, if **TED** were not defined, **Hi anyone** would be displayed, followed by **RALPH not defined**.

You can nest **#ifdef**s and **#ifndef**s to at least eight levels. The proposed ANSI C++ standard suggests that at least 256 levels of nesting be supported.

#undef

The **#undef** directive removes a previously defined definition of the macro name that follows it. That is, it "undefines" a macro. The general form for **#undef** is

   #undef *macro_name*

For example,

```
#define LEN 100
#define WIDTH 100

char array[LEN][WIDTH];

#undef LEN
#undef WIDTH
/* at this point both LEN and WIDTH are undefined */
```

Both **LEN** and **WIDTH** are defined until the **#undef** statements are encountered.

#undef is used principally to allow macro names to be localized to only those sections of code that need them.

Using defined

In addition to **#ifdef**, there is a second way to determine if a macro name is defined. You can use the **#if** directive in conjunction with the **defined** compile-time operator. The **defined** operator has this general form:

defined *macro-name*

If *macro-name* is currently defined, then the expression is true. Otherwise, it is false. For example, to determine if the macro **MYFILE** is defined, you can use either of these two preprocessing commands:

```
#if defined MYFILE
```

or

```
#ifdef MYFILE
```

You can also precede **defined** with the ! to reverse the condition. For example, the following fragment is compiled only if **DEBUG** is not defined.

```
#if !defined DEBUG
  printf("Final version!\n");
#endif
```

One reason for using **defined** is that it allows the existence of a macro name to be determined by a **#elif** statement.

#line

The **#line** directive changes the contents of _ _LINE_ _ and _ _FILE_ _, which are predefined identifiers in the compiler. The _ _LINE_ _ identifier contains the line number of the currently compiled line of code. The _ _FILE_ _ identifier is a string that contains the name of the source file being compiled. The general form for **#line** is

#line *number* "*filename*"

where *number* is any positive integer and becomes the new value of _ _LINE_ _, and the optional *filename* is any valid file identifier, which becomes the new value of _ _FILE_ _. **#line** is primarily used for debugging and special applications.

For example, the following code specifies that the line count will begin with 100 and the **printf( )** statement displays the number 102 because it is the third line in the program after the **#line 100** statement.

```
#include <stdio.h>

#line 100                      /* reset the line counter */
void main(void)                /* line 100 */
{                              /* line 101 */
   printf("%d\n",_ _LINE_ _);  /* line 102 */
}
```

#pragma

The **#pragma** directive is an implementation-defined directive that allows various instructions to be given to the compiler. For example, a compiler may have an option that supports program execution tracing. A trace option would then be specified by a **#pragma** statement. You must check the compiler's user's manual for details and options.

The # and ## Preprocessor Operators

There are two preprocessor operators: # and ##. These operators are used with the **#define** statement.

The **#** operator, which is generally called the *stringize* operator, turns the argument it precedes into a quoted string. For example, consider this program:

```
#include <stdio.h>

#define mkstr(s)   # s

void main(void)
{
   printf(mkstr(I like C++));
}
```

The C preprocessor turns the line

```
printf(mkstr(I like C++));
```

into

```
printf("I like C++");
```

The ## operator, called the *pasting* operator, concatenates two tokens. For example,

```
#include <stdio.h>

#define concat(a, b)   a ## b

void main(void)
{
  int xy = 10;
  printf("%d", concat(x, y));
}
```

The preprocessor transforms

```
printf("%d", concat(x, y));
```

into

```
printf("%d", xy);
```

If these operators seem strange to you, keep in mind that they are not needed or used in most C/C++ programs. They exist primarily to allow the preprocessor to handle some special cases.

Predefined Macro Names

C contains five built-in predefined macro names. They are

```
__LINE__
__FILE__
__DATE__
__TIME__
__STDC__
```

The __**LINE**__ and __**FILE**__ macros were discussed in the section on **#line**.

The __**DATE**__ macro contains a string of the form *month/day/year*. This string represents the date of the translation of the source file into object code.

The time of the translation of the source code into object code is contained as a string in _ _**TIME**_ _. The form of the string is *hour:minute:second*.

The macro _ _**STDC**_ _ contains the decimal constant 1. This means that the implementation conforms to the ANSI C standard. If the macro contains any other number (or is not defined), the implementation varies from the standard or is a C++ program.

> **NOTE:** *The proposed ANSI C++ standard includes the preceding predefined macros and adds one more: _ _**cplusplus**. This macro is defined (as anything) when a C++ program is being compiled. Thus, when compiling a C++ program, _ _**cplusplus** will be defined and _ _**STDC**_ _ will generally not be defined. (Technically, in C++, the meaning of _ _**STDC**_ _ is implementation-dependent, which means that it could, in theory, be defined when compiling a C++ program.)*

Comments

In C, all comments begin with the character pair /* and end with */. There must be no spaces between the asterisk and the slash. The compiler ignores any text between the beginning and ending comment symbols. For example, the following program prints only **hello** on the screen.

```
#include <stdio.h>

void main(void)
{
  printf("hello");
  /* printf("there"); */
}
```

Comments can be placed anywhere in a program, as long as they do not appear in the middle of a keyword or identifier. That is, this comment is valid:

```
x = 10+ /* add the numbers */5;
```

while

```
swi/*this will not work*/tch(c) { ...
```

is incorrect because a keyword cannot contain a comment. However, you should not generally place comments in the middle of expressions because it obscures their meaning.

Comments cannot be nested. That is, one comment cannot contain another comment. For example, the following code fragment causes a compile-time error.

```
/* this is an outer comment
   x = y/a;
   /* this is an inner comment - and causes an error */
*/
```

You should include comments whenever they are needed to explain the operation of the code. All but the most obvious functions should have a comment at the top that states what the function does, how it is called, and what it returns.

NOTE: C++ fully supports C-style comments. However, it also allows you to define a single-line comment. Single-line comments begin with // and they end at the end of the line.

PART TWO

C++-Specific Features

Part Two of this book examines the C++-specific features of C++. That is, it discusses those features of C++ that it does not have in common with C. (The C-like features of C++ are described in Part One.) C++ is essentially a superset of C, so almost everything you already know about C is applicable to C++. Because most of the C++ enhancements to C are designed to support object-oriented programming (OOP), Part Two also provides a discussion of the theory and merits of object-oriented programming.

 NOTE: *This part assumes that you know how to program in C. Knowledge of the C language is a prerequisite to learning C++, so if you don't already know C, you must take some time to learn it.*

Chapter Eleven

An Overview of C++

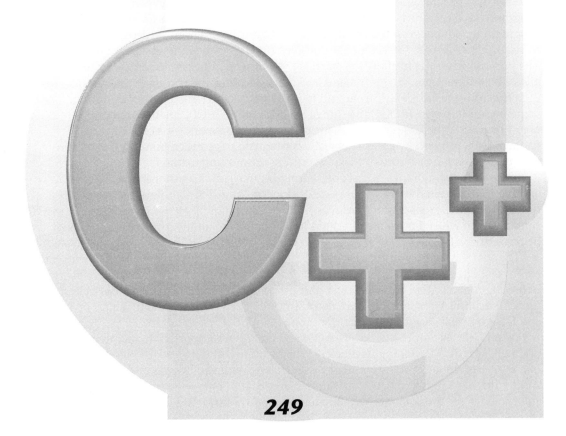

249

This chapter provides an overview of the key concepts embodied in C++. C++ is an object-oriented programming language, and its object-oriented features are highly interrelated. In several instances, this interrelatedness makes it difficult to describe one feature of C++ without implicitly involving several others. In many places, the object-oriented features of C++ are so intertwined that discussion of one feature implies prior knowledge of one or more other features. To address this problem, this chapter presents a quick overview of the most important aspects of C++. The remaining chapters in this part examine C++ in detail.

The Origins of C++

As you know, C++ is an expanded version of C. The C++ extensions to C were first invented by Bjarne Stroustrup in 1980 at Bell Laboratories in Murray Hill, New Jersey. He initially called the new language "C with Classes." However, in 1983 the name was changed to C++.

Although C++'s predecessor, C, is one of the most liked and widely used professional programming languages in the world, the invention of C++ was necessitated by one major programming factor: increasing complexity. Over the years, computer programs have become larger and more complex. Even though C is an excellent programming language, it too has its limits. In C, once a program exceeds from 25,000 to 100,000 lines of code, it becomes so complex that it is difficult to grasp as a totality. The purpose of C++ is to allow this barrier to be broken. The essence of C++ is to allow the programmer to comprehend and manage larger, more complex programs.

Most additions made by Stroustrup to C support object-oriented programming, sometimes referred to as OOP. (See the next section for a brief explanation of object-oriented programming.) Stroustrup states that some of C++'s object-oriented features were inspired by another object-oriented language called Simula67. Therefore, C++ represents the blending of two powerful programming methods.

Since the advent of C++, it has gone through three major revisions, one in 1985, another in 1989, and the third when work began on the ANSI standard for C++. The first draft of the proposed standard was created on January 25, 1994. The ANSI C++ committee (of which I am a member) has kept virtually all of the features first defined by Stroustrup and has added several new ones as well.

The standardization process is typically a slow one, and it will probably be years before the C++ standard is finally adopted. Therefore, keep in mind that C++ is still a "work in progress," and that some features are being fine-tuned. However, the material presented in this book is stable. It is also applicable to all contemporary C++ compilers and is in compliance with the currently proposed ANSI C++ standard.

When C++ was invented, Stroustrup knew that it was important to maintain the original spirit of C, including its efficiency, its flexibility, and its underlying philosophy that the programmer, not the language, is in charge, while at the same time adding support for object-oriented programming. Happily, his goals were accomplished. C++ still provides the programmer with the freedom and control of C, coupled with the power of objects. The object-oriented features in C++, to use Stroustrup's words, "allow programs to be structured for clarity, extensibility, and ease of maintenance without loss of efficiency."

Although C++ was initially designed to aid in the management of very large programs, it is in no way limited to this use. In fact, the object-oriented attributes of C++ can be effectively applied to virtually any programming task. It is not uncommon to see C++ used for projects such as editors, databases, personal file systems, and communication programs. Also, because C++ shares C's efficiency, much high-performance systems software is constructed using C++.

What Is Object-Oriented Programming?

Object-oriented programming (OOP) is a new way of approaching the job of programming. Approaches to programming have changed dramatically since the invention of the computer, primarily to accommodate the increasing complexity of programs. For example, when computers were first invented, programming was done by toggling in the binary machine instructions using the computer's front panel. As long as programs were just a few hundred instructions long, this approach worked. As programs grew, assembly language was invented so that a programmer could deal with larger, increasingly complex programs, using symbolic representations of the machine instructions. As programs continued to grow, high-level languages were introduced that gave the programmer more tools with which to handle complexity. The first widespread language was, of course, FORTRAN. Although FORTRAN was a very impressive first step, it is hardly a language that encourages clear, easy-to-understand programs.

The 1960s gave birth to structured programming. This is the method encouraged by languages such as C and Pascal. The use of structured languages made it possible to write moderately complex programs fairly easily. However, even using structured programming methods a project becomes uncontrollable once it reaches a certain size (that is, once its complexity exceeds that which a programmer can manage).

Consider this: At each milestone in the development of programming, methods were created to allow the programmer to deal with greater complexity. Each step of the way, the new approach took the best elements of the previous methods and moved forward. Today, many projects are near or at the point where the structured approach no longer works. To solve this problem, object-oriented programming was invented.

Object-oriented programming has taken the best ideas of structured programming and combined them with several powerful new concepts that encourage you to approach the task of programming in a new way. In general, when programming in an object-oriented fashion, you break down a problem into subgroups of related parts that take into account both code and data related to each group. Also, you organize these subgroups into a hierarchical structure. Finally, you translate these subgroups into self-contained units called objects.

All object-oriented programming languages have three traits in common: encapsulation, polymorphism, and inheritance. Let's examine each briefly.

Encapsulation

Encapsulation is the mechanism that binds together code and data, and that keeps both safe from outside interference or misuse. Further, it is encapsulation that allows the creation of an object. Put simply, an *object* is a logical entity that encapsulates both data and the code that manipulates that data. Within an object, some of the code and/or data may be private to the object and inaccessible to anything outside the object. In this way, an object provides a significant level of protection against some other, unrelated part of the program accidentally modifying or incorrectly using the private parts of the object.

For all intents and purposes, an object is a variable of a user-defined type. It may seem strange at first to think of an object, which links both code and data, as a variable. However, in object-oriented programming, this is precisely the case. When you define an object, you are implicitly creating a new data type.

Polymorphism

Object-oriented programming languages support *polymorphism,* which is characterized by the phrase "one interface, multiple methods." In simple terms, polymorphism is the attribute that allows one interface to be used with a general class of actions. The specific action selected is determined by the exact nature of the situation. A real-world example of polymorphism is a thermostat. No matter what type of furnace your house has (gas, oil, electric, and so on) the thermostat works the same way. In this case, the theromostat (which is the interface) is the same no matter what type of furnace (method) you have. For example, if you want a 70-degree temperature, you set the thermostat to 70 degrees. It doesn't matter what type of furnace provides the heat. This same principle can also apply to programming. For example, you might have a program that defines three types of stacks. One stack is used for integer values, one for character values, and one for floating-point values. Because of polymorphism, you can create three sets of functions called **push( )** and **pop( )**—one set for each type of data. The general concept (interface) is that of pushing and popping data onto and from a stack. The functions define the specific ways (methods) this is done for each type of data. When you push data on the stack, it is the type of the data that will determine which specific version of the **push( )** function will be called. (You will see an example of this, shortly.)

Polymorphism helps reduce complexity by allowing the same interface to be used to specify a general class of actions. It is the compiler's job to select the *specific action* (that is, method) as it applies to each situation. You, the programmer, don't need to make this selection manually. You need only remember and utilize the general interface.

The first object-oriented programming languages were interpreters, so polymorphism was, of course, supported at run time. However, C++ is a compiled language. Therefore, in C++, both run-time and compile-time polymorphism are supported.

Inheritance

Inheritance is the process by which one object can acquire the properties of another object. This is important because it supports the concept of *classification.* If you think about it, most knowledge is made manageable by hierarchical classifications. For example, a Red Delicious apple is part of the classification *apple,* which in turn is part of the *fruit* class, which is under the larger class *food.* Without the use of classifications, each object would have to define explicitly all of its characteristics. However, through the use of classifications, an object need only define those qualities that make it unique within its class. It is the inheritance mechanism that makes it possible for one object to be a specific instance of a more general case. As you will see, inheritance is an important aspect of object-oriented programming.

Programming in C++ Style

Because C++ is a superset of C, you can write C++ programs that look just like C programs. However, doing so prevents you from taking full advantage of C++. (It is something like watching a color TV with the color turned off!) Instead, most C++ programmers use a style and certain features that are unique to C++. Most of the stylistic differences between a C and a C++ program have to do with taking advantage of C++'s object-oriented capabilities. But another advantage to using a programming style unique to C++ is that it helps you begin thinking in C++ rather than in C. (That is, by adopting a different style when writing C++ code, you are telling yourself to stop thinking in C and start thinking in C++.)

Because it is important to learn to write C++ programs that *look* like C++ programs, this section introduces a few of these features. Examine this C++ program:

```
#include <iostream.h>

main()
{
  int i;

  cout << "This is output.\n";  // this is a single line comment
  /* you can still use C style comments */

  // input a number using >>
  cout << "enter a number: ";
  cin >> i;

  // now, output a number using <<
  cout << i << " squared is " << i*i << "\n";
```

```
    return 0;
}
```

As you can see, this program looks much different from the average C program found in Part One. To begin, the header file IOSTREAM.H is included. This file is defined by C++ and is used to support C++-style I/O operations. (IOSTREAM.H is to C++ what STDIO.H is to C.)

The first stylistic change is found in this line:

```
main()
```

Notice that the parameter list in **main( )** is empty. In C++, this indicates that **main( )** has no parameters. This differs from C. In C, a function that has no parameters must use **void** in its parameter list, as shown here:

```
main(void)
```

However, in C++, the use of **void** is redundant and unnecessary. As a general rule, in C++ when a function takes no parameters, its parameter list is simply empty; the use of **void** is not required.

The next difference is found in this line:

```
cout << "This is output.\n";   // this is a single line comment
```

This line introduces two new C++ features. First, the statement

```
cout << "This is output.\n";
```

causes **This is output.** to be displayed on the screen followed by a carriage return-linefeed combination. In C++, the **<<** has an expanded role. It is still the left shift operator, but when it is used as shown in this example, it is also an *output operator*. The word **cout** is an identifier that is linked to the screen. (Actually, like C, C++ supports I/O redirection, but for the sake of discussion, assume that **cout** refers to the screen.) You can use **cout** and the **<<** to output any of the built-in data types, as well as strings of characters.

Note that you can still use **printf( )** or any other of C's I/O functions in a C++ program. (Of course, you must include STDIO.H if you want to use the C-like I/O functions.) However, most programmers feel that using **cout <<** is more in the spirit of

C++. Further, while using **printf( )** to output the string is virtually equivalent to using << in this case, the C++ I/O system can be expanded to perform operations on objects that you define (something that you cannot do using **printf( )**).

What follows the output expression is a C++ comment. In C++, comments are defined in two ways. First, you can use a C-like comment, which works the same in C++ as in C. However, in C++ you can also define a *single-line comment* by using **//**. When you start a comment by using **//**, whatever follows is ignored by the compiler until the end of the line is reached. In general, C++ programmers use C-like comments when a multiline comment is being created and use C++ single-line comments when only a single line is needed.

Next, the program prompts the user for a number. The number is read from the keyboard with this statement:

```
cin >> i;
```

In C++, the **>>** operator still retains its right shift meaning. However, when used as shown, it also is C++'s *input operator.* This statement causes **i** to be given a value read from the keyboard. The identifier **cin** refers to the standard input device, which is usually the keyboard. In general, you can use **cin >>** to input a variable of any of the basic data types plus strings.

*NOTE: The line of code just described is not misprinted. Specifically, there is not supposed to be an & in front of the **i**. As you know, when inputting information using a function like **scanf( )**, you have to explicitly pass a pointer to the variable that will receive the information. This means preceding the variable name with the "address of" operator, &. However, because of the way that the **>>** operator is implemented in C++, you do not need (in fact, must not use) the &. In Chapter 17 you will learn why this is the case.*

Although it is not illustrated by the example, you are free to use any of C's input functions, such as **scanf( )**, instead of using **cin >>**. However, as with **cout**, most programmers feel that **cin >>** is more in the spirit of C++.

Another interesting line in the program is shown here:

```
cout << i << "squared is " << i*i << "\n";
```

Assuming that **i** has the value 10, this statement causes the phrase **10 squared is 100** to be displayed, followed by a carriage return-linefeed. As this line illustrates, you can run together several **<<** output operations.

Notice that the program ends with this statement:

```
return 0;
```

This causes zero to be returned to the calling process (which is usually the operating system). Returning zero indicates that the program terminated normally. Abnormal program termination should be signaled by returning a nonzero value.

There are two ways that **main( )** is commonly declared in a C++ program. It is either declared as returning nothing (that is, its return type is **void**), or it is declared as returning an integer value. Remember, it is not necessary for **main( )** to return a value. In fact, most of the programs in Part One of this book simply declared **main( )** as **void**. In Part Two, **main( )** will return a value simply as a means of illustrating the two common approaches. However, you can use either method in your own programs.

A Closer Look at the I/O Operators

As stated, when used for I/O, the **<<** and **>>** operators are capable of handling any of C++'s built-in data types. For example, this program inputs a **float**, a **double**, and a string, and then outputs them:

```
#include <iostream.h>

main()
{
  float f;
  char str[80];
  double d;

  cout << "Enter two floating-point numbers: ";
  cin >> f >> d;

  cout << "Enter a string: ";
  cin >> str;

  cout << f << " " << d << " " << str;

  return 0;
}
```

When you run this program, try entering **This is a test** when prompted for the string. When the program redisplays the information you entered, only the word "This" will be displayed. The rest of the string is not shown because the **>>** operator works relative to strings the same way that the **%s** specifier works with **scanf( )**. It stops reading input when the first white-space character is encountered. Thus, "is a test" is never read by the program.

This program also illustrates that you can string together several input operations in a single statement.

Declaring Local Variables

Another difference between how can may write C and C++ code is where local variables can be declared. In C, you must declare all local variables used within a block at the start of that block. You cannot declare a variable in a block after an "action" statement has occurred. For example, in C, this fragment is incorrect:

```
/* Incorrect in C. OK in C++. */
f()
{
  int i, k;

  for(i=0; i<10; i++) {
    k = i+1;
    int j;  /* won't compile as a C program */
    j = i*2;
    .

    .

    .

  }
}
```

Because an "action" statement precedes the declaration of **j**, a C compiler will flag an error and refuse to compile this function. However, in C++, this fragment is perfectly acceptable and will compile without error. In C++ you can declare local variables at any point within a block—not just at the beginning.

Here is another version of the program from the preceding section, in which each variable is declared as needed.

```
#include <iostream.h>

main()
{
  float f;
  double d;
  cout << "Enter two floating-point numbers: ";
  cin >> f >> d;

  cout << "Enter a string: ";
  char str[80];  // str declared here, just before 1st use
  cin >> str;

  cout << f << " " << d << " " << str;
```

```
    return 0;
}
```

Whether you declare all variables at the start of a block or at the point of first use is up to you. Since much of the philosophy behind C++ is the encapsulation of code and data, it makes sense that you can declare variables close to where they are used instead of just at the beginning of the block. In the preceding example, the declarations are separated simply for illustration. However, it is easy to imagine more complex examples in which this feature of C++ is more valuable.

Declaring variables close to where they are used can help you avoid accidental side effects. However, the greatest benefit of declaring variables at the point of first use is gained in large functions. Frankly, in short functions (like many of the examples in this book), there is little reason not to simply declare all variables at the start of a function. For this reason, this book will declare variables at the point of first use only when it seems warranted by the size or complexity of a function.

There is some debate as to the general wisdom of localizing the declaration of variables. Opponents suggest that sprinkling declarations throughout a block makes it harder, not easier, for someone reading the code to find quickly the declarations of all variables used in that block, making the program harder to maintain. For this reason, some C++ programmers do not make significant use of this feature. This book takes no stand on this issue. However, when applied properly, especially in large functions, declaring variables at the point of their first use can help you create bug-free programs more easily.

Introducing C++ Classes

This section introduces C++'s most important feature: the class. In C++, to create an object, you first must define its general form by using the keyword **class**. A **class** is similar syntactically to a structure. The following class defines a type called **stack**, which is used to create a stack:

```
#define SIZE 100

// This creates the class stack.
class stack {
  int stck[SIZE];
  int tos;
public:
  void init();
  void push(int i);
  int pop();
};
```

A **class** may contain private as well as public parts. By default, all items defined in a **class** are private. For example, the variables **stck** and **tos** are private. This means that they cannot be accessed by any function that is not a member of the **class**. This is one way that encapsulation is achieved—access to certain items of data can be tightly controlled by keeping them private. Although it is not shown in this example, you can also define private functions, which then can only be called by other members of the **class**.

To make parts of a **class** public (that is, accessible to other parts of your program), you must declare them after the **public** keyword. All variables or functions defined after **public** can be accessed by all other functions in the program. Essentially, the rest of your program accesses an object through its public functions. It should be mentioned at this time that although you can have public variables, philosophically you should try to limit or eliminate their use. Instead, you should make all data private, and control access to it through public functions. One other point: notice that the **public** keyword is followed by a colon.

The functions **init( )**, **push( )**, and **pop( )** are called *member functions* because they are part of the class **stack**. The variables **stck** and **tos** are called *member variables* (or *data members*). Remember, an object forms a bond between code and data. Only member functions have access to the private members of the class in which they are declared. Thus, only **init( )**, **push( )**, and **pop( )** can access **stck** and **tos**.

Once you have defined a **class**, you can create an object of that type by using the class name. In essence, the class name becomes a new data type specifier. For example, this creates an object called **mystack** of type **stack**.

```
stack mystack;
```

You can also create variables when the **class** is defined by putting their names after the closing curly brace, in exactly the same way as you would with a structure.

To review: In C++, **class** creates a new data type that may be used to create objects of that type. Therefore, an object is an instance of a class in just the same way that some other variable is an instance of the **int** data type, for example. Put differently, a class is a logical abstraction, an object is real. (That is, an object exists inside the memory of the computer.)

The general form of a **class** declaration is

```
class class-name {
    private data and functions
public:
    public data and functions
} object list;
```

Of course, the *object list* may be empty.

Inside the declaration of **stack**, member functions were identified using their prototypes. In C++, all functions must be prototyped. Prototypes are not optional.

When it comes time to actually code a function that is the member of a class, you must tell the compiler which class the function belongs to by qualifying its name with the name of the class of which it is a member. For example, here is one way to code the **push( )** function:

```
void stack::push(int i)
{
  if(tos==SIZE) {
    cout << "Stack is full.";
    return;
  }
  stck[tos] = i;
  tos++;
}
```

The **::** is called the *scope resolution operator.* Essentially, it tells the compiler that this version of **push( )** belongs to the **stack** class or, put differently, that this **push( )** is in **stack**'s scope. As you will soon see, in C++, several different classes can use the same function name. The compiler knows which function belongs to which class because of the scope resolution operator and the class name.

When you refer to a member of a class from a piece of code that is not part of the class, you must always do so in conjunction with an object of that class. To do so, use the object's name, followed by the dot operator, followed by the name of the member. This rule applies whether you are accessing a data member or a function member. For example, this calls **init( )** for object **stack1**.

```
stack stack1, stack2;

stack1.init();
```

This fragment creates two objects (**stack1** and **stack2**) and initializes **stack1**. At this point, it is very important to understand that **stack1** and **stack2** are two separate objects. This means, for example, that initializing **stack1** does *not* cause **stack2** to be initialized as well. The only relationship **stack1** has with **stack2** is that they are objects of the same type.

A member function can call another member function or refer to a data member directly, without using the dot operator. It is only when a member is referred to by code that does not belong to the class that the object name and the dot operator must be used.

The program shown here puts together all the pieces and missing details and illustrates the **stack** class:

```cpp
#include <iostream.h>

#define SIZE 100

// This creates the class stack.
class stack {
  int stck[SIZE];
  int tos;
public:
  void init();
  void push(int i);
  int pop();
};

void stack::init()
{
  tos = 0;
}

void stack::push(int i)
{
  if(tos==SIZE) {
    cout << "Stack is full.";
    return;
  }
  stck[tos] = i;
  tos++;
}

int stack::pop()
{
  if(tos==0) {
    cout << "Stack underflow.";
    return 0;
  }
  tos--;
  return stck[tos];
}
```

```
main()
{
  stack stack1, stack2;   // create two stack objects

  stack1.init();
  stack2.init();

  stack1.push(1);
  stack2.push(2);

  stack1.push(3);
  stack2.push(4);

  cout << stack1.pop() << " ";
  cout << stack1.pop() << " ";
  cout << stack2.pop() << " ";
  cout << stack2.pop() << "\n";

  return 0;
}
```

REMEMBER: *The private parts of an object are accessible only by functions that are members of that object. For example, a statement like*

```
stack1.tos = 0; // error
```

could not be in the **main( )** *function of the previous program because* **tos** *is private.*

By convention, most C programs have the **main( )** function as the first function in the program. However, in the **stack** program, the member functions of **stack** are defined before the **main( )** function. While there is no rule that dictates this (they could be defined anywhere in the program), it is the most common approach used in writing C++ code. (However, nonmember functions are still typically defined after **main( )**.) This book will follow that convention. Of course, in real applications, the classes associated with a program will usually be contained in a header file.

Function Overloading

One way that C++ achieves polymorphism is through the use of function overloading. In C++, two or more functions can share the same name as long as their parameter declarations are different. In this situation, the functions that share the same name are said to be *overloaded*, and the process is referred to as *function overloading*.

To see why function overloading is important, first consider three functions found in the standard library of virtually all C/C++ compilers: **abs( )**, **labs( )**, and **fabs( )**. The **abs( )** function returns the absolute value of an integer, **labs( )** returns the absolute value of a **long**, and **fabs( )** returns the absolute value of a **double**. Although these functions perform almost identical actions, in C, three slightly different names must be used to represent these essentially similar tasks. This makes the situation more complex, conceptually, than it actually is. Even though the underlying concept of each function is the same, the programmer has to remember three things, not just one. However, in C++, you can use just one name for all three functions, as the following program illustrates.

```cpp
#include <iostream.h>

// abs is overloaded three ways
int abs(int i);
double abs(double d);
long abs(long l);

main()
{
  cout << abs(-10) << "\n";

  cout << abs(-11.0) << "\n";

  cout << abs(-9L) << "\n";

  return 0;
}
int abs(int i)
{
  cout << "using integer abs()\n";

  return i<0 ? -i : i;
}

double abs(double d)
{
  cout << "using double abs()\n";

  return d<0.0 ? -d : d;
}

long abs(long l)
```

```
  {
    cout << "using long abs()\n";

    return l<0 ? -1 : 1;
  }
```

This program creates three similar but different functions called **abs( )**, each of which returns the absolute value of its argument. The compiler knows which function to call in each situation because of the type of the argument. The value of overloaded functions is that they allow related sets of functions to be accessed with a common name. Thus, the name **abs( )** represents the *general action* that is being performed. It is left to the compiler to choose the right *specific method* for a particular circumstance. The programmer need only remember the general action being performed. Due to polymorphism, three things to remember have been reduced to one. This example is fairly trivial, but if you expand the concept, you can see how polymorphism can help you manage very complex programs.

In general, to overload a function, you simply declare different versions of it. The compiler takes care of the rest. You must observe one important restriction when overloading a function: the type and/or number of the parameters of each overloaded function must differ. It is not sufficient for two functions to differ only in their return types. They must differ in the types or number of their parameters. (Return types do not provide sufficient information in all cases for the compiler to decide which function to use.) Of course, overloaded functions *may* differ in their return types too.

Here is another example that uses overloaded functions:

```
#include <iostream.h>
#include <stdio.h>
#include <string.h>

void stradd(char *s1, char *s2);
void stradd(char *s1, int i);

main()
{
  char str[80];

  strcpy(str, "Hello ");
  stradd(str, "there");
  cout << str << "\n";

  stradd(str, 100);
```

```
   cout << str << "\n";

   return 0;
}

// concatenate two strings
void stradd(char *s1, char *s2)
{
   strcat(s1, s2);
}

// concatenate a string with a "stringized" integer
void stradd(char *s1, int i)
{
   char temp[80];

   sprintf(temp, "%d", i);
   strcat(s1, temp);
}
```

In this program, the function **stradd( )** is overloaded. One version concatenates two strings (just like **strcat( )** does). The other version "stringizes" an integer and then appends that to a string. Here, overloading is used to create one interface that appends either a string or an integer to another string.

You can use the same name to overload unrelated functions, but you should not. For example, you could use the name **sqr( )** to create functions that return the *square* of an **int** and the *square root* of a **double**. However, these two operations are fundamentally different; applying function overloading in this manner defeats its purpose (and, in fact, is considered bad programming style). In practice, you should overload only closely related operations.

Operator Overloading

Polymorphism is also achieved in C++ through operator overloading. As you know, in C++, it is possible to use the << and >> operators to perform console I/O operations. They can perform these extra operations because in the IOSTREAM.H header file, these operators are overloaded. When an operator is overloaded, it takes on an additional meaning relative to a certain class. However, it still retains all of its old meanings.

In general, you can overload most of C++'s operators by defining what they mean relative to a specific class. For example, think back to the **stack** class developed earlier in this chapter. It is possible to overload the **+** operator relative to objects of type **stack** so that it appends the contents of one stack to the contents of another. However, the **+** still retains its original meaning relative to other types of data.

Because operator overloading is, in practice, somewhat more complex than function overloading, examples are deferred until Chapter 14.

Inheritance

As stated earlier in this chapter, inheritance is one of the major traits of an object-oriented programming language. In C++, inheritance is supported by allowing one class to incorporate another class into its declaration. Inheritance allows a hierarchy of classes to be built, moving from most general to most specific. The process involves first defining a *base class,* which defines those qualities common to all objects to be derived from the base. The base class represents the most general description. The classes derived from the base are usually referred to as *derived classes.* A derived class includes all features of the generic base class and then adds qualities specific to the derived class. To demonstrate how this works, the next example creates classes that categorize different types of buildings.

To begin, the **building** class is declared, as shown here. It will serve as the base for two derived classes.

```cpp
class building {
  int rooms;
  int floors;
  int area;
public:
  void set_rooms(int num);
  int get_rooms();
  void set_floors(int num);
  int get_floors();
  void set_area(int num);
  int get_area();
};
```

Because (for the sake of this example) all buildings have three common features—one or more rooms, one or more floors, and a total area—the **building** class embodies these components into its declaration. The member functions beginning with **set** set the values of the private data. The functions starting with **get** return those values.

You can now use this broad definition of a building to create derived classes that describe specific types of buildings. For example, here is a derived class called **house**:

```
// house is derived from building
class house : public building {
  int bedrooms;
  int baths;
public:
  void set_bedrooms(int num);
  int get_bedrooms();
  void set_baths(int num);
  int get_baths();
};
```

Notice how **building** is inherited. The general form for inheritance is

class *new-class-name : access inherited-class* {
   // body of new class
}

Here, *access* is optional. However, if present, it must be **public**, **private**, or **protected**. (These options are further examined in Chapter 12.) For now, all inherited classes will use **public**. Using **public** means that all the public elements of the base class will also be public in the derived class that inherits it. Therefore, in the example, members of the class **house** have access to the member functions of **building** just as if they had been declared inside **house**. However, **house**'s member functions do *not* have access to the private parts of **building**. This is an important point. Even though **house** inherits **building**, it has access only to the public members of **building**. In this way, inheritance does not circumvent the principles of encapsulation necessary to OOP.

 REMEMBER: *A derived class has direct access to both its own members and the public members of the base class.*

Here is a program illustrating inheritance. It creates two derived classes of **building** using inheritance; one is **house**, the other, **school**.

```
#include <iostream.h>

class building {
  int rooms;
  int floors;
  int area;
public:
```

```
  void set_rooms(int num);
  int get_rooms();
  void set_floors(int num);
  int get_floors();
  void set_area(int num);
  int get_area();
};

// house is derived from building
class house : public building {
  int bedrooms;
  int baths;
public:
  void set_bedrooms(int num);
  int get_bedrooms();
  void set_baths(int num);
  int get_baths();
};

// school is also derived from building
class school : public building {
  int classrooms;
  int offices;
public:
  void set_classrooms(int num);
  int get_classrooms();
  void set_offices(int num);
  int get_offices();
};

void building::set_rooms(int num)
{
  rooms = num;
}

void building::set_floors(int num)
{
  floors = num;
}

void building::set_area(int num)
{
```

```
    area = num;
}

int building::get_rooms()
{
  return rooms;
}

int building::get_floors()
{
  return floors;
}

int building::get_area()
{
  return area;
}

void house::set_bedrooms(int num)
{
  bedrooms = num;
}

void house::set_baths(int num)
{
  baths = num;
}

int house::get_bedrooms()
{
  return bedrooms;
}

int house::get_baths()
{
  return baths;
}

void school::set_classrooms(int num)
{
  classrooms = num;
}
```

```
void school::set_offices(int num)
{
  offices = num;
}

int school::get_classrooms()
{
  return classrooms;
}

int school::get_offices()
{
  return offices;
}

main()
{
  house h;
  school s;
  h.set_rooms(12);
  h.set_floors(3);
  h.set_area(4500);
  h.set_bedrooms(5);
  h.set_baths(3);

  cout << "house has " << h.get_bedrooms();
  cout << " bedrooms\n";

  s.set_rooms(200);
  s.set_classrooms(180);
  s.set_offices(5);
  s.set_area(25000);

  cout << "school has " << s.get_classrooms();
  cout << " classrooms\n";
  cout << "Its area is " << s.get_area();

  return 0;
}
```

As this program sshows, the major advantage of inheritance is that you can create a general classification that can be incorporated into more specific ones. In this way, each object can precisely represent its own classification.

When writing about C++, the terms *base* and *derived* are generally used to describe the inheritance relationship. However, you may also see the terms *parent* and *child* used.

Aside from providing the advantages of hierarchical classification, inheritance also provides support for run-time polymorphism through the mechanism of **virtual** functions. (Refer to Chapter 16 for details.)

Constructors and Destructors

It is very common for some part of an object to require initialization before it can be used. For example, think back to the **stack** class developed earlier in this chapter. Before the stack could be used, **tos** had to be set to zero. This was performed by using the function **init( )**. Because the requirement for initialization is so common, C++ allows objects to initialize themselves when they are created. This automatic initialization is performed through the use of a constructor function.

A *constructor function* is a special function that is a member of a class and has the same name as that class. For example, here is how the **stack** class looks when converted to use a constructor function for initialization:

```
// This creates the class stack.
class stack {
  int stck[SIZE];
  int tos;
public:
  stack();  // constructor
  void push(int i);
  int pop();
};
```

Notice that the constructor **stack( )** has no return type specified. In C++, constructor functions cannot return values and, thus, have no return type.

The **stack( )** function is coded like this:

```
// stack's constructor function
stack::stack()
{
```

```
    tos = 0;
    cout << "Stack Initialized\n";
}
```

Keep in mind that the message **Stack Initialized** is output as a way to illustrate the constructor. In actual practice, most constructor functions will not output or input anything. They will simply perform various initializations.

An object's constructor is automatically called when the object is created. This means that it is called when the object's declaration is executed. There is an important distinction between a C-like declaration statement and a C++ declaration. In C, variable declarations are, loosely speaking, passive and resolved mostly at compile time. Put differently, in C, variable declarations are not thought of as being executable statements. However, in C++, variable declarations are active statements that are, in fact, executed at run time. One reason for this is that an object declaration may need to call a constructor, thus causing the execution of a function. Although this difference may seem subtle and largely academic at this point, it has some important implications relative to variable initialization, as you will see later.

An object's constructor is called once for global or **static** local objects. For local objects, the constructor is called each time the object declaration is encountered.

The complement of the constructor is the *destructor*. In many circumstances, an object will need to perform some action or actions when it is destroyed. Local objects are created when their block is entered, and destroyed when the block is left. Global objects are destroyed when the program terminates. When an object is destroyed, its destructor (if it has one) is automatically called. There are many reasons why a destructor function may be needed. For example, an object may need to deallocate memory that it had previously allocated, or it may need to close a file that it had opened. In C++, it is the destructor function that handles deactivation events. The destructor has the same name as the constructor, but it is preceded by a ~. For example, here is the **stack** class and its constructor and destructor functions. (Keep in mind that the **stack** class does not require a destructor; the one shown here is just for illustration.)

```
// This creates the class stack.
class stack {
  int stck[SIZE];
  int tos;
public:
  stack();  // constructor
  ~stack(); // destructor
  void push(int i);
  int pop();
```

```
};

// stack's constructor function
stack::stack()
{
  tos = 0;
  cout << "Stack Initialized\n";
}

// stack's destructor function
stack::~stack()
{
  cout << "Stack Destroyed\n";
}
```

Notice that, like constructor functions, destructor functions do not have return values.

To see how constructors and destructors work, here is a new version of the **stack** program examined earlier in this chapter. Notice that **init( )** is no longer needed.

```
#include <iostream.h>

#define SIZE 100
// This creates the class stack.
class stack {
  int stck[SIZE];
  int tos;
public:
  stack();   // constructor
  ~stack(); // destructor
  void push(int i);
  int pop();
};

// stack's constructor function
stack::stack()
{
  tos = 0;
  cout << "Stack Initialized\n";
}
```

```cpp
// stack's destructor function
stack::~stack()
{
  cout << "Stack Destroyed\n";
}

void stack::push(int i)
{
  if(tos==SIZE) {
    cout << "Stack is full.";
    return;
  }
  stck[tos] = i;
  tos++;
}

int stack::pop()
{
  if(tos==0) {
    cout << "Stack underflow.";
    return 0;
  }
  tos--;
  return stck[tos];
}

main()
{
  stack a, b;  // create two stack objects

  a.push(1);
  b.push(2);

  a.push(3);
  b.push(4);

  cout << a.pop() << " ";
  cout << a.pop() << " ";
  cout << b.pop() << " ";
  cout << b.pop() << "\n";

  return 0;
}
```

This program displays the following:

```
Stack Initialized
Stack Initialized
3 1 4 2
Stack Destroyed
Stack Destroyed
```

The C++ Keywords

In addition to the 32 keywords that form the C language, the proposed ANSI standard for C++ adds 30 more. These keywords are shown in Table 11-1. However, at the time of this writing, the keywords **bool, const_cast, dynamic_cast, explicit, false, mutable, namespace, reinterpret_cast, static_cast, true, typeid, using,** and **wchar_t** are in the process of being defined by the ANSI C++ standards committee and may not be fully implemented by your compiler. These keywords were not part of the original specification for C++ created by Bjarne Stroustrup. They are being added primarily to allow C++ to accommodate some special situations and are subject to change. Also, the **overload** keyword is obsolete but is included for compatibility with older C++ programs. You will want to check your compiler user's manual to determine precisely what C++ keywords are supported by your compiler.

asm	overload
bool	private
catch	protected
class	public
const_cast	reinterpret_cast
delete	static_cast
dynamic_cast	template
explicit	this
false	throw
friend	true
inline	try
mutable	typeid
namespace	using
new	virtual
operator	wchar_t

Table 11-1. *The C++ Keywords*

The General Form of a C++ Program

Although individual styles will differ, most C++ programs will have this general form:

```
#includes
base-class declarations
derived class declarations
nonmember function prototypes
main( )
{
    .
    .
    .
}
nonmember function definitions
```

However, keep in mind that, in most large projects, all **class** declarations will be put into a header file and included with each module.

The remaining chapters in this section examine in greater detail the features discussed in this chapter, as well as all other C++ features.

Chapter Twelve

Classes and Objects

In C++, the class forms the basis of object-oriented programming. Specifically, it is the class that is used to define the nature of an object. In fact, the class is C++'s basic unit of encapsulation. In this chapter, classes and objects are examined in detail.

Classes

Classes are created using the keyword **class**. A class declaration defines a new type that links code and data. This new type is then used to declare objects of that class. Thus, a class is a logical abstraction, but an object has physical existence. In other words, an object is an *instance* of a class.

A class declaration is similar syntactically to a structure. In Chapter 11, a simplified general form of a class declaration was shown. Here is the entire general form of a **class** declaration that does not inherit any other class.

```
class class-name {
    private data and functions
access-specifier:
    data and functions
access-specifier:
    data and functions
    .
    .
    .
access-specifier:
    data and functions
} object-list;
```

The *object-list* is optional. If present, it declares objects of the class. Here, *access-specifier* is one of these three C++ keywords:

```
public
private
protected
```

By default, functions and data declared within a **class** are private to that class and may be accessed only by other members of the class. However, by using the **public** access specifier, you allow functions or data to be accessible to other parts of your program. Once an access specifier has been used, it remains in effect until either another access specifier is encountered or the end of the **class** declaration is reached. To switch back to private declarations, you can use the **private** access specifier. The **protected** access specifier is needed only when inheritance is involved (see Chapter 15).

You can change access specification as often as you like within a **class** declaration. That is, you can switch to **public** for some declarations and then switch back to **private** again. The **class** declaration in the following example illustrates this feature.

```cpp
#include <iostream.h>
#include <string.h>

class employee {
  char name[80];
public:
  void putname(char *n);
  void getname(char *n);
private:
  double wage;
public:
  void putwage(double w);
  double getwage();
} ;

void employee::putname(char *n)
{
  strcpy(name, n);
}

void employee::getname(char *n)
{
  strcpy(n, name);
}

void employee::putwage(double w)
{
  wage = w;
}

double employee::getwage()
{
  return wage;
}

main()
{
```

```
     employee ted;
     char name[80];

     ted.putname("Ted Jones");
     ted.putwage(75000);

     ted.getname(name);
     cout << name << " makes $";
     cout << ted.getwage() << " per year.";

     return 0;
}
```

Here, **employee** is a simple class that could be used to store an employee's name and wage. Notice that the **public** access specifier is used twice.

Actually, most C++ programmers will code the **employee** class as shown next, with all private elements grouped together and all public elements grouped together.

```
class employee {
  char name[80];
  double wage;
public:
  void putname(char *n);
  void getname(char *n);
  void putwage(double w);
  double getwage();
} ;
```

Although you can use the access specifiers as often as you like within a class declaration, the only advantage of doing so is that by visually grouping various parts of a class, you may make it easier for someone else reading the program to understand it. However, to the compiler, using multiple access specifiers makes no difference. Actually, most programmers find it easier to have only one **private**, one **protected**, and one **public** section within each class.

Functions that are declared within a class are called *member functions*. Member functions can access any element of the class of which they are a part. This includes all **private** elements. Variables that are elements of a class are called *member variables* or *data members*. Collectively, any element of a class can be referred to as a member of that class.

There are a few restrictions that apply to class members. A non-**static** member variable cannot have an initializer. No member can be an object of the class that is being declared. (Although a member can be a pointer to the class that is being declared.) No member can be declared as **auto**, **extern**, or **register**.

In general, you should make all data members of a class private to that class. This is part of the way that encapsulation is achieved. However, there may be situations in which you will need to make one or more variables public. (For example, a heavily used variable may need to be accessible globally in order to achieve faster run times.) When a variable is public, it may be accessed directly by any other part of your program. The syntax for accessing a public data member is the same as for effecting a function call: Specify the object's name, the dot operator, and the variable name. The following simple program illustrates direct access of a public variable.

```cpp
#include <iostream.h>

class myclass {
public:
  int i, j, k; // accessible to entire program
};

main()
{
  myclass a, b;
  a.i = 100;   // direct access of i, j, and k
  a.j = 4;
  a.k = a.i * a.j;

  b.k = 12;   // remember, a.k and b.k are different
  cout << a.k << " " << b.k;

  return 0;
}
```

Structures and Classes

C++ has elevated the role of the standard C structure to that of an alternative way to specify a class. In fact, the only difference between a **class** and a **struct** is that by default all members are public in a structure and private in a **class**. In all other respects, structures and **class**es are equivalent. That is, in C++, a structure also defines a class type. For example, consider the following short program, which uses a structure to declare a class that controls access to a string.

```
#include <iostream.h>
#include <string.h>

struct mystr {
  void buildstr(char *s); // public
  void showstr();
private: // now go private
  char str[255];
} ;

void mystr::buildstr(char *s)
{
  if(!*s) *str = '\0'; // initialize string
  else strcat(str, s);
}

void mystr::showstr()
{
  cout << str << "\n";
}

main()
{
  mystr s;

  s.buildstr(""); // init
  s.buildstr("Hello ");
  s.buildstr("there!");

  s.showstr();

  return 0;
}
```

This program displays the string **Hello there!**

Notice how **s** is declared in **main( )**. Because a C++ **struct** defines a class type, objects of that type can be declared using only the structure's tag name, without preceding it with the keyword **struct**. Recall that in C, structure variables have to be declared using this form:

struct *tag-name var;*

However, in C++ a structure is a class type, and its tag name describes a complete type. Thus, there is no need to precede it with **struct** when declaring objects (although it is not technically an error to do so).

The class **mystr** could be rewritten by using **class** as shown here:

```
class mystr {
  char str[255];
public:
  void buildstr(char *s); // public
  void showstr();
} ;
```

You might wonder why C++ contains the two virtually equivalent keywords **struct** and **class**. This seeming redundancy is justified for several reasons. First, there is no fundamental reason not to increase the capabilities of a structure. In C, structures already provide a means of grouping data. Therefore, it is a small step to allow them to include member functions. Second, because structures and **class**es are related, it may be easier to transport existing C programs to C++. Finally, although the two are virtually equivalent today, providing two different keywords allows the definition of a **class** to be free to evolve. However, in order for C++ to remain compatible with C, a structure declaration may not be able to evolve in the same way.

Although you can use a **struct** where you use a **class**, generally you shouldn't. For the sake of clarity, you should use a **class** when you want a class and a **struct** when you want a C-like structure. This is the style that this book will follow.

REMEMBER: *In C++, a structure declaration defines a class type.*

Unions and Classes

Like a structure, a **union** may also be used to define a class. In C++, unions may contain both member functions and variables. They may also include constructor and destructor functions. A **union** in C++ retains all of its C-like features, the most important being that all data elements share the same location in memory. Like the structure, **union** members are public by default. In the next example, a **union** is used to swap the bytes that make up an **unsigned** integer. (This example assumes that integers are 2 bytes long.)

```cpp
#include <iostream.h>

union swap_byte {
  void swap();
  void set_byte(unsigned i);
  void show_word();

  unsigned u;
  unsigned char c[2];
};

void swap_byte::swap()
{
  unsigned char t;

  t = c[0];
  c[0] = c[1];
  c[1] = t;
}

void swap_byte::show_word()
{
  cout << u;
}

void swap_byte::set_byte(unsigned i)
{
  u = i;
}

main()
{
  swap_byte b;

  b.set_byte(49034);
  b.swap();
  b.show_word();

  return 0;
}
```

It is important to understand that like a structure, a **union** declaration in C++ defines a special type of class. This means that the principle of encapsulation is preserved.

There are several restrictions that must be observed when you use C++ unions. First, a **union** cannot inherit any other classes of any type. Further, a **union** cannot be a base **class**. A **union** cannot have virtual member functions. (Virtual functions are discussed in Chapter 16.) No **static** variables can be members of a **union**. A **union** cannot have as a member any object that overloads the = operator. Finally, no object can be a member of a **union** if the object has a constructor or destructor function.

Anonymous Unions

There is a special type of **union** in C++ called an *anonymous union*. An anonymous union does not contain a type name, and no variables may be declared of this sort of **union**. Instead, an anonymous union tells the compiler that the member variables of the **union** are to share the same location. However, the variables themselves are referred to directly, without the normal dot operator syntax. For example, consider this program:

```
#include <iostream.h>
#include <string.h>

main()
{
  // define anonymous union
  union {
    long l;
    double d;
    char s[4];
  } ;

  // now, reference union elements directly
  l = 100000;
  cout << l << " ";
  d = 123.2342;
  cout << d << " ";
  strcpy(s, "hi");
  cout << s;

  return 0;
}
```

As you can see, the elements of the **union** are referenced as if they had been declared as normal local variables. In fact, relative to your program, that is exactly how you will use them. Further, even though they are defined within a **union** declaration, they are at the same scope level as any other local variable within the same block. Indeed, the members of an anonymous union can not have the same name as any other identifier known to the current scope. This implies that the names of the members of an anonymous union must not conflict with other identifiers known within the scope of the union.

All restrictions involving **union**s apply to anonymous ones, with several additions. First, the only elements contained within an anonymous union must be data. No member functions are allowed. Anonymous unions cannot contain **private** or **protected** elements. Finally, global anonymous unions must be specified as **static**.

Friend Functions

It is possible to grant a nonmember function access to the private members of a class by using a **friend**. A **friend** function has access to all **private** and **protected** members of the class for which it is a **friend**. To declare a **friend** function, include its prototype within the class, preceding it with the keyword **friend**. Consider this program:

```
#include <iostream.h>

class myclass {
  int a, b;
public:
  friend int sum(myclass x);
  void set_ab(int i, int j);
};

void myclass::set_ab(int i, int j)
{
  a = i;
  b = j;
}

// Note: sum() is not a member function of any class.
int sum(myclass x)
{
  /* Because sum() is a friend of myclass, it can
     directly access a and b. */

  return x.a + x.b;
}

main()
```

```
{
  myclass n;

  n.set_ab(3, 4);

  cout << sum(n);

  return 0;
}
```

In this example, the **sum( )** function is not a member of **myclass**. However, it still has full access to its private members. Also, notice that **sum( )** is called normally. Because it is not a member function, it does not need to be (indeed, it may not be) qualified with an object's name.

Although there is nothing gained by making **sum( )** a **friend** rather than a member function of **myclass**, there are some circumstances in which **friend** functions are quite valuable. First, friends can be useful when you are overloading certain types of operators (see Chapter 14). Second, **friend** functions make the creation of some types of I/O functions easier (see Chapter 17). The third reason that **friend** functions may be desirable is that in some cases, two or more classes may contain members that are interrelated relative to other parts of your program. Let's examine this third usage now.

To begin, imagine two different classes, each of which displays a pop-up message on the screen when error conditions occur. Other parts of your program may wish to know if a pop-up message is currently being displayed before writing to the screen so that no message is accidentally overwritten. Although you can create member functions in each class that return a value indicating whether a message is active, this means additional overhead when the condition is checked (that is, two function calls, not just one). If the condition needs to be checked frequently, this additional overhead may not be acceptable. However, using a function that is a **friend** of each class, it is possible to check the status of each object by calling only this one function. Thus, in situations like this, a **friend** function allows you to generate more efficient code. The following program illustrates this concept.

```
#include <iostream.h>

#define IDLE 0
#define INUSE 1

class C2;  // forward reference
class C1 {
  int status;  // IDLE if off, INUSE if on screen
```

```
  // ...
public:
  void set_status(int state);
  friend int idle(C1 a, C2 b);
};

class C2 {
  int status; // IDLE if off, INUSE if on screen
  // ...
public:
  void set_status(int state);
  friend int idle(C1 a, C2 b);
};

void C1::set_status(int state)
{
  status = state;
}

void C2::set_status(int state)
{
  status = state;
}

int idle(C1 a, C2 b)
{
  if(a.status || b.status) return 0;
  else return 1;
}

main()
{
  C1 x;
  C2 y;

  x.set_status(IDLE);
  y.set_status(IDLE);

  if(idle(x, y)) cout << "Screen can be used.\n";
  else cout << "In use.\n";

  x.set_status(INUSE);
```

```
    if(idle(x, y)) cout << "Screen can be used.\n";
    else cout << "In use.\n";

    return 0;
}
```

Notice that this program uses a *forward declaration* (also called a *forward reference*) for the class **C2**. This is necessary because the declaration of **idle( )** inside **C1** references **C2** before it is declared. To create a forward declaration to a class, simply use the form shown in this program.

A **friend** of one class may be a member of another. For example, here is the preceding program rewritten so that **idle( )** is a member of **C1**:

```
#include <iostream.h>

#define IDLE 0
#define INUSE 1

class C2;  // forward reference

class C1 {
  int status;  // IDLE if off, INUSE if on screen
  // ...
public:
  void set_status(int state);
  int idle(C2 b);  // now a member of C1
};

class C2 {
  int status;  // IDLE if off, INUSE if on screen
  // ...
public:
  void set_status(int state);
  friend int C1::idle(C2 b);
};

void C1::set_status(int state)
{
  status = state;
}
```

```
void C2::set_status(int state)
{
  status = state;
}

// idle() is member of C1, but friend of C2
int C1::idle(C2 b)
{
  if(status || b.status) return 0;
  else return 1;
}

main()
{
  C1 x;
  C2 y;

  x.set_status(IDLE);
  y.set_status(IDLE);

  if(x.idle(y)) cout << "Screen can be used.\n";
  else cout << "In use.\n";

  x.set_status(INUSE);

  if(x.idle(y)) cout << "Screen can be used.\n";
  else cout << "In use.\n";

  return 0;
}
```

Because **idle( )** is a member of **C1**, it can access the **status** variable of objects of type **C1** directly. Thus, only objects of type **C2** need be passed to **idle( )**.

There are two important restrictions that apply to **friend** functions. First, a derived class does not inherit **friend** functions. Second, a **friend** function cannot have a storage-class specifier. That is, they may not be declared as **static** or **extern**.

Friend Classes

It is possible for one **class** to be a **friend** of another class. When this is the case, the **friend** class has access to the private names defined within the other class. These private names may include such things as type names and enumerated constants. Consider the following example.

```
#include <iostream.h>

class coins {
  // The following is a private enumeration.
  enum units {penny, nickel, dime, quarter, half_dollar};
  friend class amount;
};

class amount {
  coins::units money; // notice use of coins::units
public:
  void setm();
  int getm();
} ob;

void amount::setm()
{
  // Enumeration units accessible here because
  // amount is friend of coins.
  money = coins::dime;
}

int amount::getm()
{
  return money;
}

main()
{
  ob.setm();

  cout << ob.getm(); // outputs the number 2

  return 0;
}
```

Here, class **amount** has access to the **units** type specifier declared within the **coins** class (and to the names defined within the **units** enumeration) because **amount** is a **friend** of **coins**.

It is critical to understand that when one class is a **friend** of another, it only has access to names defined within the other class. It does not inherit the other class. Specifically, the members of the first class do not become members of the **friend** class.

Friend classes are seldom used. They are supported to allow certain special-case situations to be handled.

Inline Functions

There is an important feature in C++, called an *inline function,* that is commonly used with classes. Since the rest of this chapter (and the rest of the book) will make heavy use of them, inline functions are examined here.

In C++, you can create short functions that are not actually called; rather, their code is expanded inline at the point of each invocation. This process is similar to using a function-like macro. To cause a function to be expanded inline rather than called, precede its definition with the **inline** keyword. For example, in the following program, the function **max( )** is expanded inline instead of called.

```
#include <iostream.h>

inline int max(int a, int b)
{
  return a>b ? a : b;
}

main()
{
  cout << max(10, 20);
  cout << " " << max(99, 88);

  return 0;
}
```

As far as the compiler is concerned, the preceding program is equivalent to this one:

```
#include <iostream.h>

main()
{

  cout << (10>20 ? 10 : 20);
  cout << " " << (99>88 ? 99 : 88);

  return 0;
}
```

The reason that **inline** functions are an important addition to C++ is that they allow you to create very efficient code. Since classes typically require several frequently executed interface functions (which provide access to private data), the efficiency of these functions is of critical concern in C++. As you probably know, each time a function is called, a significant amount of overhead is generated by the calling and return mechanism. Typically, arguments are pushed onto the stack and various registers are saved when a function is called and then restored when the function returns. The trouble is that these instructions take time. However, when a function is expanded inline, none of those operations occur. Although expanding function calls inline can produce faster run times, it also often results in larger code size because of the duplicated code. For this reason, it is best to inline only very small functions. Further, it is also a good idea to only inline those functions that will have significant impact on the performance of your program.

Like the **register** specifier, **inline** is actually just a *request*, not a command, to the compiler. The compiler can choose to ignore it. Also, some compilers may not inline all types of functions. For example, it is common for a compiler not to inline a recursive function. You will need to check your compiler's user manual for any restrictions to **inline**. Remember, if a function cannot be inlined, it will simply be called as a normal function.

Inline functions may be **class** member functions. For example, this is a perfectly valid C++ program:

```
#include <iostream.h>

class myclass {
  int a, b;
public:
  void init(int i, int j);
  void show();
};

inline void myclass::init(int i, int j)
{
  a = i;
  b = j;
}

inline void myclass::show()
{
  cout << a << " " << b << "\n";
}

main()
```

```
{
  myclass x;

  x.init(10, 20);
  x.show();

  return 0;
}
```

Defining Inline Functions Within a Class

It is possible to define short functions within a **class** declaration. When a function is defined inside a **class** declaration, it is automatically made into an **inline** function (if possible). It is not necessary (but not an error) to precede its declaration with the **inline** keyword. For example, the preceding program is rewritten here with the definitions of **init( )** and **show( )** contained within the declaration of **myclass**:

```
#include <iostream.h>

class myclass {
  int a, b;
public:
  // automatic inline
  void init(int i, int j) {a=i; b=j;}
  void show() {cout << a << " " << b << "\n";}
};

main()
{
  myclass x;

  x.init(10, 20);
  x.show();

  return 0;
}
```

Notice the format of the function code within **myclass**. Because **inline** functions are usually short, this style of coding within a **class** is fairly typical. However, you are free

to use any format you like. For example, this is a perfectly valid way to rewrite the
class declaration:

```
#include <iostream.h>

class myclass {
  int a, b;
public:
  // automatic inline
  void init(int i, int j)
  {
    a = i;
    b = j;
  }

  void show()
  {
    cout << a << " " << b << "\n";
  }
};
```

Technically, the inlining of the **show( )** function is pointless because (in general) the
amount of time the I/O statement will take far exceeds the overhead of a function call.
However, it is extremely common to see all short member functions defined inside
their **class** in C++ programs. (In fact, it is rare to see short member functions defined
outside their class declarations in professionally written C++ code.)

Keep in mind that constructor and destructor functions may also be inlined—either
by default, if defined within their **class**, or explicitly.

Parameterized Constructors

It is possible to pass arguments to constructor functions. Typically, these arguments
are used to help initialize an object when it is created. To create a parameterized
constructor, simply add parameters to it the way you would to any other function.
When you define the constructor's body, use the parameters to initialize the object.
For example, here is a simple **class** that includes a parameterized constructor:

```
#include <iostream.h>

class myclass {
```

```
   int a, b;
public:
   myclass(int i, int j) {a=i; b=j;}
   void show() {cout << a << " " << b;}
};

main()
{
   myclass ob(3, 5);

   ob.show();

   return 0;
}
```

Notice that in the definition of **myclass( )**, the parameters **i** and **j** are used to give initial values to **a** and **b**.

The program illustrates the most common way to specify arguments when you declare an object that uses a parameterized constructor function. Specifically, this statement

```
myclass ob(3, 4);
```

causes an object called **ob** to be created and passes the arguments **3** and **4** to the **i** and **j** parameters of **myclass( )**. You may also pass arguments using this type declaration statement:

```
myclass ob = myclass(3, 4);
```

However, the first method is the one generally used, and this is the approach taken by most of the examples in this book. Actually, there is a small technical difference between the two types of declarations, which relates to copy constructors. (Copy constructors are discussed in Chapter 22.)

Here is another example that uses a parameterized constructor function. It creates a **class** that keeps information about library books.

```
#include <iostream.h>
#include <string.h>
```

```
#define IN 1
#define CHECKED_OUT 0

class book {
  char author[40];
  char title[40];
  int status;
public:
  book(char *n, char *t, int s);
  int get_status() {return status;}
  void set_status(int s) {status = s;}
  void show();
};

book::book(char *n, char *t, int s)
{
  strcpy(author, n);
  strcpy(title, t);
  status = s;
}

void book::show()
{
  cout << title << " by " << author;
  cout << " is ";
  if(status==IN) cout << "in.\n";
  else cout << "out.\n";
}

main()
{
  book b1("Twain", "Tom Sawyer", IN);
  book b2("Melville", "Moby Dick", CHECKED_OUT);

  b1.show();
  b2.show();

  return 0;
}
```

Parameterized constructor functions are very useful because they allow you to avoid having to make an additional function call simply to initialize one or more variables in an object. Each function call you can avoid makes your program more efficient. Also, notice that the functions **get_status( )** and **set_status( )** are defined within the **book** class. This is a very common practice when writing C++ programs.

Constructors with One Parameter: A Special Case

If a constructor function only has one parameter, then there is a third way to pass an initial value to that constructor. For example, consider the following short program:

```
#include <iostream.h>

class X {
  int a;
public:
  X(int j) { a = j; }
  int geta() { return a; }
};

main()
{
  X ob = 99; // passes 99 to j

  cout << ob.geta(); // outputs 99

  return 0;
}
```

As this example shows, in cases where the constructor only takes one argument, you can simply use the normal initialization form. The C++ compiler will automatically assign the value on the right of the = to the constructor's parameter.

Static Class Members

Both function and data members of a class can be made **static**. This section explains what this means relative to each type of member.

Static Data Members

When you precede a member variable's declaration with static, you are telling the compiler that only one copy of that variable will exist and that all objects of the class will share that variable. Unlike regular data members, individual copies of a **static** member variable are not made for each object. No matter how many objects of a class are created, only one copy of a **static** data member exists. Thus, all objects of that class use that same variable. All **static** variables are initialized to zero when the first object is created.

When you declare a **static** data member within a class, you are *not* defining it. That is, you are not allocating storage for it. (In the language of C++, a declaration *describes* something. A definition causes something to exist.) Instead, you must provide a global definition for the static data member elsewhere, outside the class. This is done by redeclaring the **static** variable using the scope resolution operator to identify which class it belongs to. This causes storage for the variable to be allocated. (Remember, a **class** declaration is simply a logical construct that does not have physical reality.)

To understand the usage and effect of a **static** data member, consider this program:

```
#include <iostream.h>

class shared {
  static int a;
  int b;
public:
  void set(int i, int j) {a=i; b=j;}
  void show();
} ;

int shared::a; // define a

void shared::show()
{
  cout << "This is static a: " << a;
  cout << "\nThis is non-static b: " << b;
  cout << "\n";
}

main()
{
  shared x, y;

  x.set(1, 1); // set a to 1
  x.show();

  y.set(2, 2); // change a to 2
  y.show();

  x.show(); /* Here, a has been changed for both x and y
               because a is shared by both objects. */

  return 0;
}
```

This program displays the following output when run.

```
This is static a: 1
This is non-static b: 1
This is static a: 2
This is non-static b: 2
This is static a: 2
This is non-static b: 1
```

Notice that the integer **a** is declared both inside **shared** and outside of it. As mentioned earlier, this is necessary because the declaration of **a** inside **shared** does not allocate storage.

NOTE: *As a convenience, older versions of C++ did not require the second declaration of a **static** member variable. However, this convenience gave rise to serious inconsistencies, and it was eliminated several years ago. Even so, you may still find older C++ code that does not redeclare **static** member variables. In these cases, you will need to add the required definitions.*

A **static** member variable exists *before* any object of its class is created. For example, in the following short program, **a** is both **public** and **static**. Thus it can be directly accessed in **main( )**. Further, since **a** exists before an object of **shared** is created, **a** can be given a value at any time. As this program illustrates, the value of **a** is unchanged by the creation of object **x**. For this reason, both output statements display the same value: 99.

```cpp
#include <iostream.h>

class shared {
public:
  static int a;
} ;

int shared::a; // define a

main()
{
  // init a before creating any objects
  shared::a = 99;

  cout << "This is initial value of a: " << shared::a;
  cout << "\n";
```

```
   shared x;

   cout << "This is x.a: " << x.a;

   return 0;
}
```

Notice how **a** is referenced through the use of the class name and the scope resolution operator. In general, when your program references a **static** member independently of an object, you must qualify it by using the name of the **class** of which it is a member.

One of the most common uses of **static** member variables is to provide access control to some shared resource. For example, you might create several objects, each of which needs to write to a specific disk file. Clearly, however, only one object can be allowed to write to the file at a time. In this case, you will want to declare a **static** variable that indicates when the file is in use and when it is free. Each object then interrogates this variable before writing to the file. The following program shows how you might use a **static** variable of this type to control access to a scarce resource.

```
#include <iostream.h>

class cl {
   static int resource;
public:
   int get_resource();
   void free_resource() {resource = 0;}
};

int cl::resource; // define resource

int cl::get_resource()
{
   if(resource) return 0; // resource already in use
   else {
      resource = 1;
      return 1;  // resource allocated to this object
   }
}

main()
{
```

```
cl ob1, ob2;

if(ob1.get_resource()) cout << "ob1 has resource\n";

if(!ob2.get_resource()) cout << "ob2 denied resource\n";

ob1.free_resource();  // let someone else use it

if(ob2.get_resource())
  cout << "ob2 can now use resource\n";

return 0;
}
```

By using **static** member variables, you should be able to virtually eliminate any need for global variables. The trouble with global variables relative to OOP is that they almost always violate the principle of encapsulation.

Static Member Functions

Member functions may also be declared as **static**. There are several restrictions placed on **static** member functions. First, they may only access other **static** members of the class. (Of course, global functions and data may be accessed by **static** member functions.) Second, **static** member functions do not have a **this** pointer. (See Chapter 13 for information on **this**.) Third, there cannot be a **static** and a non-**static** version of the same function.

Following is a slightly reworked version of the program that concluded the previous section. Notice that **get_resource( )** is now declared as **static**. As the program illustrates, **get_resource( )** may be accessed either by itself, independent of any object using the **class** name and the scope resolution operator, or in connection with an object.

```
#include <iostream.h>

class cl {
  static int resource;
public:
  static int get_resource();
  void free_resource() {resource = 0;}
};

int cl::resource; // define resource
```

```
int cl::get_resource()
{
  if(resource) return 0; // resource already in use
  else {
    resource = 1;
    return 1;  // resource allocated to this object
  }
}

main()
{
  cl ob1, ob2;

  /* get_resource() is static so may be called independent
     of any object. */
  if(cl::get_resource()) cout << "ob1 has resource\n";

  if(!cl::get_resource()) cout << "ob2 denied resource\n";

  ob1.free_resource();

  if(ob2.get_resource()) // can still call using object syntax
    cout << "ob2 can now use resource\n";

  return 0;
}
```

Actually, **static** member functions have limited applications, but one good use for them is that they can "preinitialize" private **static** data before any object is actually created. For example, this is a perfectly valid C++ program:

```
#include <iostream.h>

class static_type {
  static int i;
public:
  static void init(int x) {i = x;}
  void show() {cout << i;}
};

int static_type::i; // define i
```

```
main()
{
  // init static data before object creation
  static_type::init(100);

  static_type x;
  x.show(); // displays 100

  return 0;
}
```

When Constructors and Destructors Are Executed

As a general rule, an object's constructor is called when the object is declared, and an object's destructor is called when the object is destroyed. Precisely when these events occur is discussed here.

A local object's constructor function is executed when the object's declaration statement is encountered. Further, when two or more objects are declared in the same statement, the constructors are called in the order in which they are encountered, from left to right. The destructor functions for local objects are executed in the reverse order of the constructor functions.

Global objects have their constructor functions execute *before* **main( )** begins execution. Global constructors are executed in order of left to right, top to bottom, within the same file. You cannot know the order of execution of global constructors spread among several files. Global destructors execute in reverse order *after* **main( )** has terminated.

The following program illustrates the execution of constructors and destructors.

```
#include <iostream.h>

class myclass {
public:
  int who;
  myclass(int id);
  ~myclass();
} glob_ob1(1), glob_ob2(2);

myclass::myclass(int id)
{
```

```
   cout << "Initializing " << id << "\n";
   who = id;
}

myclass::~myclass()
{
   cout << "Destructing " << who << "\n";
}

main()
{
  myclass local_ob1(3);

  cout << "This will not be first line displayed.\n";

  myclass local_ob2(4);

  return 0;
}
```

It displays this output:

```
Initializing 1
Initializing 2
Initializing 3
This will not be first line displayed.
Initializing 4
Destructing 4
Destructing 3
Destructing 2
Destructing 1
```

The Scope Resolution Operator

As you know, the :: operator is used to link a class name with a member name in order to tell the compiler what class the member belongs to. However, the scope resolution operator has another related use: it can allow access to a name in an enclosing scope that is "hidden" by a local declaration of the same name. For example, consider the following fragment:

```
      .
      .
      .

int i;   // global i

void f()
{
   int i; // local i

   i = 10; // uses local i
      .
      .
      .

}

      .
      .
      .
```

However, what if function **f( )** needs to access the global version of **i**? It may do so if the **i** is preceded by the :: operator, as shown here:

```
      .
      .
      .

int i;   // global i

void f()
{
   int i; // local i

   ::i = 10; // now refers to global i
      .
      .
      .

}

      .
      .
      .
```

Nested Classes

It is possible to define one **class** within another. Doing so creates a *nested* class. Since a **class** declaration does, in fact, define a scope, a nested class is valid only within the scope of the enclosing class. Nested classes are seldom used. Because of C++'s flexible and powerful inheritance mechanism, the need for nested classes is virtually nonexistent.

Local Classes

A class may be defined within a function. For example, this is a valid C++ program:

```
#include <iostream.h>

void f();

main()
{
  f();
  // myclass not known here
  return 0;
}

void f()
{
  class myclass {
    int i;
  public:
    void put_i(int n) {i=n;}
    int get_i() {return i;}
  } ob;

  ob.put_i(10);
  cout << ob.get_i();
}
```

When a class is declared within a function, it is known only to that function and unknown outside of it.

Several restrictions apply to local classes. First, all member functions must be defined within the **class** declaration. The local class may not use or access local variables of the function in which it is declared. (Except that a local class has access to **static** local variables declared within the function.) No **static** variables may be declared inside a local class. Because of these restrictions, local classes are not common in C++ programming.

Passing Objects to Functions

Objects may be passed to functions in just the same way that any other type of variable can. Objects are passed to functions through the use of the standard call-by-value mechanism. This means that a copy of an object is made when it is passed to a function. However, the fact that a copy is created means, in essence, that another object is created. This raises the questions of whether the object's constructor function is executed when the copy is made and whether the destructor function is executed when the copy is destroyed. The answer to these two questions may surprise you. To begin, here is an example:

```cpp
#include <iostream.h>

class myclass {
  int i;
public:
  myclass(int n);
  ~myclass();
  void set_i(int n) {i=n;}
  int get_i() {return i;}
};

myclass::myclass(int n)
{
  i = n;
  cout << "Constructing " << i << "\n";
}

myclass::~myclass()
{
  cout << "Destroying " << i << "\n";
}

void f(myclass ob);

main()
{
  myclass o(1);

  f(o);
```

```
    cout << "This is i in main: ";
    cout << o.get_i() << "\n";

    return 0;
}

void f(myclass ob)
{
    ob.set_i(2);

    cout << "This is local i: " << ob.get_i();
    cout << "\n";
}
```

This program produces the following output:

```
Constructing 1
This is local i: 2
Destroying 2
This is i in main: 1
Destroying 1
```

Notice that two calls to the destructor function are executed, but only one call is made to the constructor function. As the output illustrates, the constructor function is not called when the copy of **o** (in **main( )**) is passed to **ob** (within **f( )**). The reason that the constructor function is not called when the copy of the object is made is easy to understand. When you pass an object to a function, you want the current state of that object. If the constructor is called when the copy is created, initialization will occur, possibly changing the object. Thus, the constructor function cannot be executed when the copy of an object is generated in a function call.

Although the constructor function is not called when an object is passed to a function, it is necessary to call the destructor when the copy is destroyed. (The copy is destroyed like any other local variable, when the function terminates.) Remember, the copy of the object does exist as long as the function is executing. This means that the copy could be performing operations that will require a destructor function to be called when the copy is destroyed. For example, it is perfectly valid for the copy to allocate memory that must be freed when it is destroyed. For this reason, the destructor function must be executed when the copy is destroyed.

To summarize: When a copy of an object is generated because it is passed to a function, the object's constructor function is not called. However, when the copy of the object inside the function is destroyed, its destructor function is called.

By default, when a copy of an object is made, a bitwise copy occurs. This means that the new object is an exact duplicate of the original. The fact that an exact copy is made can, at times, be a source of trouble. Even though objects are passed to functions by means of the normal call-by-value parameter passing mechanism which, in theory, protects and insulates the calling argument, it is still possible for a side effect to occur that may affect, or even damage, the object used as an argument. For example, if an object used as an argument allocates memory and frees that memory when it is destroyed, then its local copy inside the function will free the same memory when its destructor is called. This will leave the original object damaged and effectively useless. As you will see later in this book, it is possible to prevent this type of problem by defining the copy operation relative to your own classes by creating a special type of constructor called a *copy constructor*. (See Chapter 22.)

Returning Objects

A function may return an object to the caller. For example, this is a valid C++ program:

```cpp
#include <iostream.h>

class myclass {
  int i;
public:
  void set_i(int n) {i=n;}
  int get_i() {return i;}
};

myclass f();  // return object of type myclass

main()
{
  myclass o;

  o = f();

  cout << o.get_i() << "\n";

  return 0;
}

myclass f()
{
  myclass x;
```

```
    x.set_i(1);
    return x;
}
```

When an object is returned by a function, a temporary object is automatically created, which holds the return value. It is this object that is actually returned by the function. After the value has been returned, this object is destroyed. The destruction of this temporary object may cause unexpected side effects in some situations. For example, if the object returned by the function has a destructor that frees dynamically allocated memory, that memory will be freed even though the object that is receiving the return value is still using it. As you will see later in this book, there are ways to overcome this problem that involve overloading the assignment operator and defining a copy constructor.

Object Assignment

Assuming that both objects are of the same type, you can assign one object to another. This causes the data of the object on the right side to be copied into the data of the object on the left. For example, the following program displays **99**.

```
#include <iostream.h>

class myclass {
  int i;
public:
  void set_i(int n) {i=n;}
  int get_i() {return i;}
};

main()
{
  myclass ob1, ob2;

  ob1.set_i(99);
  ob2 = ob1; // assign data from ob1 to ob2

  cout << "this is ob2's i: " << ob2.get_i();

  return 0;
}
```

By default, all data from one object is assigned to the other by use of a bit-by-bit copy. However, it is possible to overload the assignment operator and define some other assignment procedure (see Chapter 14).

Chapter Thirteen

Arrays, Pointers, and References

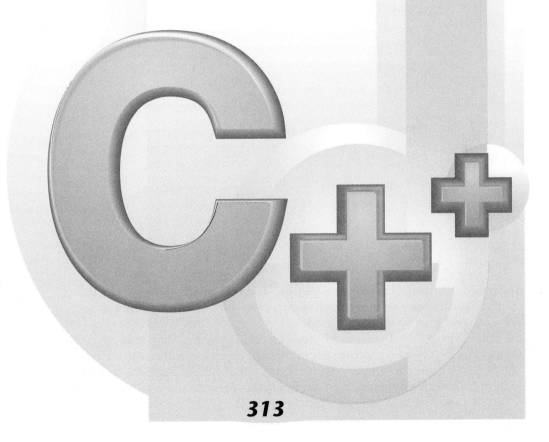

A s you know, pointers and their relatives, arrays, are important to the C language. Therefore, it should be no surprise that they are also important to the enhanced features provided by C++. In fact, pointers are so important to C++ that a new form of pointer, called a *reference*, has been added. This chapter examines arrays, pointers, and references as they relate to objects.

Arrays of Objects

In C++, it is possible to have arrays of objects. The syntax for declaring and using an object array is exactly the same as it is for any other type of variable. For example, this program uses a three-element array of objects:

```cpp
#include <iostream.h>

class cl {
  int i;
public:
  void set_i(int j) {i=j;}
  int get_i() {return i;}
};

main()
{
  cl ob[3];
  int i;

  for(i=0; i<3; i++) ob[i].set_i(i+1);

  for(i=0; i<3; i++)
    cout << ob[i].get_i() << "\n";

  return 0;
}
```

The program displays the numbers **1**, **2**, and **3** on the screen.

If a class defines a parameterized constructor, you can initialize each object in an array by specifying an initialization list like you do for other types of arrays. However, the exact form of the initialization list will be decided by the number of parameters required by the object's constructor function. For objects whose constructors take only one parameter, you can simply specify a list of initial values, using the normal array-initialization syntax. Each value in the list is passed, in order, to the constructor function as each element in the array is created. For example, here is a slightly different version of the preceding program that uses an initialization:

```
#include <iostream.h>

class cl {
  int i;
public:
  cl(int j) {i=j;}  // constructor
  int get_i() {return i;}
};

main()
{
  cl ob[3] = {1, 2, 3};  // initializers
  int i;

  for(i=0; i<3; i++)
    cout << ob[i].get_i() << "\n";

  return 0;
}
```

This program also displays the numbers **1, 2**, and **3** on the screen.

If an object's constructor requires two or more arguments, then you will have to use the slightly different initialization form, shown here:

```
#include <iostream.h>

class cl {
  int h;
  int i;
public:
  cl(int j, int k) { h=j; i=k; } // constructor
  int get_i() {return i;}
  int get_h() {return h;}
};

main()
{
```

```
cl ob[3] = {
  cl(1, 2),
  cl(3, 4),
  cl(5, 6)
}; // initializers

int i;

for(i=0; i<3; i++) {
  cout << ob[i].get_h();
  cout << ", ";
  cout << ob[i].get_i() << "\n";
}

return 0;
}
```

In this example, **cl**'s constructor has two parameters and, therefore, requires two arguments. This means that the "shorthand" initialization format cannot be used. Instead, use the "long form" shown in the example. Of course, you can use the long form in cases where the constructor requires only one argument too. It is just that the short form is easier to use when only one argument is required.

Creating Initialized Versus Uninitialized Arrays

A special-case situation occurs if you intend to create both initialized and uninitialized arrays of objects. Consider the following **class**:

```
class cl {
  int i;
public:
  cl(int j) {i=j;}
  int get_i() {return i;}
};
```

Here, the constructor function defined by **cl** requires one parameter. This implies that any array declared of this type must be initialized. That is, it precludes the following array declaration:

```
cl a[9]; // error, constructor requires initializers
```

The reason that this statement isn't valid (as **cl** is currently defined) is that it implies that **cl** has a parameterless constructor because no initializers are specified. However, as it stands, **cl** does not have a parameterless constructor. Because there is no valid constructor that corresponds to this declaration, the compiler will report an error.

To solve this problem, you need to overload the constructor function, adding one that takes no parameters. In this way, arrays that are initialized and those that are not initialized are both allowed. (Overloading is discussed in detail in Chapter 14.) For example, here is an improved version of **cl**:

```
class cl {
   int i;
public:
   cl() {i=0;}  // called for non-initialized arrays
   cl(int j) {i=j;}  // called for initialized arrays
   int get_i() {return i;}
};
```

Given this **class**, both of the following statements are permissible:

```
cl a1[3] = {3, 5, 6}; // initialized

cl a2[34]; // uninitialized
```

Pointers to Objects

Just as you can have pointers to other types of variables, you can have pointers to objects. When accessing members of a class given a pointer to an object, use the arrow (–>) operator instead of the dot operator. The next program illustrates how to access an object given a pointer to it:

```
#include <iostream.h>

class cl {
   int i;
public:
   cl(int j) {i=j;}
   int get_i() {return i;}
};

main()
{
```

```
    cl ob(88), *p;

    p = &ob;  // get address of ob

    cout << p->get_i(); // use -> to call get_i()

    return 0;
}
```

As you know, when a pointer is incremented, it points to the next element of its type. For example, an integer pointer will point to the next integer. In general, all pointer arithmetic is relative to the base type of the pointer. (That is, it is relative to the type of data that the pointer is declared as pointing to.) The same is true of pointers to objects. For example, the following program uses a pointer to access all three elements of array **ob** after being assigned **ob**'s starting address.

```
#include <iostream.h>

class cl {
    int i;
public:
    cl() {i=0;}
    cl(int j) {i=j;}
    int get_i() {return i;}
};

main()
{
    cl ob[3] = {1, 2, 3};
    cl *p;
    int i;

    p = ob;  // get start of array
    for(i=0; i<3; i++) {
        cout << p->get_i() << "\n";
        p++; // point to next object
    }

    return 0;
}
```

You can assign the address of a public member of an object to a pointer and then access that member by using the pointer. For example, this is a valid C++ program that displays the number **1** on the screen:

```
#include <iostream.h>

class cl {
public:
  int i;
  cl(int j) {i=j;}
};

main()
{
  cl ob(1);
  int *p;

  p = &ob.i;  // get address of ob.i

  cout << *p; // access ob.i via p

  return 0;
}
```

Because **p** is pointing to an integer, it is declared as an integer pointer. It is irrelevant that **i** is a member of object **ob** in this situation.

Type Checking C++ Pointers

There is one important thing to understand about pointers in C++: you may only assign one pointer to another if the two pointer types are compatible. For example, given

```
int *pi;
float *pf;
```

In C++, the following assignment is illegal.

```
pi = pf; // error--type mismatch
```

Of course, you can override any type incompatibilities using a cast, but doing so violates C++'s type-checking mechanism.

NOTE: C++'s stronger type checking where pointers are involved differs from C, in which you may assign any value to any pointer.

The this Pointer

When a member function is called, it is automatically passed an implicit argument that is a pointer to the object that generated the call (that is, the object that invoked the function). This pointer is called **this**. To understand **this**, first consider a program that creates a class called **pwr** that computes the result of a number raised to some power:

```
#include <iostream.h>

class pwr {
  double b;
  int e;
  double val;
public:
  pwr(double base, int exp);
  double get_pwr() {return val;}
};

pwr::pwr(double base, int exp)
{
  b = base;
  e = exp;
  val = 1;
  if(exp==0) return;
  for( ; exp>0; exp--) val = val * b;
}

main()
{
  pwr x(4.0, 2), y(2.5, 1), z(5.7, 0);

  cout << x.get_pwr() << " ";
  cout << y.get_pwr() << " ";
  cout << z.get_pwr() << "\n";
```

```
   return 0;
}
```

Within a member function, the members of a **class** can be accessed directly, without any object or class qualification. Thus, inside **pwr( )**, the statement

```
b = base;
```

means that the copy of **b** associated with the object that generated the call will be assigned the value contained in **base**. However, the same statement can also be written like this:

```
this->b = base;
```

Remember, the **this** pointer points to the object that invoked **pwr( )**. Thus, **this–>b** refers to that object's copy of **b**. For example, if **pwr( )** had been invoked by **x** (as in **x(4.0, 2)**), then **this** in the preceding statement would have been pointing to **x**. Keep in mind that writing the statement without using **this** is really just shorthand.

Here is the entire **pwr( )** function written using the **this** pointer:

```
pwr::pwr(double base, int exp)
{
  this->b = base;
  this->e = exp;
  this->val = 1;
  if(exp==0) return;
  for( ; exp>0; exp--)
    this->val = this->val * this->b;
}
```

Actually, no C++ programmer would write **pwr( )** as just shown because nothing is gained, and the shorthand form is easier. However, the **this** pointer is very important when operators are overloaded (see Chapter 14) and whenever a member function must utilize a pointer to the object that invoked it.

Remember, the **this** pointer is automatically passed to all member functions. Therefore, **get_pwr( )** could also be rewritten as shown here:

```
double get_pwr() {return this->val;}
```

In this case, if **get_pwr( )** is invoked like this:

```
y.get_pwr();
```

then **this** will point to object **y**.

Two final points about **this**. First, **friend** functions are not members of a class and, therefore, are not passed a **this** pointer. Second, **static** member functions do not have a **this** pointer.

Pointers to Derived Types

In general, a pointer of one type cannot point to an object of a different type. However, there is an important exception to this rule that relates only to derived classes. To begin, assume two classes called **B** and **D**. Further, assume that **D** is derived from the base class **B**. In this situation, a pointer of type **B *** may also point to an object of type **D**. More generally, a base class pointer can also be used as a pointer to an object of any class derived from that base.

Although a base class pointer can be used to point to a derived object, the opposite is not true. A pointer of type **D *** may not point to an object of type **B**. Further, although you can use a base pointer to point to a derived object, you can access only the members of the derived type that were imported from the base. That is, you won't be able to access any members added by the derived class. (You can cast a base pointer into a derived pointer and gain full access to the entire derived class, however.)

Here is a short program that illustrates this feature of C++.

```cpp
#include <iostream.h>

class base {
  int i;
public:
  void set_i(int num) {i=num;}
  int get_i() {return i;}
};

class derived: public base {
  int j;
public:
  void set_j(int num) {j=num;}
  int get_j() {return j;}
};
```

```
main()
{
  base *bp;
  derived d;

  bp = &d; // base pointer points to derived object

  // access derived object using base pointer
  bp->set_i(10);
  cout << bp->get_i() << " ";

/* This won't work. You can't access an element of
   a derived class using a base class pointer.

  bp->set_j(88);  // error
  cout << bp->get_j(); // error

*/
  return 0;
}
```

As you can see, a base pointer is used to access an object of a derived class.

Although considered poor form by most C++ programmers, it is possible to cast a base pointer into a pointer of the derived type to access a member of the derived class using the base pointer. For example, this is valid C++ code:

```
// access now allowed because of cast
((derived *)bp)->set_j(88);
cout << ((derived *)bp)->get_j();
```

It is important to remember that pointer arithmetic is relative to the base type of the pointer. For this reason, when a base pointer is pointing to a derived object, incrementing the pointer does not cause it to point to the next object of the derived type. Instead, it will point to what it thinks is the next object of the base type. For example, the following program, while syntactically correct, contains this error.

```
#include <iostream.h>

class base {
  int i;
```

```
public:
    void set_i(int num) {i=num;}
    int get_i() {return i;}
};

class derived: public base {
    int j;
public:
    void set_j(int num) {j=num;}
    int get_j() {return j;}
};

main()
{
    base *bp;
    derived d[2];

    bp = d;

    d[0].set_i(1);
    d[1].set_i(2);

    cout << bp->get_i() << " ";
    bp++;  // relative to base, not derived
    cout << bp->get_i();  // garbage value displayed

    return 0;
}
```

The use of base pointers to derived types is most useful when creating run-time polymorphism through the mechanism of virtual functions (see Chapter 16).

Pointers to Class Members

C++ allows you to generate a special type of pointer that "points" generically to a member of a class, not to a specific instance of that member in an object. This sort of pointer is called a pointer to a class member or a *pointer-to-member*, for short. A pointer to a member is not the same as a normal C++ pointer. Instead, a pointer to a member provides only an offset into an object of the member's class at which that member can be found. Since member pointers are not true pointers, the . and –> cannot be applied to them. To access a member of a class given a pointer to it, you must use the special pointer-to-member operators .* and –>*. Their job is to allow you to access a member of a class given a pointer to that member.

Here is an example:

```
#include <iostream.h>

class cl {
public:
  cl(int i) {val=i;}
  int val;
  int double_val() {return val+val;}
};

main()
{
  int cl::*data; // data member pointer
  int (cl::*func)(); // function member pointer
  cl ob1(1), ob2(2); // create objects

  data = &cl::val; // get offset of val
  func = &cl::double_val;  // get offset of double_val()

  cout << "Here are values: ";
  cout << ob1.*data << " " << ob2.*data << "\n";

  cout << "Here they are doubled: ";
  cout << (ob1.*func)() << " ";
  cout << (ob2.*func)() << "\n";

  return 0;
}
```

In **main( )**, this program creates two member pointers: **data** and **func**. Note carefully the syntax of each declaration. When declaring pointers to members, you must specify the class and use the scope resolution operator. The program also creates objects of **cl** called **ob1** and **ob2**. As the program illustrates, member pointers may point to either functions or data. Next, the program obtains the addresses of **val** and **double_val( )**. As stated earlier, these "addresses" are really just offsets into an object of type **cl**, at which point **val** and **double_val( )** will be found. Next, to display the values of each object's **val**, each is accessed through **data**. Finally, the program uses **func** to call the **double_val( )** function. The extra parentheses are necessary in order to correctly associate the .* operator.

When you are accessing a member of an object by using an object or a reference (discussed later in this chapter), you must use the .* operator. However, if you are using a pointer to the object, you need to use the ->* operator, as illustrated in the following version of the preceding program.

```cpp
#include <iostream.h>

class cl {
public:
  cl(int i) {val=i;}
  int val;
  int double_val() {return val+val;}
};

main()
{
  int cl::*data; // data member pointer
  int (cl::*func)(); // function member pointer
  cl ob1(1), ob2(2); // create objects
  cl *p1, *p2;

  p1 = &ob1;
  p2 = &ob2;

  data = &cl::val; // get offset of val
  func = &cl::double_val;  // get offset of double_val()

  cout << "Here are values: ";
  cout << p1->*data << " " << p2->*data << "\n";

  cout << "Here they are doubled: ";
  cout << (p1->*func)() << " ";
  cout << (p2->*func)() << "\n";

  return 0;
}
```

In this version, **p1** and **p2** are pointers to objects of type **cl**. Therefore, the ->* operator is used to access **val** and **double_val( )**.

Remember, pointers to members are different from pointers to specific instances of elements of an object. For example, consider the following fragment. (Assume that **cl** is declared as shown in the preceding programs.)

```
int cl::*d;
int *p;
cl o;

p = &o.val // this is address of a specific val

d = &cl::val // this is offset of generic val
```

Here, **p** is a pointer to an integer inside a *specific* object. However, **d** is simply an offset that indicates where **val** will be found in any object of type **cl**.

In general, pointer-to-member operators are applied in special-case situations. They are not typically used in day-to-day programming.

References

C++ contains a feature that is related to the pointer. This feature is called a reference. A *reference* is essentially an implicit pointer that acts as another name for an object.

Reference Parameters

One important use for a reference is to allow you to create functions that automatically use call-by-reference parameter passing rather than C++'s default call-by-value method.

As you know, in C, to create a call-by-reference you must explicitly pass the address of an argument to the function. For example, consider the following short program, which uses this approach in a function called **neg( )**, which reverses the sign of the integer variable pointed to by its argument.

```
#include <iostream.h>

void neg(int *i);

main()
{
  int x;

  x = 10;
  cout << x << " negated is ";

  neg(&x);
  cout << x << "\n";
```

```
   return 0;
}

void neg(int *i)
{
  *i = -*i;
}
```

In this program, **neg( )** takes as a parameter a pointer to the integer whose sign it will reverse. Therefore, **neg( )** is explicitly called with the address of **x**. Further, inside **neg( )** the * operator must be used to access the variable pointed to by **i**. As you know, this is how you generate a "manual" call-by-reference. However, in C++, you can automate this feature by using a reference parameter.

To create a reference parameter, precede the parameter's name with an **&**. Here is how **neg( )** is declared using a reference:

```
void neg(int &i);
```

This tells the compiler to make **i** into a reference parameter. Once this has been done, **i** essentially becomes another name for whatever argument **neg( )** is called with. That is, **i** is an implicit pointer that automatically refers to the argument used in the call to **neg( )**. Once **i** has been made into a reference, it is no longer necessary (or even legal) to apply the * operator. Instead, each time **i** is used, it is implicitly a reference to the argument. Further, when calling **neg( )**, it is no longer necessary (or legal) to precede the argument's name with the **&** operator. Instead, the compiler does this automatically. Here is the reference version of the preceding program:

```
#include <iostream.h>

void neg(int &i);  // i now a reference

main()
{
  int x;

  x = 10;
  cout << x << " negated is ";

  neg(x);  // no longer need the & operator
  cout << x << "\n";
```

```
    return 0;
}

void neg(int &i)
{
    i = -i;  // i is now a reference, don't need *
}
```

To review: When you create a reference parameter, that parameter automatically refers to (implicitly points to) the argument used to call the function. Therefore, the statement

```
    i = -i ;
```

actually operates on **x,** not on a copy of **x.** There is no need to apply the **&** operator to an argument. Also, inside the function, the reference parameter is used directly without the need to apply the ***** operator.

It is important to understand that when you assign a value to a reference, you are actually assigning that value to the variable that the reference refers to. In the case of function parameters, this will be the variable used in the call to the function.

Inside the function, it is not possible to change what the reference parameter is "pointing" to. That is, a statement like

```
    i++;
```

inside **neg( )** increments the value of the variable used in the call. It does not cause **i** to point to some new location.

Here is another example. This program uses reference parameters to swap the values of the variables it is called with. (The **swap( )** function is the classic example of call-by-reference parameter passing.)

```
#include <iostream.h>

void swap(int &i, int &j);

main()
{
    int a, b, c, d;
```

```
   a = 1;
   b = 2;
   c = 3;
   d = 4;

   cout << "a and b: " << a << " " << b << "\n";
   swap(a, b);  // no & operator needed
   cout << "a and b: " << a << " " << b << "\n";

   cout << "c and d: " << c << " " << d << "\n";
   swap(c, d);
   cout << "c and d: " << c << " " << d << "\n";

   return 0;
}

void swap(int &i, int &j)
{
   int t;

   t = i;  // no * operator needed
   i = j;
   j = t;
}
```

This program displays the following:

```
a and b: 1 2
a and b: 2 1
c and d: 3 4
c and d: 4 3
```

Passing References to Objects

In Chapter 12 it was explained that when an object is passed as an argument to a function, a copy of that object is made. Further, when the copy is made, that object's normal constructor function is *not* called. (Rather, an exact copy of the calling argument is made.) However, when the function terminates, the copy's destructor *is* called. If for some reason you do not want the destructor function to be called, simply pass the object by reference. (Later in this book you will see examples where this is the case.) When you pass by reference, no copy of the object is made. This means that no object used as a parameter is destroyed when the function terminates, and the parameter's destructor is not called. For example, try this program:

```
#include <iostream.h>

class cl {
  int id;
public:
  int i;
  cl(int i);
  ~cl();
  void neg(cl &o) {o.i = -o.i;} // no temporary created
};

cl::cl(int num)
{
  cout << "Constructing " << num << "\n";
  id = num;
}

cl::~cl()
{
  cout << "Destructing " << id << "\n";
}

main()
{
  cl o(1);

  o.i = 10;
  o.neg(o);

  cout << o.i << "\n";

  return 0;
}
```

Here is the output of the program:

```
Constructing 1
-10
Destructing 1
```

As you can see, only one call is made to **cl**'s destructor function. Had **o** been passed by value, a second object would have been created inside **neg( )**, and the destructor would have been called a second time when that object was destroyed at the time **neg( )** terminated.

When passing parameters by reference, remember that changes to the object inside the function affect the calling object.

Returning References

A function may return a reference. This has the rather startling effect of allowing a function to be used on the left side of an assignment statement! For example, consider this simple program:

```
#include <iostream.h>

char &replace(int i);  // return a reference

char s[80] = "Hello There";

main()
{

  replace(5) = 'X'; // assign X to space after Hello

  cout << s;

  return 0;
}

char &replace(int i)
{
  return s[i];
}
```

This program replaces the space between **Hello** and **There** with an **X**. That is, the program displays **HelloXThere**. Take a look at how this is accomplished.

As shown, **replace( )** is declared as returning a reference to a character array. As **replace( )** is coded, it returns a reference to the element of **s** that is specified by its argument **i**. The reference returned by **replace( )** is then used in **main( )** to assign to that element the character **X**.

Independent References

By far the most common uses for references are to pass an argument using call-by-reference and to act as a return value from a function. However, you can declare a reference that is simply a variable. This type of reference is called an *independent reference.*

When you create an independent reference, all you are creating is a second name for another variable. All independent reference variables must be initialized when they are created. The reason for this is easy to understand. Aside from initialization, you cannot change what object a reference variable points to. Therefore, it must be initialized when it is declared. (In C++, initialization is a wholly separate operation from assignment.)

The following program illustrates an independent reference.

```
#include <iostream.h>

main()
{
  int a;
  int &ref = a; // independent reference

  a = 10;
  cout << a << " " << ref << "\n";

  ref = 100;
  cout << a << " " << ref << "\n";

  int b = 19;
  ref = b; // this puts b's value into a
  cout << a << " " << ref << "\n";

  ref--;  // this decrements a
          // it does not affect what ref refers to

  cout << a << " " << ref << "\n";

  return 0;
}
```

The program displays this output:

```
10 10
100 100
19 19
18 18
```

You can use an independent reference to refer to a constant. For example,

```
int &count = 9;
```

causes **count** to point to the location in your program's constant table where the value 9 is stored.

Actually, independent references are of little real value because each one is, literally, just another name for another variable. Having two names to describe the same object is likely to confuse, not organize, your program.

Restrictions to References

There are a number of restrictions that apply to references. You cannot reference another reference. Put differently, you cannot obtain the address of a reference. You cannot create arrays of references. You cannot create a pointer to a reference. You cannot reference a bit-field.

A reference variable must be initialized when it is declared unless it is a member of a class, a function parameter, or a return value. Null references are prohibited.

A Matter of Style

When declaring pointer and reference variables, some C++ programmers use a unique coding style that associates the * or the & with the type name and not the variable. For example, here are two functionally equivalent declarations:

```
int& p; // & associated with type
int &p; // & associated with variable
```

Associating the * or & with the type name reflects the desire of some programmers for C++ to contain a separate pointer type. However, the trouble with associating the & or * with the type name rather than the variable is that, according to the formal C++ syntax, neither the & nor the * is distributive over a list of variables. Thus, misleading declarations are easily created. For example, the following declaration creates *one, not two,* integer pointers. Here, **b** is declared as an integer (not an integer pointer) because, as specified by the C++ syntax, when used in a declaration, the * (or **&**) is linked to the individual variable that it precedes, not to the type that it follows.

```
int* a, b;
```

The trouble with this declaration is that the visual message suggests that both **a** and **b** are pointer types, even though, in fact, only **a** is a pointer. This visual confusion not only misleads novice C++ programmers, but occasionally old pros too.

It is important to understand that, as far as the C++ compiler is concerned, it doesn't matter whether you write **int *p** or **int* p**. Thus, if you prefer to associate the *** or **&** with the type rather than the variable, feel free to do so. However, to avoid confusion, this book will continue to associate the *** and the **&** with the variables that they modify rather than their types.

C++'s Dynamic Allocation Operators

In C, dynamic memory allocation is achieved by using the functions **malloc( )** and **free( )**. For the sake of compatibility, the C-like dynamic allocation functions are still available in C++. However, C++ provides its own alternative dynamic allocation system based upon two operators: **new** and **delete**. As you will see, there are substantial advantages to C++'s approach to dynamic memory allocation.

The **new** operator returns a pointer to allocated memory. Like **malloc( )**, **new** allocates memory from the heap. It returns a null pointer if there is insufficient memory to fulfill the allocation request. The **delete** operator frees memory previously allocated using **new**. The general forms of **new** and **delete** are

p_var = new *type*;

delete *p_var*;

Here, *p_var* is a pointer variable that receives a pointer to memory that is large enough to hold an item of type *type*. For example, here is a program that allocates memory to hold an integer:

```
#include <iostream.h>
#include <stdlib.h>

main()
{
  int *p;

  p = new int;  // allocate space for an int

  if(!p) {
```

```
      cout << "Allocation error\n";
      exit(1);
  }

  *p = 100;

  cout << "At " << p << " ";
  cout << "is the value " << *p << "\n";

  delete p;

  return 0;
}
```

The **delete** operator must be used only with a valid pointer previously allocated by using **new**. Using any other type of pointer with **delete** is undefined and will almost certainly cause serious problems, such as a system crash.

Although **new** and **delete** perform functions similar to **malloc( )** and **free( )**, they have several advantages. First, **new** automatically allocates enough memory to hold an object of the specified type. You do not need to use the **sizeof** operator. Because the size is computed automatically, it eliminates any possibility for error in this regard. Second, **new** automatically returns a pointer of the specified type. You don't need to use an explicit type cast as you do when allocating memory by using **malloc( )**. Finally, both **new** and **delete** can be overloaded, allowing you to create customized allocation systems.

You can initialize the allocated memory to some known value by putting an initializer after the type name in the **new** statement. Here is the general form of **new** when an initialization is included:

p_var = new *var_type* (*initializer*);

For example, the following program gives the allocated integer an initial value of 87.

```
#include <iostream.h>
#include <stdlib.h>

main()
{
  int *p;
```

```
p = new int (87);   // initialize to 87

if(!p) {
  cout << "Allocation error\n";
  exit(1);
}

cout << "At " << p << " ";
cout << "is the value " << *p << "\n";

delete p;

return 0;
}
```

You can allocate arrays using **new** by using this general form:

p_var = new *array_type* [*size*];

To free an array, use this form of **delete**:

delete [ ] *p_var*;

Here, the [ ] informs **delete** that an array is being released.
For example, the next program allocates a ten-element integer array.

```
#include <iostream.h>
#include <stdlib.h>

main()
{
  int *p, i;

  p = new int [10];   // allocate 10 integer array

  if(!p) {
    cout << "Allocation error\n";
    exit(1);
  }
```

```
  for(i=0; i<10; i++ )
    p[i] = i;

  for(i=0; i<10; i++)
    cout << p[i] << " ";

  delete [] p; // release the array

  return 0;
}
```

Notice the **delete** statement. As just mentioned, when an array allocated by **new** is released, **delete** must be made aware that an array is being freed by using the [ ]. (As you will see in the next section, this is especially important when you are allocating arrays of objects.)

One restriction applies to allocating arrays: They cannot be given initial values. That is, you cannot specify an initializer when allocating arrays.

Allocating Objects

You can allocate objects dynamically by using **new**. When you do this, an object is created and a pointer is returned to it. The dynamically created object acts just like any other object. When it is created, its constructor function (if it has one) is called. When the object is freed, its destructor function is executed.

Here is a short program that creates a class called **balance** that links a person's name with his or her account balance. Inside **main( )**, an object of type **balance** is created dynamically.

```
#include <iostream.h>
#include <stdlib.h>
#include <string.h>

class balance {
  double cur_bal;
  char name[80];
public:
  void set(double n, char *s) {
    cur_bal = n;
    strcpy(name, s);
  }
```

```
    void get_bal(double &n, char *s) {
      n = cur_bal;
      strcpy(s, name);
    }
};

main()
{
  balance *p;
  char s[80];
  double n;

  p = new balance;
  if(!p) {
    cout << "Allocation error\n";
    exit(1);
  }

  p->set(12387.87, "Ralph Wilson");

  p->get_bal(n, s);

  cout << s << "'s balance is: " << n;
  cout << "\n";

  delete p;

  return 0;
}
```

Because **p** contains a pointer to an object, the arrow operator is used to access members of the object.

As stated, dynamically allocated objects may have constructors and destructors. Also, the constructor functions can be parameterized. Examine the following version of the previous program.

```
#include <iostream.h>
#include <stdlib.h>
#include <string.h>
```

```
class balance {
  double cur_bal;
  char name[80];
public:
  balance(double n, char *s) {
    cur_bal = n;
    strcpy(name, s);
  }
  ~balance() {
    cout << "Destructing ";
    cout << name << "\n";
  }
  void get_bal(double &n, char *s) {
    n = cur_bal;
    strcpy(s, name);
  }
};

main()
{
  balance *p;
  char s[80];
  double n;

  // this version uses an initializer
  p = new balance (12387.87, "Ralph Wilson");
  if(!p) {
    cout << "Allocation error\n";
    exit(1);
  }

  p->get_bal(n, s);

  cout << s << "'s balance is: " << n;
  cout << "\n";

  delete p;

  return 0;
}
```

The parameters to the object's constructor function are specified after the type name, just as in other sorts of initializations.

You can allocate arrays of objects, but there is one catch. Since no array allocated by **new** can have an initializer, you must make sure that if the **class** contains constructor functions, one will be parameterless. If you don't, the C++ compiler will not find a matching constructor when you attempt to allocate the array and will not compile your program.

In this version of the preceding program, an array of **balance** objects is allocated, and the parameterless constructor is called.

```cpp
#include <iostream.h>
#include <stdlib.h>
#include <string.h>

class balance {
  double cur_bal;
  char name[80];
public:
  balance(double n, char *s) {
    cur_bal = n;
    strcpy(name, s);
  }
  balance() {} // parameterless constructor
  ~balance() {
    cout << "Destructing ";
    cout << name << "\n";
  }
  void set(double n, char *s) {
    cur_bal = n;
    strcpy(name, s);
  }
  void get_bal(double &n, char *s) {
    n = cur_bal;
    strcpy(s, name);
  }
};

main()
{
  balance *p;
  char s[80];
  double n;
```

```
    int i;

    p = new balance [3]; // allocate entire array
    if(!p) {
      cout << "Allocation error\n";
      exit(1);
    }

    // note use of dot, not arrow operators
    p[0].set(12387.87, "Ralph Wilson");
    p[1].set(144.00, "A. C. Conners");
    p[2].set(-11.23, "I. M. Overdrawn");

    for(i=0; i<3; i++) {
      p[i].get_bal(n, s);

      cout << s << "'s balance is: " << n;
      cout << "\n";
    }

    delete [] p;
    return 0;
  }+
```

One reason that you need to use the **delete []** form when deleting an array of dynamically allocated objects is so that the destructor function can be called for each object in the array.

A final point about **new** and **delete**: Although there is no formal rule that states this, it is best not to mix **new** and **delete** with **malloc( )** and **free( )** in the same program. There is no guarantee that they are mutually compatible.

Chapter Fourteen

Function and
Operator Overloading

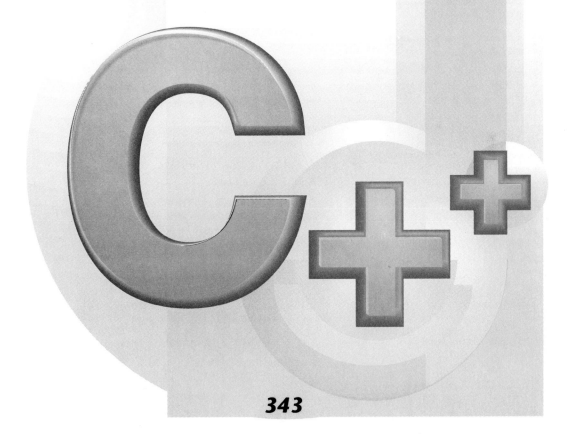

343

Function and operator overloading are crucial elements in C++ programming. Not only do these two features provide most of the support for compile-time polymorphism, they also add flexibility and extensibility to the language. For example, the overloading of the << and >> operators forms the basis of C++'s approach to I/O.

This chapter begins with function overloading and concludes by examining operator overloading. Although similar to function overloading, operator overloading introduces several nuances to the process. Therefore, before attempting to overload an operator, you should thoroughly understand function overloading.

Function Overloading

As discussed in Chapter 11, function overloading is simply the process of using the same name for two or more functions. The central point is, however, that each redefinition of the function must use either different types of parameters or a different number of parameters. It is only through these differences that the compiler knows which function to call in any given situation. For example, the following program overloads **myfunc( )** by using different types of parameters.

```
#include <iostream.h>

int myfunc(int i); // these differ in types of parameters
double myfunc(double i);

main()
{

  cout << myfunc(10) << " "; // calls myfunc(int i)
  cout << myfunc(5.4); // calls myfunc(double i)

  return 0;
}

double myfunc(double i)
{
  return i;
}

int myfunc(int i)
{
  return i;
}
```

The next program overloads **myfunc( )** using a different number of parameters.

```
#include <iostream.h>

int myfunc(int i);  // these differ in number of parameters
int myfunc(int i, int j);

main()
{
  cout << myfunc(10) << " "; // calls myfunc(int i)
  cout << myfunc(4, 5); // calls myfunc(int i, int j)

  return 0;
}

int myfunc(int i)
{
  return i;
}

int myfunc(int i, int j)
{
  return i*j;
}
```

As mentioned, the key point about function overloading is that the functions must differ in regard to the types or number of parameters. Two functions differing only in their return types cannot be overloaded. For example, this is an invalid attempt to overload **myfunc( )**:

```
int myfunc(int i);  // Error: differing return types are
float myfunc(int i);  // insufficient when overloading.
```

Sometimes, two function declarations will appear to differ, when in fact, they do not. For example, consider the following declarations:

```
void f(int *p);
void f(int p[]); // error, *p is same as p[]
```

Remember, to the compiler ***p** is the same as **p[]**. Therefore, although the two prototypes appear to differ in the types of their parameter, in actuality they do not.

Function Overloading and Ambiguity

You can create a situation in which the compiler is unable to choose between two (or more) overloaded functions. When this happens, the situation is said to be *ambiguous*. Ambiguous statements are errors, and programs containing ambiguity will not compile.

By far the main cause of ambiguity involves C++'s automatic type conversions. As you know, C++ automatically attempts to convert the arguments used to call a function into the type of arguments expected by the function. For example, consider this fragment:

```
int myfunc(double d);
  .
  .
  .
cout << myfunc('c');  // not an error, conversion applied
```

As the comment indicates, this is not an error because C++ automatically converts the character **c** into its **double** equivalent. In C++, very few type conversions of this sort are actually disallowed. Although automatic type conversions are convenient, they are also a prime cause of ambiguity. For example, consider the following program:

```
#include <iostream.h>

float myfunc(float i);
double myfunc(double i);

main()
{
  cout << myfunc(10.1) << " "; // unambiguous, calls myfunc(double)
  cout << myfunc(10);  // ambiguous

  return 0;
}

float myfunc(float i)
{
  return i;
}

double myfunc(double i)
{
  return -i;
}
```

Here, **myfunc( )** is overloaded so that it can take arguments of either type **float** or type **double**. In the unambiguous line, **myfunc(double)** is called because, unless explicitly specified as **float**, all floating-point constants in C++ are automatically of type **double**. Hence, that call is unambiguous. However, when **myfunc( )** is called by using the integer 10, ambiguity is introduced because the compiler has no way of knowing whether it should be converted to a **float** or to a **double**. This causes an error message to be displayed, and the program will not compile.

As the preceding example illustrates, it is not the overloading of **myfunc( )** relative to **double** and **float** that causes the ambiguity. Rather, it is the specific call to **myfunc( )** using an indeterminate type of argument that causes the confusion. Put differently, the error is not caused by the overloading of **myfunc( )**, but by the specific invocation.

Here is another example of ambiguity caused by C++'s automatic type conversions:

```
#include <iostream.h>

char myfunc(unsigned char ch);
char myfunc(char ch);

main()
{
  cout << myfunc('c');  // this calls myfunc(char)
  cout << myfunc(88) << " "; // ambiguous

  return 0;
}

char myfunc(unsigned char ch)
{
  return ch-1;
}

char myfunc(char ch)
{
  return ch+1;
}
```

In C++, **unsigned char** and **char** are *not* inherently ambiguous. However, when **myfunc( )** is called by using the integer 88, the compiler does not know which function to call. That is, should 88 be converted into a **char** or an **unsigned char**?

Another way you can cause ambiguity is by using default arguments in overloaded functions. (Default arguments are discussed in Chapter 21.) To see how, examine the following program:

```
#include <iostream.h>

int myfunc(int i);
int myfunc(int i, int j=1);

main()
{
  cout << myfunc(4, 5) << " ";  // unambiguous
  cout << myfunc(10);  // ambiguous

  return 0;
}

int myfunc(int i)
{
  return i;
}

int myfunc(int i, int j)
{
  return i*j;
}
```

Here, in the first call to **myfunc( )**, two arguments are specified; therefore, no ambiguity is introduced and **myfunc(int i, int j)** is called. However, when the second call to **myfunc( )** is made, ambiguity occurs because the compiler does not know whether to call the version of **myfunc( )** that takes one argument or to apply the default to the version that takes two arguments.

Some types of overloaded functions are simply inherently ambiguous even if, at first, they may not seem so. For example, consider this program:

```
// This program contains an error.
#include <iostream.h>

void f(int x);
void f(int &x); // error

main()
{
  int a=10;

  f(a); // error, which f()?
```

```
   return 0;
}

void f(int x)
{
  cout << "In f(int)\n";
}

void f(int &x)
{
  cout << "In f(int &)\n";
}
```

As the comments in the program describe, two functions cannot be overloaded when the only difference is that one takes a reference parameter and the other takes a normal, call-by-value parameter. In this situation, the compiler has no way of knowing which version of the function is intended when it is called. Remember, there is no difference in the way that an argument is specified when it will be received by a reference parameter or a value parameter.

The overload Anachronism

When C++ was created, the keyword **overload** was required to create an overloaded function. Although it is no longer needed and is considered obsolete, it is usually accepted by C++ compilers for the sake of compatibility with older C++ programs. (However, there is no requirement that guarantees this.) Because you might encounter older programs or perhaps find yourself in a situation where only an old C++ compiler is available, it is a good idea to know how **overload** was used. Here is its general form:

overload *func-name*;

Here, *func-name* is the name of the function that you will be overloading. This statement must precede the overloaded declarations. For example, this tells an old-style compiler that you will be overloading a function called **test( )**:

```
overload test;
```

Because **overload** is an anachronism, you should avoid its use in C++ programs that you create.

Overloading Constructor Functions

Aside from performing the special role of initialization, constructor functions are no different from other types of functions. This includes overloading. In fact, it is very common to find overloaded constructor functions. For example, consider the following program, which creates a **class** called **date** that holds a calendar date. Notice that the constructor is overloaded two ways.

```
#include <iostream.h>
#include <stdio.h>

class date {
  int day, month, year;
public:
  date(char *d);
  date(int m, int d, int y);
  void show_date();
};

// Initialize using string.
date::date(char *d)
{
  sscanf(d, "%d%*c%d%*c%d", &month, &day, &year);
}

// Initialize using integers.
date::date(int m, int d, int y)
{
  day = d;
  month = m;
  year = y;
}

void date::show_date()
{
  cout << month << "/" << day;
  cout << "/" << year << "\n";
}

main()
{
  date ob1(12, 4, 96), ob2("10/22/97");
```

```
   ob1.show_date();
   ob2.show_date();

   return 0;
}
```

In this program, you can initialize an object of type **date**, either by specifying the date using three digits to represent the month, day, and year, or by using a string that contains the date in this general form:

mm/dd/yy

The most common reason to overload a constructor is to allow an object to be created by using the most appropriate and natural means for each circumstance. For example, in the following **main( )**, the user is prompted for the date, which is input to array **s**. This string can then be used directly to create **d**. There is no need for it to be converted to any other form. However, if **date( )** were not overloaded to accept the string form, you would have to manually convert it into three integers each time you created an object.

```
main()
{
  char s[80];

  cout << "Enter new date: ";
  cin >> s;

  date d(s);
  d.show_date();

  return 0;
}
```

In another situation, initializing an object of type **date** by using three integers may be more convenient. For example, if the date is generated by some sort of computational method, then creating a **date** object using **date(int, int, int)** is the most natural and appropriate constructor to employ. The point here is that by overloading **date**'s constructor, you have made it more flexible and easier to use. This increased flexibility and ease of use are especially important if you are creating class libraries that will be used by other programmers.

> **NOTE:** C++ defines a special type of overloaded constructor, called a copy
> constructor, that allows you to determine how objects are copied under certain
> circumstances. Copy constructors are discussed later in this book.

Finding the Address of an Overloaded Function

As you know, in C you can assign the address of a function to a pointer and then call
that function by using the pointer. The same feature also exists in C++. However,
because of function overloading, this process is a little more complex. To understand
why, first consider the following statement, which assigns the address of some
function called **myfunc( )** to a pointer called **p.**

```
p = myfunc;
```

If this is part of a C program, then there is one and only one function called **myfunc( )**,
and the compiler has no difficulty assigning its address to **p.** However, if this statement is
part of a C++ program, then **myfunc( )** might be overloaded. Assuming that it is, how
does the compiler know which function's address to assign to **p**? The answer is that it
depends upon how **p** is declared. For example, consider this program:

```
#include <iostream.h>

int myfunc(int a);
int myfunc(int a, int b);

main()
{
  int (*fp)(int a);   // pointer to int xxx(int)

  fp = myfunc;   // points to myfunc(int)

  cout << fp(5);

  return 0;
}

int myfunc(int a)
{
```

```
  return a;
}

int myfunc(int a, int b)
{
  return a*b;
}
```

As the program illustrates, **fp** is declared as a pointer to a function that returns an integer and that takes one integer argument. C++ uses this information to select the **myfunc(int a)** version of **myfunc( )**.

Had **fp** been declared like this,

```
int (*fp)(int a, int b);
```

then **fp** would have been assigned the address of the **myfunc(int a, int b)** version of **myfunc( )**.

To review: When you assign the address of an overloaded function to a function pointer, it is the declaration of the pointer that determines which function's address is assigned. Further, the declaration of the function pointer must exactly match one and only one of the overloaded function's declarations.

Operator Overloading

Closely related to function overloading is operator overloading. In C++, you can overload most operators so that they perform special operations relative to classes that you create. For example, a **class** that maintains a stack might overload + to perform a push operation and – – to perform a pop. When an operator is overloaded, none of its original meanings are lost. Instead, the type of objects it can be applied to is expanded.

You overload operators by creating **operator** functions. An **operator** function defines the specific operations that the overloaded operator will perform relative to the class it is designed to work on. **operator** functions can be either members or nonmembers of the class that they will operate on. Nonmember **operator** functions are almost always **friend** functions of the class, however. The way **operator** functions are written differs between member and **friend** functions. Therefore, each will be examined separately, beginning with member **operator** functions.

Creating a Member operator Function

Member **operator** functions take this general form:

ret-type class-name::operator#(*arg-list*)
{
  // operations
}

Often, **operator** functions return an object of the class they operate on, but *ret-type* can be any valid type. The **#** is a placeholder. When you create an **operator** function, substitute the operator for the **#**. For example, if you are overloading the **/** operator, use **operator/**. When you are overloading a unary operator, *arg-list* will be empty. When you are overloading binary operators, *arg-list* will contain one parameter. (The reasons for this seemingly unusual situation will be made clear in a moment.)

Shown next is a simple first example of operator overloading. This program creates a **class** called **loc**, which stores longitude and latitude values. It overloads the **+** operator relative to this **class**. Examine the program carefully, paying special attention to the definition of **operator+( )**.

```
#include <iostream.h>

class loc {
  int longitude, latitude;
public:
  loc() {}
  loc(int lg, int lt) {
    longitude = lg;
    latitude = lt;
  }

  void show() {
    cout << longitude << " ";
    cout << latitude << "\n";
  }

  loc operator+(loc op2);
};

loc loc::operator+(loc op2)
{
  loc temp;
```

```
   temp.longitude = op2.longitude + longitude;
   temp.latitude = op2.latitude + latitude;

   return temp;
}

main()
{
  loc ob1(10, 20), ob2( 5, 30);

  ob1.show(); // displays 10 20
  ob2.show(); // displays 5 30

  ob1 = ob1 + ob2;
  ob1.show(); // displays 15 50

  return 0;
}
```

As you can see, **operator+( )** has only one parameter even though it overloads the binary + operator. (You might expect two parameters corresponding to the two operands of a binary operator.) The reason that **operator+( )** takes only one parameter is that the operand on the left side of the + is passed implicitly to the function using the **this** pointer. The operand on the right is passed in the parameter **op2**. The fact that the left operand is passed using **this** also implies one important point: when binary operators are overloaded, it is the object on the left that generates the call to the **operator** function.

As mentioned, it is common for an overloaded **operator** function to return an object of the class it operates upon. By doing so, it allows the operator to be used in larger C++ expressions. For example, if the **operator+( )** function returned some other type, this expression would not have been valid:

```
ob1 = ob1 + ob2;
```

In order for the sum of **ob1** and **ob2** to be assigned to **ob1**, the outcome of that operation must be an object of type **loc**.

Further, having **operator+( )** return an object of type **loc** makes possible the following statement:

```
(ob1+ob2).show();   // displays outcome of ob1+ob2
```

In this situation, **ob1+ob2** generates a temporary object that ceases to exist after the call to **show( )** terminates.

It is important to understand that an **operator** function can return any type, and that the type returned depends solely upon your specific application. It is just that, often, an **operator** function will return an object of the class upon which it operates.

One last point about the **operator+( )** function: It does not modify either operand. Because the traditional use of the + operator does not modify either operand, it makes sense for the overloaded version not to do so either. (For example, 5+7 yields 12, but neither 5 nor 7 is changed.) Also, relative to how it is used by the **loc class**, **operator+( )** should not alter either operand. Although you are free to perform any operation you want inside an **operator** function, it is usually best to stay within the context of the normal use of the operator.

The next program adds three additional overloaded operators to the **loc class**: the **–**, the **=**, and the unary **++**. Pay special attention to how these functions are defined.

```
#include <iostream.h>

class loc {
  int longitude, latitude;
public:
  loc() {} // needed to construct temporaries
  loc(int lg, int lt) {
    longitude = lg;
    latitude = lt;
  }

  void show() {
    cout << longitude << " ";
    cout << latitude << "\n";
  }

  loc operator+(loc op2);
  loc operator-(loc op2);
  loc operator=(loc op2);
  loc operator++();
};

loc loc::operator+(loc op2)
{
  loc temp;
```

```
    temp.longitude = op2.longitude + longitude;
    temp.latitude = op2.latitude + latitude;

    return temp;
}

loc loc::operator-(loc op2)
{
  loc temp;

  // notice order of operands
  temp.longitude = longitude - op2.longitude;
  temp.latitude = latitude - op2.latitude;

  return temp;
}

loc loc::operator=(loc op2)
{
  longitude = op2.longitude;
  latitude = op2.latitude;

  return *this; // i.e., return object that generated call
}

loc loc::operator++()
{
  longitude++;
  latitude++;

  return *this;
}

main()
{
  loc ob1(10, 20), ob2( 5, 30), ob3(90, 90);

  ob1.show();
  ob2.show();
```

```
    ++ob1;
    ob1.show();  // displays 11 21

    ob2 = ++ob1;
    ob1.show(); // displays 12 22
    ob2.show(); // displays 12 22

    ob1 = ob2 = ob3; // multiple assignment
    ob1.show(); // displays 90 90
    ob2.show(); // displays 90 90

    return 0;
}
```

First, examine the **operator–( )** function. Notice the order of the operands in the subtraction. In keeping with the meaning of subtraction, the operand on the right side of the minus sign is subtracted from the operand on the left. Because it is the object on the left that generates the call to the **operator–( )** function, **op2**'s data must be subtracted from the data pointed to by **this**. It is important to remember which operand generates the call to the function.

In C++, if the = is not overloaded, a default assignment operation is created automatically for any class you define. The default assignment is simply a member-by-member copy. However, by overloading the =, you can define explicitly what the assignment does relative to a class. In this example, the overloaded = does exactly the same thing as the default, but in other situations, it could perform other operations. Notice that the **operator=( )** function returns ***this**, which is the object that generated the call. This arrangement is necessary if you want to be able to use multiple assignment statements such as this:

```
    ob1 = ob2 = ob3;   // multiple assignment
```

Finally, look at the definition of **operator++( )**. As you can see, it takes no parameters. Since **++** is a unary operator, its only operand is implicitly passed by using the **this** pointer.

Notice that both **operator=( )** and **operator++( )** alter the value of an operand. In the case of assignment, the operand on the left (the one generating the call to the **operator=( )** function) is assigned a new value. In the case of the **++**, the operand is incremented. As stated previously, although you are free to make these functions do anything you please, it is almost always wisest to stay consistent with their original meanings.

Creating Prefix and Postfix Forms of the Increment and Decrement Operators

In the preceding program, only the prefix form of the increment operator was overloaded relative to the **loc class**. In older versions of C++, it was not possible to determine whether an overloaded **++** or **– –** preceded or followed its operand. For example, assuming some object called **O**, these two statements were identical:

```
O++;
++O;
```

However, modern versions of C++ provide a means for determining whether an increment or decrement prefixes or postfixes its operand. To accomplish this, define two versions of the **operator++( )** function. One is defined as shown in the foregoing program. The other is declared like this:

```
loc operator++(int x);
```

If the **++** precedes its operand, the **operator++( )** function is called. If the **++** follows its operand, the **operator++(int x)** is called and **x** has the value zero.

The preceding example can be generalized. Here are the general forms for the prefix and postfix **++** and **– –** operator functions:

```
// Prefix increment
type operator++( ) {
  // body of prefix operator
}

// Postfix increment
type operator++(int x) {
  // body of postfix operator
}

// Prefix decrement
type operator– – ( ) {
  // body of prefix operator
}

// Postfix decrement
type operator– – (int x) {
  // body of postfix operator
}
```

Overloading the Shorthand Operators

You can overload any of C++'s "shorthand" operators, such as +=, – =, and the like. For example, this function overloads += relative to **loc**:

```
loc loc::operator+=(loc op2)
{
  longitude = op2.longitude + longitude;
  latitude = op2.latitude + latitude;

  return *this;
}
```

When overloading one of these operators, keep in mind that you are simply combining an assignment with another type of operation.

Operator Overloading Restrictions

There are some restrictions that apply to operator overloading. You cannot alter the precedence of an operator. You cannot change the number of operands that an operator takes. (You can choose to ignore an operand, however.) Operator functions cannot have default arguments. Finally, these operators cannot be overloaded:

.   ::   .*   ?

Remember that technically you are free to perform any activity inside an **operator** function. For example, if you want to overload the + operator in such a way that it writes **I like C++** ten times to a disk file, you can do so. However, when you stray significantly from the default meaning of an operator, you run the risk of dangerously destructuring your program. For example, when someone reading your program sees a statement like **Ob1+Ob2**, he or she expects something resembling addition to be taking place—not a disk access, for example. Therefore, before decoupling an overloaded operator from its default meaning, be sure that you have sufficient reason to do so. One good example where decoupling is successful is found in the way C++ overloads the << and >> operators for I/O. Although the I/O operations have no relationship to bit shifting, these operators provide a visual "clue" as to their meaning relative to both I/O and bit shifting, and this decoupling works. In general, however, it is best to stay within the context of the default meaning of an operator when overloading it.

Except for the = operator, **operator** functions are inherited by any derived **class**. However, a derived **class** is free to overload any operator (including those overloaded by the base **class**) it chooses relative to itself.

Operator Overloading Using a Friend

Before looking at some examples of overloading more exotic operators, such as the [] or **new** and **delete**, a short diversion that examines operator overloading using a **friend** function is in order.

You can overload an operator relative to a class by using a **friend** function. Since a **friend** is not a member of the class, it does not have a **this** pointer. Therefore, an overloaded **friend operator** function is passed the operands explicitly. This means that a **friend** that overloads a binary operator has two parameters, and a **friend** that overloads a unary operator has one parameter. When overloading a binary operator, the left operand is passed in the first parameter and the right operand is passed in the second parameter of the **friend operator** function.

In the following program, the **operator+( )** function is made into a **friend**.

```
#include <iostream.h>

class loc {
  int longitude, latitude;
public:
  loc() {} // needed to construct temporaries
  loc(int lg, int lt) {
    longitude = lg;
    latitude = lt;
  }

  void show() {
    cout << longitude << " ";
    cout << latitude << "\n";
  }

  friend loc operator+(loc op1, loc op2);  // now a friend
  loc operator-(loc op2);
  loc operator=(loc op2);
  loc operator++();
};

// now, + is overloaded using friend function
loc operator+(loc op1, loc op2)
{
  loc temp;

  temp.longitude = op1.longitude + op2.longitude;
  temp.latitude = op1.latitude + op2.latitude;
```

```
  return temp;
}

loc loc::operator-(loc op2)
{
  loc temp;

  // notice order of operands
  temp.longitude = longitude - op2.longitude;
  temp.latitude = latitude - op2.latitude;

  return temp;
}

loc loc::operator=(loc op2)
{
  longitude = op2.longitude;
  latitude = op2.latitude;

  return *this; // i.e., return object that generated call
}

loc loc::operator++()
{
  longitude++;
  latitude++;

  return *this;
}

main()
{
  loc ob1(10, 20), ob2( 5, 30);

  ob1 = ob1 + ob2;
  ob1.show();

  return 0;
}
```

There are some restrictions that apply to **friend operator** functions. First, you may not overload the =, ( ), [], or –> operators by using a **friend** function. Second, as explained in the next section, when overloading the increment or decrement operators, you will need to use a reference parameter when using a **friend** function.

Using a friend to Overload ++ or --

If you want to use a **friend** function to overload the increment or decrement operators, you must pass the operand as a reference parameter. This is because **friend** functions do not have **this** pointers. Assuming that you stay true to the original meaning of the ++ and -- operators, these operations imply the modification of the operand they operate upon. However, if you overload these operators by using a **friend**, then the operand is passed by value as a parameter. This means that a **friend operator** function has no way to modify the operand. Since the **friend operator** function is not passed a **this** pointer to the operand, but rather a copy of the operand, no changes made to that parameter affect the operand that generated the call. However, you can remedy this situation by specifying the parameter to the **friend operator** function as a reference parameter. This causes any changes made to the parameter inside the function to affect the operand that generated the call. For example, the following program uses **friend** functions to overload the prefix versions of ++ and -- operators relative to the **loc class**.

```
#include <iostream.h>

class loc {
  int longitude, latitude;
public:
  loc() {}
  loc(int lg, int lt) {
    longitude = lg;
    latitude = lt;
  }

  void show() {
    cout << longitude << " ";
    cout << latitude << "\n";
  }

  loc operator=(loc op2);
  friend loc operator++(loc &op);
  friend loc operator--(loc &op);
};

loc loc::operator=(loc op2)
{
```

```cpp
    longitude = op2.longitude;
    latitude = op2.latitude;

    return *this; // i.e., return object that generated call
}

// now a friend - use a reference parameter
loc operator++(loc &op)
{
  op.longitude++;
  op.latitude++;

  return op;
}

// make op-- a friend - use reference
loc operator--(loc &op)
{
  op.longitude--;
  op.latitude--;

  return op;
}

main()
{
  loc ob1(10, 20), ob2;

  ob1.show();
  ++ob1;
  ob1.show(); // displays 11 21

  ob2 =  ++ob1;
  ob2.show(); // displays 12 22

  --ob2;
  ob2.show(); // displays 11 21
  return 0;
}
```

If you want to overload the postfix versions of the increment and decrement operators using a **friend**, simply specify a second, dummy integer parameter. For example, this shows the prototype for the **friend** postfix version of the increment operator relative to **loc**:

```
// friend, postfix version of ++
friend loc operator++(loc &op, int x);
```

Friend Operator Functions Add Flexibility

In many cases, whether you overload an operator by using a **friend** or a member function makes no functional difference. In those cases, to preserve the greatest degree of encapsulation, it is best to overload by using member functions. However, there is one situation in which overloading by using a **friend** increases the flexibility of an overloaded operator. Let's examine this case now.

As you know, when you overload a binary operator by using a member function, the object on the left side of the operator generates the call to the overloaded **operator** function. Further, a pointer to that object is passed in the **this** pointer. Now, assume some class called **CL** that has addition of an object to an integer defined via an overloaded member **operator** function. Given an object of that class called **Ob**, the following expression is valid.

Ob + 100 // valid

In this case, **Ob** generates the call to the overloaded **+** function, and the addition is performed. But what happens if the expression is written like this?

100 + Ob // invalid

In this case, it is the integer that appears on the left. Since an integer is a built-in type, no operation between an integer and an object of **Ob**'s type is defined. Therefore, the compiler will not compile this expression. As you can imagine, in some applications, having to always position the object on the left could be a significant burden and cause of frustration.

The solution to the preceding problem is to overload addition using a **friend**, not a member, function. When this is done, both arguments are explicitly passed to the **operator** function. Therefore, to allow both *object+integer* and *integer+object*, simply overload the function twice—one version for each situation. Thus, when you overload an operator by using two **friend** functions, the object may appear on either the left or right side of the operator.

This program illustrates how **friend** functions are used to define an operation that involves an object and built-in type.

```
#include <iostream.h>

class loc {
  int longitude, latitude;
public:
  loc() {}
  loc(int lg, int lt) {
    longitude = lg;
    latitude = lt;
  }

  void show() {
    cout << longitude << " ";
    cout << latitude << "\n";
  }

  loc operator+(loc op2);
  friend loc operator+(loc op1, int op2);
  friend loc operator+(int op1, loc op2);
};

loc loc::operator+(loc op2)
{
  loc temp;

  temp.longitude = op2.longitude + longitude;
  temp.latitude = op2.latitude + latitude;

  return temp;
}

// + is overloaded for loc + int
loc operator+(loc op1, int op2)
{
  loc temp;

  temp.longitude = op1.longitude + op2;
  temp.latitude = op1.latitude + op2;

  return temp;
}

// + is overloaded for int + loc
loc operator+(int op1, loc op2)
{
```

```
  loc temp;

  temp.longitude = op1 + op2.longitude;
  temp.latitude = op1 + op2.latitude;

  return temp;
}

main()
{
  loc ob1(10, 20), ob2( 5, 30), ob3(7, 14);

  ob1.show();
  ob2.show();
  ob3.show();

  ob1 = ob2 + 10;   // both of these
  ob3 = 10 + ob2;   // are valid

  ob1.show();
  ob3.show();

  return 0;
}
```

Overloading new and delete

It is possible to overload **new** and **delete**. You might choose to do this if you want to use some special allocation method. For example, you may want allocation routines that automatically begin using a disk file as virtual memory when the heap has been exhausted. Whatever the reason, it is a very simple matter to overload these operators.

The skeletons for the functions that overload **new** and **delete** are shown here:

```
void *operator new(size_t size)
{
  // perform allocation
  return pointer_to_memory;
}

void operator delete(void *p)
{
  // free memory pointed to by p
}
```

The type **size_t** is defined as a type capable of containing the largest single piece of memory that can be allocated. **size_t** is an unsigned integer type. The parameter **size** will contain the number of bytes needed to hold the object being allocated. The overloaded **new** function must return a pointer to the memory that it allocates, or zero if an allocation error occurs. Beyond these constraints, the overloaded **new** function can do anything else you require.

The **delete** function receives a pointer to the region of memory to free. It then releases the previously allocated memory back to the system.

The **new** and **delete** operators may be overloaded globally so that all uses of these operators call your custom versions. They may also be overloaded relative to one or more classes. Let's begin with an example of overloading **new** and **delete** relative to a class. For the sake of simplicity, no new allocation scheme will be used. Instead, the overloaded functions will simply invoke **malloc( )** and **free( )**. (In your own application, you may, of course, implement any alternative allocation scheme you like.)

To overload the **new** and **delete** operators relative to a class, simply make the overloaded **operator** functions class members. For example, here the **new** and **delete** operators are overloaded for the **loc class**:

```
#include <iostream.h>
#include <stdlib.h>

class loc {
  int longitude, latitude;
public:
  loc() {}
  loc(int lg, int lt) {
    longitude = lg;
    latitude = lt;
  }

  void show() {
    cout << longitude << " ";
    cout << latitude << "\n";
  }

  void *operator new(size_t size);
  void operator delete(void *p);
};

// new overloaded relative to loc
void *loc::operator new(size_t size)
{
  cout << "In my new\n";
```

```
   return malloc(size);
}

// delete overloaded relative to loc
void loc::operator delete(void *p)
{
  cout << "In my delete\n";
  free(p);
}

main()
{
  loc *p1, *p2;

  p1 = new loc (10, 20);
  if(!p1) {
    cout << "Allocation error\n";
    exit(1);
  }

  p2 = new loc (-10, -20);
  if(!p2) {
    cout << "Allocation error\n";
    exit(1);
  }

  p1->show();
  p2->show();

  delete p1;
  delete p2;

  return 0;
}
```

When **new** and **delete** are overloaded relative to a specific **class**, the use of these operators on any other type of data causes the original **new** or **delete** to be employed. The overloaded operators are only applied to the types for which they are defined. This means that if you add the following line to **main( )**, the default **new** will be executed.

```
int *f = new float;  // uses default new
```

You can overload **new** and **delete** globally by overloading these operators outside of any **class** declaration. When **new** and **delete** are overloaded globally, C++'s default **new** and **delete** are ignored, and the new operators are used for all allocation requests. Of course, if you have defined any versions of **new** and **delete** relative to one or more classes, then the class-specific versions are used when allocating objects of the class for which they are defined. In other words, when either **new** or **delete** is encountered, the compiler first checks to see whether they are defined relative to the **class** they are operating on. If so, those specific versions are used. If not, C++ uses the globally defined **new** and **delete**. If these have been overloaded, then the overloaded versions are used.

To see an example of overloading **new** and **delete** globally, examine this program:

```
#include <iostream.h>
#include <stdlib.h>

class loc {
  int longitude, latitude;
public:
  loc() {}
  loc(int lg, int lt) {
    longitude = lg;
    latitude = lt;
  }

  void show() {
    cout << longitude << " ";
    cout << latitude << "\n";
  }
};

// Global new
void *operator new(size_t size)
{
  return malloc(size);
}

// Global delete
void operator delete(void *p)
{
  free(p);
}

main()
```

```
{
  loc *p1, *p2;

  p1 = new loc (10, 20);
  if(!p1) {
    cout << "Allocation error\n";
    exit(1);
  }
  p2 = new loc (-10, -20);
  if(!p2) {
    cout << "Allocation error\n";
    exit(1);
  }

  float *f = new float; // uses overloaded new, too
  if(!f) {
    cout << "Allocation error\n";
    exit(1);
  }

  *f = 10.10;
  cout << *f << "\n";

  p1->show();
  p2->show();

  delete p1;
  delete p2;
  delete f;  // uses overloaded delete

  return 0;
}
```

Run this program to prove to yourself that the built-in **new** and **delete** operators have, indeed, been overloaded.

Overloading new and delete for Arrays

If you want to be able to allocate arrays of objects using your own allocation system, you will need to overload **new** and **delete** a second time. To allocate and free arrays, you must use these forms of **new** and **delete**:

```
// Allocate an array of objects.
void *operator new[](size_t size)
{
  // Perform allocation.
  return pointer_to_memory;
}

// Delete an array of objects.
void operator delete[](void *p)
{
  /* Free memory pointed to by p.
     Destructor for each element automatically
     called.
  */
}
```

When an array is allocated, the constructor function for each object in the array is automatically called. When an array is freed, each object's destructor is automatically called. You do not have to provide explicit code to accomplish these actions.

The following program allocates and frees an object and an array of objects of type **loc**.

```
#include <iostream.h>
#include <stdlib.h>

class loc {
  int longitude, latitude;
public:
  loc() {longitude = latitude = 0;}
  loc(int lg, int lt) {
    longitude = lg;
    latitude = lt;
  }

  void show() {
    cout << longitude << " ";
    cout << latitude << "\n";
  }

  void *operator new(size_t size);
  void operator delete(void *p);
```

```
    void *operator new[](size_t size);
    void operator delete[](void *p);
};

// new overloaded relative to loc
void *loc::operator new(size_t size)
{
  cout << "In my new\n";
  return malloc(size);
}

// delete overloaded relative to loc
void loc::operator delete(void *p)
{
  cout << "In my delete\n";
  free(p);
}

// new overloaded relative to loc for arrays
void *loc::operator new[](size_t size)
{
  cout << "Allocating array using my new[]\n";
  return malloc(size);
}

// delete overloaded relative to loc for arrays
void loc::operator delete[](void *p)
{
  cout << "Freeing array using my delete[]\n";
  free(p);
}

main()
{
  loc *p1, *p2;
  int i;

  p1 = new loc (10, 20); // allocate an object
  if(!p1) {
    cout << "Allocation error\n";
    exit(1);
```

```
  }

  p2 = new loc [10]; // allocate an array
  if(!p2) {
    cout << "Allocation error\n";
    exit(1);
  }

  p1->show();

  for(i=0; i<10; i++)
    p2[i].show();

  delete p1; // free an object
  delete [] p2; // free an array

  return 0;
}
```

Overloading Some Special Operators

C++ (and its predecessor, C) defines array subscripting, function calling, and de-referencing as operations. The operators that perform these functions are the [], ( ), and –>, respectively. These rather exotic operators may be overloaded in C++, opening up some very interesting uses.

One important restriction applies to overloading these three operators: they must be non-static member functions. They cannot be **friend**s.

Overloading [ ]

In C++, the [] is considered a binary operator when you are overloading it. Therefore, the general form of a member **operator[]( )** function is as shown here:

type class–name::operator[](int *i*)
{
  // ...
}

Technically, the parameter does not have to be of type **int**, but an **operator[]( )** function is typically used to provide array subscripting, and as such, an integer value is generally used.

Given an object called **O**, the expression

```
O[3]
```

translates into this call to the **operator[]( )** function:

```
operator[](3)
```

That is, the value of the expression within the subscripting operator is passed to the **operator[]( )** function in its explicit parameter. The **this** pointer will point to **O**, the object that generated the call.

In the following program, **atype** declares an array of three integers. Its constructor function initializes each member of the array to the specified values. The overloaded **operator[]( )** function returns the value of the array as indexed by the value of its parameter.

```
#include <iostream.h>

class atype {
  int a[3];
public:
  atype(int i, int j, int k) {
    a[0] = i;
    a[1] = j;
    a[2] = k;
  }
  int operator[](int i) {return a[i];}
};

main()
{
  atype ob(1, 2, 3);

  cout << ob[1];  // displays 2

  return 0;
}
```

You can design the **operator[]( )** function in such a way that the [] can be used on both the left and right sides of an assignment statement. To do this, simply specify the return value of **operator[]( )** as a reference. The following program makes this change and shows its use.

```
#include <iostream.h>

class atype {
  int a[3];
public:
  atype(int i, int j, int k) {
    a[0] = i;
    a[1] = j;
    a[2] = k;
  }
  int &operator[](int i) {return a[i];}
};

main()
{
  atype ob(1, 2, 3);

  cout << ob[1];  // displays 2
  cout << " ";

  ob[1] = 25;  // [] on left of =

  cout << ob[1];  // now displays 25

  return 0;
}
```

Because **operator[]( )** now returns a reference to the array element indexed by **i**, it can be used on the left side of an assignment to modify an element of the array. (Of course, it can still be used on the right side as well.)

One advantage of being able to overload the [] operator is that it allows a means of implementing safe array indexing in C++. As you know, in C++, it is possible to overrun (or underrun) an array boundary at run time without generating a run-time error message.

However, if you create a class that contains the array, and allow access to that array only through the overloaded [] subscripting operator, then you can intercept an out-of-range index. For example, the following program adds a range check to the preceding program and proves that it works.

```
// A safe array example.
#include <iostream.h>
```

```
#include <stdlib.h>

class atype {
  int a[3];
public:
  atype(int i, int j, int k) {
    a[0] = i;
    a[1] = j;
    a[2] = k;
  }
  int &operator[](int i);
};

// Provide range checking for atype.
int &atype::operator[](int i)
{
  if(i<0 || i> 2) {
    cout << "Boundary Error\n";
    exit(1);
  }
  return a[i];
}

main()
{
  atype ob(1, 2, 3);

  cout << ob[1];   // displays 2
  cout << " ";

  ob[1] = 25;  // [] appears on left
  cout << ob[1];   // displays 25

  ob[3] = 44; // generates runtime error, 3 out-of-range
  return 0;
}
```

In this program, when the statement

```
ob[3] = 44;
```

executes, the boundary error is intercepted by **operator[]( )**, and the program is terminated before any damage can be done. (In actual practice, some sort of error-handling function would be called to deal with the out-of-range condition; the program would not have to terminate.)

Overloading ( )

When you overload the **( )** function call operator, you are not, per se, creating a new way to call a function. Rather, you are creating an **operator** function that can be passed an arbitrary number of parameters. Let's begin with an example. Given the overloaded **operator** function declaration

```
double operator()(int a, float f, char *s);
```

and an object **O** of its **class**, then the statement

```
O(10, 23.34, "hi");
```

translates into this call to the **operator( )** function:

```
operator()(10, 23.34, "hi");
```

In general, when you overload the **( )** operator, you define the parameters that you want to pass to that function. When you use the **( )** operator in your program, the arguments you specify are copied to those parameters. As always, the object that generates the call (**O** in this example) is pointed to by the **this** pointer.

Here is an example of overloading **( )** relative to the **loc class**. It assigns the value of its two arguments to the longitude and latitude of the object it is applied to.

```
#include <iostream.h>

class loc {
  int longitude, latitude;
public:
  loc() {}
  loc(int lg, int lt) {
    longitude = lg;
    latitude = lt;
  }

  void show() {
```

```
    cout << longitude << " ";
    cout << latitude << "\n";
  }

  loc operator+(loc op2);
  loc operator()(int i, int j);
};

loc loc::operator()(int i, int j)
{
  longitude = i;
  latitude = j;

  return *this;
}

loc loc::operator+(loc op2)
{
  loc temp;

  temp.longitude = op2.longitude + longitude;
  temp.latitude = op2.latitude + latitude;

  return temp;
}

main()
{
  loc ob1(10, 20), ob2(1, 1);

  ob1.show();
  ob1(7, 8);   // can be executed by itself
  ob1.show();

  ob1 = ob2 + ob1(10, 10);   // can be used in expressions
  ob1.show();

  return 0;
}
```

REMEMBER: *When overloading ( ), you can use any type of parameters and return any type of value. These types will be dictated by the demands of your programs.*

Overloading –>

The –> pointer operator is considered a unary operator when overloading. Its general usage is shown here:

object–>element;

Here, *object* is the object that activates the call. The **operator–>( )** function must return a pointer to an object of the class that **operator–>( )** operates upon. The *element* must be some element accessible within the object returned by **operator–>( )**.

The following program illustrates overloading the –> by showing the equivalence between **ob.i** and **ob–>i** when **operator–>( )** returns the **this** pointer.

```
#include <iostream.h>

class myclass {
public:
  int i;
  myclass *operator->() {return this;}
};

main()
{
  myclass ob;

  ob->i = 10;   // same as ob.i

  cout << ob.i << " " << ob->i;

  return 0;
}
```

Overloading the Comma Operator

You can overload C++'s comma operator. The comma is a binary operator, and like all overloaded operators, you may make an overloaded comma perform any operation you want. However, if you want the overloaded comma to perform in a fashion similar to its normal operation, the overloaded comma must discard the value of the left-hand operand and make the right-hand operand the value of the comma operation. In a comma-separated list, all but the rightmost operand must be discarded. As you know, this is the way the comma works by default in C++.

Here is a program that illustrates the effect of overloading the comma operator in its default manner of operation.

```
#include <iostream.h>

class loc {
  int longitude, latitude;
public:
  loc() {}
  loc(int lg, int lt) {
    longitude = lg;
    latitude = lt;
  }

  void show() {
    cout << longitude << " ";
    cout << latitude << "\n";
  }

  loc operator+(loc op2);
  loc operator,(loc op2);
};

loc loc::operator,(loc op2)
{
  loc temp;

  temp.longitude = op2.longitude;
  temp.latitude = op2.latitude;
  cout << op2.longitude << " " << op2.latitude << "\n";

  return temp;
}

loc loc::operator+(loc op2)
{
  loc temp;

  temp.longitude = op2.longitude + longitude;
  temp.latitude = op2.latitude + latitude;

  return temp;
}

main()
{
```

```
    loc ob1(10, 20), ob2( 5, 30), ob3(1, 1);

    ob1.show();
    ob2.show();
    ob3.show();
    cout << "\n";

    ob1 = (ob1, ob2+ob2, ob3);

    ob1.show();   // displays 1 1, the value of ob3
    return 0;
}
```

This program displays the following output:

```
10 20
5 30
1 1

10 60
1 1
1 1
```

Notice that although the values of the left-hand operands are discarded, each expression is still executed by the compiler so that any desired side effects will be performed.

Remember, the left-hand operand is passed via **this**, and its value is discarded by the **operator,( )** function. The value of the right-hand operation is returned by the function. This causes the overloaded comma to behave similarly to its default operation. If you want the overloaded comma to do something else, you will have to change these two features.

Chapter Fifteen

Inheritance

Inheritance is one of the cornerstones of OOP because it allows the creation of hierarchical classifications. Using inheritance, you can create a general class that defines traits common to a set of related items. This class may then be inherited by other more specific classes, each adding only those things that are unique to the inheriting class.

In keeping with standard C++ terminology, a class that is inherited is referred to as a *base class*. The class that does the inheriting is called the *derived class*. Further, a derived class can be used as a base class for another derived class. In this way, multiple inheritance is achieved.

C++'s support of inheritance is both rich and flexible. Inheritance was introduced in Chapter 11. It is examined in detail here.

Base Class Access Control

As you know, when a class inherits another, it uses this general form:

```
class derived-class-name : access base-class-name {
  // body of class
};
```

When one class inherits another, the members of the base class become members of the derived class. The access status of the base class members inside the derived class is determined by *access*. The base class access specifier must be either **public**, **private**, or **protected**. If no access specifier is present, the access specifier is **private** by default if the derived class is a **class**. If the derived class is a **struct**, then **public** is the default in the absence of an explicit access specifier. Let's examine the ramifications of using **public** or **private** access. (The **protected** specifier is examined in the next section.)

When the access specifier for a base class is **public**, all public members of the base become public members of the derived class, and all protected members of the base become protected members of the derived class. In all cases, the base's private elements remain private to the base and are not accessible by members of the derived class. For example, as illustrated in the following program, objects of type **derived** can directly access the public members of **base**.

```
#include <iostream.h>

class base {
  int i, j;
public:
  void set(int a, int b) {i=a; j=b;}
  void show() { cout << i << " " << j << "\n";}
};
```

```
class derived : public base {
  int k;
public:
  derived(int x) {k=x;}
  void showk() {cout << k << "\n";}
};

main()
{
  derived ob(3);

  ob.set(1, 2); // access member of base
  ob.show();   // access member of base

  ob.showk(); // uses member of derived class

  return 0;
}
```

When the base class is inherited by using the **private** access-specifier, all public and protected members of the base class become private members of the derived class. For example, the following program will not even compile because both **set( )** and **show( )** are now private elements of **derived**.

```
// This program won't compile.
#include <iostream.h>

class base {
  int i, j;
public:
  void set(int a, int b) {i=a; j=b;}
  void show() { cout << i << " " << j << "\n";}
};

// Public elements of base are private in derived.
class derived : private base {
  int k;
public:
  derived(int x) {k=x;}
  void showk() {cout << k << "\n";}
};
```

```
main()
{
  derived ob(3);

  ob.set(1, 2); // error, can't access set()
  ob.show(); // error, can't access show()

  return 0;
}
```

REMEMBER: *When a base class' access specifier is **private**, public and protected members of the base become private members of the derived class. This means that they are still accessible by members of the derived class but cannot be accessed by parts of your program that are not members of either the base or derived class.*

Inheritance and protected Members

The **protected** keyword is included in C++ to provide greater flexibility in the inheritance mechanism. When a member of a class is declared as **protected**, that member is not accessible by other, nonmember, elements of the program. With one important exception, access to a protected member is the same as access to a private member—it can be accessed only by other members of its class. The sole exception to this is when a protected member is inherited. In this case, a protected member differs substantially from a private one.

As you know from the preceding section, a private member of a base class is not accessible by other parts of your program, including any derived class. However, protected members behave differently. If the base class is inherited as **public**, then the base class' protected members become protected members of the derived class and are, therefore, accessible by the derived class. In other words, by using **protected**, you can create class members that are private to their class but that can still be inherited and accessed by a derived class. Here is an example:

```
#include <iostream.h>

class base {
protected:
  int i, j; // private to base, but accessible by derived
public:
  void set(int a, int b) {i=a; j=b;}
  void show() { cout << i << " " << j << "\n";}
```

```
};

class derived : public base {
  int k;
public:
  // derived may access base's i and j
  void setk() {k=i*j;}

  void showk() {cout << k << "\n";}
};

main()
{
  derived ob;

  ob.set(2, 3);   // OK, known to derived
  ob.show(); // OK, known to derived

  ob.setk();
  ob.showk();
  return 0;
}
```

Here, because **base** is inherited by **derived** as public and because **i** and **j** are declared as **protected**, **derived**'s function **setk( )** may access them. If **i** and **j** had been declared as **private** by **base**, then **derived** would not have access to them, and the program would not compile.

When a derived class is used as a base class for another derived class, then any protected member of the initial base class that is inherited (as public) by the first derived class may also be inherited as protected again by a second derived class. For example, the following program is correct, and **derived2** does, indeed, have access to **i** and **j**.

```
#include <iostream.h>

class base {
protected:
  int i, j;
public:
  void set(int a, int b) {i=a; j=b;}
  void show() { cout << i << " " << j << "\n";}
};
```

```
// i and j inherited as protected.
class derived1 : public base {
  int k;
public:
  void setk() {k = i*j;} // legal
  void showk() {cout << k << "\n";}
};

// i and j inherited indirectly through derived1.
class derived2 : public derived1 {
  int m;
public:
  void setm() {m = i-j;} // legal
  void showm() {cout << m << "\n";}
};

main()
{
  derived1 ob1;
  derived2 ob2;

  ob1.set(2, 3);
  ob1.show();
  ob1.setk();
  ob1.showk();

  ob2.set(3, 4);
  ob2.show();
  ob2.setk();
  ob2.setm();
  ob2.showk();
  ob2.showm();

  return 0;
}
```

If, however, **base** were inherited as **private**, then all members of **base** would become private members of **derived1**, which means that they would not be accessible by **derived2**. (However, **i** and **j** would still be accessible by **derived1**.) This situation is illustrated by the following program, which is in error (and won't compile). The comments describe each error.

```
// This program won't compile.
#include <iostream.h>

class base {
protected:
  int i, j;
public:
  void set(int a, int b) {i=a; j=b;}
  void show() { cout << i << " " << j << "\n";}
};

// Now, all elements of base are private in derived1.
class derived1 : private base {
  int k;
public:
  // this is legal because i and j are private to derived1
  void setk() {k = i*j;}  // OK
  void showk() {cout << k << "\n";}
};

// Access to i, j, set(), and show() not inherited.
class derived2 : public derived1 {
  int m;
public:
  // illegal because i and j are private to derived1
  void setm() {m = i-j;}  // error
  void showm() {cout << m << "\n";}
};

main()
{
  derived1 ob1;
  derived2 ob2;

  ob1.set(1, 2);  // error, can't use set()
  ob1.show();  // error, can't use show()

  ob2.set(3, 4);  // error, can't use set()
  ob2.show();  // error, can't use show()

  return 0;
}
```

*NOTE: Even though **base** is inherited as **private** by **derived1**, **derived1** still has access to **base**'s **public** and **protected** elements. However, it cannot pass along this privilege.*

Protected Base Class Inheritance

It is possible to inherit a base class as **protected**. When this is done, all public and protected members of the base class become protected members of the derived class. Here is an example:

```
#include <iostream.h>

class base {
protected:
  int i, j; // private to base, but accessible by derived
public:
  void setij(int a, int b) {i=a; j=b;}
  void showij() { cout << i << " " << j << "\n";}
};

// Inherit base as protected.
class derived : protected base{
  int k;
public:
  // derived may access base's i and j and setij().
  void setk() {setij(10, 12); k = i*j;}

  // may access showij() here
  void showall() {cout << k << " "; showij();}
};

main()
{
  derived ob;

//  ob.setij(2, 3);  // illegal, setij() is
//                      protected member of derived

  ob.setk(); // OK, public member of derived
  ob.showall(); // OK, public member of derived
```

```
// ob.showij(); // illegal, showij() is protected
//                member of derived

    return 0;
}
```

As you can see by reading the comments, even though **setij( )** and **showij( )** are public members of **base**, they become protected members of **derived** when it is inherited using the **protected** access specifier. This means that they will not be accessible inside **main( )**.

Inheriting Multiple Base Classes

It is possible for a derived class to inherit two or more base classes. For example, here **derived** inherits both **base1** and **base2**:

```
// An example of multiple base classes.

#include <iostream.h>

class base1 {
protected:
   int x;
public:
   void showx() {cout << x << "\n";}
};

class base2 {
protected:
   int y;
public:
   void showy() {cout << y << "\n";}
};

// Inherit multiple base classes.
class derived: public base1, public base2 {
public:
   void set(int i, int j) {x=i; y=j;}
};

main()
```

```
{
  derived ob;

  ob.set(10, 20); // provided by derived
  ob.showx();  // from base1
  ob.showy();  // from base2

  return 0;
}
```

As the example illustrates, to inherit more than one base class, use a comma-separated list. Further, be sure to use an access specifier for each base inherited.

Constructors, Destructors, and Inheritance

There are two major questions that arise relative to constructors and destructors when inheritance is involved. First, when are base class and derived class constructor and destructor functions called? Second, how can parameters be passed to base class constructor functions? This section examines these two important topics.

When Constructor and Destructor Functions Are Executed

It is possible for a base class, a derived class, or both to contain constructor and/or destructor functions. It is important to understand the order in which these functions are executed when an object of a derived class comes into existence and when it goes out of existence. To begin, examine this short program:

```
#include <iostream.h>

class base {
public:
  base() {cout << "Constructing base\n";}
  ~base() {cout << "Destructing base\n";}
};

class derived: public base {
public:
```

```
    derived() {cout << "Constructing derived\n";}
    ~derived() {cout << "Destructing derived\n";}
};

main()
{
  derived ob;

  // do nothing but construct and destruct ob

  return 0;
}
```

As the comment in **main( )** indicates, this program simply constructs and then destroys an object called **ob** that is of class **derived**. When executed, this program displays

```
Constructing base
Constructing derived
Destructing derived
Destructing base
```

As you can see, first **base**'s constructor is executed followed by **derived**'s. Next (because **ob** is immediately destroyed in this program), **derived**'s destructor is called, followed by **base**'s.

The results of the foregoing experiment can be generalized. When an object of a derived class is created, if the base class contains a constructor, it will be called first, followed by the derived class' constructor. When a derived object is destroyed, its destructor is called first, followed by the base class' destructor, if it exists. Put differently, constructor functions are executed in their order of derivation. Destructor functions are executed in reverse order of derivation.

If you think about it, it makes sense that constructor functions are executed in order of derivation. Because a base class has no knowledge of any derived class, any initialization it needs to perform is separate from and possibly prerequisite to any initialization performed by the derived class. Therefore, it must be executed first.

Likewise, it is quite sensible that destructors be executed in reverse order of derivation. Because the base class underlies the derived class, the destruction of the base object implies the destruction of the derived object. Therefore, the derived destructor must be called before the object is fully destroyed.

In cases of multiple inheritance (that is, where a derived class becomes the base class for another derived class), the general rule applies: Constructors are called in order of derivation, destructors in reverse order. For example, this program

```
#include <iostream.h>

class base {
public:
  base() {cout << "Constructing base\n";}
  ~base() {cout << "Destructing base\n";}
};

class derived1 : public base {
public:
  derived1() {cout << "Constructing derived1\n";}
  ~derived1() {cout << "Destructing derived1\n";}
};

class derived2: public derived1 {
public:
  derived2() {cout << "Constructing derived2\n";}
  ~derived2() {cout << "Destructing derived2\n";}
};

main()
{
  derived2 ob;

  // construct and destruct ob

  return 0;
}
```

displays this output:

```
Constructing base
Constructing derived1
Constructing derived2
Destructing derived2
Destructing derived1
Destructing base
```

The same general rule applies in situations involving multiple base classes. For example, this program

```
#include <iostream.h>

class base1 {
public:
  base1() {cout << "Constructing base1\n";}
  ~base1() {cout << "Destructing base1\n";}
};

class base2 {
public:
  base2() {cout << "Constructing base2\n";}
  ~base2() {cout << "Destructing base2\n";}
};

class derived: public base1, public base2 {
public:
  derived() {cout << "Constructing derived\n";}
  ~derived() {cout << "Destructing derived\n";}
};

main()
{
  derived ob;

  // construct and destruct ob

  return 0;
}
```

produces this output:

```
Constructing base1
Constructing base2
Constructing derived
Destructing derived
Destructing base2
Destructing base1
```

As you can see, constructors are called in order of derivation—left to right—as specified in **derived**'s inheritance list. Destructors are called in reverse order—right to left. This means that had **base2** been specified before **base1** in **derived**'s list, as shown here:

```
class derived: public base2, public base1 {
```

then the output of this program would have looked like this:

```
Constructing base2
Constructing base1
Constructing derived
Destructing derived
Destructing base1
Destructing base2
```

Passing Parameters to Base Class Constructors

So far, none of the preceding examples have included constructor functions that require arguments. In cases where only the derived class constructor requires one or more parameters, you simply use the standard parameterized constructor syntax (see Chapter 12). However, how do you pass arguments to a constructor function in a base class? The answer is to use an expanded form of the derived class' constructor declaration that passes along arguments to one or more base class constructors. The general form of the expanded derived class constructor declaration is shown here:

derived-constructor(arg-list) : base1(arg-list),
                          base2(arg-list),

                          .

                          .

                          .

                          baseN(arg-list)
{
   // body of derived constructor
}

Here, *base1* through *baseN* are the names of the base classes inherited by the derived class. Notice that a colon separates the derived class constructor function declaration from the base classes, and that the base classes are separated from each other by commas, in the case of multiple base classes. Consider this program:

```
#include <iostream.h>

class base {
protected:
  int i;
public:
  base(int x) {i=x; cout << "Constructing base\n";}
  ~base() {cout << "Destructing base\n";}
};

class derived: public base {
  int j;
public:
  // derived uses x; y is passed along to base.
  derived(int x, int y): base(y)
    {j=x; cout << "Constructing derived\n";}

  ~derived() {cout << "Destructing derived\n";}
  void show() {cout << i << " " << j << "\n";}
};

main()
{
  derived ob(3, 4);

  ob.show();   // displays 4 3

  return 0;
}
```

Here, **derived**'s constructor is declared as taking two parameters, **x** and **y**. However, **derived( )** uses only **x**; **y** is passed along to **base( )**. In general, the derived class' constructor must declare both the parameter(s) that it requires as well as any required by the base class. As the example illustrates, any parameters required by the base class are passed to it in the base class' constructor specified after the colon.

Here is an example that uses multiple base classes:

```
#include <iostream.h>

class base1 {
protected:
  int i;
public:
```

```
    base1(int x) {i=x; cout << "Constructing base1\n";}
    ~base1() {cout << "Destructing base1\n";}
};

class base2 {
protected:
    int k;
public:
    base2(int x) {k=x; cout << "Constructing base2\n";}
    ~base2() {cout << "Destructing base1\n";}
};

class derived: public base1, public base2 {
    int j;
public:
    derived(int x, int y, int z): base1(y), base2(z)
        {j=x; cout << "Constructing derived\n";}

    ~derived() {cout << "Destructing derived\n";}
    void show() {cout << i << " " << j << " " << k << "\n";}
};

main()
{
    derived ob(3, 4, 5);

    ob.show();  // displays 4 3 5

    return 0;
}
```

It is important to understand that arguments to a base class constructor are passed via arguments to the derived class' constructor. Therefore, even if a derived class' constructor does not use any arguments, it will still need to declare one or more if the base class takes one or more arguments. In this situation, the arguments passed to the derived class are simply passed along to the base. For example, in the following program, the derived class' constructor takes no arguments, but **base1( )** and **base2( )** do.

```
#include <iostream.h>

class base1 {
```

```
protected:
  int i;
public:
  base1(int x) {i=x; cout << "Constructing base1\n";}
  ~base1() {cout << "Destructing base1\n";}
};

class base2 {
protected:
  int k;
public:
  base2(int x) {k=x; cout << "Constructing base2\n";}
  ~base2() {cout << "Destructing base2\n";}
};

class derived: public base1, public base2 {
public:
  /* Derived constructor uses no parameter,
     but still must be declared as taking them to
     pass them along to base classes.
  */

  derived(int x, int y): base1(x), base2(y)
    {cout << "Constructing derived\n";}

  ~derived() {cout << "Destructing derived\n";}
  void show() {cout << i << " " << k << "\n";}
};

main()
{
  derived ob(3, 4);

  ob.show();  // displays 3 4

  return 0;
}
```

A derived class' constructor function is free to make use of any and all parameters that it is declared as taking even if one or more are passed along to a base class. Put differently, an argument that is passed along to a base class does not preclude its use by the derived class as well. For example, this fragment is perfectly valid:

```
class derived: public base {
   int j;
public:
   // derived uses both x and y and then passes them to base.
   derived(int x, int y): base(x, y)
      {j = x*y; cout << "Constructing derived\n";}
```

One final point to keep in mind when passing arguments to base class constructors: the argument can consist of any expression valid at the time. This includes function calls and variables. This is in keeping with the fact that C++ allows dynamic initialization.

Granting Access

When a base class is inherited as **private**, all public and protected members of that class become private members of the derived class. However, in certain circumstances, you may want to restore one or more inherited members to their original access specification. For example, you might want to grant certain public members of the base class public status in the derived class even though the base class is inherited as **private**. To do this, you must use an *access declaration* within the derived class. An access declaration takes this general form:

base-class::member;

The access declaration is put under the appropriate access heading in the derived class' declaration. Notice that no type declaration is required (or, indeed, allowed) in an access declaration.

To see how an access declaration works, let's begin with this short fragment:

```
class base {
public:
   int j;  // public in base
};


// Inherit base as private.
class derived: private base {
public:

   // here is access declaration
   base::j; // make j public again

   .

   .

   .

};
```

As you know, because **base** is inherited as **private** by **derived**, the public variable **j** is made a private variable of **derived** by default. However, if

```
base::j;
```

is included as the access declaration under **derived**'s **public** heading, **j** is restored to its public status.

You can use an access declaration to restore the access rights of public and protected members. However, you cannot use an access declaration to raise or lower a member's access status. For example, a member declared as private to a base class cannot be made public by a derived class. (If C++ allowed this to occur, it would destroy its encapsulation mechanism!)

The following program illustrates the access declaration.

```
#include <iostream.h>

class base {
  int i;  // private to base
public:
  int j, k;
  void seti(int x) {i = x;}
  int geti() {return i;}
};

// Inherit base as private.
class derived: private base {
public:
  /* The next three statements override
     base's inheritance as private and restore j,
     seti(), and geti() to public access. */
  base::j; // make j public again - but not k
  base::seti; // make seti() public
  base::geti; // make geti() public

// base::i;  // illegal, you cannot elevate access

  int a; // public
};

main()
{
  derived ob;
```

```
//ob.i = 10;  // illegal because i is private in derived

  ob.j = 20;  // legal because j is made public in derived
//ob.k = 30;  // illegal because k is private in derived

  ob.a = 40;  // legal because a is public in derived
  ob.seti(10);

  cout << ob.geti() << " " << ob.j << " " << ob.a;

  return 0;
}
```

Notice how this program uses access declarations to restore **j**, **seti( )**, and **geti( )** to public status.

Access declarations are supported in C++ to accommodate those situations in which most of an inherited class is intended to be made private, but a few members are to retain their public or protected status.

NOTE: *Although the proposed ANSI C++ standard still supports access declarations, it has deprecated them. This means that while they are allowed now, they might not be supported in subsequent versions of the standard. Instead, the standard suggests achieving the same effect by applying the **using** keyword. (The **using** statement is discussed later in this book.) However, at the time of this writing, access declarations are still widely used, and no commonly available compilers accept the **using** keyword.*

Virtual Base Classes

An element of ambiguity can be introduced into a C++ program when multiple base classes are inherited. For example, consider this incorrect program:

```
// This program contains an error and will not compile.
#include <iostream.h>

class base {
public:
  int i;
};

// derived1 inherits base.
class derived1 :  public base {
```

```
public:
  int j;
};

// derived2 inherits base.
class derived2 : public base {
public:
  int k;
};

/* derived3 inherits both derived1 and derived2.
   This means that there are two copies of base
   in derived3! */
class derived3 : public derived1, public derived2 {
public:
  int sum;
};

main(void)
{
  derived3 ob;

  ob.i = 10;   // this is ambiguous, which i???
  ob.j = 20;
  ob.k = 30;

  // i ambiguous here, too
  ob.sum = ob.i + ob.j + ob.k;

  // also ambiguous, which i?
  cout << ob.i << " ";

  cout << ob.j << " " << ob.k << " ";
  cout << ob.sum;

  return 0;
}
```

As the comments in the program indicate, both **derived1** and **derived2** inherit **base**. However, **derived3** inherits both **derived1** and **derived2**. This means that there are two copies of **base** present in an object of type **derived3**. Therefore, in an expression like

```
ob.i = 20;
```

which **i** is being referred to—the one in **derived1** or the one in **derived2**? Because there are two copies of **base** present in object **ob**, there are two **ob.i**s! As you can see, the statement is inherently ambiguous.

There are two ways to remedy the preceding program. The first is to apply the scope resolution operator to **i** and manually select one **i**. For example, this version of the program does compile and run as expected:

```
// This program uses explicit scope resolution to select i.
#include <iostream.h>

class base {
public:
  int i;
};

// derived1 inherits base.
class derived1 :  public base {
public:
  int j;
};

// derived2 inherits base.
class derived2 : public base {
public:
  int k;
};

/* derived3 inherits both derived1 and derived2.
   This means that there are two copies of base
   in derived3! */
class derived3 : public derived1, public derived2 {
public:
  int sum;
};

main(void)
{
  derived3 ob;
```

```
    ob.derived1::i = 10;   // scope resolved, use derived1's i
    ob.j = 20;
    ob.k = 30;

    // scope resolved
    ob.sum = ob.derived1::i + ob.j + ob.k;

    // also resolved here
    cout << ob.derived1::i << " ";

    cout << ob.j << " " << ob.k << " ";
    cout << ob.sum;

    return 0;
}
```

As you can see, because the **::** was applied, the program has manually selected
derived2's version of **base**. However, this solution raises a deeper issue: what if only
one copy of **base** is actually required? Is there some way to prevent two copies from
being included in **derived3**? The answer, as you probably have guessed, is yes. This
solution is achieved using **virtual** base classes.

When two or more objects are derived from a common base class, you can prevent
multiple copies of the base class from being present in an object derived from those
objects by declaring the base class as **virtual** when it is inherited. You accomplish this
by preceding the base class' name with the keyword **virtual** when it is inherited. For
example, here is another version of the example program in which **derived3** contains
only one copy of **base**:

```
// This program uses virtual base classes.
#include <iostream.h>

class base {
public:
  int i;
};

// derived1 inherits base as virtual.
class derived1 : virtual public base {
public:
  int j;
```

```
};

// derived2 inherits base as virtual.
class derived2 : virtual public base {
public:
  int k;
};

/* derived3 inherits both derived1 and derived2.
   This time, there is only one copy of base class. */
class derived3 : public derived1, public derived2 {
public:
  int sum;
};

main(void)
{
  derived3 ob;

  ob.i = 10;  // now unambiguous
  ob.j = 20;
  ob.k = 30;

  // unambiguous
  ob.sum = ob.i + ob.j + ob.k;

  // unambiguous
  cout << ob.i << " ";

  cout << ob.j << " " << ob.k << " ";
  cout << ob.sum;

  return 0;
}
```

As you can see, the keyword **virtual** precedes the rest of the inherited class' access specification. Now that both **derived1** and **derived2** have inherited **base** as **virtual**, any multiple inheritance involving them will cause only one copy of **base** to be present. Therefore, in **derived3**, there is only one copy of **base**; therefore **ob.i = 10** is perfectly valid and unambiguous.

One further point to keep in mind: even though both **derived1** and **derived2** specify **base** as **virtual**, **base** is still present in any objects of either type. For example, the following sequence is perfectly valid.

```
// define a class of type derived1
derived1 myclass;

myclass.i = 88;
```

The only difference between a normal base class and a virtual one is when an object inherits the base more than once. If virtual base classes are used, then only one base class is present in the object. Otherwise, multiple copies will be found.

Chapter Sixteen

Virtual Functions
and Polymorphism

olymorphism (one interface, multiple methods) is supported by C++ both at compile time and at run time. Compile-time polymorphism, supported by overloaded functions and operators, was discussed in Chapter 14. Run-time polymorphism is accomplished by using inheritance and virtual functions, and these are the topics of this chapter.

Virtual Functions

A *virtual function* is a function that is declared as **virtual** in a base class and redefined by a derived class. To declare a function as virtual, its declaration is preceded by the keyword **virtual**. The redefinition of the function in the derived class overrides the definition of the function in the base class. In essence, a virtual function declared in the base class acts as a placeholder that specifies a general class of actions and stipulates the form of the interface. The redefinition of the virtual function by a derived class provides the actual operations performed by the function. Put differently, a virtual function defines a general class of actions. The redefined virtual function implements a specific method.

When accessed "normally," virtual functions behave just like any other type of class member function. However, what makes virtual functions important and capable of supporting run-time polymorphism is how they behave when accessed via a pointer. As discussed in Chapter 13, a base class pointer can be used to point to any class derived from that base. When a base pointer points to a derived object that contains a virtual function, C++ determines which version of that function to call based upon *the type of object pointed to* by the pointer. Thus, when different objects are pointed to, different versions of the virtual function are executed.

Before discussing any more theory, examine this short example:

```
#include <iostream.h>

class base {
public:
  virtual void vfunc() {
    cout << "This is base's vfunc().\n";
  }
};

class derived1 : public base {
public:
  void vfunc() {
    cout << "This is derived1's vfunc().\n";
  }
};
```

```
class derived2 : public base {
public:
  void vfunc() {
    cout << "This is derived2's vfunc().\n";
  }
};

main()
{
  base *p, b;
  derived1 d1;
  derived2 d2;

  // point to base
  p = &b;
  p->vfunc(); // access base's vfunc()

  // point to derived1
  p = &d1;
  p->vfunc(); // access derived1's vfunc()

  // point to derived2
  p = &d2;
  p->vfunc(); // access derived2's vfunc()

  return 0;
}
```

This program displays the following:

> This is base's vfunc( ).
> This is derived1's vfunc( ).
> This is derived2's vfunc( ).

As the program illustrates, inside **base**, the virtual function **vfunc( )** is declared. Notice that the keyword **virtual** precedes the rest of the function declaration. When **vfunc( )** is redefined by **derived1** and **derived2**, the keyword **virtual** is not needed. (However, it is not an error to include it when redefining a virtual function inside a derived class.)

In this program, **base** is inherited by both **derived1** and **derived2**. Inside each class definition, **vfunc( )** is redefined relative to that class. Inside **main( )**, four variables are declared:

Name	Type
p	Base class pointer
b	Object of base
d1	Object of derived1
d2	Object of derived2

Next, **p** is assigned the address of **b**, and **vfunc( )** is called via **p**. Since **p** is pointing to an object of type **base**, that version of **vfunc( )** is executed. Next, **p** is set to the address of **d1**, and again **vfunc( )** is called by using **p**. This time **p** points to an object of type **derived1**. This causes **derived1::vfunc( )** to be executed. Finally, **p** is assigned the address of **d2**, and **p–>vfunc( )** causes the version of **vfunc( )** redefined inside **derived2** to be executed. The key point here is that the kind of object to which **p** points determines which version of **vfunc( )** is executed. Further, this determination is made at run time, and this process forms the basis for run-time polymorphism.

Although you can call a virtual function in the "normal" manner by using an object's name and the dot operator, it is only when access is through a base class pointer that run-time polymorphism is achieved. For example, assuming the preceding example, this is syntactically valid:

```
d2.vfunc(); // calls derived2's vfunc()
```

Although calling a virtual function in this manner is not wrong, it simply does not take advantage of the virtual nature of **vfunc( )**.

At first glance, the redefinition of a virtual function by a derived class appears similar to function overloading. However, this is not the case and the term *overloading* is not applied to virtual function redefinition because several differences exist. Perhaps the most important is that the prototype for a redefined virtual function must match exactly the prototype specified in the base class. This differs from overloading a normal function, in which return types and the number and type of parameters may differ. (In fact, when you overload a function, either the number or the type of the parameters *must* differ! It is through these differences that C++ can select the correct version of an overloaded function.) However, when a virtual function is redefined, all aspects of its prototype must be the same. If you change the prototype when you attempt to redefine a virtual function, the function will simply be considered overloaded by the C++ compiler, and its virtual nature will be lost. Another important restriction is that virtual functions must be non-**static** members of the classes of which they are part. Specifically, they cannot be **friends**. Finally, constructor functions cannot be virtual, but destructor functions can.

Because of the restrictions and differences between function overloading and virtual function redefinition, the term *overriding* is used to describe virtual function redefinition by a derived class.

NOTE: *A class that includes a virtual function is called a* polymorphic class.

The Virtual Attribute Is Inherited

When a virtual function is inherited, its virtual nature is also inherited. This means that when a derived class that has inherited a virtual function is, itself, used as a base class for another derived class, the virtual function can still be overridden. Put differently, no matter how many times a virtual function is inherited, it remains virtual. For example, consider this variation on the preceding program:

```
#include <iostream.h>

class base {
public:
  virtual void vfunc() {
    cout << "This is base's vfunc().\n";
  }
};

class derived1 : public base {
public:
  void vfunc() {
    cout << "This is derived1's vfunc().\n";
  }
};

/* derived2 inherits virtual function vfunc()
   from derived1. */
class derived2 : public derived1 {
public:
  // vfunc() is still virtual
  void vfunc() {
    cout << "This is derived2's vfunc().\n";
  }
};

main()
{
  base *p, b;
  derived1 d1;
```

```
    derived2 d2;

    // point to base
    p = &b;
    p->vfunc(); // access base's vfunc()

    // point to derived1
    p = &d1;
    p->vfunc(); // access derived1's vfunc()

    // point to derived2
    p = &d2;
    p->vfunc(); // access derived2's vfunc()

    return 0;
}
```

As expected, the preceding program displays this output:

    This is base's vfunc( ).
    This is derived1's vfunc( ).
    This is derived2's vfunc( ).

Virtual Functions Are Hierarchical

As you know, when a function is declared as **virtual** by a base class, it may be overridden by a derived class. However, the function does not have to be overridden. If a derived class fails to override a virtual function, then when an object of that derived class accesses that function, the function defined by the base class is used. For example, consider this program:

```
#include <iostream.h>

class base {
public:
  virtual void vfunc() {
    cout << "This is base's vfunc().\n";
  }
};
```

```
class derived1 : public base {
public:
  void vfunc() {
    cout << "This is derived1's vfunc().\n";
  }
};

class derived2 : public base {
public:
// vfunc() not overridden by derived2, base's is used
};

main()
{
  base *p, b;
  derived1 d1;
  derived2 d2;

  // point to base
  p = &b;
  p->vfunc(); // access base's vfunc()

  // point to derived1
  p = &d1;
  p->vfunc(); // access derived1's vfunc()

  // point to derived2
  p = &d2;
  p->vfunc(); // use base's vfunc()

  return 0;
}
```

The preceding program produces this output:

    This is base's vfunc( ).
    This is derived1's vfunc( ).
    This is base's vfunc( ).

Because **derived2** does not override **vfunc( )**, the function defined by **base** is used when **vfunc( )** is referenced relative to objects of type **derived2**.

The preceding program illustrates a special case of a more general rule. Because inheritance is hierarchical in C++, it makes sense that virtual functions are also hierarchical. This means that when a derived class fails to override a virtual function, then the first redefinition found in reverse order of derivation is used. For example, in the following program, **derived2** is derived from **derived1**, which is derived from **base**. However, **derived2** does not override **vfunc( )**. This means that, relative to **derived2**, the closest version of **vfunc( )** is in **derived1**. Therefore, it is **derived1::vfunc( )** that is used when an object of **derived2** attempts to call **vfunc( )**.

```cpp
#include <iostream.h>

class base {
public:
  virtual void vfunc() {
    cout << "This is base's vfunc().\n";
  }
};

class derived1 : public base {
public:
  void vfunc() {
    cout << "This is derived1's vfunc().\n";
  }
};

class derived2 : public derived1 {
public:
/* vfunc() not overridden by derived2.
   In this case, since derived2 is derived from
   derived1, derived1's vfunc() is used.
*/
};

main()
{
  base *p, b;
  derived1 d1;
  derived2 d2;

  // point to base
  p = &b;
  p->vfunc(); // access base's vfunc()
```

```
// point to derived1
p = &d1;
p->vfunc(); // access derived1's vfunc()

// point to derived2
p = &d2;
p->vfunc(); // use derived1's vfunc()

return 0;
}
```

The preceding program displays the following:

```
This is base's vfunc( ).
This is derived1's vfunc( ).
This is derived1's vfunc( ).
```

Pure Virtual Functions

As the examples in the preceding section illustrate, when a virtual function is not redefined by a derived class, the version defined in the base class will be used. However, in many situations there can be no meaningful definition of a virtual function within a base class. For example, a base class may not be able to define an object sufficiently to allow a base class virtual function to be created. Further, in some situations you will want to ensure that all derived classes override a virtual function. To handle these two cases, C++ supports the pure virtual function.

A *pure virtual function* is a virtual function that has no definition within the base class. To declare a pure virtual function, use this general form:

virtual type func_name(parameter-list) = 0;

When a virtual function is made pure, any derived class must provide its own definition. If the derived class fails to override the pure virtual function, a compile-time error will result.

The following program contains a simple example of a pure virtual function. The base type, **number**, contains an integer called **val**, the function **setval( )**, and the pure virtual function **show( )**. The derived classes **hextype**, **dectype**, and **octtype** inherit **number** and redefine **show( )** so that it outputs the value of **val** in each respective number base (that is, hexadecimal, decimal, or octal).

```cpp
#include <iostream.h>

class number {
protected:
  int val;
public:
  void setval(int i) {val = i;}

  // show() is a pure virtual function
  virtual void show() = 0;
};

class hextype : public number {
public:
  void show() {
    cout << hex << val << "\n";
  }
};

class dectype : public number {
public:
  void show() {
    cout << val << "\n";
  }
};

class octtype : public number {
public:
  void show() {
    cout << oct << val << "\n";
  }
};

main()
{
  dectype d;
  hextype h;
  octtype o;

  d.setval(20);
  d.show();  // displays 20 - decimal
```

```
    h.setval(20);
    h.show();  // displays 14 - hexadecimal

    o.setval(20);
    o.show();  // displays 24 - octal

    return 0;
}
```

Although this example is quite simple, it illustrates how a base class may not be able to meaningfully define a virtual function. In this case, **number** simply provides the common interface for the derived types to use. However, in this example, there is no reason to define **show( )** inside **number** because the point of the derived classes is to display a number in various number bases. Of course, you can always create an arbitrary placeholder definition of a virtual function. However, making **show( )** pure also ensures that all derived classes will, indeed, redefine it to meet their own needs.

Keep in mind that when a virtual function is declared as pure, all derived classes must override it. If a derived class fails to do this, a compile-time error will result.

Abstract Classes

A class that contains at least one pure virtual function is said to be *abstract*. Because an abstract class contains one or more functions for which there are no definitions (that is, pure virtual functions), no objects may be created by using an abstract class. Instead, an abstract class constitutes an incomplete type that is used as a foundation for derived classes.

Although you cannot create objects of an abstract class, you can create pointers and references to an abstract class. This allows abstract classes to support run-time polymorphism, which relies upon base class pointers to select the proper virtual function.

Using Virtual Functions

As has been mentioned, one of the central aspects of object-oriented programming is the principle of "one interface, multiple methods." This means that a general class of actions can be defined, the interface to which is constant, with each specific instance of that general class defining the actual operations relative to its own specific situation. In concrete C++ terms, a base class can be used to define the nature of the interface to a general class. Each derived class then implements the specific operations as they relate to the type of data used by the derived type.

One of the most powerful and flexible ways to implement the "one interface, multiple methods" approach is to use virtual functions, abstract classes, and run-time polymorphism. Using these features, you create a class hierarchy that moves from general to specific (base to derived). Following this philosophy, you define all common features and interfaces in a base class. In cases where certain actions can be implemented only by the derived class, you use a virtual function to define the interface that will be used by the derived class or classes. In essence, in the base class you create and define everything you can that relates to the general case. The derived class fills in the specific details.

Following is a simple example that illustrates the value of the "one interface, multiple methods" philosophy. A class hierarchy is created that performs conversions from one system of units to another. (For example, liters to gallons.) The base class **convert** declares two variables, **val1** and **val2**, which hold the initial and converted values, respectively. It also defines the functions **getinit( )** and **getconv( )**, which return the initial value and the converted value. These elements of **convert** are fixed and applicable to all derived classes that will inherit **convert**. However, the function that will actually perform the conversion, **compute( )**, is a pure virtual function that must be defined by the classes derived from **convert**. The specific nature of **compute( )** will be determined by what type of conversion is taking place.

```
// Virtual function practical example.
#include <iostream.h>

class convert {
protected:
  double val1;  // initial value
  double val2;  // converted value
public:
  convert(double i) {
    val1 = i;
  }
  double getconv() {return val2;}
  double getinit() {return val1;}

  virtual void compute() = 0;
};

// Liters to gallons.
class l_to_g : public convert {
public:
  l_to_g(double i) : convert(i) { }
  void compute() {
    val2 = val1 / 3.7854;
  }
};
```

```
// Fahrenheit to Celsius
class f_to_c : public convert {
public:
  f_to_c(double i) : convert(i) { }
  void compute() {
    val2 = (val1-32) / 1.8;
  }
};

main()
{
  convert *p;  // pointer to base class

  l_to_g lgob(4);
  f_to_c fcob(70);

  // use virtual function mechanism to convert
  p = &lgob;
  cout << p->getinit() << " liters is ";
  p->compute();
  cout << p->getconv() << " gallons\n";  // l_to_g

  p = &fcob;
  cout << p->getinit() << " in Fahrenheit is ";
  p->compute();
  cout << p->getconv() << " Celsius\n";  // f_to_c

  return 0;
}
```

This program creates two derived classes from **convert**, called **l_to_g** and **f_to_c**. These classes perform the conversions of liters to gallons and Fahrenheit to Celsius, respectively. As you can see, each derived class overrides **compute( )** in its own way to perform the desired conversion. However, even though the actual conversion (that is, method) differs between **l_to_g** and **f_to_c**, the interface remains constant.

One of the values of derived classes and virtual functions is that handling a new case is a very easy matter. For example, assuming the preceding program, you can add a conversion from feet to meters by including this class:

```
// Feet to meters
class f_to_m : public convert {
public:
  f_to_m(double i) : convert(i) { }
  void compute() {
    val2 = val1 / 3.28;
  }
};
```

An important use of abstract classes and virtual functions is in *class libraries*. You can create a generic, extensible class library that will be used by other programmers. Another programmer will inherit your general class, which defines the interface and all common elements, and will simply define those functions specific to the derived class. By creating class libraries, you are able to create and control the interface of a general class while still letting other programmers adapt it to their specific situations.

One final point: the base class **convert** is an example of an incomplete type. The virtual function **compute( )** is not defined within **convert** because no meaningful definition can be provided. The class **convert** simply does not contain sufficient information for **compute( )** to be defined. It is only when **convert** is inherited by a derived class that a complete type is created.

Early Versus Late Binding

Before concluding this chapter on virtual functions and run-time polymorphism, there are two terms that need to be defined because they are used frequently in discussions of C++ and object-oriented programming. The terms are *early binding* and *late binding*.

Early binding refers to events that occur at compile time. In essence, early binding means that all information needed to call a function is known at compile time. (Put differently, early binding means that an object and a function call are bound during compilation.) Examples of early binding include normal function calls (including standard library functions), overloaded function calls, and overloaded operators. The main advantage to early binding is efficiency. Because all information necessary to call a function is determined at compile time, these types of function calls are very fast.

The opposite of early binding is *late binding*. As it relates to C++, late binding refers to function calls that are not resolved until run time. Virtual functions are used to achieve late binding. As you know, when access is via a base pointer, the actual virtual function called is determined by the type of object pointed to by the pointer. Because in most cases this cannot be determined at compile time, the object and the function are not linked until run time. The main advantage to late binding is flexibility. Unlike early binding, late binding allows you to create programs that can respond to events that occur while the program executes without having to create a large amount of "contingency code." Keep in mind that because a function call is not resolved until run time, late binding can make for somewhat slower execution times.

Chapter Seventeen

The C++ I/O System Basics

In addition to supporting all of C's I/O system, C++ defines its own, object-oriented I/O system. Also like C's I/O system, C++'s I/O system is fully integrated. That is, the different aspects of C++'s I/O system, such as console I/O and disk I/O, are actually just different perspectives on the same mechanism. This chapter discusses the foundations of the C++ object-oriented I/O system. Although the examples in this chapter use "console" I/O, the information is applicable to other devices, including disk files (discussed in Chapter 18).

As you know, C's I/O system is extremely rich, flexible, and powerful. You might be wondering why C++ defines yet another system. The answer is that C's I/O system knows nothing about objects. Therefore, for C++ to provide complete support for object-oriented programming, it was necessary to create an object-oriented I/O system that could operate on user-defined objects. In addition to support for objects, there are some side benefits to using C++'s I/O system even in programs that don't make extensive (or any) use of user-defined objects. You will see some examples later in this chapter.

In this chapter you will learn how to format data. You will learn how to overload C++'s << and >> I/O operators so they can be used with classes that you create. You will also see how to create special I/O functions called manipulators that can make your programs more efficient.

C++ Streams

Like C's I/O system, the C++ I/O system operates through streams. Streams were discussed in detail in Chapter 9; that discussion will not be repeated here. However, to summarize: A stream is a logical device that either produces or consumes information. A stream is linked to a physical device by the C++ I/O system. All streams behave in the same way even though the actual physical devices they are connected to may differ substantially. Because all streams behave the same, the same C++ I/O functions can operate on virtually any type of physical device. For example, you can use the same function that writes to a file to write to the printer or to the screen. The advantage to this approach is that you need learn only one interface.

The Basic Stream Classes

C++ provides support for its I/O system in the header file IOSTREAM.H. In this file, two class hierarchies are defined that support I/O operations. The lowest-level class is called **streambuf**. This class provides the basic input and output operations. Unless you are deriving your own I/O classes, you will not use **streambuf** directly. The second class hierarchy starts with **ios**. It provides support for formatted I/O. From **ios** are derived the classes **istream**, **ostream**, and **iostream**. These classes are used to create streams capable of input, output, and input/output, respectively. As you will see in subsequent chapters, many other classes are derived from **ios** to support disk files and in-RAM formatting.

The **ios** class contains many member functions and variables that control or monitor the fundamental operation of a stream. In the course of this and the next chapter, many references will be made to its members. Just keep in mind that if you are using the C++ I/O system in a normal fashion, the members of **ios** will be available for use with any stream.

C++'s Predefined Streams

When a C++ program begins execution, four built-in streams are automatically opened. They are

Stream	Meaning	Default Device
cin	Standard input	Keyboard
cout	Standard output	Screen
cerr	Standard error output	Screen
clog	Buffered version of cerr	Screen

Streams **cin**, **cout**, and **cerr** correspond to C's **stdin**, **stdout**, and **stderr**.

By default, the standard streams are used to communicate with the console. However, in environments that support I/O redirection (such as DOS, Unix, OS/2, and Windows), the standard streams can be redirected to other devices or files. However, for the sake of simplicity, the examples in this chapter assume that no I/O redirection has occurred.

NOTE: *The proposed ANSI C++ standard also defines these four additional streams: **win**, **wout**, **werr**, and **wlog**. These are wide character versions of the standard streams. Wide characters are of type wchar_t and are generally 16-bit quantities. Wide characters are used to hold the large character sets associated with some human languages.*

Formatted I/O

The C++ I/O system allows you to format I/O operations. For example, you can set a field width, specify a number base, or determine how many digits after the decimal point will be displayed. In essence, any format that you can output or input by using C's **printf( )** and **scanf( )** functions can also be output or input by using C++'s << and >> I/O operators.

There are two related but conceptually different ways that you can format data. First, you can directly access various members of the **ios** class. Specifically, you can set various format status flags defined inside the **ios** class or call various **ios** member functions. Second, you can use special functions called *manipulators* that can be included as part of an I/O expression.

We will begin the discussion of formatted I/O by using the **ios** member functions and flags.

Formatting Using the ios Members

Associated with each stream is a set of format flags that control some of the ways information is formatted by a stream. In **ios**, the flags are named and given values, typically using an enumeration, as shown in the following example.

```
// ios formatting flags
enum {
  skipws = 0x0001,
  left = 0x0002,
  right = 0x0004,
  internal = 0x0008,
  dec = 0x0010,
  oct = 0x0020,
  hex = 0x0040,
  showbase = 0x0080,
  showpoint = 0x0100,
  uppercase = 0x0200,
  showpos = 0x0400,
  scientific = 0x0800,
  fixed = 0x1000,
  unitbuf = 0x2000,
};
```

The format flags associated with a stream are encoded into some form of long integer. The proposed ANSI C++ standard specifies the type of the format flags as **fmtflags**. However, no commonly available compiler currently defines this type. (Of course, almost all will in the near future.) From a practical point of view, it is almost certain that **fmtflags** will simply be a **typedef** name for a long integer. This book will use the type **long** when referring to the format flags because this is the type that is currently used by all mainstream C++ compilers. You will want to check your compiler's user manual on this point.

When the **skipws** flag is set, leading white-space characters (spaces, tabs, and newlines) are discarded when input is performed on a stream. When **skipws** is cleared, white-space characters are not discarded.

When the **left** flag is set, output is left justified. When **right** is set, output is right justified. When the **internal** flag is set, a numeric value is padded to fill a field with spaces inserted between any sign or base character. (You will learn how to specify a field width shortly.) If none of these flags is set, output is right justified by default.

Also by default, numeric values are output in decimal. However, you can change the number base. Setting the **oct** flag causes output to be displayed in octal. Setting the **hex** flag causes output to be displayed in hexadecimal. To return output to decimal, set the **dec** flag. These flags also determine the base when integer values are input.

Setting **showbase** causes the base of numeric values to be shown. For example, if the conversion base is hexadecimal, the value 1F will be displayed as 0x1F.

By default, when scientific notation is displayed, the "e" is in lowercase. Also, when a hexadecimal value is displayed, the "x" is in lowercase. When **uppercase** is set, these characters are displayed in uppercase.

Setting **showpos** causes a leading plus sign to be displayed before positive values.

Setting **showpoint** causes a decimal point and trailing zeros to be displayed for all floating-point output—whether needed or not.

Setting the **scientific** flag causes floating-point numeric values to be displayed in scientific notation. When **fixed** is set, floating-point values are displayed in normal notation. By default, when **fixed** is set, six decimal places are displayed. When neither flag is set, the compiler chooses an appropriate method.

When **unitbuf** is set, the C++ I/O system is flushed after each output operation.

NOTE: *The format flags just described will be supported by all C++ compilers. But, at this writing, the exact nature of the **ios** format flags is still being defined by the ANSI C++ standards committee. For example, the flag **boolalpha** has been added, which permits I/O operations on the newly defined **bool** data type. This flag is not currently defined by most compilers. Check your compiler's manual to see if this or other format flags may be available for your use.*

Setting the Format Flags

To set a format flag, use the **setf( )** function. This function is a member of **ios**. Its most common form is shown here:

long setf(long *flags*);

This function returns the previous settings of the format flags and turns on those flags specified by *flags*. All other flags are unaffected.

For example, to turn on the **showpos** flag, you can use this statement:

```
stream.setf(ios::showpos);
```

Here, *stream* is the stream you wish to affect. For example, the following program displays the value 100 in hexadecimal and indicates its base.

```
#include <iostream.h>

main()
{
  cout.setf(ios::hex);
  cout.setf(ios::showbase);

  cout << 100;   // displays 0x64

  return 0;
}
```

It is important to understand that **setf( )** is a member function of the **ios** class and affects streams created by that class. Therefore, any call to **setf( )** is done relative to a specific stream. There is no concept of calling **setf( )** by itself. Put differently, there is no concept in C++ of global format status. Each stream maintains its own format status information individually.

Although there is nothing technically wrong with the preceding program, there is a more efficient way to write it. Instead of making multiple calls to **setf( )**, you can simply OR together the values of the flags you want set. For example, the following single call accomplishes the same thing.

```
// You can OR together two or more flags,
cout.setf(ios::showbase | ios::hex);
```

REMEMBER: *Because the format flags are defined within the **ios** class, you must access their values by using **ios** and the scope resolution operator. For example, **showbase** by itself will not be recognized. You must specify **ios::showbase**.*

Clearing Format Flags

The complement of **setf( )** is **unsetf( )**. This member function of **ios** is used to clear one or more format flags. Its general form is

long unsetf(long *flags*);

The flags specified by *flags* are cleared. (All other flags are unaffected.) The previous flag settings are returned.

The following program illustrates **unsetf( )**. It first sets both the **uppercase** and **scientific** flags. It then outputs 100.12 in scientific notation. In this case, the E used in the scientific notation is in uppercase. Next, it clears the **uppercase** flag and again outputs 100.12 in scientific notation, using a lowercase "e".

```
#include <iostream.h>

main()
{
  cout.setf(ios::uppercase | ios::scientific);

  cout << 100.12;  // displays 1.0012E+02

  cout.unsetf(ios::uppercase); // clear uppercase

  cout << " \n" << 100.12; // displays 1.0012e+02

  return 0;
}
```

An Overloaded Form of setf( )

There is an overloaded form of **setf( )** that takes this general form:

long setf(long *flags1*, long *flags2*);

In this version, only the flags specified by *flags2* are affected. They are first reset and then set according to the flags specified by *flags1*. Note that even if *flags1* contains other flags not specified by *flags2*, only those specified by *flags2* will be affected. The previous flags setting is returned. For example, the following program sets **showpos** and **showpoint**. It then resets both flags and sets **showpoint** again.

```
#include <iostream.h>

main()
{
  cout.setf(ios::showpos | ios::showpoint);

  cout << 10.00 << " \n"; // displays +10.000000

  cout.setf(ios::showpoint, ios::showpos | ios::showpoint);

  cout << 10.00; // showpos reset, this displays 10.00000

  return 0;
}
```

Remember, only the flags specified in *flags2* can be affected by flags specified by *flags1*. For example, the following program will not work.

```
// This program will not work.
#include <iostream.h>

main()
{
  cout.setf(ios::showbase | ios::hex);

  cout << 100;  // displays 0x64

  cout.setf(ios::oct, ios::hex);  // error, oct not set

  cout << " \n" << 100; // displays 100 - not 0144

  return 0;
}
```

Here, in the call to **setf( )**, *flags2* specifies that only **hex** can be affected. Because the value of *flags1* is **oct**, **hex** is turned off, but **oct** is not turned on. The following program shows a corrected version.

```
// This is now correct.
#include <iostream.h>

main()
{
  // you can OR together two or more flags
  cout.setf(ios::showbase | ios::hex);

  cout << 100;  // displays 0x64

  // now oct can be affected
  cout.setf(ios::oct, ios::hex | ios::oct);

  cout << " \n" << 100; // displays 0144

  return 0;
}
```

References to the **oct**, **dec**, and **hex** fields can collectively be referred to as **ios::basefield**. Similarly, the **left**, **right**, and **internal** fields can be referred to as **ios::adjustfield**. Finally, the **scientific** and **fixed** fields can be referenced as **ios::floatfield**. For example, the preceding program could have been written this way:

```
#include <iostream.h>

main()
{
  // you can OR together two or more flags
  cout.setf(ios::showbase | ios::hex);

  cout << 100;  // displays 0x64

  // use ios::basefield
  cout.setf(ios::oct, ios::basefield);

  cout << " \n" << 100; // displays 0144

  return 0;
}
```

Keep in mind that most of the time you will want to use **unsetf( )** to clear flags and the single parameter version of **setf( )**, described earlier, to set flags. The **setf(long** *flags1*, **long** *flags2*) version of **setf( )** is used in specialized situations. For example, you may have a flag template that specifies the state of all format flags but wish to alter only one or two. In this case, you could specify the template in *flags1*, and use *flags2* to specify which of those flags will be affected.

Examining the Formatting Flags

There will be times when you only want to know the current format settings but not alter any. To accomplish this goal, **ios** also includes the member function **flags( )**, which simply returns the current setting of each format flag encoded into a long integer. Its prototype is shown here:

long flags( );

The following program uses **flags( )** to display the setting of the format flags relative to **cout**. Pay special attention to the **showflags( )** function. You might find it useful in programs you write.

```cpp
#include <iostream.h>

void showflags() ;

main()
{
  // show default condition of format flags
  showflags();

  cout.setf(ios::right | ios::showpoint | ios::fixed);

  showflags();

  return 0;
}

// This function displays the status of the format flags.
void showflags()
{
  long f, i;
  int j;

  char flgs[15][12] = {
    "skipws",
    "left",
    "right",
    "internal",
    "dec",
    "oct",
    "hex",
    "showbase",
    "showpoint",
    "uppercase",
    "showpos",
    "scientific",
    "fixed",
    "unitbuf",
  };

  f = cout.flags();  // get flag settings

  // check each flag
  for(i=1, j=0; i<=0x2000; i = i<<1, j++)
```

```
    if(i & f) cout << flgs[j] << " is on \n";
    else cout << flgs[j] << " is off \n";

  cout << " \n";
}
```

The output from the program is shown here:

```
skipws is on
left is off
right is off
internal is off
dec is off
oct is off
hex is off
showbase is off
showpoint is off
uppercase is off
showpos is off
scientific is off
fixed is off
unitbuf is off

skipws is on
left is off
right is on
internal is off
dec is off
oct is off
hex is off
showbase is off
showpoint is on
uppercase is off
showpos is off
scientific is off
fixed is on
unitbuf is off
```

NOTE: *Since it is possible that your C++ compiler defines different values for the format flags than those used in the preceding program, you may see results different from those shown. If this is the case, check your compiler's user manual for the values it uses for the format flags.*

Setting All Flags

The **flags( )** function has a second form that allows you to set all format flags associated with a stream. The prototype for this version of **flags( )** is shown here:

long flags(long *f*);

When you use this version, the bit pattern found in *f* is copied to the variable used to hold the format flags associated with the stream. Thus, all format flags are affected. The function returns the previous settings.

The next program illustrates this version of **flags( )**. It first constructs a flag mask that turns on **showpos**, **showbase**, **oct**, and **right**. For most C++ implementations, these flags have the values 0x0400, 0x0080, 0x0020, and 0x0004. When added together, they produce the value used in the program, 0x04A4. All other flags are turned off. It then uses **flags( )** to set the flag variable associated with **cout** to these settings. The function **showflags( )** verifies that the flags are set as indicated. (It is the same as used in the previous program.)

```
#include <iostream.h>

void showflags() ;

main()
{
  // show default condition of format flags
  showflags();

  // showpos, showbase, oct, right are on, others off
  long f = 0x04A4;
  cout.flags(f);  // set all flags

  showflags();

  return 0;
}
```

Using width( ), precision( ), and fill( )

In addition to the formatting flags, there are three member functions defined by **ios** that set these format parameters: the field width, the precision, and the fill character. The functions that do these things are **width( )**, **precision( )**, and **fill( )**, respectively. Each is examined in turn.

By default, when a value is output, it occupies only as much space as the number of characters it takes to display it. However, you can specify a minimum field width by using the **width( )** function. Its prototype is shown here:

    int width(int *w*);

Here, *w* becomes the field width, and the previous field width is returned. In some implementations, the field width must be set before each output. If it isn't, the default field width is used.

After you set a minimum field width, when a value uses less than the specified width, the field will be padded with the current fill character (space, by default) to reach the field width. However, keep in mind that if the size of the value exceeds the minimum field width, then the field will be overrun. No values are truncated.

When outputting floating-point values, you can determine the number of digits to be displayed after the decimal point by using the **precision( )** function. Its prototype is shown here:

    int precision(int *p*);

Here, the precision is set to *p*, and the old value is returned. The default precision is 6. In some implementations, the precision must be set before each floating-point output. If it isn't, the default precision is used.

Also by default, when a field needs to be filled, it is filled with spaces. However, you can specify the fill character by using the **fill( )** function. Its prototype is

    char fill(char *ch*);

After a call to **fill( )**, *ch* becomes the new fill character, and the old one is returned.

Here is a program that illustrates these functions:

```
#include <iostream.h>

main()
{
  cout.precision(4) ;
```

```
      cout.width(10);

      cout << 10.12345 << "\n";   // displays 10.12

      cout.fill('*');

      cout.width(10);
      cout << 10.12345 << "\n"; // displays *****10.12

      // field width applies to strings, too
      cout.width(10);
      cout << "Hi!" << "\n"; // displays *******Hi!
      cout.width(10);
      cout.setf(ios::left); // left justify
      cout << 10.12345; // displays 10.12*****

      return 0;
}
```

This program's output is shown here:

```
     10.12
*****10.12
*******Hi!
10.12*****
```

Using Manipulators to Format I/O

The second way you may alter the format parameters of a stream is through the use of special functions called *manipulators* that can be included in an I/O expression. The standard manipulators are shown in Table 17-1. As you can see by examining the table, many of the I/O manipulators parallel member functions of the **ios** class.

 NOTE: *The manipulators shown in Table 17-1 are supported by all C++ compilers. However, at this writing the exact nature of the I/O manipulators is still being defined by the ANSI C++ standards committee. For example, the **boolalpha( )** manipulator has been added to permit I/O operations on the newly defined **bool** data type. This manipulator may not be supported by your current C++ compiler. Check your compiler's manual to see what other manipulators may be available for your use.*

Manipulator	Purpose	Input/Output
dec	Input/output data in decimal	Input and output
endl	Output a newline character and flush the stream	Output
ends	Output a null	Output
flush	Flush a stream	Output
hex	Input/output data in hexadecimal	Input and output
oct	Input/output data in octal	Input and output
resetiosflags(long f)	Turn off the flags specified in f	Input and output
setbase(int *base*)	Set the number base to *base*	Output
setfill(int *ch*)	Set the fill character to *ch*	Output
setiosflags(long f)	Turn on the flags specified in f	Input and output
setprecision(int p)	Set the number of digits of precision	Output
setw(int w)	Set the field width to w	Output
ws	Skip leading white space	Input

Table 17-1. *The C++ Manipulators*

To access manipulators that take parameters (such as **setw( )**), you must include IOMANIP.H in your program.

Here is an example that uses some manipulators:

```
#include <iostream.h>
#include <iomanip.h>

main()
{
  cout << hex << 100 << endl;

  cout << setfill('?') << setw(10) << 2343.0;

  return 0;
}
```

This displays

```
64
??????2343
```

Notice how the manipulators occur in the chain of I/O operations. Also notice that when a manipulator does not take an argument, such as **endl( )** in the example, it is not followed by parentheses. This is because it is the address of the function that is passed to the overloaded **<<** operator.

As a comparison, here is a functionally equivalent version of the preceding program that uses **ios** member functions to achieve the same results:

```
#include <iostream.h>
#include <iomanip.h>

main()
{
  cout.setf(ios::hex);
  cout << 100 << "\n";   // 100 in hex

  cout.fill('?');
  cout.width(10);
  cout << 2343.0;

  return 0;
}
```

As the examples suggest, the main advantage of using manipulators instead of the **ios** member functions is that they often allow more compact code to be written.

You can use the **setiosflags( )** manipulator to directly set the various format flags related to a stream. For example, this program uses **setiosflags( )** to set the **showbase** and **showpos** flags:

```
#include <iostream.h>
#include <iomanip.h>

main()
{
  cout << setiosflags(ios::showpos);
  cout << setiosflags(ios::showbase);
  cout << 123 << " " << hex << 123;

  return 0;
}
```

The manipulator **setiosflags( )** performs the same function as the member function **setf( )**.

Overloading << and >>

As you know, the **<<** and the **>>** operators are overloaded in C++ to perform I/O operations on C++'s built-in types. You can also overload these operators so that they perform I/O operations on types that you create.

In the language of C++, the **<<** output operator is referred to as the *insertion operator* because it inserts characters into a stream. Likewise, the **>>** input operator is called the *extraction operator* because it extracts characters from a stream. The operator functions that overload the insertion and extraction operators are generally called *inserters* and *extractors*, respectively.

Creating Your Own Inserters

It is quite simple to create an inserter for a class that you create. All inserter functions have this general form:

ostream &operator<<(ostream &*stream, class_type obj*)
{
  // body of inserter
  return *stream*;
}

Notice that the function returns a reference to a stream of type **ostream**. (Remember, **ostream** is a class derived from **ios** that supports output.) Further, the first parameter to the function is a reference to the output stream. The second parameter is the object being inserted. (The second parameter may also be a reference to the object being inserted.) The last thing the inserter must do before exiting is return *stream*. This allows the inserter to be used in a chain of insertions.

Within an inserter function, you may put any type of procedures or operations that you want. That is, precisely what an inserter does is completely up to you. However, for the inserter to be in keeping with good programming practices, you should limit the operations performed by an inserter to outputting information to a stream. For example, having an inserter compute pi to 30 decimal places as a side effect to an insertion operation is probably not a very good idea.

To see an example, let's create an inserter for objects of type **phonebook**:

```
class phonebook {
public:
  char name[80];
```

```
   int areacode;
   int prefix;
   int num;
   phonebook(char *n, int a, int p, int nm)
   {
     strcpy(name, n);
     areacode = a;
     prefix = p;
     num = nm;
   }
};
```

This class holds a person's name and telephone number. Here is one way to create an inserter function for objects of type **phonebook**.

```
// Display name and phone number
ostream &operator<<(ostream &stream, phonebook o)
{
  stream << o.name << " ";
  stream << "(" << o.areacode << ") ";
  stream << o.prefix << "-" << o.num << "\n";

  return stream; // must return stream
}
```

Here is a short program that illustrates the **phonebook** inserter function.

```
#include <iostream.h>
#include <string.h>

class phonebook {
public:
  char name[80];
  int areacode;
  int prefix;
  int num;
  phonebook(char *n, int a, int p, int nm)
  {
      strcpy(name, n);
      areacode = a;
```

```
      prefix = p;
      num = nm;
   }
};

// Display name and phone number.
ostream &operator<<(ostream &stream, phonebook o)
{
   stream << o.name << " ";
   stream << "(" << o.areacode << ") ";
   stream << o.prefix << "-" << o.num << "\n";

   return stream; // must return stream
}

main()
{
   phonebook a("Ted", 111, 555, 1234);
   phonebook b("Alice", 312, 555, 5768);
   phonebook c("Tom", 212, 555, 9991);

   cout << a << b << c;

   return 0;
}
```

The program produces this output:

```
Ted (111) 555-1234
Alice (312) 555-5768
Tom (212) 555-9991
```

In the preceding program, notice that the **phonebook** inserter is not a member of **phonebook**. Although this may seem weird at first, the reason is easy to understand. When an operator function of any type is a member of a class, the left operand (passed implicitly through **this**) is the object that generates the call to the operator function. Further, this object is an *object of the class* for which the operator function is a member. There is no way to change this. If an overloaded operator function is a member of a class, the left operand must be an object of that class. However, when you overload inserters, the left operand is a *stream* and the right operand is an object of the class.

Therefore, overloaded inserters cannot be members of the class for which they are overloaded. Also, the only reason the variables **name**, **areacode**, **prefix**, and **num** are public in the preceding program is so that they can be accessed by the non-member inserter.

The fact that inserters cannot be members of the class for which they are defined seems to be a serious flaw in C++. Since overloaded inserters are not members, how can they access the private elements of a class? In the foregoing program, all members were made public. However, encapsulation is an essential component of object-oriented programming. Requiring all data that will be output by using an inserter to be made public conflicts with this principle. Fortunately, there is a solution to this dilemma: make the inserter a **friend** of the class. This preserves the requirement that the first argument to the overloaded inserter be a stream and still grants the function access to private parts of the class for which it is overloaded. Here is the same program modified to make the inserter into a **friend** function:

```
#include <iostream.h>
#include <string.h>

class phonebook {
  // now private
  char name[80];
  int areacode;
  int prefix;
  int num;
public:
  phonebook(char *n, int a, int p, int nm)
  {
    strcpy(name, n);
    areacode = a;
    prefix = p;
    num = nm;
  }
  friend ostream &operator<<(ostream &stream, phonebook o);
};

// Display name and phone number.
ostream &operator<<(ostream &stream, phonebook o)
{
  stream << o.name << " ";
  stream << "(" << o.areacode << ") ";
  stream << o.prefix << "-" << o.num << "\n";

  return stream; // must return stream
```

```
}

main()
{
  phonebook a("Ted", 111, 555, 1234);
  phonebook b("Alice", 312, 555, 5768);
  phonebook c("Tom", 212, 555, 9991);

  cout << a << b << c;

  return 0;
}
```

When you define the body of an inserter function, remember to keep it as general as possible. For example, the inserter shown in the preceding example can be used with any stream because the body of the function directs its output to **stream**, which is the stream that invoked the inserter. While it would not be technically wrong to have written the line

```
stream << o.name << " ";
```

as

```
cout << o.name << " ";
```

this would have the effect of hard-coding **cout** as the output stream. The original version will work with any stream, including those linked to disk files. Although in some situations, especially where special output devices are involved, you will want to hard-code the output stream, in most cases you will not. In general, the more flexible your inserters are, the more valuable they are.

 NOTE: *The inserter for the **phonebook** class works fine unless the value of **num** is something like 0034, in which case the preceding zeros will not be displayed. To fix this, you can either make **num** into a string, or you can set the fill character to zero and use the **width( )** format function to generate the leading zeros. The solution is left to the reader as an exercise.*

Before moving on to extractors, let's look at one more example of an inserter function. An inserter need not be limited to handling only text. An inserter can be used to output data in any form that makes sense. For example, an inserter for some class that is part of a CAD system may output plotter instructions. Another inserter might generate graphics images. An inserter for a Windows-based program could display a dialog box. To taste the flavor of outputting things other than text, examine the following program, which draws boxes on the screen. (Because neither C nor C++ defines graphics, the program uses characters to draw a box, but feel free to substitute graphics if your system supports them.)

```cpp
#include <iostream.h>

class box {
  int x, y;
public:
  box(int i, int j) {x=i; y=j;}
  friend ostream &operator<<(ostream &stream, box o);
};

// Output a box.
ostream &operator<<(ostream &stream, box o)
{
  register int i, j;

  for(i=0; i<o.x; i++)
    stream << "*";

  stream << "\n";

  for(j=1; j<o.y-1; j++) {
    for(i=0; i<o.x; i++)
      if(i==0 || i==o.x-1) stream << "*";
      else stream << " ";
    stream << "\n";
  }

  for(i=0; i<o.x; i++)
    stream << "*";
  stream << "\n";

  return stream;
}

main()
{
```

```
    box a(14, 6), b(30, 7), c(40, 5);

    cout << "Here are some boxes:\n";
    cout << a << b << c;

    return 0;
}
```

The program displays the following:

```
Here are some boxes:
* * * * * * * * * * * * *
*                       *
*                       *
*                       *
*                       *
* * * * * * * * * * * * *
* * * * * * * * * * * * * * * * * * * * * * * * *
*                                               *
*                                               *
*                                               *
*                                               *
*                                               *
* * * * * * * * * * * * * * * * * * * * * * * * *
* * * * * * * * * * * * * * * * * * * * * * * * * * * * * * *
*                                                           *
*                                                           *
*                                                           *
* * * * * * * * * * * * * * * * * * * * * * * * * * * * * * *
```

Creating Your Own Extractors

Extractors are the complement of inserters. The general form of an extractor function is

```
istream &operator>>(istream &stream, class_type &obj)
{
  // body of extractor
  return stream;
}
```

Extractors return a reference to a stream of type **istream**, which is an input stream. The first parameter must also be a reference to a stream of type **istream**. Notice that the second parameter must be a reference to an object of the class for which the extractor is overloaded. This allows the object to be modified by the input (extraction) operation.

Continuing with the **phonebook** class, here is one way to write an extraction function:

```
istream &operator>>(istream &stream, phonebook &o)
{
  cout << "Enter name: ";
  stream >> o.name;
  cout << "Enter area code: ";
  stream >> o.areacode;
  cout << "Enter prefix: ";
  stream >> o.prefix;
  cout << "Enter number: ";
  stream >> o.num;
  cout << "\n";

  return stream;
}
```

Notice that although this is an input function, it performs output by prompting the user. The point is that although the main purpose of an extractor is input, it can perform any operations necessary to achieve that end. However, as with inserters, it is best to keep the actions performed by an extractor directly related to input. If you don't, you run the risk of losing much in terms of structure and clarity.

Here is a program that illustrates the **phonebook** extractor:

```
#include <iostream.h>
#include <string.h>

class phonebook {
  char name[80];
  int areacode;
  int prefix;
  int num;
public:
  phonebook() { };
  phonebook(char *n, int a, int p, int nm)
    {
```

```
      strcpy(name, n);
      areacode = a;
      prefix = p;
      num = nm;
    }
    friend ostream &operator<<(ostream &stream, phonebook o);
    friend istream &operator>>(istream &stream, phonebook &o);
};

// Display name and phone number.
ostream &operator<<(ostream &stream, phonebook o)
{
  stream << o.name << " ";
  stream << "(" << o.areacode << ") ";
  stream << o.prefix << "-" << o.num << "\n";

  return stream; // must return stream
}

// Input name and telephone number.
istream &operator>>(istream &stream, phonebook &o)
{
  cout << "Enter name: ";
  stream >> o.name;
  cout << "Enter area code: ";
  stream >> o.areacode;
  cout << "Enter prefix: ";
  stream >> o.prefix;
  cout << "Enter number: ";
  stream >> o.num;
  cout << "\n";

  return stream;
}

main()
{
  phonebook a;

  cin >> a;
```

```
   cout << a;

   return 0;
}
```

Creating Your Own Manipulator Functions

In addition to overloading the insertion and extraction operators, you can further customize C++'s I/O system by creating your own manipulator functions. Custom manipulators are important for two main reasons. First, you can consolidate a sequence of several separate I/O operations into one manipulator. For example, it is not uncommon to have situations in which the same sequence of I/O operations occurs frequently within a program. In these cases you can use a custom manipulator to perform these actions, thus simplifying your source code and preventing accidental errors. A custom manipulator can also be important when you need to perform I/O operations on a nonstandard device. For example, you might use a manipulator to send control codes to a special type of printer or to an optical recognition system.

Custom manipulators are a feature of C++ that supports OOP, but that also can benefit programs that aren't object oriented. As you will see, custom manipulators can help make any I/O-intensive program clearer and more efficient.

As you know, there are two basic types of manipulators: those that operate on input streams and those that operate on output streams. However, in addition to these two broad categories, there is a secondary division: those manipulators that take an argument and those that don't. There are some significant differences between the way a parameterless manipulator and a parameterized manipulator are created. This section discusses how to create each type, beginning with creating parameterless manipulators.

Creating Parameterless Manipulators

All parameterless manipulator output functions have this skeleton:

```
ostream &manip-name(ostream &stream)
{
  // your code here
  return stream;
}
```

Here, *manip-name* is the name of the manipulator. Notice that a reference to a stream of type **ostream** is returned. This is necessary if a manipulator is used as part of a larger

I/O expression. It is important to note that even though the manipulator has as its single argument a reference to the stream upon which it is operating, no argument is used when the manipulator is inserted in an output operation.

As a simple first example, the following program creates a manipulator called **sethex( )**, which turns on the **showbase** flag and sets output to hexadecimal.

```
#include <iostream.h>
#include <iomanip.h>

// A simple output manipulator.
ostream &sethex(ostream &stream)
{
  stream.setf(ios::showbase);
  stream.setf(ios::hex);

  return stream;
}

main()
{
  cout << 256 << " " << sethex << 256;

  return 0;
}
```

This program displays **256 0x100**. As you can see, **sethex** is used as part of an I/O expression in the same way as any of the built-in manipulators.

Custom manipulators need not be complex to be useful. For example, the simple manipulators **la( )** and **ra( )** display a left and right arrow, respectively, for emphasis, as shown here:

```
#include <iostream.h>
#include <iomanip.h>

// Right Arrow
ostream &ra(ostream &stream)
{
  stream << "------> ";
  return stream;
}
```

```
// Left Arrow
ostream &la(ostream &stream)
{
    stream << " <-------";
    return stream;
}

main()
{
    cout << "High balance " << ra << 1233.23 << "\n";
    cout << "Over draft " << ra << 567.66 << la;

    return 0;
}
```

This program displays:

```
High balance -------> 1233.23
Over draft -------> 567.66 <-------
```

If used frequently, these simple manipulators save you from some tedious typing.

Using an output manipulator is particularly useful for sending special codes to a device. For example, a printer may be able to accept various codes that change the type size or font, or that position the print head in a special location. If these adjustments are going to be made frequently, then they are perfect candidates for a manipulator.

All parameterless input manipulator functions have this skeleton:

```
istream &manip-name(istream &stream)
{
    // your code here
    return stream;
}
```

An input manipulator receives a reference to the stream for which it was invoked. This stream must be returned by the manipulator.

The following program creates the **getpass( )** input manipulator, which rings the bell and then prompts for a password.

```
#include <iostream.h>
#include <string.h>

// A simple input manipulator.
istream &getpass(istream &stream)
{
  cout << '\a';  // sound bell
  cout << "Enter password: ";

  return stream;
}

main()
{
  char pw[80];

  do {
    cin >> getpass >> pw;
  } while (strcmp(pw, "password"));

  cout << "Logon complete\n";

  return 0;
}
```

It is crucial that your manipulator return **stream**. If this is not done, your manipulator cannot be used in a series of input or output operations.

Creating Parameterized Manipulators

Creating a manipulator function that takes an argument is less straightforward than creating one that doesn't. One reason for this is that parameterized manipulators use generic classes. Generic classes are created using the **template** keyword. (Templates and generic classes are discussed in Chapter 20.) If you don't understand how generic classes operate, you will not be able to fully understand the creation of a parameterized manipulator. Another reason that parameterized manipulators are more complex is that the precise method that you use to create one currently varies from compiler to compiler. That is, what works for one compiler will not necessarily work for another. While the ANSI C++ committee is finalizing this issue, not all compilers implement parameterized manipulators in compliance with the standard. Because of these problems, you will want to consult your compiler's user manual for specific details if you will be creating your own parameterized manipulators.

NOTE: *The examples of parameterized manipulators shown in this section comply with the proposed ANSI C++ standard and will work with most modern C++ compilers.*

To create a parameterized manipulator you must include IOMANIP.H in your file. Three generic classes are defined in IOMANIP.H: **omanip**, **imanip**, and **smanip**. **omanip** is used to create output manipulators that take an argument. **imanip** is used to create parameterized input manipulators. **smanip** is used to create parameterized manipulators capable of being used in input and output streams. (You may want to look at the class definitions for these classes in the version of IOMANIP.H provided by your compiler to see how they are implemented.)

In general, whenever you need to create a manipulator that takes an argument, you will need to create two overloaded manipulator functions. In one, you need to define two parameters. The first parameter is a reference to the stream, and the second is the parameter that will be passed to the function. The second version of the manipulator defines only one parameter—the one specified when the manipulator is used in an I/O expression. This second version generates a call to the first version. For output manipulators, you will use these general forms for creating parameterized manipulators:

```
ostream &manip-name(ostream &stream, type param)
{
  // your code here
  return stream;
}
  // Overload
omanip <type> manip-name(type param) {
  return omanip <type> (manip-name, param);
}
```

Here, *manip-name* is the name of the manipulator, and *type* specifies the type of parameter used by the manipulator. Since **omanip** is a generic class, *type* also becomes the type of data operated upon by the specific **omanip** object returned by the manipulator.

The following program creates a parameterized output manipulator called **indent( )**, which indents the specified number of spaces.

```
#include <iostream.h>
#include <iomanip.h>

// Indent length number of spaces.
```

```
ostream &indent(ostream &stream, int length)
{
  register int i;

  for(i=0; i<length; i++) cout << " ";
  return stream;
}

omanip<int> indent(int length)
{
  return omanip<int>(indent, length);
}


main()
{
  cout << indent(10) << "This is a test\n";
  cout << indent(20) << "of the indent manipulator.\n";
  cout << indent(5) << "It works!\n";

  return 0;
}
```

As you can see, **indent( )** is overloaded as previously described. When **indent(10)** is encountered in the output expression, the second version of **indent( )** is executed, with value 10 passed to the **length** parameter. This version then executes the first version with the value 10 again passed in **length**. This process repeats itself for each **indent( )** call.

The type of the parameter you want your manipulator to have is under your control and is determined by the type you specify for the second parameter of the manipulator function. This same type is then used when the generic class is created for the overloaded version of the manipulator. For example, the next program shows how to pass a **double** value to a manipulator function. It then outputs the value by using a dollars-and-cents format.

```
#include <iostream.h>
#include <iomanip.h>

ostream &dollars(ostream &stream, double amount)
{
```

```
    stream.setf(ios::showpoint);
    stream << "$" << setw(10) << setprecision(2)   << amount;

    return stream;
}

omanip <double> dollars(double amount) {
    return omanip<double> (dollars, amount);
}

main()
{
    cout << dollars(123.123456);
    cout << "\n" << dollars(10.0);
    cout << "\n" << dollars(1234.23);
    cout << "\n" << dollars(0.0);

    return 0;
}
```

Input manipulators may also take a parameter. The following program improves the **getpass( )** manipulator developed earlier. This version takes an argument that specifies how many tries the user has to enter the password correctly.

```
// This program uses a manipulator to input a password.
#include <iostream.h>
#include <iomanip.h>
#include <string.h>
#include <stdlib.h>

char *password="IlikeC++";
char pw[80];

// Input a password
istream &getpass(istream &stream, int tries)
{
    do {
        cout << "Enter password: ";
        stream >> pw;
        if(!strcmp(password, pw)) return stream;
```

```
    cout << "\a"; // bell
    tries--;
  } while(tries>0);

  cout << "All tries failed!\n";
  exit(1) ; // didn't enter password

  return stream;
}

imanip<int> getpass(int tries) {
  return imanip<int>(getpass, tries);
}

main()
{
  // give 3 tries to enter password
  cin >> getpass(3);
  cout << "Login Complete!\n";

  return 0;
}
```

Notice that the format is the same as for output manipulators, with two exceptions: the input stream **istream** must be used, and the class **imanip** is specified.

As you work with C++, you will find that custom manipulators can help streamline your I/O statements.

A Short Note About the Old Stream Class Library

When C++ was invented, a smaller and somewhat different I/O class library was created. This library was defined in the file STREAM.H. However, as C++ evolved, this older I/O library was superseded by the I/O library described in this book. Most C++ compilers still support the old stream library for the sake of compatibility with older C++ programs. But you should use the modern I/O library defined in IOSTREAM.H when writing new programs.

Chapter Eighteen

C++ File I/O

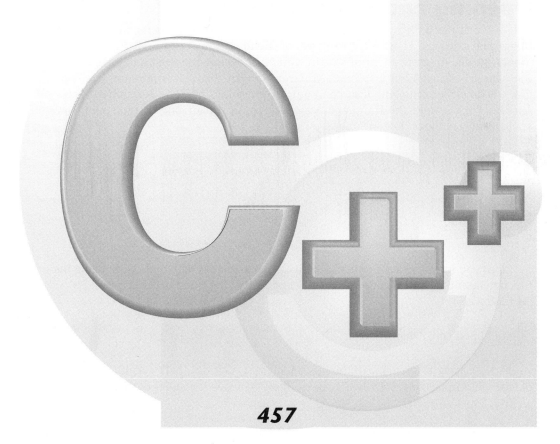

A lthough the C++ approach to I/O forms an integrated system, file I/O (specifically, disk file I/O) is sufficiently specialized that it is generally thought of as a special case, subject to its own constraints and quirks. In part, this is because the most common file is a disk file, and disk files have capabilities and features that most other devices don't. Keep in mind, however, that disk file I/O is simply a special case of a general I/O system and that most of the material discussed in this chapter also applies to streams connected to other types of devices.

fstream.h and the File Classes

To perform file I/O, you must include the header file FSTREAM.H in your program. It defines several classes, including **ifstream**, **ofstream**, and **fstream**. These classes are derived from **istream** and **ostream**, respectively. Remember, **istream** and **ostream** are derived from **ios**, so **ifstream**, **ofstream**, and **fstream** also have access to all operations defined by **ios** (discussed in the preceding chapter).

Opening and Closing a File

In C++, you open a file by linking it to a stream. Before you can open a file, you must first obtain a stream. There are three types of streams: input, output, and input/output. To create an input stream, you must declare the stream to be of class **ifstream**. To create an output stream, you must declare it as class **ofstream**. Streams that will be performing both input and output operations must be declared as class **fstream**. For example, this fragment creates one input stream, one output stream, and one stream capable of both input and output.

```
ifstream in; // input

ofstream out; // output

fstream io; // input and output
```

Once you have created a stream, one way to associate it with a file is by using the function **open( )**. This function is a member of each of the three stream classes. Its prototype is

void open(const char *filename*, int *mode*, int *access=filebuf::openprot*);

Here, *filename* is the name of the file, which may include a path specifier. The value of *mode* determines how the file is opened. It must be one (or more) of these values.

ios::app
ios::ate
ios::binary
ios::in
ios::nocreate
ios::noreplace
ios::out
ios::trunc

You can combine two or more of these values by ORing them together. Let's see what each of these values means.

Including **ios::app** causes all output to that file to be appended to the end. This value can be used only with files capable of output. Including **ios::ate** causes a seek to end-of-file to occur when the file is opened. Although **ios::ate** causes a seek to end-of-file, I/O operations can still occur anywhere within the file.

By default, files are opened in text mode. The **ios::binary** value causes a file to be opened in binary mode. When a file is opened in text mode, various character translations may take place, such as the conversion of carriage-return/linefeed sequences into newlines. However, when a file is opened in binary mode, no such character translations will occur. Any file, whether it contains formatted text or raw binary data, can be opened in either text or binary mode. The only difference is whether character translations take place.

The **ios::in** value specifies that the file is capable of input. The **ios::out** value specifies that the file is capable of output. However, creating a stream by using **ifstream** implies input and creating a stream using **ofstream** implies output, so in these cases, it is unnecessary to supply these values.

Including **ios::nocreate** causes the **open( )** function to fail if the file does not already exist. The **ios::noreplace** value causes the **open( )** function to fail if the file does already exist.

The **ios::trunc** value causes the contents of a preexisting file by the same name to be destroyed and truncates the file to zero length.

NOTE: *The proposed ANSI C++ standard specifies the type of the* mode *parameter to be* **openmode**, *which is some form of integer (generally an* **int***). Currently, most implementations simply specify the type of the* mode *parameter as* **int***.*

The value of *access* determines how the file can be accessed. Its default value is **filebuf::openprot**, which specifies a normal file. (**filebuf** is a class derived from **streambuf**.) Most of the time, you will allow *access* to default. However, you will want to check your compiler's user manual to see what other options are available for this parameter in your operating environment. For example, file sharing options are typically specified using the *access* parameter in networked environments.

The following fragment opens a normal output file.

```
ofstream out;

out.open("test", ios::out);
```

However, you will seldom (if ever) see **open( )** called as shown here, because the *mode* parameter also has default values. For **ifstream**, the default value of *mode* is **ios::in**, and for **ofstream** it is **ios::out**. Therefore, the preceding statement will usually look like this:

```
out.open("test"); // defaults to output and normal file
```

To open a stream for input and output, you must specify both the **ios::in** and the **ios::out** *mode* values, as shown in the next example. (No default value for *mode* is supplied in this case.)

```
fstream mystream;

mystream.open("test", ios::in | ios::out);
```

If **open( )** fails, **mystream** will be zero. Therefore, before using a file, you should test to make sure that the open operation succeeded. You can do so by using a statement like this:

```
if(!mystream) {
  cout << "Cannot open file.\n";
  // handle error
}
```

Although it is entirely proper to open a file by using the **open( )** function, most of the time you will not do so because the **ifstream**, **ofstream**, and **fstream** classes have constructor functions that automatically open the file. The constructor functions have the same parameters and defaults as the **open( )** function. Therefore, you will most commonly see a file opened as shown here:

```
ifstream mystream("myfile"); // open file for input
```

As stated, if for some reason the file cannot be opened, the value of the associated stream variable will be zero. Therefore, whether you use a constructor function to open the file or an explicit call to **open( )**, you will want to confirm that the file has actually been opened by testing the value of the stream.

To close a file, use the member function **close( )**. For example, to close the file linked to a stream called **mystream**, use this statement:

```
mystream.close();
```

The **close( )** function takes no parameters and returns no value.

Reading and Writing Text Files

It is very easy to read from or write to a text file. Simply use the **<<** and **>>** operators the same way you do when performing console I/O, except that instead of using **cin** and **cout**, you substitute a stream that is linked to a file. For example, this program creates a short inventory file that contains each item's name and its cost:

```
#include <iostream.h>
#include <fstream.h>

main()
{
  ofstream out("INVNTRY"); // output, normal file

  if(!out) {
    cout << "Cannot open INVENTORY file.\n";
    return 1;
  }

  out << "Radios " << 39.95 << endl;
  out << "Toasters " << 19.95 << endl;
  out << "Mixers " << 24.80 << endl;

  out.close();
  return 0;
}
```

The following program reads the inventory file created by the previous program and displays its contents on the screen.

```
#include <iostream.h>
#include <fstream.h>

main()
{
  ifstream in("INVNTRY"); // input

  if(!in) {
    cout << "Cannot open INVENTORY file.\n";
    return 1;
  }

  char item[20];
  float cost;

  in >> item >>  cost;
  cout << item << " " << cost << "\n";
  in >> item >> cost;
  cout << item << " " << cost << "\n";
  in >> item >> cost;
  cout << item << " " << cost << "\n";

  in.close();
  return 0;
}
```

In a way, reading and writing files by using **>>** and **<<** are like using C's **fprintf( )** and **fscanf( )** functions. All information is stored in the file in the same format as it would be displayed on the screen.

Following is another example of disk I/O. This program reads strings entered at the keyboard and writes them to disk. The program stops when the user enters a blank line. To use the program, specify the name of the output file on the command line.

```
#include <iostream.h>
#include <fstream.h>
#include <stdio.h>

main(int argc, char *argv[])
```

```
{
  if(argc!=2) {
    cout << "Usage: output <filename>\n";
    return 1;
  }

  ofstream out(argv[1]); // output, normal file

  if(!out) {
    cout << "Cannot open output file.\n";
    return 1;
  }

  char str[80];
  cout << "Write strings to disk, RETURN to stop.\n";

  do {
    cout << ": ";
    gets(str);
    out << str << endl;
  } while (*str);

  out.close();
  return 0;
}
```

When reading text files using the **>>** operator, keep in mind that certain character translations will occur. For example, white-space characters are omitted. If you want to prevent any character translations, you must use C++'s binary I/O functions, discussed in the next section.

When inputting, if end-of-file is encountered, the stream linked to that file will be a zero. (The next section illustrates this.)

Binary I/O

There are two ways to write and read binary data to or from a file. These two methods are explained here.

REMEMBER: *If you will be performing binary operations on a file, be sure to open it using the **ios::binary** mode specifier. Although the binary file functions will work on files opened for text mode, some character translations may occur. Character translations negate the purpose of binary file operations.*

get( ) and put( )

One way that you may read and write binary data is by using the member functions **get( )** and **put( )**. These functions are byte-oriented. That is, **get( )** will read a byte of data and **put( )** will write a byte of data. The **get( )** function has many forms, but the most commonly used version is shown here, along with **put( )**:

istream &get(char &*ch*);

ostream &put(char *ch*);

The **get( )** function reads a single character from the associated stream and puts that value in *ch*. It returns a reference to the stream. The **put( )** function writes *ch* to the stream and returns a reference to the stream.

The following program displays the contents of any file on the screen. It uses the **get( )** function.

```
#include <iostream.h>
#include <fstream.h>

main(int argc, char *argv[])
{
  char ch;

  if(argc!=2) {
    cout << "Usage: PR <filename>\n";
    return 1;
  }

  ifstream in(argv[1], ios::in | ios::binary);
  if(!in) {
    cout << "Cannot open file.";
    return 1;
  }

  while(in) { // in will be 0 when eof is reached
    in.get(ch);
```

```
    cout << ch;
  }

  return 0;
}
```

As stated in the preceding section, when the end-of-file is reached, the stream associated with the file becomes zero. Therefore, when **in** reaches the end of the file, it will be zero, causing the **while** loop to stop.

There is actually a more compact way to code the loop that reads and displays a file, as shown here:

```
while(in.get(ch))
  cout << ch;
```

This works because **get( )** returns a reference to the stream **in**, and **in** will be zero when the end of the file is encountered.

The next program uses **put( )** to write all characters from zero to 255 to a file called CHARS. As you probably know, the ASCII characters occupy only about half the available values that can be held by a **char**. The other values are generally called the *extended character set* and include such things as foreign language and mathematical symbols. (Not all systems support the extended character set, but most do.)

```
#include <iostream.h>
#include <fstream.h>

main()
{
  int i;
  ofstream out("CHARS", ios::out | ios::binary);

  if(!out) {
    cout << "Cannot open output file.\n";
    return 1;
  }

  // write all characters to disk
  for(i=0; i<256; i++) out.put((char) i);

  out.close();
```

```
    return 0;
}
```

You might find it interesting to examine the contents of the CHARS file to see what extended characters your computer has.

read( ) and write( )

The second way to read and write blocks of binary data is to use C++'s **read( )** and **write( )** functions. Their prototypes are

istream &read(unsigned char *buf*, int *num*);

ostream &write(const unsigned char *buf*, int *num*);

The **read( )** function reads *num* bytes from the associated stream and puts them in the buffer pointed to by *buf*. The **write( )** function writes *num* bytes to the associated stream from the buffer pointed to by *buf*.

NOTE: *The proposed ANSI C++ standard specifies the type of the* num *parameter by* **streamsize**, *which is a* **typedef** *for an integer type. Currently, most C++ compilers simply specify* num *as an integer, as shown in the preceding prototypes. In general, the proposed ANSI C++ standard uses* **streamsize** *as the type of any object that specifies the number of bytes transferred in an input or output operation.*

The next program writes a structure to disk, then reads it back in.

```
#include <iostream.h>
#include <fstream.h>
#include <string.h>

struct status {
  char name[80];
  float balance;
  unsigned long account_num;
};

main()
{
```

```
    struct status acc;

    strcpy(acc.name, "Ralph Trantor");
    acc.balance = 1123.23;
    acc.account_num = 34235678;

    ofstream outbal("balance", ios::out | ios::binary);

    if(!outbal) {
      cout << "Cannot open file.\n";
      return 1;
    }

    outbal.write((unsigned char *) &acc, sizeof(struct status));
    outbal.close();

    // now, read back;

    ifstream inbal("balance", ios::in | ios::binary);

    if(!inbal) {
      cout << "Cannot open file.\n";
      return 1;
    }

    inbal.read((unsigned char *) &acc, sizeof(struct status));

    cout << acc.name << endl;
    cout << "Account # " << acc.account_num;
    cout.precision(2);
    cout.setf(ios::fixed);
    cout << endl << "Balance: $" << acc.balance;

    inbal.close();
    return 0;
  }
```

As you can see, only a single call to **read( )** or **write( )** is necessary to read or write the entire structure. Each individual field need not be read or written separately. As this example illustrates, the buffer can be any type of object.

NOTE: *The type casts inside the calls to* **read( )** *and* **write( )** *are necessary when operating on a buffer that is not defined as a character array. Because of C++'s strong type checking, a pointer of one type will not automatically be converted into a pointer of another type.*

If the end of the file is reached before *num* characters have been read, then **read( )** simply stops, and the buffer contains as many characters as were available. You can find out how many characters have been read by using another member function, called **gcount( )**, which has this prototype:

    int gcount( );

It returns the number of characters read by the last binary input operation. The following program shows another example of **read( )** and **write( )** and illustrates the use of **gcount( )**.

```cpp
#include <iostream.h>
#include <fstream.h>

main(void)
{
  float fnum[4] = {99.75, -34.4, 1776.0, 200.1};
  int i;

  ofstream out("numbers", ios::out | ios::binary);
  if(!out) {
    cout << "Cannot open file.";
    return 1;
  }

  out.write((unsigned char *) &fnum, sizeof fnum);

  out.close();

  for(i=0; i<4; i++) // clear array
    fnum[i] = 0.0;

  ifstream in("numbers", ios::in | ios::binary);
  in.read((unsigned char *) &fnum, sizeof fnum);

  // see how many bytes have been read
```

```
    cout << in.gcount() << " bytes read\n";

    for(i=0; i<4; i++) // show values read from file
    cout << fnum[i] << " ";

    in.close();

    return 0;
}
```

This program writes an array of floating-point values to disk and then reads them back. After the call to **read( )**, **gcount( )** is used to determine how many bytes were just read.

More get( ) Functions

In addition to the form shown earlier, the **get( )** function is overloaded in several ways. The prototypes for the two most commonly used overloaded forms are shown here:

istream &get(char *buf, int num, char delim='\n');

int get( );

The first overloaded form reads characters into the array pointed to by buf until either num characters have been read, or the character specified by delim has been encountered. The array pointed to by buf will be null terminated by **get( )**. If no delim parameter is specified, by default a newline character acts as a delimiter. If the delimiter character is encountered in the input stream, it is *not* extracted. Instead, it remains in the stream until the next input operation.

The second overloaded form of **get( )** returns the next character from the stream. It returns EOF if the end of the file is encountered. This form of **get( )** is similar to C's **getc( )** function.

getline( )

Another member function that performs input is **getline( )**. Its prototype is

istream &getline(char *buf, int num, char delim='\n');

As you can see, this function is virtually identical to the **get(buf, num, delim)** version of **get( )**. It reads characters from input and puts them into the array pointed to by *buf* until either *num* characters have been read, or the character specified by *delim* is encountered. If not specified, *delim* defaults to the newline character. The array pointed to by *buf* is null terminated. The difference between **get(buf, num, delim)** and **getline( )** is that **getline( )** reads and removes the delimiter from the input stream.

Here is a program that demonstrates the **getline( )** function. It reads the content of a text file one line at a time and displays it on the screen.

```
// Read and display a text file line by line.

#include <iostream.h>
#include <fstream.h>

main(int argc, char *argv[])
{
  if(argc!=2) {
    cout << "Usage: Display <filename>\n";
    return 1;
  }

  ifstream in(argv[1]); // input

  if(!in) {
    cout << "Cannot open input file.\n";
    return 1;
  }

  char str[255];

  while(in) {
    in.getline(str, 255);  // delim defaults to '\n'
    cout << str << endl;
  }

  in.close();

  return 0;
}
```

Detecting EOF

You can detect when the end of the file is reached by using the member function **eof( )**, which has this prototype:

int eof( );

It returns nonzero when the end of the file has been reached; otherwise it returns zero.

NOTE: *The proposed ANSI C++ standard specifies the return type of **eof( )** to be **bool**. However, currently most available C++ compilers do not support the **bool** data type. From a practical point of view, it doesn't matter whether **eof( )**'s return type is specified as **bool** or **int** because **bool** is automatically elevated to **int** in any expression.*

The following program uses **eof( )** to display the contents of a file in both hexadecimal and ASCII.

```
/* Display contents of specified file
   in both ASCII and in hex.
*/
#include <iostream.h>
#include <fstream.h>
#include <ctype.h>
#include <iomanip.h>
#include <stdio.h>

main(int argc, char *argv[])
{
  if(argc!=2) {
    cout << "Usage: Display <filename>\n";
    return 1;
  }

  ifstream in(argv[1], ios::in | ios::binary);

  if(!in) {
    cout << "Cannot open input file.\n";
    return 1;
  }

  register int i, j;
  int count = 0;
```

```
  char c[16];

  cout.setf(ios::uppercase);
  while(!in.eof()) {
    for(i=0; i<16 && !in.eof(); i++) {
      in.get(c[i]);
    }
    if(i<16) i--; // get rid of eof

    for(j=0; j<i; j++)
      cout << setw(3) << hex << (int) c[j];
    for(; j<16; j++) cout << "   ";

    cout << "\t";
    for(j=0; j<i; j++)
      if(isprint(c[j])) cout << c[j];
      else cout << ".";

    cout << endl;

    count++;
    if(count==16) {
      count = 0;
      cout << "Press ENTER to continue: ";
      cin.get();
      cout << endl;
    }
  }

  in.close();

  return 0;
}
```

When this program is used to display itself, the first screen looks like this:

```
2F 2A 20 44 69 73 70 6C 61 79 20 63 6F 6E 74 65  /* Display conte
6E 74 73 20 6F 66 20 73 70 65 63 69 66 69 65 64  nts of specified
20 66 69 6C 65  D  A 20 20 20 69 6E 20 62 6F 74   file..    in bot
68 20 41 53 43 49 49 20 61 6E 64 20 69 6E 20 68  h ASCII and in h
65 78 2E  D  A 2A 2F  D  A 23 69 6E 63 6C 75 64  ex...*/..#includ
```

```
65 20 3C 69 6F 73 74 72 65 61 6D 2E 68 3E  D  A e <iostream.h>..
23 69 6E 63 6C 75 64 65 20 3C 66 73 74 72 65 61 #include <fstrea
6D 2E 68 3E  D  A 23 69 6E 63 6C 75 64 65 20 3C m.h>..#include <
63 74 79 70 65 2E 68 3E  D  A 23 69 6E 63 6C 75 ctype.h>..#inclu
64 65 20 3C 69 6F 6D 61 6E 69 70 2E 68 3E  D  A de <iomanip.h>..
23 69 6E 63 6C 75 64 65 20 3C 73 74 64 69 6F 2E #include <stdio.
68 3E  D  A  D  A 6D 61 69 6E 28 69 6E 74 20 61 h>....main(int a
72 67 63 2C 20 63 68 61 72 20 2A 61 72 67 76 5B rgc, char *argv[
5D 29  D  A 7B  D  A 20 20 69 66 28 61 72 67 63 ])..{..  if(argc
21 3D 32 29 20 7B  D  A 20 20 20 20 63 6F 75 74 !=2) {..    cout
20 3C 3C 20 22 55 73 61 67 65 3A 20 44 69 73 70  << "Usage: Disp
Press ENTER to continue:
```

The ignore( ) Function

You can use the **ignore( )** member function to read and discard characters from the input stream. It has this prototype:

   istream &ignore(int *num*=1, int *delim*=EOF);

It reads and discards characters until either *num* characters have been ignored (1 by default) or until the character specified by *delim* is encountered (EOF by default). If the delimiting character is encountered, it is not removed from the input stream.

   The next program reads a file called TEST. It ignores characters until either a space is encountered or 10 characters have been read. It then displays the rest of the file.

```
#include <iostream.h>
#include <fstream.h>

main()
{
  ifstream in("test");

  if(!in) {
    cout << "Cannot open file.\n";
    return 1;
  }

  /* Ignore up to 10 characters or until first
     space is found. */
  in.ignore(10, ' ');
```

```
char c;
while(in) {
  in.get(c);
  cout << c;
}

in.close();
return 0;
}
```

peek( ) and putback( )

You can obtain the next character in the input stream without removing it from that stream by using **peek( )**. It has this prototype:

int peek( );

It returns the next character in the stream or EOF if the end of the file is encountered.

You can return the last character read from a stream to that stream by using **putback( )**. Its prototype is

istream &putback(char *c*);

where *c* is the last character read.

flush( )

When output is performed, data is not necessarily immediately written to the physical device linked to the stream. Instead, information is stored in an internal buffer until the buffer is full. Only then are the contents of that buffer written to disk. However, you can force the information to be physically written to disk before the buffer is full by calling **flush( )**. Its prototype is

ostream &flush( );

Calls to **flush( )** might be warranted when a program is going to be used in adverse environments (for example, in situations where power outages occur frequently).

 NOTE: *Closing a file or normal program termination also flushes all buffers.*

Random Access

In C++'s I/O system, you perform random access by using the **seekg( )** and **seekp( )** functions. Their most common forms are

istream &seekg(streamoff *offset*, seek_dir *origin*);

ostream &seekp(streamoff *offset*, seek_dir *origin*);

Here, **streamoff** is a type defined in IOSTREAM.H that is capable of containing the largest valid value that *offset* can have. Also, **seek_dir** is an enumeration that has these values:

ios::beg
ios::cur
ios::end

The C++ I/O system manages two pointers associated with a file. One is the *get pointer*, which specifies where in the file the next input operation will occur. The other is the *put pointer*, which specifies where in the file the next output operation will occur. Each time an input or output operation takes place, the appropriate pointer is automatically sequentially advanced. However, using the **seekg( )** and **seekp( )** functions allows you to access the file in a nonsequential fashion.

The **seekg( )** function moves the associated file's current get pointer *offset* number of bytes from the specified *origin*, which must be one of these three values:

ios::beg   Beginning-of-file
ios::cur   Current location
ios::end   End-of-file

The **seekp( )** function moves the associated file's current put pointer *offset* number of bytes from the specified *origin*, which must be one of the values just shown.

The following program demonstrates the **seekp( )** function. It allows you to change a specific character in a file. Specify a file name on the command line, followed by the number of the byte in the file you want to change, followed by the new character. Notice that the file is opened for read/write operations.

```
#include <iostream.h>
#include <fstream.h>
```

```
#include <stdlib.h>

main(int argc, char *argv[])
{
  if(argc!=4) {
    cout << "Usage: CHANGE <filename> <byte> <char>\n";
    return 1;
  }

  fstream out(argv[1], ios::in | ios::out | ios::binary);
  if(!out) {
    cout << "Cannot open file.";
    return 1;
  }

  out.seekp(atoi(argv[2]), ios::beg);

  out.put(*argv[3]);
  out.close();

  return 0;
}
```

For example, to use this program to change the 12th byte of a file called TEST to a Z, use this command line:

change test 12 Z

The next program uses **seekg( )**. It displays the contents of a file beginning with the location you specify on the command line.

```
#include <iostream.h>
#include <fstream.h>
#include <stdlib.h>

main(int argc, char *argv[])
{
  char ch;

  if(argc!=3) {
```

```
      cout << "Usage: SHOW <filename> <starting location>\n";
      return 1;
    }

    ifstream in(argv[1], ios::in | ios::binary);
    if(!in) {
      cout << "Cannot open file.";
      return 1;
    }

    in.seekg(atoi(argv[2]), ios::beg);

    while(in.get(ch))
      cout << ch;

    return 0;
}
```

The following program uses both **seekp( )** and **seekg( )** to reverse the first <num> characters in a file.

```
#include <iostream.h>
#include <fstream.h>
#include <stdlib.h>

main(int argc, char *argv[])
{
  if(argc!=3) {
    cout << "Usage: Reverse <filename> <num>\n";
    return 1;
  }

  fstream inout(argv[1], ios::in | ios::out | ios::binary);

  if(!inout) {
    cout << "Cannot open input file.\n";
    return 1;
  }

  long e, i, j;
```

```
char c1, c2;
e = atol(argv[2]);

for(i=0, j=e; i<j; i++, j--) {
  inout.seekg(i, ios::beg);
  inout.get(c1);
  inout.seekg(j, ios::beg);
  inout.get(c2);

  inout.seekp(i, ios::beg);
  inout.put(c2);
  inout.seekp(j, ios::beg);
  inout.put(c1);
}

inout.close();
return 0;
}
```

To use the program, specify the name of the file that you want to reverse, followed by the number of characters to reverse. For example, to reverse the first ten characters of a file called TEST, use this command line:

reverse test 10

If the file contained this,

This is a test.

then the file would contain the following after the program executed:

a si sihTtest.

Obtaining the Current File Position

You can determine the current position of each file pointer by using these functions:

streampos tellg( );

streampos tellp( );

Here, **streampos** is a type defined in IOSTREAM.H that is capable of holding the largest value that either function can return. You can use the values returned by **tellg( )** and **tellp( )** as arguments to the following forms of **seekg( )** and **seekp( )**, respectively.

istream &seekg(streampos *pos*);

ostream &seekp(streampos *pos*);

These functions allow you to save the current file location, perform other file operations, and then reset the file location to its previously saved location.

I/O Status

The C++ I/O system maintains status information about the outcome of each I/O operation. The current state of the I/O system is held in an integer, in which the following flags are encoded:

Name	Meaning
eofbit	1 when end-of-file is encountered 0 otherwise
failbit	1 when a (possibly) nonfatal I/O error has occurred 0 otherwise
badbit	1 when a fatal I/O error has occurred 0 otherwise

These flags are enumerated inside **ios**. Also defined in **ios** is **goodbit**, which has the value 0.

There are two ways in which you can obtain I/O status information. First, you can call the **rdstate( )** member function. It has this prototype:

int rdstate( );

It returns the current status of the error flags encoded into an integer. As you can probably guess from looking at the preceding list of flags, **rdstate( )** returns zero when no error has occurred. Otherwise, an error bit is turned on.

*NOTE: The proposed ANSI C++ standard specifies the return type of **rdstate( )** as **iostate**, which is a **typedef** for some form of integer. Currently, most C++ compilers specify **rdstate( )**'s return type as **int**.*

The following program illustrates **rdstate( )**. It displays the contents of a text file. If an error occurs, the program reports it, using **checkstatus( )**.

```cpp
#include <iostream.h>
#include <fstream.h>

void checkstatus(ifstream &in);

main(int argc, char *argv[])
{
  if(argc!=2) {
    cout << "Usage: Display <filename>\n";
    return 1;
  }

  ifstream in(argv[1]);

  if(!in) {
    cout << "Cannot open input file.\n";
    return 1;
  }

  char c;
  while(in.get(c)) {
    cout << c;
    checkstatus(in);
  }

  checkstatus(in);  // check final status
  in.close();
  return 0;
}

void checkstatus(ifstream &in)
{
  int i;

  i = in.rdstate();

  if(i & ios::eofbit)
    cout << "EOF encountered\n";
  else if(i & ios::failbit)
```

```
      cout << "Non-Fatal I/O error\n";
    else if(i & ios::badbit)
      cout << "Fatal I/O error\n";
  }
```

This program will always report one "error." After the **while** loop ends, the final call to **checkstatus( )** reports, as expected, that an EOF has been encountered. You might find the **checkstatus( )** function useful in programs that you write.

The other way that you can determine if an error has occurred is by using one or more of these functions:

int bad( );

int eof( );

int fail( );

int good( );

The **eof( )** function was discussed earlier. The **bad( )** function returns true if **badbit** is set. The **fail( )** function returns true if **failbit** is set. The **good( )** function returns true if there are no errors. Otherwise, they return false.

 NOTE: *The proposed ANSI C++ standard specifies the return type of **bad( )**, **eof( )**, **fail( )**, and **good( )** to be **bool**. However, most currently available C++ compilers specify their return type as **int**. From a practical point of view, the difference is irrelevant because **bool** is automatically elevated to **int** in an expression.*

Once an error has occurred, it may need to be cleared before your program continues. To do this, use the **clear( )** function, which has this prototype:

void clear(int *flags*=0);

If *flags* is zero (as it is by default), all error flags are cleared (reset to zero). Otherwise, set *flags* to the flags or values you want to clear.

Customized I/O and Files

In Chapter 17 you learned how to overload the insertion and extraction operators relative to your own classes. In that chapter, only console I/O was performed. However, because all C++ streams are the same, you can use the same overloaded inserter function to output to the screen or to a file with no changes whatsoever. As an example, the following program reworks the phone book example in Chapter 17 so that it stores a list on disk. The program is very simple: it allows you to add names to the list or to display the list on the screen. However, as an exercise, you might find it interesting to enhance the program so that it will find a specific number and delete unwanted numbers.

```cpp
#include <iostream.h>
#include <fstream.h>
#include <string.h>

class phonebook {
  char name[80];
  char areacode[4];
  char prefix[4];
  char num[5];
public:
  phonebook() { };
  phonebook(char *n, char *a, char *p, char *nm)
  {
    strcpy(name, n);
    strcpy(areacode, a);
    strcpy(prefix, p);
    strcpy(num, nm);
  }
  friend ostream &operator<<(ostream &stream, phonebook o);
  friend istream &operator>>(istream &stream, phonebook &o);
};

// Display name and phone number.
ostream &operator<<(ostream &stream, phonebook o)
{
  stream << o.name << " ";
  stream << "(" << o.areacode << ") ";
  stream << o.prefix << "-";
  stream << o.num << "\n";
  return stream; // must return stream
}

// Input name and telephone number.
istream &operator>>(istream &stream, phonebook &o)
```

```
{
  cout << "Enter name: ";
  stream >> o.name;
  cout << "Enter area code: ";
  stream >> o.areacode;
  cout << "Enter prefix: ";
  stream >> o.prefix;
  cout << "Enter number: ";
  stream >> o.num;
  cout << "\n";
  return stream;
}

main()
{
  phonebook a;
  char c;

  fstream pb("phone", ios::in | ios::out | ios::app);

  if(!pb) {
    cout << "Cannot open phone book file.\n";
    return 1;
  }

  for(;;) {
    do {
      cout << "1. Enter numbers\n";
      cout << "2. Display numbers\n";
      cout << "3. Quit\n";
      cout << "\nEnter a choice: ";
      cin >> c;
    } while(c<'1' || c>'3');

    switch(c) {
      case '1':
        cin >> a;
        cout << "Entry is: ";
        cout << a;  // show on screen
        pb << a;  // write to disk
```

```
        break;
      case '2':
        char ch;
        pb.seekg(0, ios::beg);
        while(!pb.eof()) {
          pb.get(ch);
          cout << ch;
        }
        pb.clear();  // reset eof
        cout << endl;
        break;
      case '3':
        pb.close();
        return 0;
    }
  }
}
```

Notice that the overloaded << operator can be used to write to a disk file or to the screen without any changes. This is one of the most important and useful features of C++'s approach to I/O.

Chapter Nineteen

Array-Based I/O

In addition to console and file I/O, C++'s stream-based I/O system allows *array-based I/O*. *Array-based I/O* uses RAM as the input device, the output device, or both. Array-based I/O is performed through normal C++ streams. In fact, all the information presented in the two preceding chapters is applicable to array-based I/O. What makes array-based I/O unique is that the device linked to the stream is memory.

In some C++ literature, array-based I/O is referred to as *in-RAM I/O*. Also, because the streams are, like all C++ streams, capable of handling formatted information, array-based I/O is sometimes called *in-RAM formatting*. (Sometimes the archaic term *incore formatting* is also used. However, because core memory is largely a thing of the past, this book uses the terms *in-RAM* and *array-based*.)

C++'s array-based I/O is similar in effect to C's **sprintf( )** and **sscanf( )** functions. Both approaches use memory as an input or output device.

To use array-based I/O in your programs, you must include STRSTREA.H.

The Array-Based Classes

The array-based I/O classes are **istrstream**, **ostrstream**, and **strstream**. These classes are used to create input, output, and input/output streams, respectively. All of these classes have **strstreambuf** as one of their base classes. This class defines several low-level details that are used by the derived classes. In addition to **strstreambuf**, the **istrstream** class also has **istream** as a base. The **ostrstream** class is also derived from **ostream**, and the **strstream** class also contains the **iostream** classes. Therefore, all array-based classes have access to the same member functions that the "normal" I/O classes do.

Creating an Array-Based Output Stream

To link an output stream to an array, use this **ostrstream** constructor:

ostrstream ostr(char *buf, int size, int mode=ios::out)

Here, *buf* is a pointer to the array that will be used to collect characters written to the stream. The size of the array is passed in the *size* parameter. By default, the stream is opened for normal output, but you can OR various other options with it to create the mode that you need. (For example, you might include **ios::app** to cause output to be written at the end of any information already contained in the array.) For most purposes, *mode* will be allowed to default.

Once you have opened an array-based output stream, all output to that stream is put into the array. However, no output will be written outside the bounds of the array. An attempt to do so results in an error.

Here is a simple program that demonstrates an array-based output stream:

```
#include <strstrea.h>
#include <iostream.h>

main()
{
  char str[80];

  ostrstream outs(str, sizeof(str));

  outs << "Hello ";
  outs << 99-14 << hex << " ";
  outs.setf(ios::showbase);
  outs << 100 << ends;
  cout << str;  // display string on console

  return 0;
}
```

This program displays **Hello 85 0x64**. Keep in mind that **outs** is a stream like any other stream; it has the same capabilities as any of the other types of streams that have been described. The only difference is that the device it is linked to is memory. Because **outs** is a stream, manipulators such as **hex** and **ends** are perfectly valid. Also, **ostream** member functions such as **setf( )** are also available for use.

If you want the output array to be null terminated, you must explicitly write a null. In the preceding program, the **ends** manipulator was used to null terminate the string, but you could also have used '\0'.

If you're not quite sure what is really happening in the preceding program, compare it to the following C program. This program is functionally equivalent to the C++ version. However, it uses **sprintf( )** to construct an output array.

```
#include <stdio.h>

main()
{
  char str[80];

  sprintf(str, "Hello %d %#x", 99-14, 100);
  printf(str);

  return 0;
}
```

You can determine how many characters are in the output array by calling the **pcount( )** member function. It has this prototype:

int pcount( );

The number returned by **pcount( )** also includes the null terminator, if it exists.

The next program illustrates **pcount( )**. It reports that 17 characters are in **outs**—16 characters plus the null terminator.

```cpp
#include <strstrea.h>
#include <iostream.h>

main()
{
  char str[80];

  ostrstream outs(str, sizeof(str));

  outs << "Hello ";
  outs << 34 << " " << 1234.23;
  outs << ends;  // null terminate

  cout << outs.pcount(); // display how many chars in outs

  cout << " " << str;

  return 0;
}
```

Using an Array as Input

To link an input stream to an array, use this **istrstream** constructor:

istrstream istr(char *buf);

Here, *buf* is a pointer to the array that will be used as a source of characters each time input is performed on the stream. The contents of the array pointed to by *buf* must be null terminated. However, the null terminator is never read from the array.

Here is an example that uses a string as input:

```
#include <iostream.h>
#include <strstrea.h>

main()
{
  char s[] = "10 Hello 0x88 12.23 done";

  istrstream ins(s);

  int i;
  char str[80];
  float f;

  // reading: 10 Hello
  ins >> i;
  ins >> str;
  cout << i << " " << str << endl;

  // reading 0x88 12.23 done
  ins >> i;

  ins >> f;
  ins >> str;

  cout << hex << i << " " << f << " " << str;

  return 0;
}
```

If you want only part of a string to be used for input, use this form of the
istrstream constructor:

istrstream istr(char *buf*, int *size*);

Here, only the first *size* elements of the array pointed to by *buf* will be used. This string
need not be null terminated because it is the value of *size* that determines the size of
the string.

Streams linked to memory behave just like those linked to other devices. For
example, the following program illustrates how contents of any text array may be
read. When the end of the array (same as end-of-file) is reached, **ins** will be zero.

```
/* This program shows how to read the contents of any
   array that contains text.  */
#include <iostream.h>
#include <strstrea.h>

main()
{
  char s[] = "10.23 this is a test !#?@\n";

  istrstream ins(s);

  char ch;

  /* This will read and display the contents
     of any text array. */
  ins.unsetf(ios::skipws); // don't skip spaces
  while (ins) {  // 0 when end of array is reached
    ins >> ch;
    cout << ch;
  }

  return 0;
}
```

Using ios Member Functions on Array-Based Streams

Array-based streams can also be accessed with the standard **ios** member functions, such as **get( )** and **put( )**. The status of an array-based stream can be determined with functions such as **rdstate( )**, **good( )**, **bad( )**, and so on. You can also use **eof( )** to determine when the end of the array has been reached. For example, the following program shows how to read the contents of any array by using **get( )**.

```
#include <iostream.h>
#include <strstrea.h>

main()
{
  char s[] = "abcdefghijklmnop";

  istrstream ins(s);
```

```
    char ch;

    // This will read the contents of any type of array.
    while (!ins.eof()) {
      ins.get(ch);
      cout << ch;
    }

    return 0;
}
```

One especially good use of the **ios** member functions is when you need to read or write buffers of data. Specifically, you can use **read( )** to read a buffer and **write( )** to write a buffer.

Input/Output Array-Based Streams

To create an array-based stream that can perform both input and output, use this **strstream** constructor function:

strstream iostr(char *buf, int size, int mode);

Here, *buf* points to the string that will be used for I/O operations. The value of *size* specifies the size of the array. The value of *mode* determines how the stream operates. For normal input/output operations, *mode* will be **ios::in ¦ ios::out**. For input, the array must be null terminated.

Here is a program that uses an array to perform both input and output:

```
// Perform both input and output.
#include <iostream.h>
#include <strstrea.h>

main()
{
  char iostr[80];

  strstream ios(iostr, sizeof(iostr), ios::in ¦ ios::out);

  int a, b;
  char str[80];
```

```
ios << "10 20 testing";
ios >> a >> b >> str;
cout << a << " " << b << " " << str << endl;

return 0;
}
```

It first writes **10 20 testing** to **iostr** and reads this information from **iostr**.

Random Access Within Arrays

Remember that all normal I/O operations apply to array-based I/O. This includes random access using **seekg( )** and **seekp( )**. For example, the next program seeks the eighth character inside **iostr** and displays it. (It outputs **h**.)

```
#include <iostream.h>
#include <strstrea.h>

main()
{
  char iostr[80];

  strstream ios(iostr, sizeof(iostr), ios::in | ios::out);

  char ch;

  ios << "abcdefghijklmnopqrstuvwxyz";
  ios.seekg(7, ios::beg);
  ios >> ch;
  cout << "Character at 7: " << ch;

  return 0;
}
```

You can seek anywhere *inside* the I/O array. However, you are not allowed to seek past an array boundary.

You can also apply functions like **tellg( )** and **tellp( )** to array-based streams.

Using Dynamic Arrays

In the first part of this chapter, when you linked a stream to an output array, the array and its size were passed to the **ostrstream** constructor. This approach is fine as long as you know the maximum number of characters that you will be outputting to that array. However, what if you don't know how large the output array needs to be? The solution to this problem is to use a second form of the **ostrstream** constructor, shown here:

```
ostrstream( );
```

When this constructor is used, **ostrstream** creates and maintains a dynamically allocated array. This array is allowed to grow in length to accommodate the output that it must store.

Notice that the **ostrstream** constructor does *not* return a pointer to the allocated array. To access the dynamically allocated array, you must use a second function, called **str( )**. This function "freezes" the array and returns a pointer to it. Once a dynamic array is frozen, it cannot be used for output again. Therefore, wait to freeze the array until you are through outputting characters to it.

Here is a program that uses a dynamic output array:

```cpp
#include <strstrea.h>
#include <iostream.h>

main()
{

  char *p;

  ostrstream outs;  // dynamically allocate array

  outs << "I like C++ ";
  outs << -10 << hex << " ";
  outs.setf(ios::showbase);
  outs << 100 << ends;

  p = outs.str(); /* Freeze dynamic buffer and return
                      pointer to it. */

  cout << p;

  delete p;  // Free dynamic buffer created by ostrstream().
  return 0;
}
```

As this program illustrates, once a dynamic array has been frozen, it is your responsibility to release its memory back to the system when you are through with it. However, if you never freeze the array, the memory is automatically freed when the stream is destroyed.

You can also use dynamic I/O arrays with the **strstream** class, which may perform both input and output on an array. To create a dynamic array using **strstream**, use this constructor:

```
strstream( );
```

This will cause a dynamic array capable of input and output to be created.

Manipulators and Array-Based I/O

Because array-based streams are the same as any other stream, manipulators that you create for I/O in general can be used with array-based I/O with no changes whatsoever. For example, in Chapter 17, the output manipulators **ra( )** and **la( )** (right arrow and left arrow, respectively) were created for console I/O. The following program shows that they are just as effective on array-based I/O.

```cpp
// This program uses custom manipulators with
// array-based I/O.

#include <strstrea.h>
#include <iostream.h>

// Right Arrow
ostream &ra(ostream &stream)
{
   stream << "-------> ";
   return stream;
}

// Left Arrow
ostream &la(ostream &stream)
{
   stream << " <-------";
   return stream;
}

main()
{
```

```
    char str[80];

    ostrstream outs(str, sizeof(str));

    outs << ra << "Look at this number: ";
    outs << 1000000 << la << ends; // null terminate

    cout << " " << str;

    return 0;
}
```

This program displays the following output:

```
-------> Look at this number: 1000000 <-------
```

Custom Extractors and Inserters

Because array-based streams are just like other streams, you can create your own extractor and inserter functions the same way you create them for other types of streams. For example, the following program creates a class called **plot**, which maintains the x, y coordinates of a point in two-dimensional space. The overloaded inserter for this class displays a small coordinate plane and plots the location of the point. For simplicity, the range of the x, y coordinates is restricted to 0 through 5.

```
#include <iostream.h>
#include <strstrea.h>

const int size = 5;

class plot {
  int x, y;
public:
  plot(int i, int j) {
    // for sake of example, restrict x and y to 0 through size
    if(i>size) i = size;  if (i<0) i=0;
    if(j>size) j = size;  if (j<0) j=0;
    x=i; y=j;
  }
  // An inserter for plot.
```

```cpp
    friend ostream &operator<<(ostream &stream, plot o);
};

ostream &operator<<(ostream &stream, plot o)
{
  register int i, j;

  for(j=size; j>=0; j--) {
    stream << j;
    if(j == o.y) {
      for(i=0; i<o.x; i++) stream << "   ";
      stream << '*';
    }
    stream << "\n";
  }

  for(i=0; i<=size; i++) stream << " " << i;
  stream << "\n";

  return stream;
}

main()
{
  plot a(2, 3), b(1, 1);
  char str[200];

  // output first using cout
  cout << "Output using cout:\n";
  cout << a << "\n" << b << "\n\n";

  // now use RAM-based I/O
  ostrstream outs(str, sizeof(str));

  // now output using outs and in-RAM formatting
  outs << a << b << ends;

  cout << "Output using in-RAM formatting:\n";
  cout << str;

  return 0;
}
```

This program produces the following output:

```
Output using cout:
5
4
3     *
2
1
0
  0 1 2 3 4 5


5
4
3
2
1  *
0
  0 1 2 3 4 5


Output using in-RAM formatting:
5
4
3     *
2
1
0
  0 1 2 3 4 5
5
4
3
2
1  *
0
  0 1 2 3 4 5
```

Uses for Array-Based Formatting

In C, the in-RAM I/O functions **sprintf( )** and **sscanf( )** were particularly useful for preparing output to or reading input from nonstandard devices. However, because of C++'s ability to overload inserters and extractors relative to a class and to create custom manipulators, many exotic devices can be easily handled with these features. This makes the need for in-RAM formatting less important. Still, there are many uses for array-based I/O.

One common use of array-based formatting is to construct a string to be used as input by either a standard library or third-party function. For example, you may need to construct a string that will be parsed by the **strtok( )** standard library function. (The **strtok( )** function "tokenizes"—that is, decomposes to its elements—a string.) Another place where array-based I/O can be used is in text editors that perform complex formatting operations. Often it is easier to use C++'s array-based formatted I/O to construct a complex string than it is to do so by "manual" means. Constructing a string using array-based formatting is also particularly useful in Windows programming. Windows does not contain any standard functions that provide formatted output to a window. Instead, you need to construct all formatted output ahead of time.

Chapter Twenty

Templates

A relatively new feature of C++ is the *template*. With a template, it is possible to create *generic functions* and *generic classes*. In a generic function or class, the type of data upon which the function or class operates is specified as a parameter. Thus, you can use one function or class with several different types of data without having to explicitly recode specific versions for different data types. Both generic functions and generic classes are discussed here.

NOTE: *Templates were not part of the original specification for C++, but were added in 1990. Templates are defined by the proposed ANSI C++ standard and are supported by most C++ compilers available today.*

Generic Functions

A generic function defines a general set of operations that will be applied to various types of data. A generic function has the type of data that it will operate upon passed to it as a parameter. Using this mechanism, the same general procedure can be applied to a wide range of data. As you probably know, many algorithms are logically the same no matter what type of data is being operated upon. For example, the Quicksort sorting algorithm is the same whether it is applied to an array of integers or an array of **float**s. It is just that the type of the data being sorted is different. By creating a generic function, you can define, independent of any data, the nature of the algorithm. Once this is done, the compiler automatically generates the correct code for the type of data that is actually used when you execute the function. In essence, when you create a generic function, you are creating a function that can automatically overload itself.

A generic function is created with the keyword **template**. The normal meaning of the word "template" accurately reflects its use in C++. It is used to create a template (or framework) that describes what a function will do, leaving it to the compiler to fill in the details as needed. Here is the general form of a **template** function definition:

```
template <class Ttype> ret-type func-name(parameter list)
{
  // body of function
}
```

Ttype is a placeholder name for the data type used by the function. This name may be used within the function definition. However, it is only a placeholder that the compiler will automatically replace with an actual data type when it creates a specific version of the function.

The following short example creates a generic function that swaps the values of the two variables with which it is called. Because the general process of exchanging two values is independent of the type of the variables, it is a good choice to be made into a generic function.

data: integers, **floats**, and **char**s. Because swap( ) is a generic function, the compiler automatically creates three versions of swap( )—one that will exchange integer values, one that will exchange floating-point values, and one that will swap characters.

Here are some other terms that are sometimes used when discussing templates that you may encounter in other C++ literature. First, a generic function (that is, a function definition preceded by a **template** statement) is also called a *template function*. When the compiler creates a specific version of this function, it is said to have created a *generated function*. The act of generating a function is referred to as *instantiating* it. Put differently, a generated function is a specific instance of a template function.

Technically, the **template** portion of a generic function definition does not have to be on the same line as the function's name. For example, the following is also a common way to format the swap( ) function.

```
template <class X>
void swap(X &a, X &b)
{
    X temp;

    temp = a;
    a = b;
    b = temp;
}
```

If you use this form, it is important to understand that no other statements can occur between the **template** statement and the start of the generic function definition. For example, the fragment shown next will not compile.

```
// This will not compile.
template <class X>
int i; // this is an error
void swap(X &a, X &b)
{
    X temp;

    temp = a;
    a = b;
    b = temp;
}
```

```
// Function template example.
#include <iostream.h>

// This is a function template.
template <class X> void swap(X &a, X &b)
{
   X temp;

   temp = a;
   a = b;
   b = temp;
}

main()
{
   int i=10, j=20;
   float x=10.1, y=23.3;
   char a='x', b='z';

   cout << "Original i, j: " << i << ' ' << j << endl;
   cout << "Original x, y: " << x << ' ' << y << endl;
   cout << "Original a, b: " << a << ' ' << b << endl;

   swap(i, j); // swap integers
   swap(x, y); // swap floats
   swap(a, b); // swap chars

   cout << "Swapped i, j: " << i << ' ' << j << endl;
   cout << "Swapped x, y: " << x << ' ' << y << endl;
   cout << "Swapped a, b: " << a << ' ' << b << endl;

   return 0;
}
```

Let's look closely at this program. The line

```
template <class X> void swap(X &a, X &b)
```

tells the compiler two things: that a template is being created and that a gene···
definition is beginning. Here, **X** is a generic type that is used as a placeholde···
template portion, the function **swap( )** is declared, using **X** as the data type···
values that will be swapped. In **main( )**, the **swap( )** function is called with···

As the comments imply, the **template** specification must directly precede the function definition.

A Function with Two Generic Types

You can define more than one generic data type in the **template** statement, using a comma-separated list. For example, the following program creates a generic function that has two generic types.

```
#include <iostream.h>

template <class type1, class type2>
void myfunc(type1 x, type2 y)
{
  cout << x << ' ' << y << endl;
}

main()
{
  myfunc(10, "hi");

  myfunc(0.23, 10L);

  return 0;
}
```

In this example, the placeholder types **type1** and **type2** are replaced by the compiler with the data types **int** and **char *** and **double** and **long**, respectively, when the compiler generates the specific instances of **myfunc( )** within **main( )**.

 REMEMBER: When you create a generic function, you are, in essence, allowing the compiler to generate as many different versions of that function as necessary to handle the various ways that your program calls that function.

Explicitly Overloading a Generic Function

Even though a template function overloads itself as needed, you can explicitly overload one too. If you overload a generic function, then that overloaded function overrides (or "hides") the generic function relative to that specific version. For example, consider this version of the first example.

```cpp
// Overriding a template function.
#include <iostream.h>

template <class X> void swap(X &a, X &b)
{
  X temp;

  temp = a;
  a = b;
  b = temp;
}

// This overrides the generic version of swap().
void swap(int &a, int &b)
{
  int temp;

  temp = a;
  a = b;
  b = temp;
  cout << "Inside overloaded swap(int &, int &).\n";
}

main()
{
  int i=10, j=20;
  float x=10.1, y=23.3;
  char a='x', b='z';

  cout << "Original i, j: " << i << ' ' << j << endl;
  cout << "Original x, y: " << x << ' ' << y << endl;
  cout << "Original a, b: " << a << ' ' << b << endl;

  swap(i, j); // this calls the explicitly overloaded swap()
  swap(x, y); // swap floats
  swap(a, b); // swap chars

  cout << "Swapped i, j: " << i << ' ' << j << endl;
  cout << "Swapped x, y: " << x << ' ' << y << endl;
  cout << "Swapped a, b: " << a << ' ' << b << endl;

  return 0;
}
```

As the comments indicate, when **swap(i, j)** is called, it invokes the explicitly overloaded version of **swap( )** defined in the program. Thus, the compiler does not generate this version of the generic **swap( )** function because the generic function is overridden by the explicit overloading.

Manual overloading of a template, as shown in this example, allows you to specially tailor a version of a generic function to accommodate a special situation. However, in general, if you need to have different versions of a function for different data types, you should use overloaded functions rather than templates.

Generic Function Restrictions

Generic functions are similar to overloaded functions except that they are more restrictive. When functions are overloaded, you may have different actions performed within the body of each function. But a generic function must perform the same general action for all versions—only the type of data may differ. For example, in the following program, the overloaded functions could not be replaced by a generic function because they do not do the same thing.

```
#include <iostream.h>
#include <math.h>

void myfunc(int i)
{
  cout << "value is: " << i << "\n";
}

void myfunc(double d)
{
  double intpart;
  double fracpart;

  fracpart = modf(d, &intpart);
  cout << "Fractional part: " << fracpart;
  cout << "\n";
  cout << "Integer part: " << intpart;
}

main()
{
  myfunc(1);
  myfunc(12.2);

  return 0;
}
```

Here are some other restrictions to template functions. A virtual function cannot be a template function. Destructors cannot be templates. A template function must use C++ linkage. (That is, it cannot use a linkage specification. See Chapter 22.)

Applying Generic Functions

Generic functions are one of C++'s most useful features. They can be applied to all types of situations. As mentioned earlier, whenever you have a function that defines a generalizable algorithm, you can make it into a template function. Once you have done so, you can use it with any type of data without having to recode it. Before moving on to generic classes, two examples of applying generic functions will be given. They illustrate how easy it is to take advantage of this powerful C++ feature.

A Generic Sort

Sorting is exactly the type of operation that generic functions were designed for. Within wide latitude, a sorting algorithm is the same no matter what type of data is being sorted. The following program illustrates this by creating a generic bubble sort. While the bubble sort is a rather poor sorting algorithm, its operation is clear and uncluttered, and it makes an easy-to-understand example. (You might want to try creating a generic version of your own favorite sorting algorithm on your own.) The **bubble( )** function will sort any type of array. It is called with a pointer to the first element in the array and the number of elements in the array.

```
// A Generic bubble sort.
#include <iostream.h>

template <class X> void bubble(
  X *items,  // pointer to array to be sorted
  int count) // number of items in array
{
  register int a, b;
  X t;

  for(a=1; a<count; a++)
    for(b=count-1; b>=a; b--)
      if(items[b-1] > items[b]) {
        // exchange elements
        t = items[b-1];
        items[b-1] = items[b];
        items[b] = t;
      }
```

```
}

main()
{
  int iarray[7] = {7, 5, 4, 3, 9, 8, 6};
  double darray[5] = {4.3, 2.5, -0.9, 100.2, 3.0};

  int i;

  cout << "Here is unsorted integer array: ";
  for(i=0;  i<7; i++)
    cout << iarray[i] << ' ';
  cout << endl;

  cout << "Here is unsorted double array: ";
  for(i=0;  i<5; i++)
    cout << darray[i] << ' ';
  cout << endl;

  bubble(iarray, 7);
  bubble(darray, 5);

  cout << "Here is sorted integer array: ";
  for(i=0;  i<7; i++)
    cout << iarray[i] << ' ';
  cout << endl;

  cout << "Here is sorted double array: ";
  for(i=0;  i<5; i++)
    cout << darray[i] << ' ';
  cout << endl;

  return 0;
}
```

This program generates the following output:

```
Here is unsorted integer array: 7 5 4 3 9 8 6
Here is unsorted double array: 4.3 2.5 -0.9 100.2 3
Here is sorted integer array: 3 4 5 6 7 8 9
Here is sorted double array: -0.9 2.5 3 4.3 100.2
```

As you can see, the preceding program creates two arrays: one integer and one **double**. It then sorts each. Because **bubble( )** is a template function, it is automatically overloaded to accommodate the two different types of data.

Compacting an Array

Another function that benefits from being made into a template function is called **compact( )**. This function compacts the elements in an array. As you may know from your programming experience, it is not uncommon to want to remove elements from the middle of an array and then move the remaining elements down so that all unused elements are at the end. This sort of operation is the same for all types of arrays because it is independent of the type of data actually being operated upon. The generic **compact( )** function shown in the following program is called with a pointer to the first element in the array, the number of elements in the array, and the starting and ending indexes of the elements to be removed. The function then removes those elements and compacts the array. For the purposes of illustration, it also zeros the unused elements at the end of the array that have been freed by the compaction.

```cpp
// A Generic array compaction function.
#include <iostream.h>

template <class X> void compact(
  X *items,  // pointer to array to be compacted
  int count, // number of items in array
  int start, // starting index of compacted region
  int end)   // ending index of compacted region
{
  register int i;

  for(i=end+1; i<count; i++, start++)
    items[start] = items[i];

  /* For the sake of illustration, the remainder of
     the array will be zeroed. */
```

```
    for( ; start<count; start++) items[start] = (X) 0;
}

main()
{
  int nums[7] = {0, 1, 2, 3, 4, 5, 6};
  char str[18] = "Generic Functions";

  int i;

  cout << "Here is uncompacted integer array: ";
  for(i=0;  i<7; i++)
    cout << nums[i] << ' ';
  cout << endl;

  cout << "Here is uncompacted string: ";
  for(i=0;  i<18; i++)
    cout << str[i] << ' ';
  cout << endl;

  compact(nums, 7, 2, 4);
  compact(str, 18, 6, 10);

  cout << "Here is compacted integer array: ";
  for(i=0;  i<7; i++)
    cout << nums[i] << ' ';
  cout << endl;

  cout << "Here is compacted string: ";
  for(i=0;  i<18; i++)
    cout << str[i] << ' ';
  cout << endl;

  return 0;
}
```

This program compacts two types of arrays. One is an integer array and the other is a string. However, the **compact( )** function will work for any type of array. The output from this program in shown here:

```
Here is uncompacted integer array: 0 1 2 3 4 5 6
Here is uncompacted string: G e n e r i c   F u n c t i o n s
Here is compacted integer array: 0 1 5 6 0 0 0
Here is compacted string: G e n e r i c t i o n s
```

As the preceding examples illustrate, once you begin to start thinking in terms of templates, many uses will naturally suggest themselves. As long as the underlying logic of a function is independent of the data, then it can be made into a generic function.

Generic Classes

In addition to generic functions, you can also define a generic class. When you do this, you create a class that defines all algorithms used by that class, but the actual type of the data being manipulated will be specified as a parameter when objects of that class are created.

Generic classes are useful when a class contains generalizable logic. For example, the same algorithm that maintains a queue of integers will also work for a queue of characters. Also, the same mechanism that maintains a linked list of mailing addresses will also maintain a linked list of auto part information. By using a generic class, you can define the operations that will maintain a queue, linked list, and so on, for any type of data. The compiler will automatically generate the correct type of object based upon the type you specify when the object is created.

The general form of a generic class declaration is shown here:

```
template <class Ttype> class class-name {
    .
    .
    .
}
```

Here, *Ttype* is the placeholder type name that will be specified when a class is instantiated. If necessary, you can define more than one generic data type using a comma-separated list.

Once you have created a generic class, you create a specific instance of that class using this general form:

```
class-name <type> ob;
```

Here, *type* is the type name of the data that the class will be operating upon. Member functions of a generic class are, themselves, automatically generic.

In the following program, the **stack** class (first introduced in Chapter 11) is reworked into a generic class. Thus, it can be used to provide a stack for any type of object. In the example shown here, a character stack, an integer stack, and a floating-point stack are created.

```cpp
// Demonstrate a generic stack class.
#include <iostream.h>

const int SIZE = 100;

// This creates the generic class stack.
template <class SType> class stack {
  SType stck[SIZE];
  int tos;
public:
  stack();
  ~stack();
  void push(SType i);
  SType pop();
};

// stack's constructor function
template <class SType> stack<SType>::stack()
{
  tos = 0;
  cout << "Stack Initialized\n";
}

/* stack's destructor function
   This function is not required.  It is included
   for illustration only. */
template <class SType> stack<SType>::~stack()
{
  cout << "Stack Destroyed\n";
}

// Push an object onto the stack.
template <class SType> void stack<SType>::push(SType i)
{
  if(tos==SIZE) {
```

```
      cout << "Stack is full.";
      return;
    }
    stck[tos] = i;
    tos++;
}

// Pop an object off the stack.
template <class SType> SType stack<SType>::pop()
{
    if(tos==0) {
     . cout << "Stack underflow.";
      return 0;
    }
    tos--;
    return stck[tos];
}

main()
{
    stack<int> a; // create integer stack
    stack<double> b; // create a double stack
    stack<char> c; // create a character stack

    int i;

    // use the integer and double stacks
    a.push(1);
    b.push(99.3);
    a.push(2);
    b.push(-12.23);

    cout << a.pop() << " ";
    cout << a.pop() << " ";
    cout << b.pop() << " ";
    cout << b.pop() << "\n";

    // demonstrate the character stack
    for(i=0; i<10; i++) c.push((char) 'A'+i);
    for(i=0; i<10; i++) cout << c.pop();
    cout << "\n";
```

```
    return 0;
}
```

As you can see, the declaration of a generic class is similar to that of a generic function. The generic data type is used in the class declaration and in its member functions. It is not until an object of the stack is declared that the actual data type is determined. When a specific instance of **stack** is declared, the compiler automatically generates all the necessary functions and variables to handle the actual data. In this example, three types of stacks are declared (one for integers, one for **double**s, and one for characters). Pay special attention to these declarations:

```
stack<int> a; // create integer stack
stack<double> b; // create a double stack
stack<char> c; // create a character stack
```

Notice how the desired data type is passed inside the angle brackets. By changing the type of data specified when **stack** objects are created, you can change the type of data stored by that stack. For example, you could create another stack that stores character pointers by using this declaration:

```
stack<char *> chrptrstck;
```

You can also create stacks to store data types that you create. For example, if you want to store address information, use this structure:

```
struct addr {
   char name[40];
   char street[40];
   char city[30];
   char state[3];
   char zip[12];
}
```

Then, to use **stack** to generate a stack that will store objects of type **addr**, use a declaration like this:

```
stack<addr> obj;
```

As the **stack** class illustrates, generic functions and classes provide a powerful tool that you can use to maximize your programming effort because they allow you to define the general form of an object that can be used with any type of data. You are saved from the tedium of creating separate implementations for each data type that you want the class to work with. The compiler automatically creates the specific versions of the class for you.

An Example with Two Generic Data Types

A template class can have more than one generic data type. Simply declare all the data types required by the class in a comma-separated list within the **template** specification. For example, the following short example creates a class that uses two generic data types.

```
/* This example uses two generic data types in a
   class definition.
*/
#include <iostream.h>

template <class Type1, class Type2> class myclass
{
  Type1 i;
  Type2 j;
public:
  myclass(Type1 a, Type2 b) { i = a; j = b; }
  void show() { cout << i << ' ' << j << '\n'; }
};

main()
{
  myclass<int, double> ob1(10, 0.23);
  myclass<char, char *> ob2('X', "This is a test");

  ob1.show(); // show int, double
  ob2.show(); // show char, char *

  return 0;
}
```

This program produces the following output:

```
10 0.23
X This is a test
```

The program declares two types of objects. **ob1** uses integer and **double** data. **ob2** uses a character and a character pointer. For both cases, the compiler automatically generates the appropriate data and functions to accommodate the way the objects are created.

Creating a Generic Array Class

Let's look at a common application of a generic class. As you saw in Chapter 14, you can overload the [] operator. Doing so allows you to create your own array implementations. This allows the creation of "safe arrays," which provide run-time boundary checking. As you know, in C++, it is possible to overrun (or underrun) an array boundary at run time without generating a run-time error message. However, if you create a class that contains the array and allow access to that array only through the overloaded [] subscripting operator, then you can intercept an out-of-range index.

By combining operator overloading with a generic class, it is possible to create a generic safe array type that can be used to create safe arrays of any data type. The following program illustrates this.

```
// A generic safe array example.
#include <iostream.h>
#include "stdlib.h"

const int SIZE = 10;

template <class AType> class atype {
  AType a[SIZE];
public:
  atype() {
    register int i;
    for(i=0; i<SIZE; i++) a[i] = i;
  }
  AType &operator[](int i);
};

// Provide range checking for atype.
template <class AType> AType &atype<AType>::operator[](int i)
{
```

```
    if(i<0 || i> SIZE-1) {
      cout << "\nIndex value of ";
      cout << i << " is out-of-bounds.\n";
      exit(1);
    }
    return a[i];
}

main()
{
  atype<int> intob; // integer array
  atype<double> doubleob; // double array

  int i;

  cout << "Integer array: ";
  for(i=0; i<SIZE; i++) intob[i] = i;
  for(i=0; i<SIZE; i++) cout << intob[i] << "  ";
  cout << '\n';

  cout << "Double array: ";
  cout.precision(2);
  for(i=0; i<SIZE; i++) doubleob[i] = (double) i/3;
  for(i=0; i<SIZE; i++) cout << doubleob[i] << "  ";
  cout << '\n';

  intob[12] = 100; // generates runtime error

  return 0;
}
```

This program implements a generic safe array type and then demonstrates its use by creating an array of integers and an array of **double**s. (You might want to try creating other types of arrays.) As this example shows, part of the power of generic classes is that they allow you to write the code once, debug it, and then apply it to any type of data without having to reengineer it for each application.

For simplicity, the preceding program uses fixed-size arrays. However, you can change the **atype** class so that arrays of varying dimensions can be declared. To accomplish this, specify the array dimension as a parameter to the **atype** constructor function and dynamically allocate the array.

NOTE: *For another example of class templates, refer to Chapter 25. It uses a template class to create a generic doubly linked list capable of storing any type of object.*

Chapter Twenty-One

Exception Handling

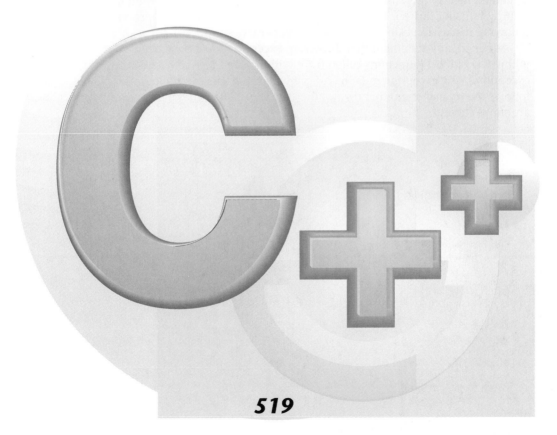

519

This chapter discusses C++-style *exception handling. Exception handling* allows you to manage run-time errors in an orderly fashion. Using C++ exception handling, your program can automatically invoke an error-handling routine when an error occurs. The principal advantage of exception handling is that it automates much of the error-handling code that previously had to be coded "by hand" in any large program.

NOTE: *Exception handling was not part of the original specification for C++. It evolved from 1984 through 1989. Exception handling is defined by the proposed ANSI C++ standard and is supported by most C++ compilers available today.*

Exception-Handling Fundamentals

C++ exception handling is built upon three keywords: **try**, **catch**, and **throw**. In the most general terms, program statements that you want to monitor for exceptions are contained in a **try** block. If an exception (that is, an error) occurs within the **try** block, it is thrown (using **throw**). The exception is caught, using **catch**, and processed. The following discussion elaborates upon this general description.

As stated, any statement that throws an exception must have been executed from within a **try** block. (Functions called from within a **try** block may also throw an exception.) Any exception must be caught by a **catch** statement that immediately follows the **try** statement that throws the exception. The general forms of **try** and **catch** are shown here:

```
try {
    // try block
}
catch (type1 arg) {
    // catch block
}
catch (type2 arg) {
    // catch block
}
catch (type3 arg) {
    // catch block
}
    .
    .
    .
catch (typeN arg) {
```

```
    // catch block
}
```

The **try** block must contain that portion of your program that you want to monitor for errors. This can be as short as a few statements within one function or as all-encompassing as enclosing the **main( )** function code within a **try** block (which effectively causes the entire program to be monitored).

When an exception is thrown, it is caught by its corresponding **catch** statement, which processes the exception. There can be more than one **catch** statement associated with a **try**. Which **catch** statement is used is determined by the type of the exception. That is, if the data type specified by a **catch** matches that of the exception, then that **catch** statement is executed (and all others are bypassed). When an exception is caught, *arg* will receive its value. Any type of data may be caught, including classes that you create. If no exception is thrown (that is, no error occurs within the **try** block), then no **catch** statement is executed.

The general form of the **throw** statement is shown here:

throw *exception*;

throw must be executed either from within the **try** block, proper, or from any function called (directly or indirectly) from within the **try** block. *exception* is the value thrown.

If you throw an exception for which there is no applicable **catch** statement, an abnormal program termination may occur. If your compiler complies with the proposed ANSI C++ standard, then throwing an unhandled exception causes the **terminate( )** function to be invoked. By default, **terminate( )** calls **abort( )** to stop your program, but you can specify your own termination handler if you like. You will need to refer to your compiler's library reference for details.

Here is a very simple example that shows the way C++ exception handling operates:

```cpp
// A simple exception handling example.
#include <iostream.h>

main()
{
  cout << "Start\n";

  try { // start a try block
    cout << "Inside try block\n";
    throw 100; // throw an error
    cout << "This will not execute";
  }
```

```
  catch (int i) { // catch an error
    cout << "Caught an exception -- value is: ";
    cout << i << "\n";
  }

  cout << "End";

  return 0;
}
```

This program displays the following output:

```
Start
Inside try block
Caught an exception -- value is: 100
End
```

Look carefully at the preceding program. As you can see, there is a **try** block containing three statements and a **catch(int i)** statement that processes an integer exception. Within the **try** block, only two of the three statements will execute: the first **cout** statement and the **throw**. Once an exception has been thrown, control passes to the **catch** expression and the **try** block is terminated. That is, **catch** is *not* called. Rather, program execution is transferred to it. (The program's stack is automatically reset as needed to accomplish this.) Thus, the **cout** statement following the **throw** will never execute.

Usually, the code within a **catch** statement attempts to remedy an error by taking appropriate action. If the error can be fixed, then execution will continue with the statements following the **catch**. However, often an error cannot be fixed and a **catch** block will terminate the program with a call to **exit( )** or **abort( )**.

As mentioned, the type of the exception must match the type specified in a **catch** statement. For example, in the preceding example, if you change the type in the **catch** statement to **double**, then the exception will not be caught and abnormal termination will occur. This change is shown here:

```
// This example will not work.
#include <iostream.h>

main()
{
  cout << "Start\n";

  try { // start a try block
```

```
    cout << "Inside try block\n";
    throw 100; // throw an error
    cout << "This will not execute";
  }
  catch (double i) { // Won't work for an int exception
    cout << "Caught an exception -- value is: ";
    cout << i << "\n";
  }

  cout << "End";

  return 0;
}
```

This program produces the following output because the integer exception will not be caught by the **catch(double i)** statement.

```
Start
Inside try block
Abnormal program termination
```

An exception can be thrown from a statement that is outside the **try** block as long as it is within a function that is called from within the **try** block. For example, this is a valid program:

```
/* Throwing an exception from a function outside the
   try block.
*/
#include <iostream.h>

void Xtest(int test)
{
  cout << "Inside Xtest, test is: " << test << "\n";
  if(test) throw test;
}

main()
{
  cout << "Start\n";

  try { // start a try block
    cout << "Inside try block\n";
```

```
    Xtest(0);
    Xtest(1);
    Xtest(2);
  }
  catch (int i) { // catch an error
    cout << "Caught an exception -- value is: ";
    cout << i << "\n";
  }

  cout << "End";

  return 0;
}
```

This program produces the following output:

```
Start
Inside try block
Inside Xtest, test is: 0
Inside Xtest, test is: 1
Caught an exception -- value is: 1
End
```

A **try** block can be localized to a function. When this is the case, each time the function is entered, the exception handling relative to that function is reset. For example, examine this program:

```
#include <iostream.h>

// A try/catch can be inside a function other than main().
void Xhandler(int test)
{
  try{
    if(test) throw test;
  }
  catch(int i) {
    cout << "Caught Exception #: " << i << '\n';
  }
}
```

```
main()
{
  cout << "Start\n";

  Xhandler(1);
  Xhandler(2);
  Xhandler(0);
  Xhandler(3);

  cout << "End";

  return 0;
}
```

This program displays the following output:

```
Start
Caught Exception #: 1
Caught Exception #: 2
Caught Exception #: 3
End
```

As you can see, three exceptions are thrown. After each exception, the function returns. When the function is called again, the exception handling is reset.

It is important to understand that the code associated with a **catch** statement will only be executed if it catches an exception. Otherwise, execution simply bypasses a **catch** statement. (That is, execution never flows into a **catch** statement.) For example, in the following program, no exception is thrown, so the **catch** statement does not execute.

```
#include <iostream.h>

main()
{
  cout << "Start\n";

  try { // start a try block
    cout << "Inside try block\n";
//    throw 100; // this throw does not execute
```

```
    cout << "Still inside try block\n";
  }
  catch (int i) { // catch an error
    cout << "Caught an exception -- value is: ";
    cout << i << "\n";
  }

  cout << "End";

  return 0;
}
```

This program produces the following output:

```
Start
Inside try block
Still inside try block
End
```

As you see, the **catch** statement is bypassed by the flow of execution.

Using Multiple catch Statements

As stated, you can associate more than one **catch** with a **try**. In fact, it is common to do so. However, each **catch** must catch a different type of exception. For example, this program catches both integers and strings.

```
#include <iostream.h>

// Different types of exceptions can be caught.
void Xhandler(int test)
{
  try{
    if(test) throw test;
    else throw "Value is zero";
  }
  catch(int i) {
    cout << "Caught Exception #: " << i << '\n';
  }
  catch(char *str) {
```

```
        cout << "Caught a string: ";
        cout << str << '\n';
    }
}

main()
{
  cout << "Start\n";

  Xhandler(1);
  Xhandler(2);
  Xhandler(0);
  Xhandler(3);

  cout << "End";

  return 0;
}
```

This program produces the following output:

```
Start
Caught Exception #: 1
Caught Exception #: 2
Caught a string: Value is zero
Caught Exception #: 3
End
```

As you can see, each **catch** statement responds only to its own type.

In general, **catch** expressions are checked in the order in which they occur in a program. Only a matching statement is executed. All other **catch** blocks are ignored.

Exception-Handling Options

There are several additional features and nuances to C++ exception handling that make it easier and more convenient to use. These attributes are discussed here.

Catching All Exceptions

In some circumstances you will want an exception handler to catch all exceptions instead of just a certain type. This is easy to accomplish. Simply use this form of **catch**:

```
catch(...) {
  // process all exceptions
}
```

Here, the ellipsis matches any type of data.

The following program illustrates **catch(...)**.

```cpp
// This example catches all exceptions.
#include <iostream.h>

void Xhandler(int test)
{
  try{
    if(test==0) throw test; // throw int
    if(test==1) throw 'a'; // throw char
    if(test==2) throw 123.23; // throw double
  }
  catch(...) { // catch all exceptions
    cout << "Caught One!\n";
  }
}

main()
{
  cout << "Start\n";

  Xhandler(0);
  Xhandler(1);
  Xhandler(2);

  cout << "End";

  return 0;
}
```

This program displays the following output:

```
Start
Caught One!
Caught One!
Caught One!
End
```

As you can see, all three **throw**s were caught using the one **catch** statement.

One very good use for **catch(...)** is as the last **catch** of a cluster of catches. In this capacity it provides a useful default or "catch all" statement. For example, this slightly different version of the preceding program explicitly catches integer exceptions but relies upon **catch(...)** to catch all others.

```
// This example uses catch(...) as a default.
#include <iostream.h>

void Xhandler(int test)
{
  try{
    if(test==0) throw test; // throw int
    if(test==1) throw 'a'; // throw char
    if(test==2) throw 123.23; // throw double
  }
  catch(int i) { // catch an int exception
    cout << "Caught an integer\n";
  }
  catch(...) { // catch all other exceptions
    cout << "Caught One!\n";
  }
}

main()
{
  cout << "Start\n";

  Xhandler(0);
  Xhandler(1);
  Xhandler(2);

  cout << "End";

  return 0;
}
```

The output produced by this program is shown here:

```
Start
Caught an integer
Caught One!
Caught One!
End
```

As this example suggests, using **catch(...)** as a default is a good way to catch all exceptions that you don't want to handle explicitly. Also, by catching all exceptions, you prevent an unhandled exception from causing an abnormal program termination.

Restricting Exceptions

When a function is called from within a **try** block, you can restrict what type of exceptions that function can throw. In fact, you can also prevent that function from throwing any exceptions whatsoever. To accomplish these restrictions, you must add a **throw** clause to a function definition. The general form of this is shown here:

ret-type func-name(arg-list) throw(*type-list*)
{
  // ...
}

Here, only those data types contained in the comma-separated *type-list* may be thrown by the function. Throwing any other type of expression will cause abnormal program termination. If you don't want a function to be able to throw *any* exceptions, then use an empty list.

If your compiler complies with the proposed ANSI C++ standard, then attempting to throw an exception that is not supported by a function will cause the **unexpected( )** function to be called. By default, this causes **abort( )** to be called, which causes abnormal program termination. However, you can specify your own termination handler, if you like. You will need to refer to your compiler's library reference for details.

The following program shows how to restrict the types of exceptions that can be thrown from a function.

```
// Restricting function throw types.
#include <iostream.h>

// This function can only throw ints, chars, and doubles.
void Xhandler(int test) throw(int, char, double)
{
  if(test==0) throw test; // throw int
  if(test==1) throw 'a'; // throw char
  if(test==2) throw 123.23; // throw double
}

main()
{
```

```
  cout << "start\n";

  try{
    Xhandler(0); // also, try passing 1 and 2 to Xhandler()
  }
  catch(int i) {
    cout << "Caught an integer\n";
  }
  catch(char c) {
    cout << "Caught char\n";
  }
  catch(double d) {
    cout << "Caught double\n";
  }

  cout << "end";

  return 0;
}
```

In this program, the function **Xhandler( )** may only throw integer, character, and **double** exceptions. If it attempts to throw any other type of exception, then an abnormal program termination will occur. (That is, **unexpected( )** will be called.) To see an example of this, remove **int** from the list and retry the program.

It is important to understand that a function can only be restricted in what types of exceptions it throws back to the **try** block that called it. That is, a **try** block *within* a function may throw any type of exception so long as it is caught *within* that function. The restriction applies only when throwing an exception outside of the function.

The following change to **Xhandler( )** prevents it from throwing any exceptions.

```
// This function can throw NO exceptions!
void Xhandler(int test) throw()
{
  /* The following statements no longer work. Instead,
     they will cause an abnormal program termination. */
  if(test==0) throw test;
  if(test==1) throw 'a';
  if(test==2) throw 123.23;
}
```

Rethrowing an Exception

If you wish to rethrow an exception from within an exception handler, you may do so by calling **throw**, by itself, with no exception. This causes the current exception to be passed on to an outer **try/catch** sequence. The most likely reason for doing so is to allow multiple handlers access to the exception. For example, perhaps one exception handler manages one aspect of an exception and a second handler copes with another. An exception can only be rethrown from within a **catch** block (or from any function called from within that block). When you rethrow an exception, it will not be recaught by the same **catch** statement. It will propagate to the next **catch** statement. The following program illustrates rethrowing an exception. It rethrows a **char *** exception.

```
// Example of "rethrowing" an exception.
#include <iostream.h>

void Xhandler()
{
  try {
    throw "hello"; // throw a char *
  }
  catch(char *) { // catch a char *
    cout << "Caught char * inside Xhandler\n";
    throw ; // rethrow char * out of function
  }
}

main()
{
  cout << "Start\n";

  try{
    Xhandler();
  }
  catch(char *) {
    cout << "Caught char * inside main\n";
  }

  cout << "End";

  return 0;
}
```

This program displays the following output:

```
Start
Caught char * inside Xhandler
Caught char * inside main
End
```

Applying Exception Handling

Exception handling is designed to provide a structured means by which your program can handle abnormal events. This implies that the error handler must do something rational when an error occurs. For example, consider the following simple program. It inputs two numbers and divides the first by the second. It uses exception handling to manage a divide-by-zero error.

```cpp
#include <iostream.h>

void divide(double a, double b);

main()
{
  double i, j;

  do {
    cout << "Enter numerator (0 to stop): ";
    cin >> i;
    cout << "Enter denominator: ";
    cin >> j;
    divide(i, j);
  } while(i != 0);

  return 0;
}

void divide(double a, double b)
{
  try {
    if(!b) throw b; // check for divide-by-zero
    cout << "Result: " << a/b << endl;
  }
  catch (double b) {
    cout << "Can't divide by zero.\n";
  }
}
```

While the preceding program is a very simple example, it does illustrate the essential nature of exception handling. Since division by zero is illegal, the program cannot continue if a zero is entered for the second number. In this case, the exception is handled by not performing the division (which would have caused abnormal program termination) and notifying the user of the error. The program then reprompts the user for two more numbers. Thus, the error has been handled in an orderly fashion, and the user may continue with the program. The same basic concepts will apply to more complex applications of exception handling.

Exception handling is especially useful for exiting from a deeply nested set of routines when a catastrophic error occurs. In this regard, C++'s exception handling is designed to replace the rather clumsy C-based **setjmp( )** and **longjmp( )** functions.

REMEMBER: *The main reason for using exception handling is to provide an orderly means of handling errors. This means rectifying the situation, if possible.*

Chapter Twenty-Two

Miscellaneous Issues and Advanced Topics

This chapter discusses several C++ topics not examined elsewhere in this book. Topics include conversion functions, copy constructors, default function arguments, linkage specifications, new features added by the proposed ANSI C++ standard, and differences between C and C++.

Default Function Arguments

C++ allows a function to assign a parameter a default value when no argument corresponding to that parameter is specified in a call to that function. The default value is specified in a manner syntactically similar to a variable initialization.

The following example declares **myfunc( )** as taking one **double** argument with a default value of 0.0.

```
void myfunc(double d = 0.0)
{
    .
    .
    .
}
```

Now, **myfunc( )** can be called one of two ways, as the following examples show.

```
myfunc(198.234);   // pass an explicit value
myfunc();   // let function use default
```

The first call passes the value 198.234 to **d**. The second call automatically gives **d** the default value zero.

One reason that default arguments are included in C++ is because they provide another method for the programmer to manage greater complexity. To handle the widest variety of situations, quite frequently a function contains more parameters than are required for its most common usage. Thus, when the default arguments apply, you need only remember and specify the arguments that are meaningful to the most common situation, not to the most general case. For example, many of the C++ I/O functions described in preceding chapters use default arguments for just this reason.

A simple illustration of how useful a default function argument can be is shown by the **clrscr( )** function in the following program. The **clrscr( )** function clears the screen by outputting a series of linefeeds (not the most efficient way, but sufficient for this example). Because a very common video mode displays 25 lines of text, the default argument of 25 is provided. However, because some terminals can display more or fewer than 25 lines (often depending upon what type of video mode is used), you can override the default argument by specifying one explicitly.

```
#include <iostream.h>

void clrscr(int size=25);

main()
{
  register int i;

  for(i=0; i<30; i++ ) cout << i << endl;
  cin.get();
  clrscr(); // clears 25 lines

  for(i=0; i<30; i++ ) cout << i << endl;
  cin.get();
  clrscr(10); // clears 10 lines

  return 0;
}

void clrscr(int size)
{
    for(; size; size--) cout << endl;
}
```

As this program illustrates, when the default value is appropriate to the situation, no argument need be specified when **clrscr( )** is called. However, it is still possible to override the default and give **size** a different value when needed.

A default argument can also be used as a flag telling the function to reuse a previous argument. To illustrate this type of usage, a simple function called **iputs( )** is developed here that automatically indents a string by a specified amount. To begin, here is a version of this function that does not use a default argument:

```
void iputs(char *str, int indent)
{
  if(indent < 0) indent = 0;

  for( ; indent; indent--) cout << " ";

  cout << str << "\n";
}
```

This version of **iputs( )** is called with the string to output as the first argument and the amount to indent as the second. Although there is nothing wrong with writing **iputs( )** this way, you can improve its usability by providing a default argument for the **indent** parameter that tells **iputs( )** to indent to the previously specified level. It is quite common to display a block of text with each line indented the same amount. In this situation, instead of having to supply the same **indent** argument over and over, you can give **indent** a default value that tells **iputs( )** to indent as previously specified. This approach is illustrated in the following program:

```cpp
#include <iostream.h>

/* Default indent to -1.  This value tells the function
   to reuse the previous value. */
void iputs(char *str, int indent = -1);

main()
{
  iputs("Hello there", 10);
  iputs("This will be indented 10 spaces by default");
  iputs("This will be indented 5 spaces", 5);
  iputs("This is not indented", 0);

  return 0;
}

void iputs(char *str, int indent)
{
  static i = 0;  // holds previous indent value

  if(indent>=0)
    i = indent;
  else    // reuse old indent value
    indent = i;

  for( ; indent; indent--) cout << " ";

  cout << str << "\n";
}
```

This program displays the following output:

```
        Hello there
        This will be indented 10 spaces by default
    This will be indented 5 spaces
This is not indented
```

When you are creating functions that have default argument values, it is important to remember that the default values must be specified only once, and this must be the first time the function is declared within the file. In the preceding example, the default argument was specified in **iputs( )**'s prototype. If you try to specify a new (or even the same) default value in **iputs( )**'s definition, the compiler will display an error and not compile your program. Even though default arguments for the same function may not be redefined, you can specify different default arguments for each version of an overloaded function.

All parameters that take default values must appear to the right of those that do not. For example, it is incorrect to define **iputs( )** like this:

```
// wrong!
void iputs(int indent = -1, char *str);
```

Once you begin to define parameters that take default values, you may not specify a nondefaulting parameter. That is, a declaration like this is also wrong and will not compile:

```
int myfunc(float f, char *str, int i=10, int j);
```

Because **i** has been given a default value, **j** must be given one too.

You can also use default parameters in an object's constructor function. For example, the **cube** class shown here maintains the integer dimensions of a cube. Its constructor function defaults all dimensions to zero if no other arguments are supplied, as shown here:

```
#include <iostream.h>

class cube {
  int x, y, z;
public:
  cube(int i=0, int j=0, int k=0) {
    x=i;
    y=j;
    z=k;
```

```
  }

  int volume() {
    return x*y*z;
  }
};

main()
{
  cube a(2,3,4), b;

  cout << a.volume() << endl;
  cout << b.volume();

  return 0;
}
```

There are two advantages to including default arguments, when appropriate, in a constructor function. First, they prevent you from having to provide a parameterless constructor. For example, if the parameters to **cube( )** were not given defaults, the second constructor shown here would be needed to handle the declaration of **b** (which specified no arguments):

```
cube() {x=0; y=0; z=0}
```

Second, defaulting common initial values is more convenient than specifying them each time an object is declared.

Using Default Arguments Correctly

Although default arguments can be very powerful tools when used correctly, they can be misused. The point of default arguments is to allow a function to perform its job in an efficient, easy-to-use manner while still allowing considerable flexibility. Toward this end, all default arguments should represent the way the function is used most of the time. For example, a default argument makes sense if the default value will be used 90 percent of the time. However, if a common value will occur in only 10 percent of the calls and the rest of the time the arguments corresponding to that parameter vary widely, it is probably not a good idea to provide a default argument. The point of default arguments is that their values are those that the programmer will normally associate with a given function. When there is no single value that is normally associated with a parameter, there is no reason for a default argument. In fact, declaring default arguments when there is an insufficient basis destructures your code—it misleads and confuses anyone reading your program. Where, between 10 percent and 90 percent, you should elect to use a default argument is, of course, subjective, but 51 percent would seem a reasonable break point.

One other important guideline you should follow when using default arguments is this: no default argument should cause a harmful or destructive action. That is, the accidental use of a default argument should not cause a catastrophe.

Default Arguments Versus Overloading

Before leaving the topic of default arguments, one other application will be discussed. In some situations, default arguments can be used as a shorthand form of function overloading. To see why, imagine that you want to create two customized versions of the standard **strcat( )** function. The first version will operate like **strcat( )** and concatenate the entire contents of one string to the end of another. The second version takes a third argument that specifies the number of characters to concatenate. That is, the second version will only concatenate a specified number of characters from one string to the end of another. Thus, assuming that you call your customized functions **mystrcat( )**, they will have the following prototypes:

```
void mystrcat(char *s1, char *s2, int len);
void mystrcat(char *s1, char *s2);
```

The first version would copy **len** characters from **s2** to the end of **s1**. The second version would copy the entire string pointed to by **s2** onto the end of the string pointed to by **s1** and would operate like **strcat( )**.

While it would not be wrong to implement two versions of **mystrcat( )** to create the two versions that you desire, there is an easier way. Using a default argument, you can create only one version of **mystrcat( )** that performs both functions. The following program demonstrates this.

```
// A customized version of strcat().
#include <iostream.h>
#include <string.h>

void mystrcat(char *s1, char *s2, int len = 0);

main()
{
  char str1[80] = "This is a test";
  char str2[80] = "0123456789";
```

```
    mystrcat(str1, str2, 5); // concatenate 5 chars
    cout << str1 << '\n';

    strcpy(str1, "This is a test"); // reset str1

    mystrcat(str1, str2); // concatenate entire string
    cout << str1 << '\n';

    return 0;
}

// A custom version of strcat().
void mystrcat(char *s1, char *s2, int len)
{
    // find end of s1
    while(*s1) s1++;

    if(len==0) len = strlen(s2);

    while(*s2 && len) {
        *s1 = *s2; // copy chars
        s1++;
        s2++;
        len--;
    }

    *s1 = '\0'; // null terminate s1
}
```

Here, **mystrcat( )** concatenates up to **len** characters from the string pointed to by **s2** onto the end of the string pointed to by **s1**. However, if **len** is zero, as it will be when it is allowed to default, **mystrcat( )** concatenates the entire string pointed to by **s2** onto **s1**. (Thus, when **len** is zero, the function operates like the standard **strcat( )** function.) By using a default argument for **len**, it is possible to combine both operations into one function. In this way, default arguments sometimes provide a shorthand form of function overloading.

Creating Conversion Functions

In some situations, you will want to use an object of a class in an expression involving other types of data. Sometimes, overloaded operator functions can provide the means of doing this. However, in other cases, all that you want is a simple type conversion from the class type to the target type. To handle these cases, C++ allows you to create custom *conversion functions.* A conversion function converts your class into a type compatible with that of the rest of the expression. The general format of a type conversion function is

operator *type*( ) { return *value*; }

Here, *type* is the target type that you are converting your class to, and *value* is the value of the object after conversion. Conversion functions return data of type *type,* and no other return type specifier is allowed. Also, no parameters may be included. A conversion function must be a member of the class for which it is defined. Conversion functions are inherited and they may be virtual.

The following illustration of how to create a conversion function uses the **stack** class developed in Chapter 11. Suppose that you want to be able to mix objects of type **stack** with an integer expression. Further, suppose that the value of a **stack** object used in an integer expression is the number of values currently on the stack. (You might want to do something like this if, for example, you are using **stack** objects in a simulation and are monitoring how quickly the stacks fill up.) One way to approach this is to convert an object of type **stack** into an integer that represents the number of items on the stack. To accomplish this, you use a conversion function that looks like this:

```
operator int() {return tos;}
```

Here is a program that illustrates how the conversion function works:

```
#include <iostream.h>

const int SIZE=100;

// this creates the class stack
class stack {
  int stck[SIZE];
  int tos;
public:
  stack() {tos=0;}
  void push(int i);
  int pop(void);
  operator int() {return tos;} // conversion of stack to int
};
```

```cpp
void stack::push(int i)
{
  if(tos==SIZE) {
    cout << "Stack is full.";
    return;
  }
  stck[tos] = i;
  tos++;
}

int stack::pop()
{
  if(tos==0) {
    cout << "Stack underflow.";
    return 0;
  }
  tos--;
  return stck[tos];
}

main()
{
  stack stck;
  int i, j;

  for(i=0; i<20; i++)  stck.push(i);

  j = stck; // convert to integer

  cout << j << " items on stack\n";

  cout << SIZE - stck << " spaces open\n";
  return 0;
}
```

This program displays the following output:

```
20 items on stack
80 spaces open
```

As the program illustrates, when a **stack** object is used in an integer expression, such as **j = stck**, the conversion function is applied to the object. In this specific case, the conversion function returns the value 20. Also, when **stck** is subtracted from **SIZE**, the conversion function is also called.

Here is another example of a conversion function. This program creates a class called **pwr( )** that stores and computes the outcome of some number raised to some power. It stores the result as a **double**. By supplying a conversion function to type **double** and returning the result, you can use objects of type **pwr** in expressions involving other **double** values.

```
#include <iostream.h>

class pwr {
  double b;
  int e;
  double val;
public:
  pwr(double base, int exp);
  pwr operator+(pwr o) {
    double base;
    int exp;
    base = b + o.b;
    exp = e + o.e;

    pwr temp(base, exp);
    return temp;
  }
  operator double() {return val;}  // convert to double
};

pwr::pwr(double base, int exp)
{
  b = base;
  e = exp;
  val = 1;
  if(exp==0) return;
  for( ; exp>0; exp--) val = val * b;
}

main()
{
```

```
    pwr x(4.0, 2);
    double a;

    a = x; // convert to double
    cout << x + 100.2; // convert x to double and add 100.2
    cout << "\n";

    pwr y(3.3, 3), z(0, 0);

    z = x + y;  // no conversion
    a = z;  // convert to double
    cout << a;

    return 0;
}
```

As you can see, when **x** is used in the expression **x + 100.2**, the conversion function is used to produce the **double** value. Notice also that in the expression **x + y**, no conversion is applied because the expression involves only objects of type **pwr**.

As you can infer from the foregoing examples, there are many situations in which it is beneficial to create a conversion function for a class. Often, conversion functions provide a more natural syntax when class objects are mixed with the built-in types. Specifically, in the case of the **pwr** class, the availability of the conversion to **double** makes objects of that class in "normal" mathematical expressions both easier to program and easier to understand.

You can create different conversion functions to meet different needs. You could define one that converts to **long**, for example. Each will be applied automatically as determined by the type of each expression.

Copy Constructors

By default, when one object is used to initialize another, C++ performs a bitwise copy. That is, an identical copy of the initializing object is created in the target object. Although this is perfectly adequate for many cases—and generally exactly what you want to happen—there are situations in which a bitwise copy cannot be used. One of the most common situations in which you must avoid a bitwise copy is when an object allocates memory when it is created. For example, assume two objects, *A* and *B*, of the same class called *ClassType*, which allocates memory when an object is created. Also, assume that *A* already exists. This means that *A* has already allocated its memory. Further, assume that *A* is used to initialize *B*, as shown here:

ClassType B = A;

If a simple bitwise copy is performed, then *B* will be an exact copy of *A*. This means that *B* will be using the same piece of allocated memory that *A* is using, instead of allocating its own. Clearly, this is not the desired outcome. For example, if *ClassType* includes a destructor that frees the memory, then the same piece of memory will be freed twice when *A* and *B* are destroyed!

The same type of problem can occur in two additional ways. The first way is when a copy of an object is made when it is passed as an argument to a function. The second way is when a temporary object is created as a return value from a function. (Remember, temporary objects are automatically created to hold the return value of a function, and they may also be created in certain other circumstances.)

To solve the type of problem just described, C++ allows you to create a *copy constructor*, which the compiler uses when one object is used to initialize another. When a copy constructor exists, the bitwise copy is bypassed. The general form of a copy constructor is

```
classname (const classname &o) {
    // body of constructor
}
```

Here, *o* is a reference to the object on the right side of the initialization. It is permissible for a copy constructor to have additional parameters as long as they have default arguments defined for them. However, in all cases the first parameter must be a reference to the object doing the initializing.

Initialization occurs three ways: when one object initializes another, when a copy of an object is made to be passed to a function, or when a temporary object is generated (most commonly, as a return value). For example, each of the following statements involves initialization.

```
myclass x = y; // initialization
func(x); // parameter passing
y = func();  // receiving temporary object
```

Following is an example where an explicit copy constructor function is needed. This program creates a (very) limited "safe" integer array type that prevents array boundaries from being overrun. Storage for each array is allocated by the use of **new**, and a pointer to the memory is maintained within each array object.

```
/* This program creates a "safe" array class.  Since space
   for the array is allocated using new, a copy constructor
   is provided to allocate memory when one array object is
   used to initialize another.
*/
#include <iostream.h>
#include <stdlib.h>

class array {
  int *p;
  int size;
public:
  array(int sz) {
    p = new int[sz];
    if(!p) exit(1);
    size = sz;
  }
  ~array() {delete [] p;}

  // copy constructor
  array(const array &a);

  void put(int i, int j) {
    if(i>=0 && i<size) p[i] = j;
  }
  int get(int i) {
    return p[i];
  }
};

// copy constructor
array::array(const array &a) {
  int i;

  p = new int[a.size];
  if(!p) exit(1);
  for(i=0; i<a.size; i++) p[i] = a.p[i];
}

main()
{
  array num(10);
```

```
    int i;

    for(i=0; i<10; i++) num.put(i, i);
    for(i=9; i>=0; i--) cout << num.get(i);
    cout << "\n";

    // create another array and initialize with num
    array x=num;  // invokes copy constructor
    for(i=0; i<10; i++) cout << x.get(i);

    return 0;
}
```

When **num** is used to initialize **x**, the copy constructor is called, memory for the new array is allocated and stored in **x.p**, and the contents of **num** are copied to **x**'s array. In this way, **x** and **num** have arrays that have the same values, but each array is separate and distinct. (That is, **num.p** and **x.p** do not point to the same piece of memory.) If the copy constructor had not been created, the default bitwise initialization would have resulted in **x** and **num** sharing the same memory for their arrays. (That is, **num.p** and **x.p** would have, indeed, pointed to the same location.)

The copy constructor is called only for initializations. For example, the following sequence does not call the copy constructor defined in the preceding program.

```
array a(10);

    .
    .
    .

array b(10);

b = a; // does not call copy constructor
```

In this case, **b = a** performs the assignment operation. If = is not overloaded (as it is not here), a bitwise copy will be made. Therefore, in some cases, you may need to overload the = operator as well as create a copy constructor to avoid problems.

Dynamic Initialization

Dynamic initialization is the process by which variables are initialized at run time rather than at compile time. Further, dynamic initialization allows a variable to be initialized through the use of any expression valid at the point of that initialization, including other variables and function calls. Both C and C++ allow local variables to be dynamically initialized. However, in C++, you may also dynamically initialize global variables. For example, this program is perfectly valid:

```
#include <iostream.h>
#include <stdlib.h>

int i = atoi("1233");  // valid in C++, not C
int x = i * 2;  // valid in C++, not C

main()
{
  cout << "value of i is " << i << endl;
  cout << "value of x is " << x << endl;
  return 0;
}
```

As expected, the program displays this output:

```
value of i is 1233
value of x is 2466
```

const and volatile Member Functions

Class member functions may be declared as **const**, **volatile**, or both. A few rules apply. First, objects declared as **volatile** may call only member functions also declared as **volatile**. A **const** object may not invoke a non-**const** member function. However, a **const** member function can be called by either **const** or non-**const** objects. A **const** member function cannot modify the object that invokes it. The rules combine for functions that are both **const** and **volatile**.

To specify a member function as **const** or **volatile**, use the forms shown in this example:

```
class X {
public:
  int f1() const; // const member function
  void f2(int a) volatile; // volatile member function
  char *f3() const volatile; // const volatile member function
};
```

Using the asm Keyword

You can embed assembly language directly into your C++ program by using the **asm** keyword. The **asm** keyword has this syntax:

asm ("*string*");

Here, *string* is passed, untouched, to the assembler.

Several compilers accept three slightly different general forms of the **asm** statement, which are shown here:

asm *instruction*;
asm *instruction* newline
asm {
  instruction sequence
}

Here, *instruction* is any valid assembly language instruction.

As a simple (and fairly "safe") example, this program uses **asm** to execute an **INT 5** instruction, which invokes the PC's print-screen function:

```
// Print the screen.
#include <iostream.h>

main(void)
{
  asm int 5;  // use asm int 5
  return 0;
}
```

CAUTION: *You must have a thorough working knowledge of assembly language programming to use the **asm** statement. If you are not proficient at assembly language, it is best to avoid using it, because very nasty errors may result.*

Linkage Specification

In C++, you may specify how a function is linked. For example, you can tell the compiler to link a function as a C function, as a C++ function, or, depending upon the implementation of your C++ compiler, as a function produced by another language altogether, such as FORTRAN. By default, functions are linked as C++ functions.

However, by using a *linkage specification,* you can cause a function to be linked as a different type of language function. The general form of a linkage specifier is

> extern *"language" function-prototype*

where *language* denotes the desired language. All C++ compilers will support C and C++ linkage. Some will support additional languages.

The following program causes **myCfunc( )** to be linked as a C function.

```
#include <iostream.h>

extern "C" void myCfunc(void);

main(void)
{
  myCfunc();

  return 0;
}

// This will link as a C function.
void myCfunc(void)
{
  cout << "This links as a C function.\n";
}
```

NOTE: *The **extern** keyword is a necessary part of the linkage specification. Further, the linkage specification must be global; it cannot be used inside a function.*

You can specify more than one function at a time by using this form of the linkage specification:

> extern *"language"* {
>   *prototypes*
> }

The use of a linkage specification is rare, and you will probably not need to use one.

New Features Added by the Proposed ANSI C++ Standard

In the process of standardization, the ANSI C++ committee has added several new features to C++ that were not part of its original specification. Not all of these additions are currently implemented by any mainstream C++ compiler. (However, these new features will be available in virtually all C++ compilers in the near future.) Although none of these new features are technically necessary to fully utilize the C++ language, some give you more control over certain situations. Also, some are included for convenience. In this section, a brief overview of these features is presented. However, since the exact nature of these new features is still being defined, you will need to check your compiler's user manual for details concerning their implementation.

NOTE: Since the standard for C++ is still in the development stage, there is no guarantee that any or all of the features described in this section will be defined by the final version of the standard. But the most likely outcome is that all these features will be part of standardized C++.

New Casting Operators

Although C++ still fully supports the traditional casting operator, the proposed ANSI C++ standard defines four new casting operators. They are **const_cast**, **dynamic_cast**, **reinterpret_cast**, and **static_cast**. Their general forms are

const_cast<*type*> (*object*)
dynamic_cast<*type*> (*object*)
reinterpret_cast<*type*> (*object*)
static_cast<*type*> (*object*)

Here, *type* specifies the target type of the cast, and *object* is the object being cast into the new type.

The **const_cast** operator is used to explicitly override **const** and/or **volatile** in a cast. The target type must be the same as the source type, except for the alteration of its **const** or **volatile** attributes. The most common use of **const_cast** is to remove **const**ness.

dynamic_cast performs a run-time cast that verifies the validity of the cast. If the cast cannot be made, the cast fails and the expression evaluates to null. Its main use is for performing casts on polymorphic types. (Polymorphic classes are classes that contain virtual functions.) For example, **dynamic_cast** can return a pointer to a derived object given a pointer to a polymorphic base class. If the object pointed to is not an object of the base class or of a derived class, then **dynamic_cast** evaluates to null.

The **static_cast** operator performs a nonpolymorphic cast. For example, it can be used to cast a base class pointer into a derived class pointer. It can also be used for any standard conversion. The **reinterpret_cast** operator changes one type into a fundamentally different type. For example, it can be used to change a pointer into an integer. A **reinterpret_cast** should be used for casting inherently incompatible types.

Only **const_cast** can cast away **const**ness. That is, neither **dynamic_cast**, **static_cast**, nor **reinterpret_cast** can alter the **const**ness of an object.

The following program demonstrates the use of **reinterpret_cast**.

```
// An example that uses reinterpret_cast.
#include <iostream.h>

main()
{
  int i;
  char *p = "This is a string";

  i = reinterpret_cast<int> (p); // cast pointer to integer

  cout << i;

  return 0;
}
```

The bool Data Type

Although technically unnecessary, the proposed ANSI C++ standard has added the **bool** data type, which is capable of holding a Boolean value. Objects of type **bool** may have only the values **true** and **false**. (The values **true** and **false** are keywords that are now part of the C++ language.) Values of type **bool** are automatically elevated to integers when used in a non-Boolean expression.

Using a Namespace

The proposed C++ standard has added the keyword **namespace**, which may be used to define a scope. The general form of **namespace** is shown here:

namespace *name* {
  // *object declarations*
}

For example,

```
namespace MyNameSpace {
   int i, k;
   void myfunc(int j) { cout << j; }
}
```

Here, **i**, **k**, and **myfunc( )** are part of the scope defined by the **MyNameSpace** namespace.

Since a namespace defines a scope, you need to use the scope resolution operator to refer to objects defined within a namespace. For example, to assign the value 10 to **i**, you must use this statement:

```
MyNameSpace::i = 10;
```

If the members of a namespace will be frequently used, you can use a **using** directive to simplify their access. The **using** statement has these two general forms:

using namespace *name*;

using *name::member*;

In the first form, *name* specifies the name of the namespace you want to access. All of the members defined within the specified namespace may be used without qualification. In the second form, only a specific member of the namespace is made visible. For example, assuming **MyNameSpace** as just shown, the following **using** statements and assignments are valid:

```
using MyNameSpace::k; // only k is made visible
k = 10; // OK because k is visible

using namespace MyNameSpace; // all members of MyNameSpace are visible
i = 10; // OK because all members of MyNameSpace are now visible
```

NOTE: *The exact form and nature of the **namespace** and the **using** statements are being finalized. You should check your compiler's user manual for implementation details relating to these two features.*

Run-time Type Identification

One of the most important additions being added by the proposed ANSI C++ standard is *run-time type identification* (RTTI). Using run-time type identification, you can determine the type of an object during program execution. To obtain an object's type, use **typeid**. You must include the header file TYPEINFO.H in order to use **typeid**. Its general form is

typeid(*object*)

Here, *object* is the object whose type you will be obtaining. **typeid** returns a reference to an object of type **type_info** that describes the type of object defined by *object*. The **type_info** class defines the following public members:

bool operator==(const type_info &ob) const;
bool operator!=(const type_info &ob) const;
bool before(const type_info &ob) const;
const char *name( ) const;

The overloaded == and != provide for the comparison of types. The **before( )** function returns true if the invoking object is before the object used as a parameter in collation order. (This function is mostly for internal use only. Its return value has nothing to do with inheritance or class hierarchies.) The **name( )** function returns a pointer to the name of the type. (Since **typeid** is in the process of being defined, you will need to consult your compiler's user manual for details on any other types of operations defined by the **type_info** class.)

When **typeid** is applied to a base class pointer of a polymorphic class, it will automatically return the type of the object being pointed to, including any classes derived from that base. (Remember, a polymorphic class is one that contains at least one virtual function.)

The following program demonstrates **typeid**.

```
// An example that uses typeid.
#include <iostream.h>
#include <typeinfo.h>

class BaseClass {
  int a, b;
  virtual void f() {}; // make BaseClass polymorphic
};

class Derived1: public BaseClass {
```

```
   int i, j;
};

class Derived2: public BaseClass {
  int k;
};

main()
{
  int i;
  BaseClass *p, baseob;
  Derived1 ob1;
  Derived2 ob2;

  // First, display type name of a built in type.
  cout << "Typeid of i is ";
  cout << typeid(i).name() << endl;

  // Demonstrate typeid with polymorphic types.
  p = &baseob;
  cout << "p is pointing to an object of type ";
  cout << typeid(*p).name() << endl;

  p = &ob1;
  cout << "p is pointing to an object of type ";
  cout << typeid(*p).name() << endl;

  p = &ob2;
  cout << "p is pointing to an object of type ";
  cout << typeid(*p).name() << endl;

  return 0;
}
```

The output produced by this program is shown here:

```
Typeid of i is int
p is pointing to an object of type BaseClass
p is pointing to an object of type Derived1
p is pointing to an object of type Derived2
```

As mentioned, when **typeid** is applied to a base class pointer of a polymorphic type, the type of object pointed to will be determined at run time, as the output produced by the program shows. (For an experiment, comment out the virtual function **f( )** in **BaseClass** and observe the results.)

Run-time type identification is not something that every program will use. However, when working with polymorphic types, it allows you to know what type of object is being operated upon in any given situation.

Explicit Constructors

The proposed ANSI C++ standard has defined the keyword **explicit**. It is used to create "nonconverting constructors." For example, given the following class,

```
class MyClass {
   int i;
public:
   MyClass(int j) {i = j;}
   // ...
};
```

MyClass objects can be declared as shown here:

```
MyClass ob1(1);
MyClass ob2 = 10;
```

In this case, the statement

```
MyClass ob2 = 10;
```

is automatically converted into the form

```
MyClass ob2(10);
```

However, if the **MyClass** constructor is declared as **explicit**, this automatic conversion will not be supplied. Here is **MyClass** shown using an **explicit** constructor:

```
class MyClass {
   int i;
public:
```

```
   explicit MyClass(int j) {i = j;}
   // ...
};
```

Now, only constructors of the form

```
MyClass ob(110);
```

will be allowed.

Using mutable

The proposed ANSI C++ standard defines the keyword **mutable**. It is used to allow a member of an object to override **const**ness. That is, a **mutable** member of a **const** object is not **const** and can be modified.

The wchar_t Type

The proposed ANSI C++ standard defines the type **wchar_t**, which can hold wide characters. Wide characters are typically 16-bit values. They are used to represent the character sets of languages that have more than 255 characters.

New Headers

The proposed ANSI C++ standard has defined a new way to specify header files. However, the traditional style (which is used by this book) is still fully supported. The new style does not require the use of an actual filename. Instead, a standard header identifier is used, which will be mapped to a filename by the compiler, if necessary. For example, the new-style header format to include the header for the I/O system is

```
#include <iostream>
```

As you can see, the **.h** has been left off. This example can be generalized. For instance, using the new-style header format, the following statement includes the header for file I/O.

```
#include <fstream>
```

You will need to check your compiler manual to see if it supports new-style header specifications.

Differences Between C and C++

For the most part, C++ is a superset of ANSI standard C, and virtually all C programs are also C++ programs. However, a few differences do exist, the most important of which are discussed here.

In C++, local variables can be declared anywhere within a block. In C, they must be declared at the start of a block, before any "action" statements occur.

One of the most important yet subtle differences between C and C++ is that in C, a function declared like this

```
int f();
```

says *nothing* about any parameters to that function. That is, when there is nothing specified between the parentheses following the function's name, in C this means that nothing is being stated, one way or the other, about any parameters to that function. It might have parameters, it might not. However, in C++, a function declaration like this means that the function does *not* have parameters. That is, in C++, these two declarations are equivalent:

```
int f();

int f(void);
```

In C++, **void** is optional. Many C++ programmers include **void** as a means of making it completely clear to anyone reading the program that a function does not have any parameters, but this is technically unnecessary.

In C++, all functions must be prototyped. This is an option in C (although good programming practice suggests full prototyping be used in a C program).

A small but potentially important difference between C and C++ is that in C, a character constant is automatically elevated to an integer. In C++, it is not.

In C, it is not an error to declare a global variable several times, even though this is bad programming practice. In C++, it is an error.

In C, an identifier may be up to 31 characters long. In C++, no such limit exists. However, from a practical point of view, extremely long identifiers are unwieldy and seldom needed.

In C, although it is unusual, you can call **main( )** from within your program. This is not allowed by C++.

In C, you cannot take the address of a **register** variable. In C++, this is allowed.

PART THREE

Some C++ Applications

Part Three of this book provides a sampling of applications written in C++. The purpose of this section is twofold. First, the examples help illustrate the benefits of object-oriented programming, including the advantages of polymorphism, encapsulation, and inheritance, and the creation of class libraries. Second, the examples show how C++ can be applied to solve various types of programming problems—whether object-oriented or not. Remember, C++ is an enhanced and expanded version of C that gives the programmer more power and flexibility, independent of object-oriented methodologies. So, whether you will be using C++ to pursue OOP or just to give you an edge over your normal programming tasks doesn't really matter.

Chapter Twenty-Three

A String Class

A s you know, in C++, strings are implemented as null-terminated character arrays and not as a separate data type. This approach makes C++ strings powerful, elegant, and efficient. Also, the close relationship between arrays and pointers allows you to write many "lean and mean" string operations. However, there are many times when you need to use a string, but don't need an extremely high level of efficiency and power. In these cases, working with C++ strings can become a tiresome chore. Fortunately, with C++, it is possible to create a string type that trades a little efficiency for a big gain in ease of use.

In this chapter, a string class is developed that makes creating, using, and manipulating strings much easier.

NOTE: At this writing, the ANSI C++ standardization committee is in the process of defining a standard string class. (However, its exact form has not yet been finalized.) The purpose of this chapter is not to develop an alternative to this class. Instead, the purpose of this chapter is to give you insight into how any new data type can be easily added and integrated into the C++ environment. The creation of a string class is a quintessential example of this process. While the example string class developed in this chapter is much simpler than the one being developed for the C++ standard, it does have one advantage: it gives you full control over how strings are implemented and manipulated. You may find it useful in a variety of situations.

Defining a String Type

First, it is important to define what is meant by a string type and what sorts of operations can be performed on it. Fortunately, other languages have defined string types that can be looked to as models on which to base the string type discussed here. It may seem strange at first, but one very good model for a string type is BASIC. Although most C++ programmers are unenthusiastic about BASIC as a programming language in general, the way that it handles strings is intuitive and easy to use. BASIC is also a good model because virtually all programmers know it.

The string class developed in this chapter does not "clone" BASIC's approach, but it does borrow its most important features, which are examined here.

In BASIC, to give a string a value, you simply assign it a quoted string by using BASIC's assignment operator, the =. For example, this is a valid BASIC string assignment:

```
A$ = "This is a string"
```

(All string variables in BASIC must end with a dollar sign. Of course, the string class developed in this chapter does not have this restriction.) This statement assigns to **A$** the string "This is a string".

You can also assign one string variable to another. For example, this copies into **B$** the string contained in **A$**.

```
B$ = A$
```

As you can see, the main difference between BASIC and C++ in terms of assigning a string variable a string is that BASIC uses an operator, whereas C++ uses a call to the **strcpy( )** function (although C++ allows character arrays to be *initialized* with the = operator).

The + operator is used to concatenate two strings in BASIC. For example, this sequence causes **C$** to contain the value "Hi there".

```
A$ = "Hi "
B$ = "there"
C$ = A$ + B$
```

Actually, the preceding sequence could have been simplified like this:

```
A$ = "Hi "
C$ = A$ + "there"
```

Here, a string variable is concatenated with a quoted string. Thus, BASIC allows string variables to be concatenated with other string variables or with quoted strings.

One difference between BASIC string concatenation and the standard **strcat( )** function is that the **strcat( )** function modifies one of the strings it is called with so that it contains the result. However, when you add two strings in BASIC, a temporary string containing their concatenation is produced, and the original strings are left unchanged.

String comparisons in BASIC are straightforward because they use the same relational operators used when comparing other data types. All string comparisons are performed in dictionary order. For example, this determines if **A$** is greater than **B$**.

```
IF A$ > B$ THEN PRINT "A$ is greater than B$"
```

As the preceding examples show, the major advantage of BASIC's approach to strings is that it allows all major string operations to be performed with the same operators used by other data types. In a sense, BASIC overloads its assignment, addition, and relational operators so that they also work with strings. It is this basic concept that will be implemented by the string class in this chapter. The string type developed here will substitute overloaded operators for calls to library functions.

With BASIC's approach to strings as a backdrop, we are now ready to develop a string class for C++.

The StrType Class

The string class defined here will meet the following requirements:

- Strings can be assigned by use of the assignment operator.

- String objects can be assigned other string objects or quoted strings.

- Concatenation of two string objects is accomplished with the + operator.

- The – operator can be used to subtract a substring from a string.

- String comparisons are performed with the relational operators.

- A string object can be initialized by use of either a quoted string or another string object.

- Strings must be able to be of arbitrary and variable lengths. This implies that storage for each string is dynamically allocated.

- A method of converting string objects to null-terminated strings will be provided.

The class that will manage strings is called **StrType**. Its declaration is shown here:

```cpp
class StrType {
  char *p;
  int size;
public:
  StrType(char *str);
  StrType();
  StrType(const StrType &o);  // copy constructor

  ~StrType() {delete [] p;}

  friend ostream &operator<<(ostream &stream, StrType &o);
  friend istream &operator>>(istream &stream, StrType &o);

  StrType operator=(StrType &o);  // assign a StrType object
  StrType operator=(char *s);  // assign a quoted string
```

```
    StrType operator+(StrType &o); // concatenate a StrType object
    StrType operator+(char *s); // concatenate a quoted string
    friend StrType operator+(char *s, StrType &o); /*  concatenate
          a quoted string with a StrType object */

    StrType operator-(StrType &o); // subtract a substring
    StrType operator-(char *s);  // subtract a quoted substring

    // relational operations between StrType objects
    int operator==(StrType &o) {return !strcmp(p, o.p);}
    int operator!=(StrType &o) {return strcmp(p, o.p);}
    int operator<(StrType &o) {return strcmp(p, o.p) < 0;}
    int operator>(StrType &o) {return strcmp(p, o.p) > 0;}
    int operator<=(StrType &o) {return strcmp(p, o.p) <= 0;}
    int operator>=(StrType &o) {return strcmp(p, o.p) >= 0;}

    // operations between StrType objects and quoted strings
    int operator==(char *s) {return !strcmp(p, s);}
    int operator!=(char *s) {return strcmp(p, s);}
    int operator<(char *s) {return strcmp(p, s) < 0;}
    int operator>(char *s) {return strcmp(p, s) > 0;}
    int operator<=(char *s) {return strcmp(p, s) <= 0;}
    int operator>=(char *s) {return strcmp(p, s) >= 0;}

    int strsize() {return strlen(p);} // return size of string
    void makestr(char *s) {strcpy(s, p);} // make quoted string

    operator char *() {return p;}  // conversion to char *
};
```

The private part of **StrType** contains only two items: **p** and **size**. When a string object is created, memory to hold the string is dynamically allocated by **new**, and a pointer to that memory is put in **p**. The string pointed to by **p** will be a normal, null-terminated character array. Although it is not technically necessary, the size of the string is held in **size**. Because the string pointed to by **p** is a normal string, it would be possible to compute the size of the string each time it is needed. However, as you will see, this value is used so often by the **StrType** member functions that the repeated calls to **strlen( )** cannot be justified.

The next several sections detail how the **StrType** class works.

The Constructor and Destructor Functions

A **StrType** object can be declared in three ways. It can be declared without any initialization, and it can be declared with a quoted string as an initializer or with a **StrType** object as an initializer. The constructors that support these three operations are shown here:

```
// No explicit initialization.
StrType::StrType() {
  size = 1;  // make room for null terminator
  p = new char[size];
  if(!p) {
    cout << "Allocation error\n";
    exit(1);
  }
  *p = '\0';
}

// Initialize using a null-terminated, quoted string.
StrType::StrType(char *str) {
  size = strlen(str) + 1;  // make room for null terminator
  p = new char[size];
  if(!p) {
    cout << "Allocation error\n";
    exit(1);
  }
  strcpy(p, str);
}

// Initialize using a StrType object.
StrType::StrType(const StrType &o) {
  size = o.size;
  p = new char[size];
  if(!p) {
    cout << "Allocation error\n";
    exit(1);
  }
  strcpy(p, o.p);
}
```

When a **StrType** object is created with no initializer, it is assigned a null-string. Although the string could have been left undefined, knowing that all **StrType** objects contain a valid, null-terminated string simplifies several other member functions.

When a **StrType** object is initialized by a quoted string, first the size of the string is determined. This value is stored in **size**. Next, sufficient memory is allocated by **new**. After the safety check that confirms that **p** is not null, the initializing string is copied into the memory pointed to by **p**.

When a **StrType** object is used to initialize another, the process is similar to using a quoted string. The only difference is that the size of the string is known and does not have to be computed. This version of the **StrType** constructor is also the class' copy constructor. This constructor will be invoked whenever one **StrType** object is used to initialize another. This means that it is called when temporary objects are created and when objects of type **StrType** are passed to functions. (See Chapter 22 for a discussion of copy constructors.)

Given the three preceding constructors, the following declarations are allowed.

```
StrType x("my string"); // use quoted string
StrType y(x); // use another object
StrType z; // no explicit initialization
```

The **StrType** destructor function simply frees the memory pointed to by **p**.

I/O on Strings

Because it is very common to want to input or output strings, the **StrType** class overloads the << and >> operators, as shown here:

```
// Output a string.
ostream &operator<<(ostream &stream, StrType &o)
{
  stream << o.p;
  return stream;
}

// Input a string.
istream &operator>>(istream &stream, StrType &o)
{
  char t[255];  // arbitrary size - change if necessary
  int len;
```

```
   for(len=0; len<255; len++) {
     stream.get(t[len]);
     if(t[len]=='\n') break;
     if(t[len]=='\b')
       if(len) {
         len--;
         cout << "'\b'";
       }
   }
   t[len] = '\0';
   len++;

   if(len > o.size) {
     delete o.p;
     o.p = new char[len];
     if(!o.p) {
       cout << "Allocation error\n";
       exit(1);
     }
     o.size = len;
   }
   strcpy(o.p, t);
   return stream;
}
```

As you can see, output is very simple. However, notice that the parameter **o** is passed by reference. Since **StrType** objects can be quite large, passing one by reference is more efficient than passing one by value. For this reason, all **StrType** parameters are passed by reference. (Any function you create that takes **StrType** parameters should probably do the same.)

Inputting a string proves to be a little more difficult than outputting one. The reason is that a statement like the following cannot be used to read input.

```
stream >> t;
```

This is because the normal input operation that reads C++-style strings stops reading input when the first white-space character is encountered. Therefore, it is necessary to read a string by inputting one character at a time. The version of **>>** overloaded for the **StrType** type reads characters until a newline is encountered.

Once the string has been read, if the size of the new string exceeds that of the one currently held by **o**, that memory is released and a larger amount is allocated. The new string is then copied into it.

The Assignment Functions

You can assign a **StrType** object a string in two ways. First, you can assign another **StrType** object to it. Second, you can assign it a quoted string. The two overloaded **operator=( )** functions that accomplish these operations are shown here:

```
// Assign a StrType object to a StrType object.
StrType StrType::operator=(StrType &o)
{
  StrType temp(o.p);

  if(o.size > size) {
    delete p;  // free old memory
    p = new char[o.size];
    size = o.size;
    if(!p) {
      cout << "Allocation error\n";
      exit(1);
    }
  }

  strcpy(p, o.p);
  strcpy(temp.p, o.p);

  return temp;
}

// Assign a quoted string to a StrType object.
StrType StrType::operator=(char *s)
{
  int len = strlen(s) + 1;
  if(size < len) {
    delete p;
    p = new char[len];
    size = len;
    if(!p) {
```

```
        cout << "Allocation error\n";
        exit(1);
      }
    }
  strcpy(p, s);
  return *this;
}
```

These two functions work by first checking to see if the memory currently pointed to by **p** of the target **StrType** object is sufficiently large to hold what will be copied to it. If not, the old memory is released and new memory is allocated. Then the string is copied into the object and the result is returned. These functions allow the following types of assignments:

```
StrType x("test"), y;

y = x; // StrType object to StrType object

x = "new string for x"; // quoted string to StrType object
```

Each assignment function must return the value assigned (that is, the right-hand value) so that multiple assignments like this can be supported:

```
StrType x, y, z;

x = y = z = "test";
```

Concatenation

Concatenation of two strings is accomplished with the **+** operator. The **StrType** class allows for the following three distinct concatenation situations.

- Concatenation of a **StrType** object with another **StrType** object
- Concatenation of a **StrType** object with a quoted string
- Concatenation of a quoted string with a **StrType** object

When used in these situations, the **+** operator produces as its outcome a **StrType** object that is the concatenation of its two operands. It does not actually modify either operand. (This approach differs from the **strcat( )** function, which modifies its first argument.)

The overloaded **operator+( )** functions are shown here:

```
// Concatenate two StrType objects.
StrType StrType::operator+(StrType &o)
{
  int len;
  StrType temp;

  delete temp.p;
  len = strlen(o.p) + strlen(p) + 1;
  temp.p = new char[len];
  temp.size = len;
  if(!temp.p) {
    cout << "Allocation error\n";
    exit(1);
  }
  strcpy(temp.p, p);

  strcat(temp.p, o.p);
  return temp;
}

// Concatenate a StrType object and a quoted string.
StrType StrType::operator+(char *s)
{
  int len;
  StrType temp;

  delete temp.p;

  len = strlen(s) + strlen(p) + 1;
  temp.p = new char[len];
  temp.size = len;
  if(!temp.p) {
    cout << "Allocation error\n";
    exit(1);
  }
  strcpy(temp.p, p);

  strcat(temp.p, s);

  return temp;
}
```

```
// Concatenate a quoted string and a StrType object.
StrType operator+(char *s, StrType &o)
{
  int len;
  StrType temp;

  delete temp.p;

  len = strlen(s) + strlen(o.p) + 1;
  temp.p = new char[len];
  temp.size = len;
  if(!temp.p) {
    cout << "Allocation error\n";
    exit(1);
  }
  strcpy(temp.p, s);

  strcat(temp.p, o.p);

  return temp;
}
```

All three functions work in basically the same way. First, a temporary **StrType** object called **temp** is created. This object will contain the outcome of the concatenation, and it is the object returned by the functions. Next, the memory pointed to by **temp.p** is freed. The reason for this is that when **temp** is created, only 1 byte of memory is allocated (as a placeholder) because there is no explicit initialization. Next, enough memory is allocated to hold the concatenation of the two strings. Finally, the two strings are copied into the memory pointed to by **temp.p**, and **temp** is returned.

Substring Subtraction

A useful string function not found in many other computer languages is substring subtraction. As implemented by the **StrType** class, *substring subtraction* removes all occurrences of a specified substring from another string. Substring subtraction is accomplished with the – operator.

The **StrType** class supports two cases of substring subtraction. One allows a **StrType** object to be subtracted from another **StrType** object. The other allows a quoted string to be removed from a **StrType** object. The two **operator–( )** functions are shown in the following example:

```
// Subtract a substring from a string using StrType objects.
StrType StrType::operator-(StrType &substr)
{
  StrType temp(p);
  char *s1;
  int i, j;

  s1 = p;
  for(i=0; *s1; i++) {
    if(*s1!=*substr.p) { // if not first letter of substring
      temp.p[i] = *s1;   // then copy into temp
      s1++;
    }
    else { // might be substring
      for(j=0; substr.p[j]==s1[j] && substr.p[j]; j++) ;
      if(!substr.p[j]) {  // is substring, so remove it
        s1 += j;
        i--;
      }
      else {  // is not substring, continue copying
        temp.p[i] = *s1;
        s1++;
      }
    }
  }
  temp.p[i] = '\0';
  return temp;
}

// Subtract quoted string from a StrType object.
StrType StrType::operator-(char *substr)
{
  StrType temp(p);
  char *s1;
  int i, j;

  s1 = p;
  for(i=0; *s1; i++) {
    if(*s1!=*substr) { // if not first letter of substring
      temp.p[i] = *s1; // then copy into temp
      s1++;
    }
    else {
```

```
      for(j=0; substr[j]==s1[j] && substr[j]; j++) ;
      if(!substr[j]) { // is substring, so remove it
        s1 += j;
        i--;
      }
      else { // is not substring, continue copying
        temp.p[i] = *s1;
        s1++;
      }
    }
  }
  temp.p[i] = '\0';
  return temp;
}
```

These functions work by copying the contents of the left-hand operand into **temp**, removing any occurrences of the substring specified by the right-hand operand during the process. The resulting **StrType** object is returned. Understand that neither operand is modified by the process.

The **StrType** class allows substring subtractions like these:

```
StrType x("I like C++"), y("like");
StrType z;

z = x - y;  // z will contain "I C++"

z = x - "C++"; // z will contain "I like "

// multiple occurrences are removed
z = "ABCDABCD";
x = z -"A"; // x contains "BCDBCD"
```

The Relational Operators

The **StrType** class allows the full range of relational operations to be applied to strings. The overloaded relational operators are defined within the **StrType** class declaration. They are repeated here for your convenience:

```
// relational operations between StrType objects
int operator==(StrType &o) {return !strcmp(p, o.p);}
```

```
int operator!=(StrType &o) {return strcmp(p, o.p);}
int operator<(StrType &o) {return strcmp(p, o.p) < 0;}
int operator>(StrType &o) {return strcmp(p, o.p) > 0;}
int operator<=(StrType &o) {return strcmp(p, o.p) <= 0;}
int operator>=(StrType &o) {return strcmp(p, o.p) >= 0;}

// operations between StrType objects and quoted strings
int operator==(char *s) {return !strcmp(p, s);}
int operator!=(char *s) {return strcmp(p, s);}
int operator<(char *s) {return strcmp(p, s) < 0;}
int operator>(char *s) {return strcmp(p, s) > 0;}
int operator<=(char *s) {return strcmp(p, s) <= 0;}
int operator>=(char *s) {return strcmp(p, s) >= 0;}
```

The relational operations are very straightforward; you should have no trouble understanding their implementation. However, keep in mind that the **StrType** class only implements comparisons between two **StrType** objects, or comparisons that have a **StrType** object as the left operand and a quoted string as the right operand. If you want to be able to put the quoted string on the left and a **StrType** object on the right, you will need to add additional relational functions.

Given the overloaded relational operator functions defined by **StrType**, the following types of string comparisons are allowed.

```
StrType x("one"), y("two"), z("three");

if(x < y) cout << "x less than y";

if(z=="three")  cout << "z equals three";

y = "o";
z = "ne";
if(x==(y+z)) cout << "x equals y+z";
```

Miscellaneous String Functions

The **StrType** class defines three functions that make **StrType** objects integrate more completely with normal C++-style strings. They are **strsize( )**, **makestr( )**, and the conversion function **operator char *( )**, and they are defined within the **StrType** declaration. These functions are shown next:

```
int strsize() {return strlen(p);} // return size of string
void makestr(char *s) {strcpy(s, p);} // make quoted string

operator char *() {return p;}  // conversion to char *
```

The first two functions are easy to understand. As you can see, the **strsize( )** function returns the length of the string pointed to by **p**. The **makestr( )** function copies into a character array the string pointed to by **p**. This function is useful when you want to obtain a null-terminated string given a **StrType** object.

The conversion function **operator char *( )** returns **p**, which is, of course, a pointer to the string contained within the object. This function allows a **StrType** object to be used anywhere that a null-terminated string can be used. For example, this is valid code:

```
StrType x("Hello");

// output the string using a standard C++ function
puts(x); // automatic conversion to char *
```

Recall that a conversion function is automatically executed when an object is involved in an expression for which the conversion is defined. In this case, because the prototype for the **puts( )** function tells the compiler that its argument is of type **char ***, the conversion from **StrType** to **char *** is automatically performed, causing a pointer to the string contained within **x** to be returned. Because of the conversion function, you can use a **StrType** object in place of a normal quoted string as an argument to any function that takes an argument of type **char ***.

 NOTE: *The conversion to **char** * does circumvent encapsulation, because once a function has a pointer to the object's string, it is possible for that function to modify the string directly, bypassing the **StrType** member functions and without that object's knowledge. For this reason, you must use the conversion to **char** * with care. (If you don't need this conversion, simply delete it from the class specification.) The loss of encapsulation in this case is offset by increased utility and integration with existing library functions. However, this trade-off is not always warranted.*

The Entire StrType Class

Here is a listing of the entire **StrType** class along with a short **main( )** function that demonstrates its features.

```
#include <iostream.h>
#include <string.h>
#include <stdlib.h>
#include <conio.h>
#include <stdio.h>

class StrType {
  char *p;
  int size;
public:
  StrType(char *str);
  StrType();
  StrType(const StrType &o);  // copy constructor

  ~StrType() {delete [] p;}

  friend ostream &operator<<(ostream &stream, StrType &o);
  friend istream &operator>>(istream &stream, StrType &o);

  StrType operator=(StrType &o);  // assign a StrType object
  StrType operator=(char *s);  // assign a quoted string

  StrType operator+(StrType &o); // concatenate a StrType object
  StrType operator+(char *s); // concatenate a quoted string
  friend StrType operator+(char *s, StrType &o); /*  concatenate
          a quoted string with a StrType object */

  StrType operator-(StrType &o); // subtract a substring
  StrType operator-(char *s);  // subtract a quoted substring

  // relational operations between StrType objects
  int operator==(StrType &o) {return !strcmp(p, o.p);}
  int operator!=(StrType &o) {return strcmp(p, o.p);}
  int operator<(StrType &o) {return strcmp(p, o.p) < 0;}
  int operator>(StrType &o) {return strcmp(p, o.p) > 0;}
  int operator<=(StrType &o) {return strcmp(p, o.p) <= 0;}
  int operator>=(StrType &o) {return strcmp(p, o.p) >= 0;}

  // operations between StrType objects and quoted strings
  int operator==(char *s) {return !strcmp(p, s);}
  int operator!=(char *s) {return strcmp(p, s);}
```

```cpp
  int operator<(char *s) {return strcmp(p, s) < 0;}
  int operator>(char *s) {return strcmp(p, s) > 0;}
  int operator<=(char *s) {return strcmp(p, s) <= 0;}
  int operator>=(char *s) {return strcmp(p, s) >= 0;}

  int strsize() {return strlen(p);} // return size of string
  void makestr(char *s) {strcpy(s, p);} // null-terminated string
  operator char *() {return p;}  // conversion to char *
};

// No explicit initialization.
StrType::StrType() {
  size = 1;  // make room for null terminator
  p = new char[size];
  if(!p) {
    cout << "Allocation error\n";
    exit(1);
  }
  strcpy(p, "");
}

// Initialize using a quoted string.
StrType::StrType(char *str) {
  size = strlen(str) + 1;  // make room for null terminator
  p = new char[size];
  if(!p) {
    cout << "Allocation error\n";
    exit(1);
  }
  strcpy(p, str);
}

// Initialize using a StrType object.
StrType::StrType(const StrType &o) {
  size = o.size;
  p = new char[size];
  if(!p) {
    cout << "Allocation error\n";
    exit(1);
  }
  strcpy(p, o.p);
}
```

```
// Output a string.
ostream &operator<<(ostream &stream, StrType &o)
{
  stream << o.p;
  return stream;
}

// Input a string.
istream &operator>>(istream &stream, StrType &o)
{
  char t[255];  // arbitrary size - change if necessary
  int len;

  for(len=0; len<255; len++) {
    stream.get(t[len]);
    if(t[len]=='\n') break;
    if(t[len]=='\b')
      if(len) {
        len--;
        cout << "'\b'";
      }
  }
  t[len] = '\0';
  len++;

  if(len > o.size) {
    delete o.p;
    o.p = new char[len];
    if(!o.p) {
      cout << "Allocation error\n";
      exit(1);
    }
    o.size = len;
  }
  strcpy(o.p, t);
  return stream;
}

// Assign a StrType object to a StrType object.
StrType StrType::operator=(StrType &o)
{
  StrType temp(o.p);
```

```
  if(o.size > size) {
    delete p;   // free old memory
    p = new char[o.size];
    size = o.size;
    if(!p) {
      cout << "Allocation error\n";
      exit(1);
    }
  }

  strcpy(p, o.p);
  strcpy(temp.p, o.p);

  return temp;
}

// Assign a quoted string to a StrType object.
StrType StrType::operator=(char *s)
{
  int len = strlen(s) + 1;
  if(size < len) {
    delete p;
    p = new char[len];
    size = len;
    if(!p) {
      cout << "Allocation error\n";
      exit(1);
    }
  }
  strcpy(p, s);
  return *this;
}

// Concatenate two StrType objects.
StrType StrType::operator+(StrType &o)
{
  int len;
  StrType temp;

  delete temp.p;
  len = strlen(o.p) + strlen(p) + 1;
  temp.p = new char[len];
```

```cpp
  temp.size = len;
  if(!temp.p) {
    cout << "Allocation error\n";
    exit(1);
  }
  strcpy(temp.p, p);

  strcat(temp.p, o.p);

  return temp;
}

// Concatenate a StrType object and a quoted string.
StrType StrType::operator+(char *s)
{
  int len;
  StrType temp;

  delete temp.p;

  len = strlen(s) + strlen(p) + 1;
  temp.p = new char[len];
  temp.size = len;
  if(!temp.p) {
    cout << "Allocation error\n";
    exit(1);
  }
  strcpy(temp.p, p);

  strcat(temp.p, s);

  return temp;
}

// Concatenate a quoted string and a StrType object.
StrType operator+(char *s, StrType &o)
{
  int len;
  StrType temp;

  delete temp.p;
```

```
  len = strlen(s) + strlen(o.p) + 1;
  temp.p = new char[len];
  temp.size = len;
  if(!temp.p) {
    cout << "Allocation error\n";
    exit(1);
  }
  strcpy(temp.p, s);

  strcat(temp.p, o.p);

  return temp;
}

// Subtract a substring from a string using StrType objects.
StrType StrType::operator-(StrType &substr)
{
  StrType temp(p);
  char *s1;
  int i, j;

  s1 = p;
  for(i=0; *s1; i++) {
    if(*s1!=*substr.p) { // if not first letter of substring
      temp.p[i] = *s1;    // then copy into temp
      s1++;
    }
    else {
      for(j=0; substr.p[j]==s1[j] && substr.p[j]; j++) ;
      if(!substr.p[j]) { // is substring, so remove it
        s1 += j;
        i--;
      }
      else {  // is not substring, continue copying
        temp.p[i] = *s1;
        s1++;
      }
    }
  }
  temp.p[i] = '\0';
  return temp;
}
```

```
// Subtract quoted string from a StrType object.
StrType StrType::operator-(char *substr)
{
  StrType temp(p);
  char *s1;
  int i, j;

  s1 = p;
  for(i=0; *s1; i++) {
    if(*s1!=*substr) { // if not first letter of substring
      temp.p[i] = *s1; // then copy into temp
      s1++;
    }
    else {
      for(j=0; substr[j]==s1[j] && substr[j]; j++) ;
      if(!substr[j]) { // is substring, so remove it
        s1 += j;
        i--;
      }
      else { // is not substring, continue copying
        temp.p[i] = *s1;
        s1++;
      }
    }
  }
  temp.p[i] = '\0';
  return temp;
}

main()
{
  StrType s1("A sample session using string objects.\n");
  StrType s2(s1);
  StrType s3;
  char s[80];

  cout << s1 << s2;

  s3 = s1;
  cout << s1;

  s3.makestr(s);
```

```
cout << "Convert to a string: " << s;

s2 = "This is a new string.";
cout << s2 << endl;

StrType s4(" So is this.");
s1 = s2+s4;
cout << s1 << endl;

if(s2==s3) cout << "Strings are equal.\n";
if(s2!=s3) cout << "Strings are not equal.\n";
if(s1<s4) cout << "s1 less than s4\n";
if(s1>s4) cout << "s1 greater than s4\n";
if(s1<=s4) cout << "s1 less than or equals s4\n";
if(s1>=s4) cout << "s1 greater than or equals s4\n";

if(s2 > "ABC") cout << "s2 greater than ABC\n\n";

s1 = "one two three one two three\n";
s2 = "two";
cout << "Initial string: " << s1;
cout << "String after subtracting two: ";
s3 = s1 - s2;
cout << s3;

cout << endl;
s4 = "Hi there!";
s3 = s4 + " C++ strings are fun\n";
cout << s3;
s3 = s3 - "Hi there!";
s3 = "Aren't" + s3;
cout << s3;

s1 = s3 - "are ";
cout << s1;
s3 = s1;

cout << "Enter a string: ";
cin >> s1;
cout << s1 << endl;
cout << "s1 is " << s1.strsize() << " characters long.\n";
```

```
    puts(s1);  // convert to char *

  s1 = s2 = s3;
  cout << s1 << s2 << s3;

  s1 = s2 = s3 = "Bye ";
  cout << s1 << s2 << s3;

  return 0;
}
```

The preceding program produces this output:

```
A sample session using string objects.
A sample session using string objects.
A sample session using string objects.
Convert to a string: A sample session using string objects.
This is a new string.
This is a new string. So is this.
Strings are not equal.
s1 greater than s4
s1 greater than or equals s4
s2 greater than ABC

Initial string: one two three one two three
String after subtracting two: one three one three

Hi there! C++ strings are fun
Aren't C++ strings are fun
Aren't C++ strings fun
Enter a string: I like C++
s1 is 10 characters long.
I like C++
Aren't C++ strings fun
Aren't C++ strings fun
Aren't C++ strings fun
Bye Bye Bye
```

This output assumes that the string "I like C++" was entered by the user when prompted for input.

To have easy access to the **StrType** class, remove the **main( )** function and put the rest of the preceding listing into a file called STR.H. Then, just include this header file with any program in which you want to use **StrType**.

Using the StrType Class

To conclude this chapter, two short examples are given that illustrate how the **StrType** class can be used. The first example creates a simple thesaurus by using **StrType** objects. It first creates a two-dimensional array of **StrType** objects. Within each pair of strings, the first contains the keyword, which can be looked up. The second string contains a list of alternative or related words. The program prompts for a word, and if the word is in the thesaurus, alternatives are displayed. This program is very simple, but notice how clean and clear the string handling is because of the use of the **StrType** class and its operators. (Remember, the header file STR.H contains the **StrType** class.)

```
#include "str.h"
#include <iostream.h>

StrType thesaurus[][2] = {
   "book", "volume, tome",
   "store", "merchant, shop, warehouse",
   "pistol", "gun, handgun, firearm",
   "run", "jog, trot, race",
   "think", "muse, contemplate, reflect",
   "compute", "analyze, work out, solve"
   "", ""
};

main()
{
  StrType x;

  cout << "Enter word: ";
  cin >> x;

  int i;
  for(i=0; thesaurus[i][0]!=""; i++)
    if(thesaurus[i][0]==x) cout << thesaurus[i][1];

  return 0;
}
```

The next example uses a **StrType** object to find out if there is an executable version of a program, given its filename. To use the program, specify the filename without an extension on the command line. The program then repeatedly tries to find an executable file of that name by adding an extension, trying to open that file, and reporting the results. (If the file does not exist, it cannot be opened.) After each extension is tried, the extension is subtracted from the filename and a new extension is added. Again, the **StrType** class and its operators make the string manipulations clean and easy to follow.

```
#include "str.h"
#include <iostream.h>
#include <fstream.h>

// executable file extensions
char ext[3][4] = {
  "EXE",
  "COM",
  "BAT"
};

main(int argc, char *argv[])
{
  StrType fname;
  int i;

  if(argc!=2) {
    cout << "Usage: fname\n";
    return 1;
  }

  fname = argv[1];

  fname = fname + ".";  // add period
  for(i=0; i<3; i++) {
    fname = fname + ext[i];  // add extension
    cout << "Trying " << fname << " ";
    ifstream f(fname);
    if(f) {
      cout << "- Exists\n";
      f.close();
    }
    else cout << "- Not found\n";
    fname = fname - ext[i]; // subtract extension
```

```
   }

   return 0;
}
```

For example, if this program is called ISEXEC, and assuming that TEST.EXE exists, the command line **ISEXEC TEST** produces this output:

```
Trying TEST.EXE - Exists
Trying TEST.COM - Not found
Trying TEST.BAT - Not found
```

One thing to notice about the program is that a **StrType** object is used in the call to **open( )**. This works because the conversion function **operator char *( )** is automatically invoked. As this situation illustrates, by the careful application of C++ features, you can achieve significant integration between C++'s standard types and types that you create.

Chapter Twenty-Four

A Pop-up Window Class

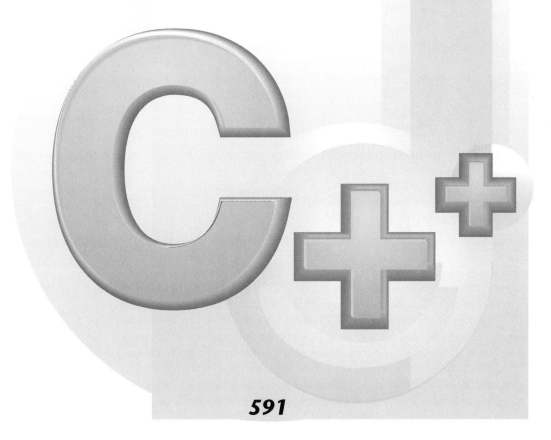

591

The pop-up window has become one of the most recognizable features in modern computing. It is hard to imagine writing a commercial application today that does not use one or more windows. The paradigm of the window is pervasive. The pop-up window also provides a classic example of object-oriented programming using C++. For this reason, this chapter develops a text-based window class and provides all the necessary functions to support a simple, yet effective windowing system.

Since Microsoft's Windows has become the dominant PC-based operating system, you might ask if there is any practical value in developing yet another windowing system. The answer is yes, for three reasons. First, the system created in this chapter is text-based (not graphics-based as is Windows). It is specifically designed to run under DOS or the DOS emulator provided by Windows. It is small and efficient, and makes text-based windowing very easy. The second reason to create your own windowing system is that you are in complete control of a system you create. Because hardware is continually evolving, you can enhance your windowing system to take advantage of new video modes or devices before support for those devices becomes generally available. You can also make it work under new operating environments and systems. Finally, the windowing system developed in this chapter interfaces directly with the video hardware of the PC. As such, it illustrates how C++ is capable of low-level device interfacing as well as high-level programming. The same general methods used to interface to the video hardware can be used to interface to other types of devices.

NOTE: *Windowing systems are extremely device dependent. This chapter assumes a PC environment, and several of the functions interface directly with ROM BIOS (Basic I/O System) or the hardware itself. However, by changing only a few functions, you can modify the window system to work in any environment.*

Before beginning, it is important to define what a windowing system will do.

Pop-up Windows

A pop-up window is a portion of the screen that is used for a specific purpose. When the window comes into existence, what is currently on the screen is saved and the window is displayed. When the application using that window is finished, the window is removed and the original contents of the screen are restored. It is possible to have several windows on the screen at the same time.

One important feature of a windowing system is that it must not allow an application using the window to write past the boundaries of the window. Because the size of the window is not necessarily known to the application, it is the job of the window routines, not the application, to prevent overwriting. Therefore, all of C++'s normal console I/O routines (such as **printf( )** and **gets( )**) and the **cout** and **cin** streams cannot be used, and alternative window-specific I/O functions must be substituted. In fact, the window-specific I/O functions form a major part of any windowing system.

To understand how pop-up windows might be effectively used, imagine that you have written a text editor that includes some extra features. One of these extra features is a calculator. Because using the calculator is not actually part of text editing, it makes sense to use a pop-up window whenever it is activated. Thus, when the calculator is used, text editing is simply suspended; it is not completely disrupted. Once the calculations have been performed, the calculator window is removed and text editing continues.

Creating Some Video Support Functions

Before creating the window system, it is necessary to develop some support functions. Because the creation of pop-up windows requires direct and intimate control of the screen, specialized functions are needed that perform screen I/O. As stated, it is not possible to use C++'s normal output functions and operators. The specialized functions will bypass both DOS and BIOS and write directly to the video hardware itself. This is the only way that sufficiently fast screen updates can be accomplished.

To begin, here is a short overview of the PC's video system.

> **NOTE:** *The discussion of the PC's video system presented in this chapter is sufficient to understand how the windowing system works. Consult other texts to learn more about the topic of video interfacing, in general.*

The PC Video System

All PCs contain some type of video adapter that outputs images to the monitor. The four most common types of adapters are the monochrome adapter, the color/graphics adapter (CGA), the enhanced graphics adapter (EGA), and the video graphics array (VGA). (There are also a number of Super VGA adapters available that support extended video modes. For the purposes of this chapter, VGAs and Super VGAs are equivalent.) The CGA, EGA, and VGA have several modes of operation. The windowing system developed in this chapter requires that the video system be in 80-column text mode. This mode is usually the default mode of operation for general-purpose console-based applications. The monochrome adapter uses mode 7 for 80-column text mode. The CGA/EGA/VGA adapters use either mode 2 or mode 3.

The characters displayed on the screen are held in RAM that is reserved for the display adapters. The location of the video RAM used by the monochrome adapter is B000:0000H, and the CGA/EGA/VGA video RAM starts at B800:0000H. Although the CGA, EGA, and VGA function differently in some modes, they are the same in modes 2 and 3.

Each character displayed on the screen requires 2 bytes of video memory. The first byte holds the actual character, and the second holds its *screen attribute*. For color adapters, the attribute byte is interpreted as shown in Table 24-1. The primary colors can be combined to produce additional colors. If you have a CGA, EGA, or VGA, by default the characters are displayed with an attribute byte value of 7. This turns the three foreground colors on, producing white. To produce reverse video, the foreground bits are turned off and the three background bits are turned on, producing a value of 70H.

The monochrome adapter recognizes the blinking and intensity bits. Fortunately, it is designed to interpret an attribute of 7 as normal, and 70H produces reverse video. Also, the value 1 produces underlined characters.

Each adapter actually has four times as much memory as it needs to display text in 80-column mode. The reasons for this are twofold. First, the extra memory is needed for graphics (except in the monochrome adapter, of course). Second, it allows multiple screens to be held in RAM and then simply switched in when needed. Each region of memory is called a *video page,* and the effect of switching the active video page is quite dramatic. By default, DOS and Windows use page 0 and virtually all applications use page 0. For this reason it will be used in the routines in this chapter. However, you can use other pages if you desire.

There are three ways to access the video adapter. The first is through calls to the operating system, a method that is far too slow for pop-up windows. The second way is through BIOS routines, which is quicker, and on faster machines it may be fast enough if the windows are small. The third way is by reading from and writing to the video RAM directly, which is very fast but requires more programming effort. However, for pop-up windows to really "pop up," direct access of the video RAM is necessary. Therefore, this is the approach taken in the windowing system developed here.

To allow the windowing system to access the video RAM, a pointer to it is needed. However, when running a program under DOS (or Windows' DOS emulator), the

Bit	Value	Meaning When Set
0	1	Blue foreground
1	2	Green foreground
2	4	Red foreground
3	8	Low intensity
4	16	Blue background
5	32	Green background
6	64	Red background
7	128	Blinking character

Table 24-1. *The Video Attribute Byte*

video RAM lies in a segment different than that used by the typical program. This means that a FAR pointer must be used. FAR pointers can be supported in one of two ways by a C++ compiler. First, the **far** keyword extension is provided by many compilers. (Some compilers call this extended keyword **_far** or **__far**, so be sure to check your compiler's user manual.) It allows a pointer to be declared as FAR. The second way is to compile your program using a large memory model, in which case all pointers are FAR by default. The routines used in this chapter use the **far** type modifier. If you like, you can remove it and simply compile the code using a large memory model.

Accessing the BIOS

Although the video functions that actually read or write information will bypass DOS and BIOS and access the video RAM directly, the BIOS will still be used for a few operations. Calls are made to BIOS by using a software interrupt. The function that generates a software interrupt is **int86( )**. The **int86( )** function is specific to DOS environments. It has this prototype:

int int86(int *num*, union REGS *inregs*, union REGS *outregs*);

The BIOS uses several different interrupts for varying purposes, and it is beyond the scope of this chapter to discuss them. However, the one related to the video adapter is interrupt 16 (10H). Like many BIOS interrupts, interrupt 16 has several options, which are selected based upon the value of the AH register. If the BIOS function returns a value, it is generally returned in AX. However, sometimes other registers are used if several values are returned. The return value of **int86( )** is the value of the **AX** register.

The structure **REGS** is supplied in the header DOS.H. The **REGS** structure is defined as follows.

```
struct BYTEREGS {
  unsigned char al;
  unsigned char ah;
  unsigned char bl;
  unsigned char bh;
  unsigned char cl;
  unsigned char ch;
  unsigned char dl;
  unsigned char dh;
};

struct WORDREGS {
```

```
    unsigned ax;
    unsigned bx;
    unsigned cx;
    unsigned dx;
    unsigned si;
    unsigned di;
    unsigned cflag;
    unsigned flags; // This is not defined by all versions of WORDREGS
};

union REGS {
  struct BYTEREGS h;
  struct WORDREGS x;
};
```

As you can see, **REGS** is a union of two structures. Using the **WORDREGS** structure allows you to access the registers of the CPU as 16-bit quantities. **BYTEREGS** gives you access to the individual 8-bit registers.

NOTE: *Microsoft C++ calls the **int86( )** function **_int86( )** and refers to **REGS** as **_REGS**.*

Determining the Location of the Video RAM

When reading and writing directly to the video RAM, you first need to overcome the problem caused by the fact that the monochrome adapter has its video RAM at B000:0000H, while the others have theirs at B800:0000H. For the window routines to operate correctly for each adapter, they need to know which adapter is in the system. Fortunately, there is an easy way to do this. The BIOS interrupt 16, function 15, returns the current video mode. As stated earlier, the routines developed in this chapter require that the mode be 2, 3, or 7. Modes 2 and 3 can be used only by the CGA, EGA, or VGA, and these adapters cannot use mode 7—only the monochrome adapter can. Therefore, if the current video mode is 7, there is a monochrome adapter in use; otherwise, it is a CGA, EGA, or VGA. For windowing purposes, the CGA, EGA, and VGA function the same in text mode, so it doesn't matter which is in the system. Therefore, by using the current video mode, it is possible to set a global FAR pointer to the address of the video RAM. The following functions perform this job.

```
    char far *vid_mem; // pointer to screen memory when in text mode
```

```
void set_v_ptr()
{
  int vmode;

  vmode = video_mode();
  if((vmode!=2) && (vmode!=3) && (vmode!=7)) {
    cout << "Video must be in 80 column text mode.";
    exit(1);
  }
  // set proper address of video RAM
  if(vmode==7) vid_mem = (char far *) 0xB0000000;
  else vid_mem = (char far *) 0xB8000000;
}

// Returns the current video mode.
video_mode()
{
  union REGS r;

  r.h.ah = 15;  // get video mode
  return int86(0x10, &r, &r) & 255;
}
```

The **video_mode( )** function uses BIOS interrupt 16, function 15, to obtain the current video mode. This value is then used to determine where **vid_mem**, declared as a global **char far ***, will point (that is, either to the memory used by the monochrome adapter or to the memory used by the other adapters). This pointer will then be used by the window-based routines that access the video RAM.

Writing to the Video RAM

Once the video mode has been determined and a pointer to the video RAM has been obtained, two direct video RAM output functions can be created. These functions are not, per se, part of the windowing system. However, they are needed because they provide extremely fast output. The functions write a character or a string to the specific X,Y location. The attribute byte is also written. They are shown here:

```
// Write character with specified attribute.
void write_char(int x, int y, char ch, int attrib)
{
```

```
    char far *v;

  v = vid_mem;
  v += (y*160) + x*2;
  *v++ = ch; // write the character
  *v = attrib; // write the attribute
}

// Display a string with specified attribute.
void write_string(int x, int y, char *p, int attrib)
{
  register int i;
  char far *v;

  v = vid_mem;
  v += (y*160) + x*2; // compute the address
  for(i=y; *p; i++) {
    *v++ = *p++; // write the character
    *v++ = attrib; // write the attribute
  }
}
```

Because, in 80-column text mode, each line of the screen holds 80 characters, 160 bytes (80 characters plus 80 attribute bytes) are used per line. The address of the correct location in the video RAM is then 160 times the Y coordinate plus 2 times the X coordinate.

Positioning the Cursor

When I/O is performed using direct video RAM I/O, the cursor's location is not automatically updated. This means that the window routines will need to move the cursor manually. The following function performs this operation. (The function is also not actually part of the windowing class, but it is used by it. The function uses BIOS interrupt 16, function 2.)

```
// Send the cursor to the specified X,Y position.
void goto_xy(int x, int y)
{
  union REGS r;

  r.h.ah = 2; // cursor addressing function
```

```
   r.h.dl = x; // column coordinate
   r.h.dh = y; // row coordinate
   r.h.bh = 0; // video page
   int86(0x10, &r, &r);
}
```

Many compilers supply a "goto xy" function. If yours does, feel free to substitute it.

The Window Class

Now that the stage has been set, the windowing system can be developed. The windowing system is managed by the **wintype** class. Its declaration is shown here:

```
class wintype {
  // define where window goes on the screen
  int leftx;  // upper left coordinates
  int upy;
  int rightx; // lower right coordinates
  int downy;

  int border;  // if non-zero, border displayed
  int active;  // non-zero if window is currently on screen
  char *title; // title message

  int curx, cury; // current cursor location in window

  char *buf; // points to window's buffer
  char color; // text color

  // private functions
  void save_screen(); // save screen so it can be restored
  void restore_screen(); // restore the original screen
  void draw_border(); // draw a window's border
  void display_title(); // display title
public:
  wintype(int lx, int uy, // upper left
          int rx, int ly, // lower right
          int b = 1, // non-zero for border
          char *mess = "" // title message
  );
```

```
~wintype() {winremove(); delete [] buf;}

void winput(); // display a window
void winremove(); // remove a window
int winputs(char *s); // write a string to the window
int winxy(int x, int y); // go to X,Y relative to window
void wingets(char *s); // input string from a window
int wingetche();  // input a character from a window
void wincls(); // clears the window
void wincleol(); // clears to end-of-line

void setcolor(char c) {color = c;}
char getcolor() {return color;}
void setbkcolor(char c) {color = color | (c<<4);}
char getbkcolor() {return (color>>4) & 127;}

friend wintype &operator<<(wintype &o, char *s);
friend wintype &operator>>(wintype &o, char *s);
};
```

The position of the window on the screen and its size are determined by the variables **leftx**, **upy**, **rightx**, and **downy**. These hold the coordinates of the upper-left and lower-right corners of the window.

If the window will have a border, then **border** must be set to nonzero. Whenever the window is on the screen, **active** is set to nonzero. When the window is not displayed, **active** is zero. The title to the window (if any) is pointed to by **title**.

The current cursor location within the window is stored in **curx** and **cury**. All output sent to a window is positioned relative to the window. That is, **curx** and **cury** are relative to the window, not to the screen. This means that if **curx** is 5 and **cury** is 3, then no matter where the window is on the screen, the cursor is located at 5,3 *within the window.* Further, the upper-left corner of the window is 0,0.

When a window is displayed, whatever is currently on the screen is saved in the memory pointed to by **buf**. (This memory is dynamically allocated when the window is created.) The color of the text is determined by the value of **color**. It must be one of the following enumerated values:

```
/* Text colors, first 7 can also be used to specify
   background color.
*/
const enum clr {black, blue, green, cyan, red, magenta,
                brown, lightgray, darkgray, lightblue,
```

```
                    lightgreen, lightcyan, lightred,
                    lightmagenta, yellow, white, blink=128};
```

The **wintype** constructor function is shown here:

```
// Construct a window.
wintype::wintype(int lx, int uy, // upper left
          int rx, int ly, // lower right
          int b, // non-zero for border
          char *mess // title message
  )
{
  if(lx<0) lx = 0;
  if(rx>79) rx = 79;
  if(uy<0) uy = 0;
  if(ly>24) ly = 24;

  leftx = lx; upy = uy;
  rightx = rx, downy = ly;
  border = b;
  title = mess;
  active = 0;
  curx = cury = 0;
  buf = new char[2*(rightx-leftx+1)*(downy-upy+1)];
  if(!buf) {
    cout << "Allocation error.\n";
    exit(1);
  }
  color = white;
}
```

The constructor first makes sure that the four coordinate values are within range. It then initializes the private data. It also allocates the memory that will be used to save the current contents of the screen when the window is activated. When the window is deactivated, the original contents will then be restored.

Notice that by default, the text color is white, the cursor is located at 0,0, and the window is inactive.

NOTE: *The **wintype( )** constructor only constructs a window. It does not display that window. Displaying the window is a separate operation from constructing it.*

The ~**wintype( )** destructor removes the window (if needed) and then frees the memory pointed to by **buf**.

Displaying and Removing a Window

Once a window has been constructed, it can be displayed by a call to **winput( )**. This function is shown here:

```
// Display a window.
void wintype::winput()
{
  // get active window
  if(!active) { // not currently in use
    save_screen(); // save the current screen
    active = 1; // set active flag
  }
  else return;  // already on screen

  if(border) draw_border();
  display_title();

  // position cursor in upper left corner
  goto_xy(leftx + curx + 1, upy + cury + 1);
}
```

This function first checks to see if the window is already on the screen. If the window is active, the call to **winput( )** is ignored. Otherwise, the current contents of the portion of the screen where the window will be displayed are saved by calling **save_screen( )**, and **active** is set to 1. If **border** is nonzero, a border for the window is drawn. Next, the title is displayed. Finally, the cursor is positioned at the current cursor location. Since the values of **curx** and **cury** are relative to the window, they must be added to **leftx** and **upy**, respectively, so that the cursor can be displayed in the correct screen-relative location.

The **save_screen( )** function is shown next. (It is a private function of **wintype( )**.) It simply copies, byte for byte, the contents of the video RAM where the window will be displayed into the memory pointed to by **buf**. It also clears that portion of the screen.

```
// Save screen so it can be restored after window is removed.
void wintype::save_screen()
{
  register int i,j;
```

```
    char *buf_ptr;
    char far *v, far *t;

    buf_ptr = buf;
    v = vid_mem;
    for(i=upy; i<downy+1; i++)
      for(j=leftx; j<rightx+1; j++) {
        t = (v + (i*160) + j*2);
        *buf_ptr++ = *t++;
        *buf_ptr++ = *t;
        *(t-1) = ' ';   // clear the window
      }
}
```

The **draw_border( )** and **display_title( )** functions are shown next. These are also private functions of **wintype**.

```
// Draw a border around the window.
void wintype::draw_border()
{
  register int i;
  char far *v, far *t;

  v = vid_mem;
  t = v;
  for(i=leftx+1; i<rightx; i++) {
     v += (upy*160) + i*2;
     *v++ = 196;
     *v = color;
     v = t;
     v += (downy*160) + i*2;
     *v++ = 196;
     *v = color;
     v = t;
  }
  for(i=upy+1; i<downy; i++) {
     v += (i*160) + leftx*2;
     *v++ = 179;
     *v = color;
     v = t;
     v += (i*160) + rightx*2;
```

```
      *v++ = 179;
      *v = color;
      v = t;
   }
   // draw the corners
   write_char(leftx, upy, 218, color);
   write_char(leftx, downy, 192, color);
   write_char(rightx, upy, 191, color);
   write_char(rightx, downy, 217, color);
}

// Display the window's title.
void wintype::display_title()
{
   register int  x, len;

   x = leftx;

   /* Calculate the correct starting position to center
      the title message - if negative, message won't
      fit.
   */
   len = strlen(title);
   len = (rightx - x - len) / 2;
   if(len<0) return; // don't display it
   x = x + len + 1;

   write_string(x, upy,
                title, color);
}
```

The values 196 and 179 correspond to horizontal and vertical lines in the PC's extended character set. The values used at the end of **draw_border( )** are corner pieces in the extended character set. The title is only displayed if it can fit.

To remove a window from the screen, use the **winremove( )** function, shown next. It copies what is stored in the memory pointed to by **buf** back into the video RAM.

```
// Remove the window and restore prior screen contents.
void wintype::winremove()
{
   if(!active) return; // can't remove a non-active window
```

```
    restore_screen(); // restore the original screen
    active = 0; // restore_video
}
```

Aside from setting **active** to zero, the main purpose of the function is to restore the original contents of the screen by calling the private **restore_screen( )** function, as shown here:

```
// Restore a portion of the screen.
void wintype::restore_screen()
{
  register int i,j;
  char far *v, far *t;
  char *buf_ptr;

  buf_ptr = buf;
  v = vid_mem;
  t = v;
  for(i=upy; i<downy+1; i++)
    for(j=leftx; j<rightx+1; j++) {
    v = t;
    v += (i*160) + j*2;
    *v++ = *buf_ptr++;  // write the character
    *v = *buf_ptr++;    // write the attribute
    }
}
```

Window I/O

Input from and output to a window can be performed either with member functions or with the overloaded << and >> operators. All window I/O must be performed through window-based routines that prevent the boundaries of the window from being overwritten.

The lowest-level input function is called **wingetche( )**. This function reads a character from the keyboard and echos it to the window, as shown here:

```
/* Input a keystroke inside a window.
   Returns full 16-bit keyboard code.
*/
```

```cpp
int wintype::wingetche()
{
  union inkey {
    char ch[2];
    int i;
  } c;
  union REGS r;
  if(!active) return 0; // window not active

  winxy(curx, cury);

  r.h.ah = 0; // read a key
  c.i = int86(0x16, &r, &r);

  if(c.ch[0]) {
    switch(c.ch[0]) {
      case '\r': // the ENTER key is pressed
        break;
      case '\b': // back space
        break;
      default:
        if(curx+leftx < rightx-1) {
          write_char(leftx+ curx+1,
          upy+cury+1, c.ch[0], color);
          curx++;
        }
    }
    if(cury < 0) cury = 0;
    if(cury+upy > downy-2)
      cury--;
    winxy(curx, cury);
  }
  return c.i;
}
```

This function calls BIOS interrupt 16, function 0, which waits for a keypress and returns the full 16-bit keyboard code. The keyboard code is divided into two parts: the character and the position code. If the key pressed is a character key, the character is returned in the low-order 8 bits. However, if a special key is pressed for which no character code exists, such as an arrow key, then the low-order byte is zero and the high-order byte contains that key's position code. For example, the position codes for the up and down arrows are 72 and 80. Although none of the window functions make use of the position code, it is provided here because your window applications will very likely need access to both the character and the position codes.

As you can see by examining the function, no keystrokes will be echoed past the boundary of the window. Also, keystrokes are echoed in the color currently defined for the window. Finally, the window must be active.

To read a string from the keyboard, use **wingets( )**, shown here:

```
// Read a string from a window.
void wintype::wingets(char *s)
{
  char ch, *temp;

  temp = s;
  for(;;) {
    ch = wingetche();
    switch(ch) {
      case '\r':  // the ENTER key is pressed
        *s = '\0';
        return;
      case '\b': // backspace
        if(s>temp) {
          s--;
          curx--;
          if(curx<0) curx = 0;
          winxy(curx, cury);
          write_char(leftx+ curx+1,upy+cury+1, ' ', color);
        }
        break;
      default: *s = ch;
        s++;
    }
  }
}
```

This function calls **wingetche( )** to input each character. Because **wingetche( )** prevents keystrokes from overrunning a window boundary, no input from **wingets( )** can overrun a window boundary either.

To output a string to a window, use **winputs( )**, shown here:

```
/* Write a string at the current cursor position
   in the specified window.
   Returns 0 if window not active;
```

```
   1 otherwise.
*/
int wintype::winputs(char *s)
{
  register int x, y;
  char far *v;

  // make sure window is active
  if(!active) return 0;
  x = curx + leftx + 1;
  y = cury + upy + 1;

  v = vid_mem;
  v += (y*160) + x*2; // compute starting address

  for( ; *s; s++) {
    if(y >= downy) {
      return 1;
    }
    if(x >= rightx) {
      return 1;
    }

    if(*s=='\n') {
      y++;
      x = leftx+1;
      v = vid_mem;
      v += (y*160) + x*2; // compute the address
      cury++;  // increment Y
      curx = 0; // reset X
    }
    else {
      curx++;
      x++;
      *v++ = *s;   // write the character
      *v++ = color; // color
    }
    winxy(curx, cury);
  }
  return 1;
}
```

This function outputs the specified string beginning at the current cursor location (as defined by **curx** and **cury**) in the current color. No output will be allowed beyond the bounds of the window.

As mentioned, in addition to the I/O member functions, you can also output a string by using << and input a string by using >>. These overloaded operators are shown next. Their operation is straightforward.

```
// Output to a window.
wintype &operator<<(wintype &o, char *s)
{
  o.winputs(s);
  return o;
}


// Input from a window.
wintype &operator>>(wintype &o, char *s)
{
  o.wingets(s);
  return o;
}
```

If you want to input other types of data, simply overload << and >> again.

Three additional window output functions are **wincls( )**, which clears the window, **wincleol( )**, which clears from the current cursor position to the end of the line, and **winxy( )**, which positions the cursor at the window-relative X,Y position. These functions are shown here:

```
// Clear a window.
void wintype::wincls()
{
  register int i,j;
  char far *v, far *t;

  v = vid_mem;
  t = v;
  for(i=upy+1; i<downy; i++)
    for(j=leftx+1; j<rightx; j++) {
      v = t;
      v += (i*160) + j*2;
      *v++ = ' ';   // write a space
      *v = color;   // in background color
```

```
    }
  curx = 0;
  cury = 0;
}

// Clear to end of line.
void wintype::wincleol()
{
  register int i, x, y;

  x = curx;
  y = cury;
  winxy(curx, cury);

  for(i=curx; i<rightx-1; i++)
    winputs(" ");
  winxy(x, y);
}

/* Position cursor in a window at specified location.
   Returns 0 if out of range; non-zero otherwise.
*/
int wintype::winxy(int x, int y)
{
  if(x<0 || x+leftx >= rightx-1)
    return 0;
  if(y<0 || y+upy >= downy-1)
    return 0;
  curx = x;
  cury = y;
  goto_xy(leftx+x+1, upy+y+1);
  return 1;
}
```

You can set the foreground color by using **setcolor( )** and the background color by using **setbkcolor( )**. These functions are defined inside the declaration of **wintype**. For **setcolor( )**, you can use any color specified in the **clr** enumeration. For **setbkcolor( )**, you can use the first seven colors. The functions **getcolor( )** and **getbkcolor( )** return the foreground and background colors, respectively. These functions are defined inline within the **wintype** class.

The Entire Window System

Here is the entire windowing system, plus support functions and a **main( )** function that demonstrates the window functions:

```
// A window class.

#include <iostream.h>
#include <conio.h>
#include <stdlib.h>
#include <string.h>
#include <dos.h>
#include <bios.h>

// Global functions
int video_mode();
void goto_xy(int x, int y);
void set_v_ptr();
void write_char(int x, int y, char ch, int attrib);
void write_string(int x, int y, char *p, int attrib);

/* Text colors, first 7 can also be used to specify
   background color. */
const enum clr {black, blue, green, cyan, red, magenta,
                brown, lightgray, darkgray, lightblue,
                lightgreen, lightcyan, lightred,
                lightmagenta, yellow, white, blink=128};

char far *vid_mem; // pointer to screen memory when in text mode

class wintype {
  // define where window goes on the screen
  int leftx;  // upper left coordinates
  int upy;
  int rightx; // lower right coordinates
  int downy;
  int border;  // if non-zero, border displayed
  int active;  // non-zero if window is currently on screen
  char *title; // title message

  int curx, cury; // current cursor location in window
```

```
    char *buf; // points to window's buffer

    char color; // text color

    // private functions
    void save_screen(); // save screen so it can be restored
    void restore_screen(); // restore the original screen
    void draw_border(); // draw a window's border
    void display_title(); // display title
  public:
    wintype(int lx, int uy, // upper left
            int rx, int ly, // lower right
            int b = 1, // non-zero for border
            char *mess = "" // title message
    );

    ~wintype() {winremove(); delete [] buf;}

    void winput(); // display a window
    void winremove(); // remove a window
    int winputs(char *s); // write a string to the window
    int winxy(int x, int y); // go to X,Y relative to window
    void wingets(char *s); // input string from a window
    int wingetche();  // input a character from a window
    void wincls(); // clears the window
    void wincleol(); // clears to end-of-line

    void setcolor(char c) {color = c;}
    char getcolor() {return color;}
    void setbkcolor(char c) {color = color | (c<<4);}
    char getbkcolor() {return (color>>4) & 127;}

    friend wintype &operator<<(wintype &o, char *s);
    friend wintype &operator>>(wintype &o, char *s);
};

// Construct a window.
wintype::wintype(int lx, int uy, // upper left
        int rx, int ly, // lower right
        int b, // non-zero for border
        char *mess // title message
  )
```

```
{
  if(lx<0) lx = 0;
  if(rx>79) rx = 79;
  if(uy<0) uy = 0;
  if(ly>24) ly = 24;
  leftx = lx; upy = uy;
  rightx = rx, downy = ly;
  border = b;
  title = mess;
  active = 0;
  curx = cury = 0;

  buf = new char[2*(rightx-leftx+1)*(downy-upy+1)];
  if(!buf) {
    cout << "Allocation error.\n";
    exit(1);
  }
  color = white;
}

//
Display a window.
void wintype::winput()
{
  // get active window
  if(!active) { // not currently in use
    save_screen(); // save the current screen
    active = 1; // set active flag
  }
  else return;  // already on screen

  if(border) draw_border();
  display_title();

  // position cursor in upper left corner
  goto_xy(leftx + curx + 1, upy + cury + 1);
}

// Remove the window and restore prior screen contents.
void wintype::winremove()
{
  if(!active) return; // can't remove a non-active window
```

```
      restore_screen(); // restore the original screen
      active = 0; // restore_video
    }

    // Draw a border around the window.
    void wintype::draw_border()
    {
      register int i;
      char far *v, far *t;

      v = vid_mem;
      t = v;
      for(i=leftx+1; i<rightx; i++) {
          v += (upy*160) + i*2;
          *v++ = 196; *v = color;
          v = t;
          v += (downy*160) + i*2;
          *v++ = 196;
          *v = color;
          v = t;
      }
      for(i=upy+1; i<downy; i++) {
          v += (i*160) + leftx*2;
          *v++ = 179;
          *v = color;
          v = t;
          v += (i*160) + rightx*2;
          *v++ = 179;
          *v = color;
          v = t;
      }
      // draw the corners
      write_char(leftx, upy, 218, color);
      write_char(leftx, downy, 192, color);
      write_char(rightx, upy, 191, color);
      write_char(rightx, downy, 217, color);
    }

    // Display the window's title.
    void wintype::display_title()
    {
      register int x, len;
```

```
  x = leftx;

  /* Calculate the correct starting position to center
     the title message - if negative, message won't
     fit.
  */
  len = strlen(title);
  len = (rightx - x - len) / 2;
  if(len<0) return; // don't display it
  x = x + len + 1;

  write_string(x, upy, title, color);
}

// Save screen so it can be restored after window is removed.
void wintype::save_screen()
{
  register int i,j;
  char *buf_ptr;
  char far *v, far *t;

  buf_ptr = buf;
  v = vid_mem;
  for(i=upy; i<downy+1; i++)
    for(j=leftx; j<rightx+1; j++) {
      t = (v + (i*160) + j*2);
      *buf_ptr++ = *t++;
      *buf_ptr++ = *t;
      *(t-1) = ' ';  // clear the window
    }
}

// Restore a portion of the screen.
void wintype::restore_screen()
{
  register int i,j;
  char far *v, far *t;
  char *buf_ptr;

  buf_ptr = buf;
  v = vid_mem;
```

```
  t = v;
  for(i=upy; i<downy+1; i++)
    for(j=leftx; j<rightx+1; j++) {
      v = t;
      v += (i*160) + j*2;
      *v++ = *buf_ptr++;  // write the character
      *v = *buf_ptr++;    // write the attribute
    }
}

/* Write a string at the current cursor position
   in the specified window.
   Returns 0 if window not active;
   1 otherwise.
*/
int wintype::winputs(char *s)
{
  register int x, y;
  char far *v;

  // make sure window is active
  if(!active) return 0;

  x = curx + leftx + 1;
  y = cury + upy + 1;

  v = vid_mem;
  v += (y*160) + x*2; // compute starting address

  for( ; *s;  s++)  {
    if(y >= downy) {
      return 1;
    }
    if(x >= rightx) {
      return 1;
    }
    if(*s=='\n') {
      y++;
      x = leftx+1;
      v = vid_mem;
      v += (y*160) + x*2; // compute the address
      cury++;  // increment Y
```

```
      curx = 0; // reset X
    }
    else {
      curx++;
      x++;
      *v++ = *s;   // write the character
      *v++ = color; // color
    }
    winxy(curx, cury);
  }
  return 1;
}

/* Position cursor in a window at specified location.
   Returns 0 if out of range; non-zero otherwise.
*/
int
wintype::winxy(int x, int y)
{
  if(x<0 || x+leftx >= rightx-1)
    return 0;
  if(y<0 || y+upy >= downy-1)
    return 0;
  curx = x;
  cury = y;
  goto_xy(leftx+x+1, upy+y+1);
  return 1;
}

// Read a string from a window.
void wintype::wingets(char *s)
{
  char ch, *temp;

  temp = s;
  for(;;) {
    ch = wingetche();
    switch(ch) {
      case '\r':  // the ENTER key is pressed
        *s = '\0';
        return;
      case '\b': // backspace
```

```
        if(s>temp) {
          s--;
          curx--;
          if(curx<0) curx = 0;
          winxy(curx, cury);
          write_char(leftx+ curx+1, upy+cury+1, ' ', color);
        }
        break;
      default: *s = ch;
        s++;
    }
  }
}

/* Input keystrokes inside a window.
   Returns full 16-bit keyboard code.
*/
wintype::wingetche()
{
  union inkey {
    char ch[2];
    int i;
  } c;
  union REGS r;

  if(!active) return 0; // window not active

  winxy(curx, cury);

  r.h.ah = 0; // read a key
  c.i = int86(0x16, &r, &r);

  if(c.ch[0]) {
    switch(c.ch[0]) {
      case '\r': // the ENTER key is pressed
        break;
      case '\b': // back space
        break;
      default:
        if(curx+leftx < rightx-1) {
          write_char(leftx+ curx+1,
          upy+cury+1, c.ch[0], color);
```

```
        curx++;
      }
    }
  if(cury < 0) cury = 0;
  if(cury+upy > downy-2)
    cury--;
  winxy(curx, cury);
  }
  return c.i;
}

// Clear a window.
void wintype::wincls()
{
  register int i,j;
  char far *v, far *t;

  v = vid_mem;
  t = v;
  for(i=upy+1; i<downy; i++)
    for(j=leftx+1; j<rightx; j++) {
      v = t;
      v += (i*160) + j*2;
      *v++ = ' ';  // write a space
      *v = color;  // in background color
    }
  curx = 0;
  cury = 0;
}

// Clear to end of line.
void wintype::wincleol()
{
  register int i, x, y;

  x = curx;
  y = cury;
  winxy(curx, cury);

  for(i=curx; i<rightx-1; i++)
    winputs(" ");
  winxy(x, y);
```

```
}

// Output to a window.
wintype &operator<<(wintype &o, char *s)
{
  o.winputs(s);
  return o;
}

// Input from a window.
wintype &operator>>(wintype &o, char *s)
{
  o.wingets(s);
  return o;
}

main()
{
  char s[80];

  set_v_ptr(); // set the video memory pointer

  wintype w1(1, 10, 20, 20, 1, "My Window #1");
  wintype w2(40, 1, 60, 20, 1, "My Window #2");
  wintype w3(40, 5, 60, 20, 1, "My Window #3");

  w1.winput();
  w2.winput();
  w1.setcolor(red);
  w2.setcolor(green);
  w1 >> s;
  w1.winxy(0, 0);
  w1.winputs("Hi there\n");
  w1.winputs("Windows are fun");
  w1 << "\n";
  w1 >> s;
  w1 << "This \nis " << "a test" << "\n";
  w2 << "this is a test";
  w2.winxy(3, 4);
  w2 << "at location 3, 4";
  w1 << "This is another test for you to see\n";
  w1 >> s;
```

```cpp
  w3.winput();  // overlap another window
  w3 >> s;
  w3.winremove();
  w1.winxy(0, 0);
  w1.setcolor(red);
  w1.setbkcolor(cyan);
  w1.winputs("PROMPT: ");
  w1.setcolor(white);
  w1.setbkcolor(black);
  w1 >> s;
  w2.winxy(0, 4);
  w2.setcolor(yellow);
  w2.setbkcolor(green);
  w2.winputs(s);
  w2 >> s;
  w2.wincls();
  w1.winxy(5, 0);
  w1.wincleol();
  w2 >> s;
  w1.winremove();
  w2.winremove();
  w1.winput();
  w1 >> s;

  return 0;
}

void set_v_ptr()
{
  int vmode;

  vmode = video_mode();
  if((vmode!=2) && (vmode!=3) && (vmode!=7)) {
    cout << "Video must be in 80 column text mode.";
    exit(1);
  }
  // set proper address of video RAM
  if(vmode==7) vid_mem = (char far *) 0xB0000000;
  else vid_mem = (char far *) 0xB8000000;
}
```

```cpp
// Returns the current video mode.
video_mode()
{
  union REGS r;

  r.h.ah = 15;  // get video mode
  return int86(0x10, &r, &r) & 255;
}

// Write character with specified attribute.
void write_char(int x, int y, char ch, int attrib)
{
  char far *v;

  v = vid_mem;
  v += (y*160) + x*2;
  *v++ = ch; // write the character
  *v = attrib; // write the attribute
}

// Send the cursor to the specified X,Y position.
void goto_xy(int x, int y)
{
  union REGS r;

  r.h.ah = 2; // cursor addressing function
  r.h.dl = x; // column coordinate
  r.h.dh = y; // row coordinate
  r.h.bh = 0; // video page
  int86(0x10, &r, &r);
}

// Display a string with specified attribute.
void write_string(int x, int y, char *p, int attrib)
{
  register int i;
  char far *v;

  v = vid_mem;
  v += (y*160) + x*2; // compute the address
  for(i=y; *p; i++) {
    *v++ = *p++; // write the character
```

```
        *v++ = attrib; // write the attribute
    }
}
```

This program produces the output shown in Figure 24-1.

Things to Try

Although the windowing system is fully functional, there are some modifications you might want to try. As it stands, when a window is removed, the contents of that window are lost. It is possible, however, to save the contents of the window so they can be restored when the window is redisplayed. This modification may prove valuable for some situations. You might want to overload the << and >> operators so that they can handle more types of data than just strings. You can overload the = operator relative to objects of type **wintype**. If you do, make sure that each object uses its own memory to hold the contents of a window. Finally, if you want to be able to use one window object to initialize another, you will need to create a copy constructor that ensures that each object allocates its own memory. If you don't, the same piece of memory will be freed twice when the objects are destroyed.

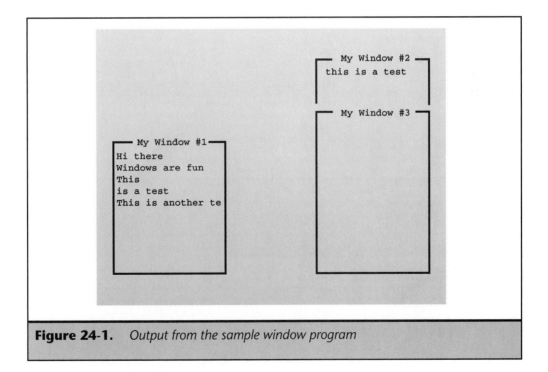

Figure 24-1.   *Output from the sample window program*

Chapter Twenty-Five

A Generic Linked List Class

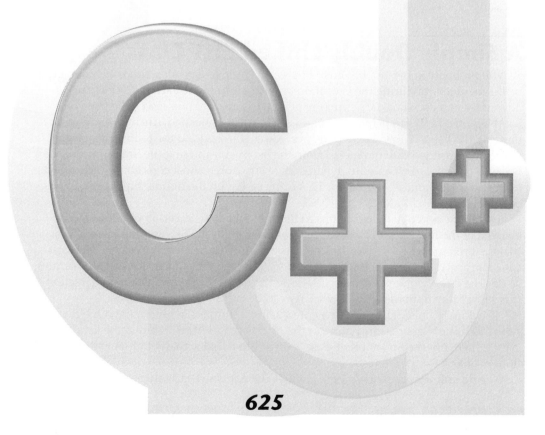

The final chapter in this book examines the issues that arise when implementing a generic doubly linked list class. Generic classes are one of the most important features of C++ — especially in professional programming environments. Although a doubly linked list is just one of several methods used to store information, the problems and solutions associated with creating a generic doubly linked list class can be generalized to any storage method.

REMEMBER: *A generic class is one that is formed using the keyword* **template**. *The type of data upon which it operates is specified as a parameter when each object of the class is instantiated.*

The creation of a generic linked list class requires the use of some of C++'s most advanced and abstract features. For this reason, this chapter will begin by implementing a nongeneric doubly linked list class. This first implementation creates a doubly linked list for a specific type of data—that is, the data held by the list is hard-coded into the class. This specific version of the linked list is used to develop, illustrate, and explain the basic linked list mechanism. Next, this specific version of the doubly linked list class is modified into a generic doubly linked list class that can work with any type of data.

A Simple Doubly Linked List Class

As you probably know, doubly linked lists are dynamic data structures that may grow or shrink in length during the execution of your program. In fact, the principal advantage of a dynamic data structure is that its size does not need to be fixed at compile time. Rather, it is free to expand or contract, as needed, during run time. Each object in the list contains a link to the preceding object and to the following object. Objects are inserted into or deleted from the list by rearranging the links appropriately. Because doubly linked lists are dynamic data structures, most commonly each object in the list is dynamically allocated. This is the case with the doubly linked list classes developed in this chapter.

Each item stored in a doubly linked list contains three parts: a pointer to the next element in the list, a pointer to the previous element in the list, and the information that is stored in the list. Figure 25-1 depicts a doubly linked list. A doubly linked list can store any data type, including characters, integers, structures, classes, unions, and so on. The doubly linked list class developed in this section simply stores characters (for ease of illustration), but any other type of data could have been used.

The doubly linked list is implemented using a simple class hierarchy. One class, called **dblinkob**, defines the nature of the objects that will be stored in the list. This class is then inherited by another class, called **dllist**, that actually implements the doubly linked list mechanism.

The **dblinkob** class, shown here, defines the nature of each element in the list:

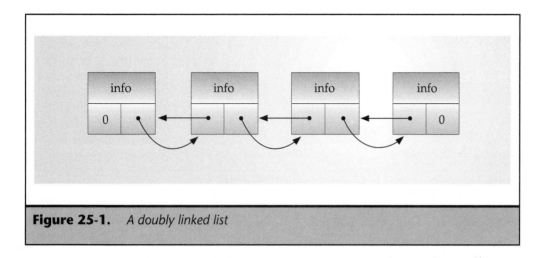

Figure 25-1. *A doubly linked list*

```
// This class defines each element in the list.
class dblinkob {
public:
  char info; // information
  dblinkob *next;  // pointer to next object
  dblinkob *prior; // pointer to previous object
  dblinkob() {
    info = 0;
    next = NULL;
    prior = NULL;
  };
  dblinkob(char c) {
    info = c;
    next = NULL;
    prior = NULL;
  }
  dblinkob *getnext() {return next;}
  dblinkob *getprior() {return prior;}
  void getinfo(char &c) { c = info;}
  void change(char c) { info = c; } // change an element

  // Overload << for object of type dblinkob.
  friend ostream &operator<<(ostream &stream, dblinkob o)
  {
    stream << o.info << "\n";
```

```
    return stream;
  }

  // Overload << for pointer to object of type dblinkob.
  friend ostream &operator<<(ostream &stream, dblinkob *o)
  {
    stream << o->info << "\n";
    return stream;
  }

  // Overload >> for dblinkob references.
  friend istream &operator>>(istream &stream, dblinkob &o)
  {
    cout << "Enter information: ";
    stream >> o.info;
    return stream;
  }
};
```

As you can see, **dblinkob** has three data members. The member **info** holds the
information stored by the list. Remember, for now, the data is simply hard-coded as
a **char**. Thus, the linked list will only be able to hold characters. The **next** pointer will
point to the next element in the list, and **prior** will point to the previous element in the
list. Notice that the data members of **dblinkob** are public. They are declared as public
only for the sake of illustration and to allow all aspects of a linked list to be easily
demonstrated. However, you might want to make them private or protected for
your own application.

Also defined within **dblinkob** are a number of operations that can be performed
on **dblinkob** objects. Specifically, the information associated with an object can be
retrieved or modified, and pointers to the next or previous elements can be obtained.
Also, objects of type **dblinkob** can be input or output using the overloaded **<<** and **>>**
operators. Keep in mind that the operations defined within **dblinkob** are independent
of the list-keeping mechanism, itself. **dblinkob** only defines the nature of the data to
be stored in the list.

When each object is constructed, the **prior** and **next** fields are initialized to **NULL**.
These pointers are null until the object is put into a list. If an initializer is included, it is
copied into **info**. Otherwise, **info** is initialized to zero.

The **getnext( )** function returns a pointer to the next element in the list. This will be
NULL if the end of the list has been reached. The **getprior( )** function returns a pointer
to the previous element in the list, if it exists; it returns **NULL** otherwise. These
functions are technically unnecessary since both **next** and **prior** are public. However,
they will be needed if you make **next** and **prior** private in your own application.

Notice that the << operator is overloaded for both objects of type **dblinkob** and pointers to objects of **dblinkob**. This is because it is extremely common, when using a linked list, to access members of the list using a pointer. Therefore it is necessary to overload << so that it operates when given a pointer to the object. However, since there is no reason to preclude an object being output, the second form, which operates directly on an object, is also included.

While **dblinkob** defines the nature of doubly linked objects, it does not, itself, create a linked list. Instead, the linked list mechanism is implemented by **dllist**, shown here. As you can see, it inherits **dblinkob** and operates on objects of that type.

```cpp
// This class actually implements the doubly linked list.
class dllist : public dblinkob {
  dblinkob *start, *end;
public:
  dllist() { start = end = NULL; }
  void store(char c);
  void remove(dblinkob *ob); // delete entry
  void frwdlist(); // display the list from beginning
  void bkwdlist(); // display the list from the end

  dblinkob *find(char c); // return pointer to matching element

  dblinkob *getstart() { return start; }
  dblinkob *getend() { return end; }
};
```

The **dllist** class maintains two pointers: one to the start of the list and one to the end of the list. As you can see, these are pointers to **dblinkob** objects. These pointers are initialized to **NULL** when a list is first created. The **dllist** class supports several doubly linked list operations, including

- Putting an item in the list
- Removing an item from the list
- Following the list in either the forward or backward direction
- Finding a specific element
- Obtaining pointers to the start and end of the list

Each of these procedures is examined next.

The store( ) Function

Information is added to the list using the **store( )** function. It is implemented as shown here:

```
// Add the next entry.
void dllist::store(char c)
{
  dblinkob *p;

  p = new dblinkob;
  if(!p) {
    cout << "Allocation error.\n";
    exit(1);
  }

  p->info = c;

  if(start==NULL) { // first element in list
    end = start = p;
  }
  else { // put on end
    p->prior = end;
    end->next = p;
    end = p;
  }
}
```

Before a new item can be put into the list, a **dblinkob** object is needed to hold it. Since linked lists are dynamic data structures, it makes sense that **store( )** obtains an object dynamically, using **new**. After a **dblinkob** object has been allocated, **store( )** assigns the information passed in **c** to the **info** member of the new object and then adds the object to the end of the list. Notice that the **start** and **end** pointers are updated as needed. In this way, **start** and **end** will always point to the beginning and end of the list.

Because objects are always added to the end of the list, the list is not sorted. However, you can modify **store( )** so that it maintains a sorted list if you like.

As the **store( )** function makes clear, the linked list managed by the **dllist** class maintains a list of *objects of type* **dblinkob**. The type of data stored within an object of type **dblinkob** is irrelevant to the **store( )** function. That is, the fact that, as currently defined, **dblinkob** contains a data field that holds a character is not relevant to the **store( )** function. (This fact will be used later to help construct a generic doubly linked list class.)

The remove( ) Function

The **remove( )** function removes an object from the list. It is shown here:

```
/* Remove an element from the list and update start and
   end pointers.
*/
void dllist::remove(dblinkob *ob)
{
  if(ob->prior) { // not deleting first element
    ob->prior->next = ob->next;
    if(ob->next) // not deleting last element
      ob->next->prior = ob->prior;
    else // otherwise, are deleting last element
      end = ob->prior;  // update end pointer
  }
  else {  // deleting first element
    if(ob->next) { // list not empty
      ob->next->prior = NULL;
      start = ob->next;
    }
    else // list now empty
      start = end = NULL;
  }
}
```

The **remove( )** function deletes the object pointed to by its parameter, **p**. (**p** must be a valid pointer to a **dblinkob** object.) There are three places where an item to be deleted can be located (see Figure 25-2). It can be the first item, the last item, or somewhere in between. The **remove( )** function handles all three cases.

Keep in mind that **remove( )** removes an object from the list, but that object is not destroyed. It is simply "delinked." (Of course, you can destroy it if you like, using **delete**.)

Like **store( )**, the operation of **remove( )** does not depend upon the type of data actually stored in the list.

Displaying the List

The functions **frwdlist( )** and **bkwdlist( )** display the contents of the list in a forward and backward direction, respectively. These functions are included to illustrate how the **dllist** class works. They also make convenient debugging aids.

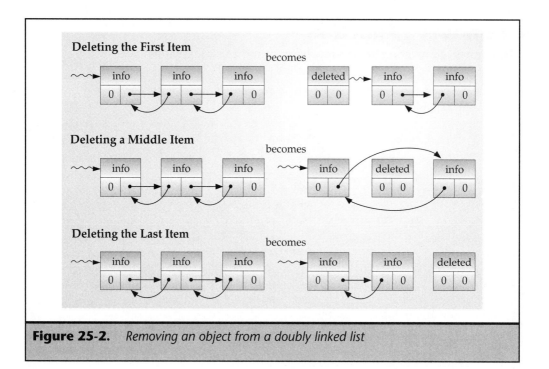

Figure 25-2. *Removing an object from a doubly linked list*

```cpp
// Walk through list in forward direction.
void dllist::frwdlist()
{
  dblinkob *temp;

  temp = start;
  do {
    cout << temp->info << " ";
    temp = temp->getnext();
  } while(temp);
  cout << "\n";
}

// Walk through list in backward direction.
void dllist::bkwdlist()
{
  dblinkob *temp;
```

```
  temp = end;
  do {
    cout << temp->info << " ";
    temp = temp->getprior();
  } while(temp);
  cout << "\n";
}
```

Finding an Object in the List

The **find( )** function, shown here, returns a pointer to the object in the list that contains information that matches that specified in its parameter. It will return **NULL** if no matching object is found.

```
// Find an object given info.
dblinkob *dllist::find(char c)
{
  dblinkob *temp;

  temp = start;

  while(temp) {
    if(c==temp->info) return temp; // found
    temp = temp->getnext();
  }
  return NULL; // not in list
}
```

A Sample Doubly Linked List Program

Here are the entire **dblinkob** and **dllist** classes, along with a **main( )** function that illustrates their use:

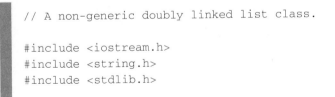

```
// A non-generic doubly linked list class.

#include <iostream.h>
#include <string.h>
#include <stdlib.h>
```

```
class dblinkob {
public:
  char info; // information
  dblinkob *next;  // pointer to next object
  dblinkob *prior; // pointer to previous object
  dblinkob() {
    info = 0;
    next = NULL;
    prior = NULL;
  };
  dblinkob(char c) {
    info = c;
    next = NULL;
    prior = NULL;
  }
  dblinkob *getnext() {return next;}
  dblinkob *getprior() {return prior;}
  void getinfo(char &c) { c = info;}
  void change(char c) { info = c; } // change an element

  // Overload << for object of type dblinkob.
  friend ostream &operator<<(ostream &stream, dblinkob o)
  {
    stream << o.info << "\n";
    return stream;
  }

  // Overload << for pointer to object of type dblinkob.
  friend ostream &operator<<(ostream &stream, dblinkob *o)
  {
    stream << o->info << "\n";
    return stream;
  }

  // Overload >> for dblinkob references.
  friend istream &operator>>(istream &stream, dblinkob &o)
  {
    cout << "Enter information: ";
    stream >> o.info;
    return stream;
  }
```

```
};

class dllist : public dblinkob {
  dblinkob *start, *end;
public:
  dllist() { start = end = NULL; }
  void store(char c);
  void remove(dblinkob *ob); // delete entry
  void frwdlist(); // display the list from beginning
  void bkwdlist(); // display the list from the end

  dblinkob *find(char c); // return pointer to matching element

  dblinkob *getstart() { return start; }
  dblinkob *getend() { return end; }
};

// Add the next entry.
void dllist::store(char c)
{
  dblinkob *p;

  p = new dblinkob;
  if(!p) {
    cout << "Allocation error.\n";
    exit(1);
  }

  p->info = c;

  if(start==NULL) { // first element in list
    end = start = p;
  }
  else { // put on end
    p->prior = end;
    end->next = p;
    end = p;
  }
}

/* Remove an element from the list and update start and
```

```
   end pointers.
*/
void dllist::remove(dblinkob *ob)
{
  if(ob->prior) { // not deleting first element
    ob->prior->next = ob->next;
    if(ob->next) // not deleting last element
      ob->next->prior = ob->prior;
    else // otherwise, are deleting last element
      end = ob->prior;  // update end pointer
  }
  else {  // deleting first element
    if(ob->next) { // list not empty
      ob->next->prior = NULL;
      start = ob->next;
    }
    else // list now empty
      start = end = NULL;
  }
}

// Walk through list in forward direction.
void dllist::frwdlist()
{
  dblinkob *temp;

  temp = start;
  do {
    cout << temp->info << " ";
    temp = temp->getnext();
  } while(temp);
  cout << "\n";
}

// Walk through list in backward direction.
void dllist::bkwdlist()
{
  dblinkob *temp;

  temp = end;
  do {
```

```
      cout << temp->info << " ";
      temp = temp->getprior();
  } while(temp);
  cout << "\n";
}

// Find an object given info.
dblinkob *dllist::find(char c)
{
  dblinkob *temp;

  temp = start;

  while(temp) {
    if(c==temp->info) return temp; // found
    temp = temp->getnext();
  }
  return NULL; // not in list
}

main()
{
  dllist list;
  char c;
  dblinkob *p;

  list.store('1');
  list.store('2');
  list.store('3');

  // use member functions to display the list
  cout << "Here is list forwards, then backwards.\n";
  list.frwdlist();
  list.bkwdlist();

  cout << endl;

  // "manually" walk through the list
  cout << "Manually walk through the list.\n";
  p = list.getstart();
  while(p) {
```

```
    p->getinfo(c);
    cout << c << " ";
    p = p->getnext(); // get next one
  }

  cout << endl << endl;

  // look for an item
  cout << "Looking for item 2.\n";
  p = list.find('2');
  if(p) {
    p->getinfo(c);
    cout << "Found: " << c << endl;
  }

  cout << endl;

  // remove an item
  p->getinfo(c);
  cout << "Removing item " << c << ".\n";
  list.remove(p);
  cout << "Here is list forwards.\n";
  list.frwdlist();

  cout << endl;

  // add another entry
  cout << "Adding an item.\n";
  list.store('4');
  cout << "Here is list forwards.\n";
  list.frwdlist();

  cout << endl;

  // change information
  p = list.find('1');
  if(!p) {
    cout << "Error, item not found.\n";
    return 1; // error
  }
```

```
    p->getinfo(c);
    cout << "Changing " << c << " to 5.\n";
    p->change('5');
    cout << "Here is list forwards, then backwards.\n";
    list.frwdlist();
    list.bkwdlist();

    cout << endl;

    // demonstrate << and >>
    cin >> *p;
    cout << p;

    cout << "Here is list forwards.\n";
    list.frwdlist();

    cout << endl;

    // remove head of list
    cout << "After removing head of list:\n";
    p = list.getstart();
    list.remove(p);
    list.frwdlist();

    cout << endl;

    // remove end of list
    cout << "After removing tail of list:\n";
    p = list.getend();
    list.remove(p);
    list.frwdlist();

    return 0;
}
```

Here is the output produced by this example. (When the program prompted for input, **X** was entered.)

```
Here is list forwards, then backwards.
1 2 3
3 2 1

Manually walk through the list.
1 2 3

Looking for item 2.
Found: 2

Removing item 2.
Here is list forwards.
1 3

Adding an item.
Here is list forwards.
1 3 4

Changing 1 to 5.
Here is list forwards, then backwards.
5 3 4
4 3 5

Enter information: X
Here is list forwards.
X 3 4

After removing head of list:
3 4

After removing tail of list:
3
```

Creating a Generic Doubly Linked List Class

Although the linked list class created in the preceding section is perfectly valid, it can only be used to manage a list of characters because this is the type of data defined by **dblinkob**. If you wanted to store another type of data, you would need to change the type specifier for **info** and modify several of the functions to accommodate the new data type. Of course, making these changes for each new type of data is both error-prone and tedious. A better solution is to create a generic linked list class, using a template, that is able to automatically handle any type of data. This is precisely what this section does.

One advantage of creating a generic doubly linked list class is that it decouples the mechanism (that is, the algorithms that maintain a linked list) from the data actually stored in the list. Thus, the mechanism can be created once and reused over and over.

NOTE: *The essentials of creating and using a generic class are discussed in Chapter 20. If you are not familiar with the use of the* **template** *keyword or generic classes in general, you will need to read Chapter 20 before attempting to understand the creation of a generic linked list class.*

The Generic Versions of the Linked List Classes

The first step in converting **dblinkob** and **dllist** into generic classes is to make them into templates. When this has been done, the data type upon which they will operate is passed as a parameter whenever an object of these classes is created. The generic versions of **dblinkob** and **dllist** are shown here:

```
template <class DataT> class dblinkob {
public:
  DataT info; // information
  dblinkob<DataT> *next;  // pointer to next object
  dblinkob<DataT> *prior; // pointer to previous object
  dblinkob() {
    info = 0;
    next = NULL;
    prior = NULL;
  };
  dblinkob(DataT c) {
    info = c;
    next = NULL;
    prior = NULL;
  }
  dblinkob<DataT> *getnext() {return next;}
  dblinkob<DataT> *getprior() {return prior;}
  void getinfo(DataT &c) { c = info;}
  void change(DataT c) { info = c; }  // change an element

  // Overload << for object of type dblinkob.
  friend ostream &operator<<(ostream &stream, dblinkob<DataT> o)
  {
```

```
      stream << o.info << "\n";
      return stream;
    }

    // Overload << for pointer to object of type dblinkob.
    friend ostream &operator<<(ostream &stream, dblinkob<DataT> *o)
    {
      stream << o->info << "\n";
      return stream;
    }

    // Overload >> for dblinkob references.
    friend istream &operator>>(istream &stream, dblinkob<DataT> &o)
    {
      cout << "Enter information: ";
      stream >> o.info;
      return stream;
    }
};

template <class DataT> class dllist : public dblinkob<DataT> {
  dblinkob<DataT> *start, *end;
public:
  dllist() { start = end = NULL; }
  void store(DataT c);
  void remove(dblinkob<DataT> *ob); // delete entry
  void frwdlist(); // display the list from beginning
  void bkwdlist(); // display the list from the end

  dblinkob<DataT> *find(DataT c); // return pointer to matching
                                  //                  element

  dblinkob<DataT> *getstart() { return start; }
  dblinkob<DataT> *getend() { return end; }
};
```

As you can see, the generic data type is called **DataT**. It is used as the type specifier for all references to the data stored in **dblinkob**. This type is replaced by the actual type specified when an object is created.

For example, to create a linked list called **mylist** that can store **unsigned long** values, you would use this declaration:

```
dllist<unsigned long> mylist;
```

This instantiates a specific version of **dllist** that is capable of storing unsigned long integers. In the declarations of **dblinkob** and **dllist** pay special attention to the way in which the generic type **DataT** is handled when **dblinkob** is inherited by **dllist**. Specifically, the type of data used to instantiate **dllist** is also passed to **dblinkob**. Therefore, in the previous declaration, the data type **unsigned long** is passed to **dllist**, which also passes it to **dblinkob**. This means that, in this case, the type of data stored in a **dblinkob** object will be **unsigned long**.

To create another type of list, simply change the data type specification. For example, this creates a list for storing character pointers:

```
dllist<char *> CharPtrList;
```

The Complete Generic Doubly Linked List Class

The entire generic doubly linked list class and sample **main( )** function are shown next. Note the way the generic data type is used throughout the function definitions. As you can see, in all cases, the data operated on by the list has been specified using the generic **DataT** type. It is not until an actual list is instantiated in **main( )** that the specific nature of the data is resolved.

```
// A generic doubly linked list class.

#include <iostream.h>
#include <string.h>
#include <stdlib.h>

template <class DataT> class dblinkob {
public:
  DataT info; // information
  dblinkob<DataT> *next;  // pointer to next object
  dblinkob<DataT> *prior; // pointer to previous object
  dblinkob() {
    info = 0;
    next = NULL;
    prior = NULL;
  };
  dblinkob(DataT c) {
    info = c;
```

```cpp
      next = NULL;
      prior = NULL;
    }
    dblinkob<DataT> *getnext() {return next;}
    dblinkob<DataT> *getprior() {return prior;}
    void getinfo(DataT &c) { c = info;}
    void change(DataT c) { info = c; }  // change an element

    // Overload << for object of type dblinkob.
    friend ostream &operator<<(ostream &stream, dblinkob<DataT> o)
    {
      stream << o.info << "\n";
      return stream;
    }

    // Overload << for pointer to object of type dblinkob.
    friend ostream &operator<<(ostream &stream, dblinkob<DataT> *o)
    {
      stream << o->info << "\n";
      return stream;
    }

    // Overload >> for dblinkob references.
    friend istream &operator>>(istream &stream, dblinkob<DataT> &o)
    {
      cout << "Enter information: ";
      stream >> o.info;
      return stream;
    }
};

template <class DataT> class dllist : public dblinkob<DataT> {
  dblinkob<DataT> *start, *end;
public:
  dllist() { start = end = NULL; }
  void store(DataT c);
  void remove(dblinkob<DataT> *ob); // delete entry
  void frwdlist(); // display the list from beginning
  void bkwdlist(); // display the list from the end

  dblinkob<DataT> *find(DataT c); // return pointer to matching
                                               element
```

```
    dblinkob<DataT> *getstart() { return start; }
    dblinkob<DataT> *getend() { return end; }
};

// Add the next entry.
template <class DataT> void dllist<DataT>::store(DataT c)
{
  dblinkob<DataT> *p;

  p = new dblinkob<DataT>;
  if(!p) {
    cout << "Allocation error.\n";
    exit(1);
  }

  p->info = c;

  if(start==NULL) { // first element in list
    end = start = p;
  }
  else { // put on end
    p->prior = end;
    end->next = p;
    end = p;
  }
}

/* Remove an element from the list and update start and
   end pointers.
*/
template <class DataT> void dllist<DataT>::remove(dblinkob<DataT> *ob)
{
  if(ob->prior) { // not deleting first element
    ob->prior->next = ob->next;
    if(ob->next) // not deleting last element
      ob->next->prior = ob->prior;
    else // otherwise, are deleting last element
      end = ob->prior;  // update end pointer
  }
  else {  // deleting first element
    if(ob->next) { // list not empty
      ob->next->prior = NULL;
```

```
        start = ob->next;
      }
      else // list now empty
        start = end = NULL;
    }
}

// Walk through list in forward direction.
template <class DataT> void dllist<DataT>::frwdlist()
{
  dblinkob<DataT> *temp;

  temp = start;
  do {
    cout << temp->info << " ";
    temp = temp->getnext();
  } while(temp);
  cout << "\n";
}

// Walk through list in backward direction.
template <class DataT> void dllist<DataT>::bkwdlist()
{
  dblinkob<DataT> *temp;

  temp = end;
  do {
    cout << temp->info << " ";
    temp = temp->getprior();
  } while(temp);
  cout << "\n";
}

// Find an object given info.
template <class DataT> dblinkob<DataT> *dllist<DataT>::find(DataT c)
{
  dblinkob<DataT> *temp;

  temp = start;

  while(temp) {
    if(c==temp->info) return temp; // found
```

```
      temp = temp->getnext();
  }
  return NULL; // not in list
}

main()
{
  dllist<char> list;
  char c;
  dblinkob<char> *p;

  list.store('1');
  list.store('2');
  list.store('3');

  // use member functions to display the list
  cout << "Here is list forwards, then backwards.\n";
  list.frwdlist();
  list.bkwdlist();

  cout << endl;

  // "manually" walk through the list
  cout << "Manually walk through the list.\n";
  p = list.getstart();
  while(p) {
    p->getinfo(c);
    cout << c << " ";
    p = p->getnext(); // get next one
  }

  cout << endl << endl;

  // look for an item
  cout << "Looking for item 2.\n";
  p = list.find('2');
  if(p) {
    p->getinfo(c);
    cout << "Found: " << c << endl;
  }

  cout << endl;
```

```cpp
  // remove an item
  p->getinfo(c);
  cout << "Removing item " << c << ".\n";
  list.remove(p);
  cout << "Here is list forwards.\n";
  list.frwdlist();

  cout << endl;

  // add another entry
  cout << "Adding an item.\n";
  list.store('4');
  cout << "Here is list forwards.\n";
  list.frwdlist();

  cout << endl;

  // change information
  p = list.find('1');
  if(!p) {
    cout << "Error, item not found.\n";
    return 1; // error
  }

  p->getinfo(c);
  cout << "Changing " << c << " to 5.\n";
  p->change('5');
  cout << "Here is list forwards, then backwards.\n";
  list.frwdlist();
  list.bkwdlist();

  cout << endl;

  // demonstrate << and >>
  cin >> *p;
  cout << p;

  cout << "Here is list forwards.\n";
  list.frwdlist();

  cout << endl;
```

```
   // remove head of list
   cout << "After removing head of list:\n";
   p = list.getstart();
   list.remove(p);
   list.frwdlist();

   cout << endl;

   // remove end of list
   cout << "After removing tail of list:\n";
   p = list.getend();
   list.remove(p);
   list.frwdlist();

   return 0;
}
```

The preceding program uses the generic doubly linked list to store character data and is functionally equivalent to the nongeneric version of the program shown earlier in this chapter. However, the point of making the doubly linked list classes generic was to allow them to be used on any type of data. To see how easy this is, try substituting the following **main( )** into the preceding program. It creates a doubly linked list of **double** values.

```
main()
{
  dllist<double> list; // create a linked list of doubles
  double c;
  dblinkob<double> *p;

  list.store(1.1);
  list.store(2.2);
  list.store(3.3);

  // use member functions to display the list
  cout << "Here is list forwards, then backwards.\n";
  list.frwdlist();
  list.bkwdlist();

  cout << endl;
```

```
// "manually" walk through the list
cout << "Manually walk through the list.\n";
p = list.getstart();
while(p) {
  p->getinfo(c);
  cout << c << " ";
  p = p->getnext(); // get next one
}

cout << endl << endl;

// look for an item
cout << "Looking for item 2.2.\n";
p = list.find(2.2);
if(p) {
  p->getinfo(c);
  cout << "Found: " << c << endl;
}

cout << endl;

// remove an item
p->getinfo(c);
cout << "Removing item " << c << ".\n";
list.remove(p);
cout << "Here is list forwards.\n";

list.frwdlist();

cout << endl;

// add another entry
cout << "Adding an item.\n";
list.store(4.4);
cout << "Here is list forwards.\n";
list.frwdlist();

cout << endl;
```

```
// change information
p = list.find(1.1);
if(!p) {
  cout << "Error, item not found.\n";
  return 1; // error
}

p->getinfo(c);
cout << "Changing " << c << " to 5.5.\n";
p->change(5.5);
cout << "Here is list forwards, then backwards.\n";
list.frwdlist();
list.bkwdlist();

cout << endl;

// demonstrate << and >>
cin >> *p;
cout << p;

cout << "Here is list forwards.\n";
list.frwdlist();

cout << endl;

// remove head of list
cout << "After removing head of list:\n";
p = list.getstart();
list.remove(p);
list.frwdlist();

cout << endl;

// remove end of list
cout << "After removing tail of list:\n";
p = list.getend();
list.remove(p);
list.frwdlist();

return 0;
}
```

After you substitute this **main( )** into the program, it will produce the following output:

```
Here is list forwards, then backwards.
1.1 2.2 3.3
3.3 2.2 1.1

Manually walk through the list.
1.1 2.2 3.3

Looking for item 2.2.
Found: 2.2

Removing item 2.2.
Here is list forwards.
1.1 3.3

Adding an item.
Here is list forwards.
1.1 3.3 4.4

Changing 1.1 to 5.5.
Here is list forwards, then backwards.
5.5 3.3 4.4
4.4 3.3 5.5

Enter information: 99.99
Here is list forwards.
99.99 3.3 4.4

After removing head of list:
3.3 4.4

After removing tail of list:
3.3
```

On your own, you should try creating lists of other types of data. Remember, even compound data types, such as a structure that contains a mailing address, can be stored in the list.

Other Implementations

There are many ways to implement a linked list class. You may want to experiment on your own. Here are some ideas you can start with.

The lists in this chapter simply add objects to the end of the list. For many applications, this is acceptable (indeed, desirable). However, you might want to modify **store( )** so that it creates a sorted list. Or you can create another version of **store( )** that adds elements to the beginning of the list. In fact, you could define several versions of **store( )** (each with an appropriately descriptive name) that store elements in various ways. For example, you could define functions called **StoreEnd( )**, **StoreStart( )**, and **StoreSort( )**, which add elements to the end, the beginning, or in sorted order, respectively.

One function you might want to add is called **getlength( )**. Have it return the number of elements in the list.

As mentioned earlier, the pointers **next** and **prior** in **dblinkob** were intentionally made public as a means of simplifying the linked list routines and to fully illustrate the linked list classes. However, you could make these pointers private, thereby preventing their accidental misuse.

One final thought: Although the linked lists developed in this chapter store characters and floating-point numbers, remember that any type of data can be stored.

Appendix A

The Proposed Standard Class Libraries

The ANSI C++ standardization committee is in the process of defining a standard set of class libraries. At the time of this writing, these libraries are still "a work in progress" and are not fully implemented by any currently available C++ compiler. Therefore, it is not feasible to discuss the class libraries in this edition of the book. (The exception to this is the I/O library, which all C++ compilers currently implement, and which is fully discussed in Part Two.) However, since future compilers will implement these class libraries, it is important for you to know what will become available. For this reason, the libraries currently being defined by the proposed ANSI C++ standard are listed here:

- Language support
- Diagnostics
- General utilities
- Strings
- Localization
- Containers
- Iterators
- Algorithms
- Numerics
- Input/Output

Although the ANSI C++ standard is still in the development stage, you will want to check your compiler manuals to see which of these class libraries are supported.

REMEMBER: *The class libraries are in addition to the standard function library, which is included in all C++ compilers.*

Index

The NEW CLASSICS

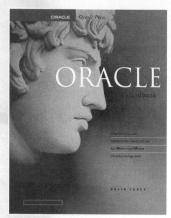

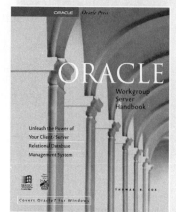
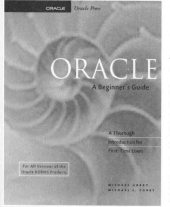

ORACLE: THE COMPLETE REFERENCE

Third Edition

by George Koch
and Kevin Loney

Get true encyclopedic coverage of Oracle with this book. Authoritative and absolutely up-to-the-minute.

Price: $34.95 U.S.A.
Available Now
ISBN: 0-07-882097-9
Pages: 1104, paperback

ORACLE BACKUP AND RECOVERY HANDBOOK

by Rama Velpuri

Keep your database running smoothly and prepare for the possibility of system failure with this comprehensive resource and guide.

Price: $29.95 U.S.A.
Available Now
ISBN: 0-07-882106-1
Pages: 400, paperback

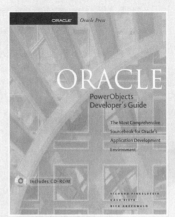

ORACLE POWER OBJECTS DEVELOPER'S GUIDE

by Richard Finkelstein,
Kasu Sista, and Rick Greenwald

Integrate the flexibility and power of Oracle Power Objects into your applications development with this results-oriented handbook.

Price: $39.95 U.S.A.
Includes One CD-ROM
Available September, 1995
ISBN: 0-07-882163-0
Pages: 656, paperback

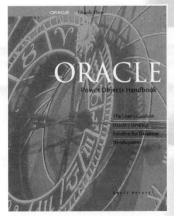

ORACLE POWER OBJECTS HANDBOOK

by Bruce Kolste
and David Petersen

Th's is the only book available on Oracle's new single/multi-user database product.

Price: $29.95 U.S.A.
Available August, 1995
ISBN: 0-07-882089-8
Pages: 512, paperback

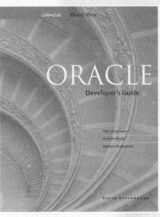

ORACLE DEVELOPER'S GUIDE

by David McClanahan

Learn to develop a database that is fast, powerful, and secure with this comprehensive guide.

Price: $29.95 U.S.A.
Available November, 1995
ISBN: 0-07-882087-1
Pages: 608, paperback

EXTRATERRESTRIAL CONNECTIONS

THESE DAYS, ANY CONNECTION IS POSSIBLE...
WITH THE INNOVATIVE BOOKS FROM LAN TIMES AND OSBORNE/McGRAW-HILL

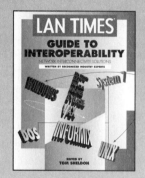

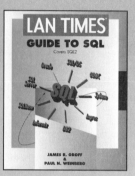

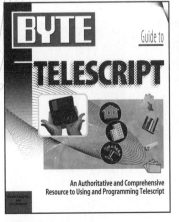